MODERN ETHICS IN 77 ARGUMENTS

MODERN ETHICS
IN 77
ARGUMENTS

A STONE READER

Edited by

PETER CATAPANO
AND SIMON CRITCHLEY

LIVERIGHT PUBLISHING CORPORATION
A Division of W. W. NORTON & COMPANY
Independent Publishers Since 1923
NEW YORK   LONDON

Preface by Peter Catapano

Selected essays previously published in the book
The Stone Reader: Modern Philosophy in 133 Arguments

For information about permission to reproduce selections
from this book, write to Permissions,
Liveright Publishing Corporation, a division of
W. W. Norton & Company, Inc.,
500 Fifth Avenue, New York, NY 10110

For information about special discounts for bulk purchases, please
contact W. W. Norton Special Sales at specialsales@wwnorton.com
or 800-233-4830

Manufacturing by Quad Graphics, Fairfield
Production manager: Beth Steidle

Library of Congress Cataloging-in-Publication Data

Names: Catapano, Peter, editor. | Critchley, Simon, 1960– editor.
Title: Modern ethics in 77 arguments : a Stone reader / edited by Peter
    Catapano and Simon Critchley.
Other titles: New York times.
Description: New York : Liveright Publishing Corporation, 2017.
Identifiers: LCCN 2017018086 | ISBN 9781631492983 (hardcover)
Subjects: LCSH: Ethics, Modern—21st century. | Newspapers—Sections,
    columns, etc.—Ethics.
Classification: LCC BJ301 .M63 2017 | DDC 170—dc23
LC record available at https://lccn.loc.gov/2017018086

ISBN 978-1-63149-399-7 pbk

Liveright Publishing Corporation
500 Fifth Avenue, New York, N.Y. 10110
www.wwnorton.com

W. W. Norton & Company Ltd.
15 Carlisle Street, London W1D 3BS

1 2 3 4 5 6 7 8 9 0

CONTENTS

ON MORALITY

ON RELIGION

ON GOVERNMENT

ON WOMEN

ON FAMILY

ON EATING

ON THE FUTURE

PREFACE

The seventy-seven essays in this volume have been selected from *The New York Times'* philosophy series, The Stone, to represent the best and most accessible writing on ethical questions by philosophers and thinkers working today. The book builds on the popular success of both the *Times'* series, founded in 2010, and the book *The Stone Reader: Modern Philosophy in 133 Arguments*, published in December 2015 by Liveright.

In putting together this volume we had a primary goal: to create a less expensive, more portable volume than the original *Stone Reader*, distilled to meet the growing interest in ethics, both in universities and the public sphere. To do this, we didnot simply carve out a subset of the larger anthology, but instead selected the most fitting entries from that book, and updated that grouping with more than thirty newer Stone essays, compiled exclusively for this volume.

The essays here tackle questions of existence, morality, religion, race, family, gender, economics, government and citizenship—nearly every topic of human concern—and reflect a range of viewpoints, writing styles and rhetorical strategies. Each one either directly or indirectly raises a question to be explored: *Is humanity getting better? Is real inclusiveness possible? How should we respond to evil? Who needs a gun?* They sit very comfortably in the tradition of philosophy as a practical tool for the navigation of life, and hence, in this case, under the heading of Modern Ethics.

The key components of the essays—clarity, brevity, integrity and jargon-free language—have been at the editorial core goal of The Stone since its founding. At their best, these works are useful not only for general readers looking to get beneath the surface of an issue but also for the student or teacher aiming to bring the practices of philosophy and writing together in the project of public engagement. We hope they can and will be read in philosophy courses and seminars, but also at kitchen tables and cafés, in libraries and airports, on road trips and summer vacations.

The Stone, which exists primarily as an entity of the *Times* opinion section, has become a well-traveled bridge from academia to the public square. It has given professors, scholars and students a vehicle to share their work and views with millions of readers in all walks of life. The conversations typically sparked by these essays—which appear weekly on the *Times* website, and occasionally in our national and international print editions—extend over a broad geographical and ideological spectrum, and have given us at least some reason to believe that philosophical thinking is not only *not dead*, it is a robust, living practice woven into the entire human experience.

The idea of using The Stone in classrooms is not entirely new. Very early on in the project, Simon and I began receiving appreciative notes from teachers using the essays in both high school and university settings, with good results, as well as from students inspired to write essays of their own after engaging with the series. We have also used Stone essays in our own teaching, and have found that the shift that occurs in the educational process is essentially a dynamic one: teaching short, accessible works by living philosophers can foster the sense among students that philosophy is not an esoteric practice to be observed from a distance but a shared activity in a common space, one in which the author of a text may actually be praised, challenged or argued with in person, only a lecture hall or an e-mail away.

It should be noted that *Modern Ethics in 77 Arguments* is not an ethics reader in the typical academic sense. It does not break down the work into the usual academic divisions—meta-, normative and applied ethics—but rather more broadly by topic. Anyone who has compiled a table of contents for an anthology knows that categories, while certainly not useless, are often fluid, and the boundaries they imply often porous. We hope at the very least that those we have provided will help in the navigation of these essays.

As products of a news organization, each Stone piece is a response to the environment. While particular pieces may use important or canonical work in the history of philosophy as a springboard, or to position or fortify an argument, they must by necessity look forward, because the energy that drives this project is a journalistic one. Its reason for being is relevancy. It weds philosophy and journalism in their shared pursuit of, and loyalty to, the truth.

What we hope to have produced is a new text that will be useful both inside and outside the classroom—in the academy and on the road, as it were, whether it is the road to enlightenment, or somewhere else entirely.

—Peter Catapano,
New York
2017

ON EXISTENCE

The Meaningfulness of Lives

—Todd May

WHO AMONG US HAS NOT ASKED WHETHER HIS OR HER LIFE IS A meaningful one? Who has not wondered—on a sleepless night, during a long stretch of dull or taxing work, or when a troubled child seems a greater burden than one can bear—whether in the end it all adds up to anything? On this day, too, ten years after the September 11 attacks, when many are steeped in painful reminders of personal loss, it is natural to wonder about the answers.

The philosopher Jean-Paul Sartre thought that without God, our lives are bereft of meaning. He tells us in his essay "Existentialism," "If God does not exist, we find no values or commands to turn to which legitimize our conduct. So, in the bright realm of values, we have no excuse behind us, nor justification before us." On this view, God gives our lives the values upon which meaning rests. And if God does not exist, as Sartre claims, our lives can have only the meaning we confer upon them.

This seems wrong on two counts. First, why would the existence of God guarantee the meaningfulness of each of our lives? Is a life of unremitting drudgery or unrequited struggle really redeemed if there's a larger plan, one to which we have no access, into which it fits? That would be small compensation for a life that would otherwise feel like a waste—a point not lost on thinkers like Karl Marx, who called religion the "opium of the people." Moreover, does God actually ground the values by which we live? Do we not, as Plato recognized 2,500 years ago, already have to think of those values as good in order to ascribe them to God?

Second, and more pointedly, must the meaningfulness of our lives depend on the existence of God? Must meaning rely upon articles of faith? Basing life's meaningfulness on the existence of a deity not only leaves all atheists out of the picture but also leaves different believers out of one another's picture. What seems called for is an approach to thinking about meaning that can draw us together, one that exists alongside or instead of religious views.

A promising and more inclusive approach is offered by Susan Wolf in her recent and compelling book, *Meaning in Life and Why It Matters*. A meaningful life, she claims, is distinct from a happy life or a morally good one. In her view, "meaning arises when subjective attraction meets objective attractiveness." A meaningful life must, in some sense then, *feel* worthwhile. The person living the life must be engaged by it. A life of commitment to causes that are generally defined as worthy—like feeding and clothing the poor or ministering to the ill—but that do not move the person participating in them will lack meaningfulness in this sense. However, for a life to be meaningful, it must also *be* worthwhile. Engagement in a life of tiddlywinks does not rise to the level of a meaningful life, no matter how gripped one might be by the game.

Often one defends an idea by giving reasons for it. However, sometimes the best defense is not to give reasons at the outset but instead to pursue the idea in order to see where it leads. Does it capture something important if we utilize it to understand ourselves? It's this latter tack that I would like to try here. The pursuit of this core idea—that a meaningful life is both valued and valuable—allows us to understand several important aspects of our attitudes toward ourselves and others.

In this pursuit, the first step we might take beyond what Wolf tells us is to recognize that lives unfold over time. A life is not an unrelated series of actions or projects or states of being. A life has, we might say, a trajectory. It is lived in a temporal thickness. Even if my life's trajectory seems disjointed or to lack continuity, it is *my* life that is disconnected in its unfolding, not elements of several different lives.

If a life has a trajectory, then it can be conceived narratively. A human life can be seen as a story, or as a series of stories that are more or less related. This does not mean that the person whose life it is must conceive it or live it narratively. I needn't say to myself, "Here's the story I want to construct," or, "This is the story so far." What it means, rather, is that, if one reflected on one's life, one could reasonably see it in terms of various story lines, whether parallel or intersecting or distinct. This idea can be traced back to Aristotle's *Ethics* but has made a reappearance with some recent narrative conceptions of what a self is.

What makes a trajectory a meaningful one? If Wolf is right, it has to feel worthwhile and, beyond that, has to be engaged in projects that are objectively worthwhile. There is not much difficulty in knowing what feels worthwhile. Most of us are good at sensing when we're onto something and when we're not. Objective worthiness is more elusive. We don't want to reduce it simply to a morally good life, as though a meaningful life were simply an unalienated moral life. Meaningful lives are not so limited and, as we shall see, are sometimes more vexed. So we must ask what lends objective worthiness to a life outside the moral realm. Here is where the narrative character of a life comes into play.

There are values we associate with a good narrative and its characters that are distinct from those we associate with good morals. A fictional character can be intense, adventurous, steadfast, or subtle. Think here of the adventurousness of Ishmael in *Moby-Dick*, the quiet intensity of Kip in *The English Patient*, the steadfastness of Dilsey in *The Sound and the Fury* or the subtlety of Marco Polo in *Invisible Cities*. As with these fictional characters, so with our lives. When a life embodies one or more of these values (or others) and feels engaging to the one who lives it, it is to that extent meaningful. There are narrative values expressed by human lives that are not reducible to moral values. Nor are they reducible to happiness; they are not simply matters of subjective feeling. Narrative values are not felt; they are lived. And they constitute their own arena of value, one that has not been generally recognized by philosophers who reflect on life's meaningfulness.

An intense life, for instance, can be lived with abandon. One might move from engagement to engagement, or stick with a single engagement, but always (well, often) by diving into it, holding nothing back. One throws oneself into swimming or poetry or community organizing or fundraising, or perhaps all of them at one time or another. Such a life is likely a meaningful one. And this is true even where it might not be an entirely moral one.

We know of people like this, people whose intensity leads them to behavior that we might call morally compromised. Intense lovers can leave bodies in their wake when the embers of love begin to cool. Intense athletes may not be the best of teammates. Our attitudes toward people like this are conflicted. There is a sense in which we might admire them and another sense in which we don't. This is because meaningful lives don't always coincide with good ones. Meaningful lives can be morally compromised, just as morally good lives can feel meaningless to those who live them.

We should not take this to imply that there is no relationship between meaningfulness and morality. They meet at certain moral limits. An evil life, no matter how intense or steadfast, is not one we would want to call meaningful. But within the parameters of those moral limits, the relationship between a meaningful life and a moral one is complicated. They do not map directly onto each other.

Why might all this matter? What is the point of understanding what makes lives meaningful? Why not just live them? On one level, the answer is obvious. If we want to live meaningful lives, we might want to know something about what makes a life so. Otherwise, we're just taking stabs in the dark. And in any event, for most of us it's just part of who we are. It's one of the causes of our lying awake at night.

There is another reason as well. This one is more bound to the time in which we live. In an earlier column for The Stone, I wrote that we are currently encouraged to think of ourselves either as consumers or as entrepreneurs. We are told to be shoppers for goods or investors for return. Neither of these types of lives, if they are the dominant character of those lives, strike me as particularly meaningful. This is because their narrative themes—buying, investing— are rarely the stuff of which a compelling life narrative is made. (I say "rarely" because there may be, for example, cases of intensely lived but morally compromised lives of investment that do not cross any moral limit to meaningfulness.) They usually lack what Wolf calls "objective attractiveness." To be sure, we must buy things and may even enjoy shopping. And we should not be entirely unconcerned with where we place our limited energies or monies. But are these the themes of a meaningful life? Are we likely to say of someone that he or she was a great networker or shopper and so really knew how to live?

In what I have called an age of economics, it is even more urgent to ask the question of a meaningful life: what it consists in, how we might live one. Philosophy cannot prescribe the particular character of meaning that each of us should embrace. It cannot tell each of us individually how we might trace the trajectory that is allotted to us. But it can, and ought to, reflect upon the framework within which we consider these questions, and in doing so perhaps offer a lucidity we might otherwise lack. This is as it should be. Philosophy can assist us in understanding how we might think about our lives, while remaining modest enough to leave the living of them to us.

SEPTEMBER 11, 2011

There Is No Theory of Everything

—Simon Critchley

OVER THE YEARS, I HAVE HAD THE GOOD FORTUNE TO TEACH A lot of graduate students, mostly in philosophy, and have noticed a recurring fact. Behind every new graduate student stands an undergraduate teacher. This is someone who opened the student's eyes and ears to the possibility of the life of the mind that they had perhaps imagined but scarcely believed was within their reach. Someone who, through the force of their example, animated a desire to read more, study more and know more. Someone in whom the student heard something fascinating or funny or just downright strange. Someone who heard something significant in what the student said in a way that gave them confidence and self-belief. Such teachers are the often unknown and usually unacknowledged (and underpaid) heroes of the world of higher education.

Some lucky people have several such teachers. This was the case with me. But there is usually one teacher who sticks out and stays in one's mind, and whose words resound down through the years. These are teachers who become repositories for all sorts of anecdotes, who are fondly recalled through multiple bon mots and jokes told by their former students. It is also very often the case that the really good teachers don't write or don't write that much. They are not engaged in "research," whatever that benighted term means with respect to the humanities. They teach. They talk. Sometimes they even listen and ask questions.

In relation to philosophy, this phenomenon is hardly new. The activity of philosophy begins with Socrates, who didn't write and about whom many stories were told. Plato and others, like Xenophon, wrote them down and we still read them. It is very often the case that the center of a vivid philosophical culture is held by figures who don't write but who exist only through the stories that are told about them. One thinks of Sidney Morgenbesser, long-time philosophy professor at Columbia, whom I once heard described as a "mind on the loose." The philosopher Robert Nozick said of his undergraduate education that he "majored in Sidney Morgenbesser." On his deathbed, Morgenbesser is said to have asked: "Why is God making me suffer so much? Just because I don't believe in him?"

These anecdotes seem incidental, but they are very important. They become a way of both revering the teacher and humanizing them, both building them up and belittling them, giving us a feeling of intimacy with them, keeping them within human reach. Often the litmus test of an interesting philosopher is how many stories circulate about them.

I want to talk here about an undergraduate teacher of mine about whom many stories were told, but who is not so widely known. His name was Frank Cioffi (1928–2012), an Italian-American from a peasant family who spent his early years close to Washington Square. His mother died giving birth to him, and his distraught father died when Frank was an infant. He was then brought up by his grandparents, who spoke in a Neapolitan dialect. He dropped out of high school, spent time with the United States Army in Japan and then in France trying to identify dug-up corpses of American soldiers for the war grave commission. In 1950, he somehow managed to get into Ruskin College, Oxford, on the G.I. Bill, where he began to study philosophy and discovered the work of Wittgenstein, whose later thinking was just then beginning to circulate. After teaching in Singapore and Kent, he became the founding professor of the philosophy department at the University of Essex in the early 1970s. I encountered him there in 1982. It was memorable.

Frank (which is how he was always referred to) has recently

become the subject of an interesting book by David Ellis, *Frank Cioffi: The Philosopher in Shirt Sleeves*. It gives a very good sense of what it felt like to be in a room with Frank. Truth to tell, Ellis's title is deceptive, as I never recall Frank in shirtsleeves. He wore a sweater, usually inside out. He never had laces in the work boots he always wore, and strangest of all, because of an acute sensitivity to fabrics, he wore pajamas underneath his clothes at all times. The word "disheveled" doesn't begin to describe the visual effect that Frank had on the senses. He was a physically large, strong-looking man, about six-foot-four. The pajamas were clearly visible at the edges of his sweater, his fly was often undone (some years later, his only word of teaching advice to me was "always check your fly") and he sometimes seemed to hold his pants up with a piece of string. In his pockets would be scraps of paper with typewritten quotations from favorite writers like George Eliot, Tolstoy or Arthur Conan Doyle's Sherlock Holmes, whom he revered.

He walked the few miles to the brutal architectural dystopia that was the University of Essex from his home in Colchester wearing an early version of a Sony Walkman. I always assumed he was listening to music, only to discover years later that he was listening to recordings of himself reading out passages from books. I remember him saying during a lecture that he was "not a publishing philosopher." This is not quite true, but although his books, like *Wittgenstein on Freud and Frazer* (1998), are fascinating, his rather tangled prose gives no sense of what it was like to listen to one of his lectures. They were amazing, unscripted and hugely funny performances, where he would move about over a vast range of quotations and reflections, his considerable bulk straining to control the passion of his thinking. Occasionally he would suddenly perch himself on the edge of a student's desk, smoking a small, Indian cigarette (yes, it was that long ago). We were at once terrified and enthralled.

I was studying English and European literature in my first year at college, but my friend Will and I were considering switching to philosophy, partly because of Frank. We went to see him in his office for advice. I don't remember him giving any. We sat with him for about

an hour and I remember a story about how, when he had been teaching in Singapore, he used to put down poison to deal with the many
cockroaches that infested his office. One day, while watching an
insect die in agony in the corner of his room, he thought to himself:
"There is a problem with other minds after all. It is a real issue. I
knew that the bug was dying in pain and felt profound sympathy and
stopped doing it." Will and I both switched to philosophy immediately and never looked back.

Some years later, I went back into his office to ask permission to
switch from one course to another. "Which courses?" he said indif-
ferently. "I'm meant to be reading Foucault, but I want to do a course
on Derrida." "Man" he replied "that's like going from horseshit to
bullshit." In fact, as others can confirm, the latter word was his most
common term of reference and it also expresses his approach to philosophy: No BS.

IN THE PREFACE to *Varieties of Religious Experience*, William James
said that it was his belief that "a large acquaintance with particulars
makes us wiser than the possession of abstract formulas, however
deep." This was Frank's pedagogical credo and his teaching moved
from particular to particular, often working from the quotations
written on small slips of paper and stuck into his pockets, to be
pulled out with great dramatic effect. He hated big theories and any
kind of metaphysical pretention and he would use little quotations to
pick away relentlessly at grand explanations. He used the particular
to scratch away at the general, like picking at a scab.

Frank's special loathing was reserved for Freud, whom he thought
a writer of great perceptiveness and expressive power but completely
deluded about the theoretical consequences of his views. "Imagine a
world in which, like ours," Frank wrote in *Wittgenstein on Freud and
Frazer*, "people laughed at jokes, but unlike ours did not know what
they were laughing at until they discovered the unconscious ener-
gic processes hypothesized by Freud." For Frank, such was the world
that Freud beguiled himself and us into believing he was living in.

He compared the twentieth-century fascination with psychoanalysis to the nineteenth-century fascination with phrenology, the "science" of bumps on the head. I think he would have come to very similar conclusions about the early 21st-century fad for neuroscience and our insatiable obsession with the brain.

Despite the astonishing breadth of his interests, Frank's core obsession in teaching turned on the relation between science and the humanities. More particularly, his concern was with the relation between the causal explanations offered by science and the kinds of humanistic description we find, say, in the novels of Dickens or Dostoevsky, or in the sociological writings of Erving Goffman and David Riesman. His quest was to try and clarify the occasions when a scientific explanation was appropriate and when it was not, and we need instead a humanistic remark. His conviction was that our confusions about science and the humanities had wide-ranging and malign societal consequences.

Let me give an example. Imagine that you are depressed, because of the death of a loved one, heartbreak or just too much hard and seemingly pointless work. You go to see a doctor. After trying to explain what ails you, with the doctor fidgeting and looking at his watch, he exclaims: "Ah, I see the problem. Take this blue pill and you will be cured." However efficacious the blue pill might be, in this instance the doctor's casual diagnosis is the wrong one. What is required is for you to be able to talk, to feel that someone understands your problems and perhaps can offer some insight or even suggestions on how you might move forward in your life. This, one imagines, is why people go into therapy.

But let's flip it around. Let's imagine that you are on a ferry crossing the English Channel during a terrible winter storm. Your nausea is uncontrollable and you run out onto the deck to vomit the contents of your lunch, breakfast and the remains of the previous evening's dinner. You feel so wretched that you no longer fear death—you wish you were dead. Suddenly, on the storm-tossed deck, appears R.D. Laing, the most skilled, charismatic and rhetorically gifted existential psychiatrist of his generation, in a blue velvet suit. He proceeds to give you an intense phenomenological description of how your guts feel, the sense of disorientation, the corpselike coldness of your flesh, the sudden loss of the will to live. This is also an error. On a ferry you want a blue pill that is going to alleviate the symptoms of seasickness and make you feel better.

Frank's point is that our society is deeply confused by the occasions when a blue pill is required and not required, or when we need a causal explanation and when we need a further description, clarification or elucidation. We tend to get muddled and imagine that one kind of explanation (usually the causal one) is appropriate in all occasions when it is not.

What is in play here is the classical distinction made by Max Weber between explanation and clarification, between causal or causal-sounding hypotheses and interpretation. Weber's idea is that natural phenomena require causal explanation, of the kind given by physics, say, whereas social phenomena require elucidation—richer, more expressive descriptions. In Frank's view, one major task of philosophy is help us get clear on this distinction and to provide the right response at the right time. This, of course, requires judgment, which is no easy thing to teach.

Let me push this a little further. At the end of his book on Wittgenstein, Frank tells a story about a philosophical paper (imagined or real, it is not clear) with the title "Qualia and Materialism—Closing the Explanatory Gap." The premise of the paper is twofold: first, there is a gap between how we experience the world—our subjective, conscious experiences (qualia)—and the scientific explanation of the material forces that constitute nature; and, second, that such a gap can potentially be closed through one, overarching theoretical explanation. Frank goes on to point out that if we can imagine such a paper, then we can also imagine papers called "The Big Bang and Me—Closing the Explanatory Gap" or "Natural Selection and Me—Closing the Explanatory Gap."

This is the risk of what some call "scientism"—the belief that natural science can explain everything, right down to the detail of our subjective and social lives. All we need is a better form of science, a more complete theory, a theory of everything. Lord knows, there are even Oscar-winning Hollywood movies made about this topic. Frank's point, which is still hugely important, is that there is no theory of everything, nor should there be. There is a gap between nature and society. The mistake, for which scientism is the name, is the belief that this gap can or should be filled.

One huge problem with scientism is that it invites, as an almost allergic reaction, the total rejection of science. As we know to our cost, we witness this every day with climate change deniers, flat-earthers and religious fundamentalists. This is what is called obscurantism, namely that the way things are is not explained by science, but with reference to occult forces like God, all-conquering Zeus, the benign earth goddess or fairies at the bottom of my garden. Now, in order to confront the challenge of obscurantism, we do not simply need to run into the arms of scientism. What is needed is a clearer overview of the occasions when a scientific remark is appropriate and when we need something else, the kind of elucidation we find in stories, poetry or indeed when we watch a movie or good TV (Frank watched a lot of TV).

PEOPLE OFTEN WONDER WHY there appears to be no progress in philosophy, unlike in natural science, and why it is that after some three millenniums of philosophical activity no dramatic changes seem to have been made to the questions philosophers ask. The reason is because people keep asking the same questions and are perplexed by the same difficulties. Wittgenstein puts the point rather directly: "Philosophy hasn't made any progress? If somebody scratches the spot where he has an itch, do we have to see some progress?" Philosophy scratches at the various itches we have, not in order that we might find some cure for what ails us, but in order to scratch in the right place and begin to understand why we engage in such apparently irritating activity. Philosophy is not Neosporin. It is not some healing balm. It is an irritant, which is why Socrates described himself as a gadfly.

This is one way of approaching the question of life's meaning. Human beings have been asking the same kinds of questions for millenniums and this is not an error. It testifies to the fact that human being are rightly perplexed by their lives. The mistake is to believe that there is an answer to the question of life's meaning. As Douglas Adams established quite some time ago, the answer to the question of life, the universe and everything will always be "42" or some variation of 42. Namely, it will be something really rather disappointing.

The point, then, is not to seek an answer to the meaning of life, but to continue to ask the question. This is what Frank did in his life and teaching. David Ellis tells a story of when Frank was in hospital, and a friend came to visit him. When the friend could not find Frank's room, he asked a nurse where he might find Professor Cioffi. "Oh," the nurse replied, "you mean the patient that knows all the answers." At which point, a voice was heard from under some nearby bedclothes, "No, I know all the questions."

We don't need an answer to the question of life's meaning, just as we don't need a theory of everything. What we need are multifarious descriptions of many things, further descriptions of phenomena that change the aspect under which they are seen, that light them up and let us see them anew. That is what Frank was doing with his quotations, with his rich variety of particulars. They allow us to momentarily clarify and focus the bewilderment that is often what passes for our "inner life" and give us an overview on things. We might feel refreshed and illuminated, even slightly transformed, but it doesn't mean we are going to stop scratching that itch. In 1948, Wittgenstein wrote, "When you are philosophizing you have to descend into primeval chaos and feel at home there."

Allow me an odd postscript. Shortly after I learned the news of Frank's death in 2012, I opened my email one morning to find a message from "Frank Cioffi." I suddenly paused, as if someone had walked over my grave or scratched my skin with their nails. I then discovered that his namesake was Frank's nephew, a professor of English at City University of New York, who was doing research into his uncle's work. But that's the great thing about one's teachers. They never really die. They live on in the stories that we tell about them.

SEPTEMBER 12, 2015

The Light at the End of Suffering

—Peg O'Connor

HOW MUCH MORE CAN I TAKE?
This question has been at the root of the human experience for as long as we have been able to record it, if not longer. It was the lament of Job—or at least one of them—and is asked with no less frequency today in response to circumstances ranging from devastating loss and grief to the typical hardships of a trying job or a long winter.

But where is that actual point at which a person "breaks" or comes to believe not only that her life is devoid of value or meaning, but that the world is, too? The truth is that most people really do not want to ascertain just how much more they can suffer. A vast majority of people would look askance at someone who really wanted to experiment with her limits for suffering. But what if we are to treat it as a genuine question? In some of my recent work in the area of addiction and philosophy, I've found that many active addicts of all sorts confront that limit every day in ways that those fortunate enough to be free of addiction may never know. For some of them, the process of reaching that limit becomes an opportunity to effect radical transformation of their lives.

A broader understanding of this concept can be found in the work of William James, whose famous work, *The Varieties of Religious Experience*, provides significant insight about the limits of misery and its transformative potential. *Varieties* is a product of lectures James delivered at the University of Edinburgh in 1901 and 1902. His focus is the experience of individuals "for whom religion exists not as a dull habit, but as an acute fever." By "religion," James does not mean religious institutions and their long entrenched theological debates, but rather something more akin to an individual spiritual state, which may or may not include belief in a god.

James was uniquely suited to deliver these lectures. He was a physician, philosopher and a psychologist before the field of psychology was part of academe, and someone with a deep, abiding interest in psychic events. He was, in all senses, a student of human nature. He explored this question of what we may call the "misery threshold" because he wanted to know if some people were more capable or more prone to experience "the acute fever" of religious belief. His answer: it is those who suffer most who are inclined to experience that fever. These are the people who fascinated him: those who toed right up to and sometimes over the line of despair and meaninglessness.

James claims in *Varieties* that there are two kinds of people, differentiated from where they live in relation to their misery threshold. Each person, he argued, has a threshold for emotional pain akin to a threshold for physical pain. While some people at the slightest physical pain tend to run to the ibuprofen or painkillers, others seem able to tolerate excruciating physical pain. The same holds for misery.

James calls those who live on the sunnier side of their misery threshold "healthy-minded." Optimism fills their lives, though there are degrees of optimism. Some of the healthy-minded see the glass half full while others see it as half full with something really delicious. These are the sort of people who always look for the bright side and have a soul with "a sky-blue tint, whose affinities are rather with the flowers and birds and all enchanting innocencies than with dark human passions." Though the sunny-side people can be miserable at times, they have a low tolerance for misery. It would take something catastrophic for them to stay on the dark side of their misery lines.

The sunny-siders are somewhat interesting to James, if only because they constitute a type that is almost completely foreign to him. James knew himself and many of his family members to belong to the second category—"sick souls" and "divided selves," who live on the dark side of their misery threshold. Sick souls tend to say no to life, according to James, and are governed by fear. Sick souls tend to become anxious and melancholic, with apprehension that opportunistically spreads.

The person with a divided self suffers from what James calls "world sickness." This sickness is progressive, and James charts its development keenly and compassionately. Those with divided self experience a war within; their lives are "little more than a series of zig zags," their "spirit wars with their flesh, they wish for incompatibles," and "their lives are one long drama of repentance and of effort to repair misdemeanors and mistakes."

Perhaps not coincidentally, this is an accurate description of addiction. James knew a great deal about drunkenness or inebriety, to use the language of his time. For years, his brother Robertson (Bob) was in and out of asylums for the inebriate and spent his final years with James and his wife. This may explain why some of the most compelling first-person accounts in James's work of divided selves and sick souls who were later transformed come from people who were drunkards. (This may also explain why Bill Wilson, one of the founders of Alcoholics Anonymous, was so taken with William James. He was able to see himself in these stories and as a consequence, make sense of his own conversion experience when he sobered up for good in 1934.)

James's description tracks our knowledge of addiction accordingly. The first stage of world sickness is what I would call "pleasure diminished." What had previously brought joy or pleasure before now brings it less often and to lesser degrees. For an addict, the buzz just isn't as much fun. It just isn't the same, yet she will continue to seek it.

"Pleasure destroyed" is the second stage. More and more things are seen as or end in disappointments; pessimism becomes the most frequent response. The pessimism grows, though at this point it still attaches to particular situations in life rather than to the whole of life. An addict will take any disappointment as a reason to use. As more things become disappointing, the more a person will understand herself to have reasons to use.

The final stage in this world sickness is best described as "patho-logical melancholy." The progression in this final stage is signifi-cant. First a person is no longer able to recognize joy and happiness. She experiences a melancholy and dreariness about life that makes her incapable of generating any joy for herself. The next phase is a melancholy in which a person generates an acute anguish about herself and the world. In this stage, a person feels self-loathing and acute anxiety. Her entire being, James would say, is choked with these feelings. Quite significantly, not only does the person see her-self as having no meaning or significance, but nothing in the world has meaning. This melancholy leads to a kind of utter hopelessness about the particular conditions in which one lives and the meaning of life in general. With this hopelessness, the drama of repentance and effort to repair will end. It would take too much energy and it just isn't worth it. Nothing is worth anything.

The person in the grips of the worst melancholy experiences a frightening anxiety about the universe and everything in it. At this point, panic and fright completely govern a person. James describes a man who admitted that a "horrible fear of my own existence" came upon him one night. The man suddenly remembered an epileptic patient he had seen in an asylum who had greenish skin and sat "like some sort of Egyptian cat or Peruvian mummy, moving nothing but his black eyes and looking absolutely nonhuman. This image and my fear entered a combination with each other. *That shape am I*, I felt potentially . . . I awoke morning after morning with a horrible dread at the pit of my stomach, and with a sense of the insecurity of life that I never knew before, and that I have never felt since." In a let-ter to a friend after the publication of *Varieties*, James admitted this was his very own experience as a young man. He himself had walked right up to the edge of a yawning abyss. James scholars debate the exact date of this crisis, but most locate it sometime when James was in his late twenties.

Nietzsche recognized that "when you gaze long into an abyss the abyss also gazes into you." Kierkegaard realized that some people were more afraid of jumping into that abyss than falling. James understood this fear and saw the potential for transformation "through a passion of renunciation of the self and surrender to the higher power." It is after this renunciation that one can experience "the acute fever" of a spiritual life.

The terms *surrender* and *higher power* and *powerlessness* are apt to leave some people uneasy (they are key phrases and concepts in twelve-step programs everywhere). To surrender, in more Jamesian terms, is to make oneself open to new possibilities. To surrender is to stop clutching core beliefs or parts of one's identity so tightly. When one loosens her grip, she makes it possible to hold something—perhaps very tentatively—in her hands. In the case of a person whose self-worth or humanity has been decimated, it is a matter of being open to the possibility that just *maybe* she is worthy of a little dignity and respect. Surrendering can be simultaneously liberating and terrifying.

The when, where and how of surrender depends on a person's misery threshold. Someone with a low threshold cannot suffer long and so is willing to make changes. Others will be able to suffer enormously and not surrender until there is nothing left to lose. Each person's "rock bottom" is the point where misery can no longer be tolerated.

"Higher power" may leave even more people uneasy. James, however, uses the term in an elastic way. He does admit that "we Christians" call this higher power "God." But to illustrate what he calls a "higher and friendly power," James uses Henry David Thoreau's description of walking in the gentle mist at Walden Pond. Thoreau wrote, "Every little pine-needle expanded and swelled with sympathy and befriended me." Higher power can be nature, moral principles, patriotism, or a sense of fellowship or good will to others. For some, higher power is "enthusiasm for humanity." Each of these, James might say, takes a person outside or beyond herself and connects her to others and thus can be a higher power.

It is easy to identify the ways that "the acute fever" burned in the Christian saints who engaged in all sorts of acts of self-mortification. But it is not easily spotted in someone who has surrendered to and embraced a higher power about their addictive behaviors; there is no equivalent of sackcloth. There is, however, a unification of a previously divided self. People who know addicts in recovery often see this before the addict herself. A person with the acute fever of sobriety or recovery comes to have a firmness of mind and character. She has clear beliefs and principles and acts from them. She also has stability that is achieved and maintained by keeping various relationships with relatives, friends congruent with personal history, commitments, goals and beliefs. Each of these helps to hold the others steady. Finally, a person who burns with the acute fever of sobriety has equilibrium. She is able to strike the balance between opposing forces, some of which are in her control and others not.

No one person will be immune from all suffering. However, the acute fever transforms a person's life so that the drama, chaos and despair are, as James says, "severed like cobwebs, broken like bubbles." And this, James would proclaim, shows that hope and redemption are just as much part of the human condition.

APRIL 7, 2013

Being There: Heidegger on Why Our Presence Matters

—Lawrence Berger

A COGNITIVE SCIENTIST AND A GERMAN PHILOSOPHER WALK into the woods and come upon a tree in bloom: What does each one see? And why does it matter?

While that may sound like the set-up to a joke making the rounds at a philosophy conference, I pose it here sincerely, as a way to explore the implications of two distinct strains of thought—that of cognitive science and that of phenomenology, in particular, the thought of Martin Heidegger, who offers a most compelling vision of the ultimate significance of our being here, and what it means to be fully human.

It can be argued that cognitive scientists tend to ignore the importance of what many consider to be essential features of human existence, preferring to see us as information processors rather than full-blooded human beings immersed in worlds of significance. In general, their intent is to explain human activity and life as we experience it on the basis of physical and physiological processes, the implicit assumption being that this is the domain of what is ultimately real. Since virtually everything that matters to us as human beings can be traced back to life as it is experienced, such thinking is bound to be unsettling.

For instance, an article in the *Times* last year by Michael S. A. Graziano, a professor of psychology and neuroscience at Princeton, about whether we humans are "really conscious," argued, among other things, that "we don't actually have inner feelings in the way most of us think we do."

One feature of this line of thought that may strike us as particularly strange is that rather than being in direct contact with people and things, we are said to process bits of information that go to form representations of the world that are the basis for any relations that we have with our fellows. That would appear to be quite different from the way we actually experience things, but we are told to trust that science is more reliable because experience is often misleading in this regard.

This is not to say that all cognitive scientists see things this way; in fact there is a burgeoning school of thought referred to as the "4 E's" (embedded, embodied, extended and enactive), inspired in part by Heidegger and like-minded philosophers, that seeks to develop a richer view of life than is found in the cognitive science mainstream. But for now, I would like to focus on how Heidegger treats a topic of considerable importance in cognitive science, which is the phenomenon of attention.

On this basis I will show that, for Heidegger, not only are we in direct contact with the people and things of this world, but also that our presence matters for how they are made manifest—how they *come into presence*—in the full potential that is associated with the sort of beings that they are. This is not our presence in a physical sense, but rather in the sense of how we are engaged as living, experiencing human beings—what Heidegger famously refers to as our "being in the world." The thought is that our worldly presence matters for how things actually unfold, well beyond any physical or physiological processes that would purport to be the ultimate basis for human activity. So, for example, when we feel that someone is really listening to us, we feel more alive, we feel our true selves coming to the surface—this is the sense in which worldly presence matters.

Attention is one of the more intensively studied areas in cognitive science. As is well recognized in this literature, we cannot take in all of the stimuli that impinge upon the senses at a given time, so there must be some sort of filtering mechanism (that goes by the name of attention) before we get down to the business of representing reality. The question of attention has to do with all possible modes of human existence—all senses (visual, auditory, etc.) and other modalities such as thought, emotion and the imagination. Any information processing that provides access to things so they can be represented must first go through the filter of attention.

Heidegger similarly sees attention as the way we gain access to things, but otherwise he sees it quite differently from how it is conceived in cognitive science. For Heidegger attention is how things come into presence for us. (His most sustained meditation on attention can be found in his lectures, "What Is Called Thinking?") To see this, note that if we stay with the movement of attention from moment to moment, we see that it moves from entity to entity; that is, things come into presence at the foreground and then recede into the background.

For example, suppose I have to write a report, but there is noise in the other room, I have a pain in my leg, and I am worried that my spouse's eye may be wandering. To get the report done attention has to stay with the task, but there are competing influences that can take over the foreground and relegate the task to the background. All of these are potential foci of attention that come to the surface and then withdraw as another comes to the fore.

Heidegger's approach is to inquire into the nature of "being," which is simply understood to be how things in general come into presence and then withdraw. This means that attention is the human side of a universal process of manifestation of entities, with an associated effort that is referred to as *vigilance* in the cognitive science literature. This effort of *staying with* the entities that we encounter is crucially important for Heidegger, for if attention is how we gain access to anything at all, then staying with an entity would enable a deeper revelation of its nature. In this regard he emphasizes the fact that entities are made manifest over the course of time (hence his famous 1927 work, *Being and Time*). The idea is that staying with an entity as it unfolds affects the manner in which it is made manifest.

For instance, if I pay better attention to my spouse over the course of our relationship, I see more deeply into what she is about, she may respond in kind, and our relationship develops in unanticipated ways as a result. The same general principle applies to a purely physical object such as a stone. The manner in which such an object is made manifest can be affected by the quality of my presence, which explains why Heidegger was so interested in how poets experience the world in a fresh manner and bring that experience to language.

To verify the truth of such an assertion, it would be necessary to put it to the test of experience; that is, it would be necessary to see what happens when we deal with an entity such as a stone with an acute and sustained attentiveness, just staying open to what may be made manifest in the encounter. The hypothesis is that acute attentiveness can lead to a sense of an entity that goes beyond the way it is typically experienced. I can feel something more deeply because I come in direct contact with it in my worldly presence.

For instance, in one of the lectures mentioned above, Heidegger considers what it is to stand before a tree in bloom in a meadow. He asks how science decides which dimensions of the tree are considered to be real; is it the tree viewed at the cellular level, or as a mechanical system of sustenance, or is it the tree *as we experience it*? Indeed, how does science derive the authority to opine on such matters? He writes:

> We are today rather inclined to favor a supposedly superior physical and physiological knowledge, and to drop the blooming tree . . . The thing that matters first and foremost . . . is not to drop the tree in bloom, but for once to let it stand where it stands . . . To this day thought has never let the tree stand where it stands.

This means that staying with the experience of the tree enables it to come to full fruition, and that such experience matters in the overall scheme of being itself. For we are more deeply alive and in profound contact with all of the entities that we encounter when such a state is achieved, which means that we participate more fully in this universal process of manifestation.

At this point the objection will undoubtedly be raised, "Surely you don't mean to say that a tree or a stone can be made manifest in a more profound fashion. How can our presence affect the being of a such an entity?" This brings us to the depth of Heidegger's thought and his notion of being as a process of manifestation. For it is not unreasonable to ask, *given that* I experience a stone in a more profound manner, what does that have to do with the being of the stone itself?

We have come up against a deeply ingrained view of what it is to be a human being (which lends credence to views that our experience ultimately does not matter), which is that subjective experience takes place in a private realm that is cut off from the rest of reality. But Heidegger does not even make the distinction between the mental and the physical; for him our experience is an event in the world. The experience of the stone that I come to is part of the process of its manifestation in all of its possibilities. In this manner we are intimately related to the stone in our worldly presence, which is the site of its more profound manifestation. The claim is that the being of the stone itself is not independent of such an event.

For the question is, what is the stone and how are we related to it? The being of the stone and our relation to it cannot be conceived independently of the whole context in which we arise. The prevailing view is that the universe consists of discrete entities that are ultimately related by physical laws. We relate to other entities by way of mental representations of the whole—something like scientific observers who don't really belong here. Heidegger, on the other hand, offers a holistic view of all that is. We belong here together with the trees and the stones, for we are made manifest together. Rather than being discrete entities, the relation comes first, and the extent to which we are related matters for what we and the stone ultimately *are*.

Such an approach is bound to seem strange to modern sensibilities, but we have to look at what is at stake. On one view we are fundamentally cut off from the world, while on the other we are in direct and potentially profound relation with the people and things that we encounter. On this latter view there is unlimited potential for what can be made manifest by way of the effort that is called for; indeed, Heidegger suggests that there may be glimmers of the divine that await those who prepare the way. There can be little doubt that our presence matters if this is any indication of our true vocation.

MARCH 30, 2015

Against Invulnerability

—Todd May

LIKE MANY OF US, I AM OFTEN TROUBLED. I AM DISTRESSED BY my failure to be more than I am: a better philosopher, a better family member, a better person. And I know that if I could take a little more distance on the daily goings-on in my world that trouble me, I would probably be better in many if not all of these ways. This knowledge leads me to think of those philosophies that counsel rising above the things that disturb me so that I may arrive at a tranquil state of mind. Philosophies like Buddhism, Stoicism, Taoism, and possibly Epicureanism (the ancient philosophy, not its modern association with pleasures of the flesh) offer different ways of achieving such a tranquil state, and so they are tempting. I believe, however, that for most of us they are a false if beguiling path.

Buddhism, at least in its official doctrine, argues that if we abandon our desires by coming to understand the true nature of the cosmos and follow the Noble Eightfold Path, the end of suffering will follow. Stoicism similarly (but distinctly) counsels that we rid ourselves of emotion, and similarly (but again distinctly) offers a path of recognition of our place in the universe to help us get there. I do not wish to claim that either or both of these or related doctrines are mistaken. Instead, I want to say that most of us, when we really reflect upon our lives, would not want what is officially on offer, but instead something else.

In their official guise, these doctrines are examples of what I am going to label "invulnerabilism." They say that we can, and we should, make ourselves immune to the world's vicissitudes. What is central to invulnerabilist views is the belief that we can extricate ourselves from the world's contingencies so that they do not affect us. We are capable of making ourselves immune to the fortunes of our bodies, our thoughts, and our environment, and we will live better or happier or more pure lives if we do so. Whether the task involves the abolition of desire, the elimination of emotion or the recognition of the ultimate oneness of all things, the guiding idea is that we can and ought to make ourselves invulnerable to the world's vagaries.

For invulnerabilist views, what matters is only the present. After all, as they argue, the present is all there is, and therefore the only thing we can have an effect upon. Moreover, we can only be assured of having an effect upon ourselves in the present. Our effects upon the world are always uncertain. The task of invulnerabilism, then, is for us to inhabit the present fully and without reserve, letting go of the grip of our past and our desires for the future. Only if we do this can we render ourselves immune to the predations of our psychological tendencies, tendencies tied up with hope, regret, expectation and mourning.

Invulnerabilism recommends that we secrete a distance between ourselves and the world so that ultimately it cannot touch us. The extremity of such a view can be illustrated by reference to the Stoic's ratification of the ancient philosopher Anaxagoras's reported remark upon hearing of his son's death: "I always knew that my child was a mortal." It is possible perhaps that some few among us can reach this degree of distance from the world. But the question is, do we want it? I suspect I am not alone in thinking that the death of one of my children should shatter me, even if it should not ultimately destroy me.

Most of us want to feel caught up in the world. We want to feel gripped by what we do and those we care about, involved with them, taken up by them. The price of this involvement is our vulnerability. We must stand prepared to feel the loss of what we care about, because that is part of what it means to care. Caring requires desiring for the sake of others, which in an uncertain world entails that that desiring can be frustrated.

There are those who will argue that doctrines like Buddhism do not actually embrace the invulnerabilism I have saddled them with here. There are many Buddhists who feel the world deeply, and in particular are deeply compassionate about others. This is certainly true. I have in my life known two people I would call wise. One described himself as a Buddhist and the other as a Taoist. And both of them made themselves vulnerable to the world, and especially to those around them. So what then am I arguing here?

I am arguing that even many people who describe themselves or their goals in invulnerablist terms do not actually live or seek to live that way. The official doctrines, the ones that offer ultimate peace with oneself, a place of stillness that cannot be shaken, are in most cases a misrepresentation of what people are like or even what they want. Instead, something else is happening, something that involves some of the insights of invulnerabilist doctrines but does not embrace them in what I'm calling their official form.

As far as I can tell, the way to think about these things has less to do with the invulnerability promoted by the official doctrines, and more to do with, one might say, using these doctrines to take the edge off of vulnerability, to allow one to experience life without becoming overwhelmed or depressed or resentful or bitter, except perhaps at the extremity of loss. There is some combination of embedding oneself in the world in a vulnerable way and not being completely undone by that vulnerability that is pointed at, if not directly endorsed, by the official doctrines.

It seems to me that Taoism, Buddhism, Stoicism, etc. work not by making one invulnerable but rather by allowing one to step back from the immediacy of the situation so that the experience of pain or suffering is seen for what it is, precisely as part of a contingent process, a process that could have yielded a very different present but just happened to yield this one. This, of course, is not the official doctrine either, especially for Stoicism, for which the unfolding of the cosmos is a rational one. (Buddhists will periodically refer to the contingency of the cosmos' unfolding; however, the concept of nirvana bends that contingency toward something more nearly rational, or at least just.) But it does seem to me to capture their common insight that there is so much about the world that we cannot control; seeking to master it is an illusion. We must learn instead to live with the process in all its contingency, even where we hope to change it for the better. And we must understand that for most of us suffering is inevitable. We can recognize all this and take solace from it without having to take the step of removing ourselves from the desires that lead to suffering.

For instance, I am a New Yorker born and bred, and have lived largely as a foreigner for the past two decades in suburban South Carolina. (New Yorkers, I suspect, rarely thrive for long periods outside the city, or at least some major city.) Sometimes I tell myself that my life is certainly far better here than most other lives on the planet. And this is certainly true. But it rarely seems to me to be helpful in those periods where I feel an exile. Instead, it leads more to an attitude of "it's bad for almost everyone, except the lucky few." That hardly counts as wisdom, and does little to comfort me. But suppose I think of it differently. Life is contingent. The very same trajectory that led me to South Carolina also gave me my family, my opportunity to study philosophy, many of the friends I have and much else.

Now it might be that a slightly different process would have led to a better life (in whatever sense of better one wants to use, which itself is a vexed issue). It also might have led to a much worse one. The fact is, here I am, with this life trajectory and these goods and ills and there you have it. Because that is how things work. This doesn't make me immune to feeling myself a foreigner, and it doesn't imply that I should not try to improve my life or the lives of those around me, but it does give me solace that exile is not all there is to the contingency of this life, my particular life.

Now apply that attitude toward a more difficult situation, that of losing a job or the end of a love relationship. It seems to me apt that these things should hurt more than the gnawing sense that one isn't at home in one's environment. In any event, I wouldn't conclude that someone who felt these losses keenly was lacking in proper insight. But perhaps knowing that the world is contingent, that everything comes and goes, and that we have only so much control over our lives will help us come to terms with these losses, and while not draining them of suffering, remove some of the searing character often associated with them.

Of course this will not work for every situation. I don't know how one copes with the death of a child, although people do. Nor do I think that this should be much solace to those who live under dire oppression or in grinding poverty. The cure for these latter two ills is a more just political order. But for those of us who find ourselves neither entirely blessed nor entirely bereft, there is something to be said for taking this perspective on the troubles that plague us. What I have argued here is that such a taking of perspective is not a matter of making ourselves invulnerable to the world. There may be those who seek invulnerability, and even those who achieve it. But for the rest of us who want something other than immunity, the lessons of invulnerabilist approaches should be something other than their official doctrines. Or, to put it another way, in taking on those lessons, such as a focus on the present moment or a recognition of the contingency of things, they should be seen as exercises rather than as goals.

These exercises help us live with rather than overcome what we cannot control, come to some sort of terms with what inevitably helps define us. But for those who choose to remain vulnerable, life is not and cannot be undergone as anything other than a fraught trajectory, one hedged about by an inescapable contingency, and one that is likely to leave scars alongside its joys. And for most of us, most of the time, we would not want it to be any other way.

DECEMBER 27, 2014

Why Life Is Absurd

—Rivka Weinberg

A Consideration of Time, Space, Relativity, Meaning and Absurdity (Yep, All of It)

I. RELATIVITY

DZIGAN: Professor Einstein said, "In the world, there is time. And just as there is time, there is another thing: space. Space and time, time and space. And these two things," he said, "are relative."

Do you know what "relative" means?
SHUMACHER: Sigh. Nu? The point? Continue.
DZIGAN: There is no person these days who doesn't know what "relative" means. I will explain it to you with an analogy and soon you will also know. Relativity is like this: If you have seven hairs on your head, it's very few but if you have seven hairs in your milk, it's very many.*

*Excerpt from the comedy routine "Einstein/Weinstein," by the Yiddish comedy duo Shimon Dzigan and Yisroel Shumacher, audio recording, Savethemusic.com, the Jewish Music Archive, Jewish songs performed by Shimon Dzigan and Yisroel Shumacher. Translated from the Yiddish audio by Rivka Weinberg.

II. ABSURDITY

In the 1870s, Leo Tolstoy became depressed about life's futility. He had it all but so what? In *My Confession*, he wrote: "Sooner or later there will come diseases and death (they had come already) to my dear ones and to me, and there would be nothing left but stench and worms. All my affairs, no matter what they might be, would sooner or later be forgotten, and I myself should not exist. So why should I worry about these things?"

Life's brevity bothered Tolstoy so much that he resolved to adopt religious faith to connect to the infinite afterlife, even though he considered religious belief "irrational" and "monstrous." Was Tolstoy right? Is life so short as to make a mockery of people and their purposes and to render human life absurd?

In a famous 1971 paper, "The Absurd," Thomas Nagel argues that life's absurdity has nothing to do with its length. If a short life is absurd, he says, a longer life would be even more absurd: "Our lives are mere instants even on a geological time scale, let alone a cosmic one; we will all be dead any minute. But of course none of these evident facts can be what makes life absurd, if it is absurd. For suppose we lived forever; would not a life that is absurd if it lasts 70 years be infinitely absurd if it lasted through eternity?"

This line of reasoning has a nice ring to it but whether lengthening an absurd thing will relieve it of its absurdity depends on why the thing is absurd and how much you lengthen it. A longer life might be less absurd even if an infinite life would not be. As short poem that is absurd because it is written in gibberish would be even more absurd if it prattled on for longer. But, say I decided to wear a skirt so short it could be mistaken for a belt. On my way to teach my class, a colleague intercepts me:

"Your skirt," she says, "is absurd."

"Absurd? Why?" I ask.

"Because it is so short!" she replies.

"If a short skirt is absurd, a longer skirt would be even more absurd," I retort.

Now who's being absurd? The skirt is absurd *because* it is so short. A longer skirt would be less absurd. Why? Because it does not suffer from the feature that makes the short skirt absurd, namely, a ridiculously short length. The same goes for a one-hour hunger strike. The point of a hunger strike is to show that one feels so strongly about something that one is willing to suffer a lack of nourishment for a long time in order to make a point. If you only "starve" for an hour, you have not made your point. Your one-hour hunger strike is absurd because it is too short. If you lengthened it to one month or one year, you might be taken more seriously. If life is absurd *because* it's short, it might be less absurd if it were suitably longer.

Absurdity occurs when things are so ill-fitting or ill-suited to their purpose or situation as to be ridiculous, like wearing a clown costume to a (non-circus) job interview or demanding that your dog tell you what time it is. Is the lifespan of a relatively healthy and well-preserved human, say somewhere between seventy-five and eighty-five, so short as to render it absurd, ill-suited to reasonable human purposes?

III. TIME

Time, as we all knew before Einstein elaborated, is relative. It flies when we are having fun; it "creeps in this petty pace from day to day" when we are wracked with guilt. Five minutes is too short a time to explain Einstein's theory of relativity but it's just the right length of time for the Dzigan and Shumacher routine about it. Our perception of time is relative to space, yes, but also to purpose, to other spans of time, to task and probably to other things I have not thought of.

To assess whether human life is usually too short, consider human aims and purposes. People are commonly thought to have two central concerns: love and work. So much has been written about how little time there is to do both that we need not elaborate. Suffice it to say that when people ask me how I manage to be a philosopher, mother, teacher, wife, writer, etc., the answer is obvious: by doing everything badly. We could abandon love or abandon work, but giving up one fundamental human pursuit in order to have time for a better shot at the other leaves us with, at best, half a life. And even half a life is not really accessible to most of us—life is too short for work alone.

By the time we have an inkling about what sort of work we might enjoy and do well, most of us have little time to do it. By the time we figure anything out, we are already losing our minds. Age-related cognitive decline begins in our *twenties*, just as our prefrontal cortex, which is responsible for judgment, is finally completing its lengthy maturation process. The rate of cognitive decline increases as we age, with a steep increase after age sixty.

We don't fare much better with time to love. It takes time and experience to develop the wisdom and maturity to choose an appropriate partner and love him or her in a way that doesn't make everyone miserable. Relationships need attention, and attention takes time. Children take lots of time too, and some reflection and experience, yet we are biologically made to bear children when we are young and unwise.

Maybe the problem is not that we don't have enough time but that we waste the time we have. Seneca famously thought this. ("It is not that we have a short time to live, but that we waste a lot of it.") Most of us seem unable to refrain from "wasting" time. It is the rare person indeed who can be maximally efficient and productive. For the rest of us—that is, for almost all of us—Seneca's advice about not wasting time seems true but useless.

If we devoted our entire lives to one great painting or one beautiful melody, even if that work was a masterpiece, we might feel absurd to have spent our entire lives on it. A life so spent is bound to have been narrow, confining and oddly obsessive. That doesn't seem to be a reasonable way to spend one's entire life. It seems out of scale. But if life were much longer, we might have enough time to write many books, paint many paintings, compose many melodies and, over a couple of hundred years or so, get really good at it. We might even feel fulfilled, accomplished and decidedly non-absurd. Maybe not, but we would have more of a chance than we do now, in our fleeting, ludicrous, minute lifespan.

What if we lived for, say, 500 or 1,000 years? Would our ambition tend to grow to scale, making life seem absurdly short for human purposes, whatever its length? Is it human nature to adopt outsized ambitions, condemning ourselves to absurdity by having conceptions of reasonable achievement that we don't have the time to realize? Why haven't we scaled down our ambitions to fit the time we have? Is the problem our nature or our lifespan?

There may be no way to be sure but consider the fact that, although we have ambitions unsuited to our lifespan, we don't seem to consistently adopt ambitions unsuited to our species in respects other than time. It's not absurd to us that we cannot fly or hibernate. We don't think the fact that we can hold our breath for minutes rather than hours or memorize a few pages rather than a tome makes human life meaningless. We don't find that our inability to read each other's minds, speak to animals, glow in the dark, run sixty miles an hour, solve complex equations in our heads simultaneously or lift thousand-pound weights makes a sad mockery of human existence. This makes it more likely that, given a longer lifespan, life might seem less absurdly short for our purposes.

Just as a lifespan can be too short, it can be too long. For many, it is far too long already. Many people are bored with life, irritated by the human condition, exhausted from suffering, tired of living. For those for whom life is too long, a longer life would be worse and, quite possibly, more absurd. For some, however, life seems too long because it's too short, meaning life is rendered so absurd by being short that even a short absurd life feels too long because it is pointless. A life made absurd because it is too short would be rendered less absurd if it were significantly longer.

A million-year or infinite life might be too long for human nature and purposes too, though such a life would be so radically different that we can only speculate. An infinite life might become tedious, and people world-weary. Lifetime love commitments, a source of meaning now, would likely cease to exist. A million-year or infinite lifespan might be too long and slip into absurdity. To everything its time. Both a too short lifespan and a too long lifespan present absurdist challenges to a meaningful life.

For a 500- or 1,000-year lifespan to work to reduce life's absurdity, we would have to be able to sustain a sense of self over that time. So long as our memories function well and our psychological continuity can be maintained, our sense of identity might hold up (at least to a degree not all that different from our current condition). There is also the matter of perception. As we age, time seems to pass more quickly, probably because we become accustomed to life and pay less attention. If life were much longer, we would have to find a way to notice so that it didn't seem to still pass in a flash of our inattention. And then there is our health. Clearly, it will not be less absurd to lengthen our period of decrepitude. The longer lifespan would have to be mostly spent in decent health. An appropriately lengthened lifespan might make life much less absurd.

IV. SPACE

In the scheme of things, humans take up very little space. The Earth is a miniscule part of the universe. And each individual takes up so little space on this miniscule part of the universe as to occupy almost no space at all, relative to the entire universe or even to the planet Earth. Our physical smallness relative to the Earth and the universe is taken by some to imply insignificance and, in turn, our absurdity.

But absurdity occurs when things are ill-suited to their purposes, and neither human size nor the space allotted to humans is ill-suited to human purposes. Unlike the time of a human lifespan, which is ill-suited to our purposes, the space allotted to humans isn't. We're neither too small nor too large to do what we want to do. We are not forced to live cramped in tiny caves; we are not so light as to be blown around by the wind. If we had to stand on each other's backs to reach the leaves that we needed for sustenance, that might make us feel absurdly small. But we'd probably adapt to accommodate this feature of our physiology or build ladders for easier foraging. If the atmosphere thinned out at four feet, we might feel absurdly large, crawling awkwardly on our bellies in order to breathe. Yet, if we were belly crawlers that would seem normal to us and our bodies would adapt to crawling. We have evolved and adapted to our space, both to the space we take up and to the space available to us.

Space is more manipulable than time. We build chairs and tables to human size; we blast through mountains to clear space for roads. We build living space horizontally and vertically so that we can live in densely populated cities. To some extent, we've conquered space by increasing the speed of human travel and developing technologies to enable us to communicate easily across great distances. This has made life more convenient but not less absurd because the absurdity of human life is not a space problem. Given enough time, we could cover more space, but more space will not solve our time-related difficulties.

People have spatial needs, but, given that we can manipulate or adapt to our spatial parameters, our size and the space we have to live in do not seem crucial to our sense of ourselves. Very short lives seem incomplete, even tragic, but we don't have comparable views about people who are very large or very small. So who cares if we are small? That is an idiosyncrasy, if you care to note it. It does not entail our insignificance. The fact that we're miniscule relative to the vast universe is not a way of showing that our relationship to space makes our lives absurd. It's just a long way of saying we are small (small is a relative term, and this long way of saying we are small specifies what we are small in relation to). Our size does not matter.

The English poet Andrew Marvell, in his famous poem "To His Coy Mistress," begins his request for seizing the day for love by saying that if he could, he would wait and woo far longer before going at it: "Had we but world enough, and time / This coyness lady, were no crime." Marvell was right about time but wrong about the world. We have too little time, but there's world aplenty.

V. MEANING

The absurdity of human life poses a challenge to its meaning. Absurdity and meaningfulness don't go together. This, however, does not mean that if life were not absurd then it would have meaning. Removing the obstacle of absurdity does not entail that meaning rushes in. But if we cannot remove the obstacle of absurdity then it will be hard to conclude that life has meaning or determine what that meaning might be. The clown suit is standing in our way.

JANUARY 11, 2015

A Life Beyond "Do What You Love"

—Gordon Marino

STUDENT ADVISEES OFTEN COME TO MY OFFICE, RUBBING THEIR hands together, furrowing their brows and asking me to walk along with them as they ponder life after graduation. Just the other day, a sophomore made an appointment because he was worrying about whether he should become a doctor or a philosophy professor. A few minutes later, he nervously confessed that he had also thought of giving standup comedy a whirl.

As an occupational counselor, my kneejerk reaction has always been, "What are you most passionate about?" Sometimes I'd even go into a sermonette about how it is important to distinguish between what we think we are supposed to love and what we really love.

But is "do what you love" wisdom or malarkey?

In a much discussed article in *Jacobin* magazine early this year, the writer Miya Tokumitsu argued that the "do what you love" ethos so ubiquitous in our culture is in fact elitist because it degrades work that is not done from love. It also ignores the idea that work itself possesses an inherent value, and most importantly, severs the traditional connection between work, talent and duty.

When I am off campus and informally counseling economically challenged kids in Northfield, Minn., a city of about 20,000, the theme is not "do what you love." Many of them are used to delivering papers at 5 a.m., slinging shingles all day or loading trucks all night. They are accustomed to doing whatever they need to do to help out their families. For them, the notion of doing what you love or find meaningful is not the idea that comes first to mind; nor should it. We put our heads together and consider, "What are you best at doing?" or "What job would most improve your family's prospects?" Maybe being licensed as a welder or electrician? Maybe the military? Passion and meaning may enter into the mix of our chats with the understanding that they sharpen your focus and make you more successful.

My father didn't do what he loved. He labored at a job he detested so that he could send his children to college. Was he just unenlightened and mistaken to put the well-being of others above his own personal interests? It might be argued that his idea of self-fulfillment was taking care of his family, but again, like so many other less than fortunate ones, he hated his work but gritted his teeth and did it well.

It could, I suppose, be argued that my father turned necessity into a virtue, or that taking the best care you can of your family is really a form of self-service. But getting outside yourself enough to put your own passions aside for the benefit of a larger circle, be it family or society, does not come naturally to everyone.

Not all take this path. You may know the tale of Dr. John Kitchin, aka Slomo, who quit his medical practice for his true passion—skating along the boardwalk of San Diego's Pacific Beach. But is it ethical for the doctor to put away his stethoscope and lace up his skates?

Thinkers as profound as Kant have grappled with this question. In the old days, before the death of God, the faithful believed that their talents were gifts from on high, which they were duty-bound to use in service to others. In his treatise on ethics, "The Groundwork for the Metaphysics of Morals," Kant ponders: Suppose a man "finds in himself a talent which might make him a useful man in many respects. But he finds himself in comfortable circumstances and prefers to indulge in pleasure rather than take pains in enlarging his happy natural capacities." Should he?

Kant huffs, no—one cannot possibly will that letting one's talents rust for the sake of pleasure should be a universal law of nature. "[A]s a rational being," he writes, "he necessarily wills that his faculties be developed, since they serve him, and have been given him, for all sorts of purposes." To Kant, it would be irrational to will a world that abided by the law "do what you love."

Perhaps, unlike Kant, you do not believe that the universe is swimming with purposes. Then is "do what you love," or "do what you find most meaningful" the first and last commandment? Not necessarily.

The faith that my likes and dislikes or our sense of meaning alone should decide what I do is part and parcel with the gospel of self-fulfillment. Philosophy has always been right to instruct that we can be as mistaken about our views on happiness as anything else. The same holds for the related notion of self-fulfillment. Suppose that true self-fulfillment comes in the form of developing into "a mature human being." This is of course not to claim that we ought to avoid work that we love doing just because we love doing it. That would be absurd. For some, a happy harmony exists or develops in which they find pleasure in using their talents in a responsible, other-oriented way.

The universally recognized paragons of humanity—the Nelson Mandelas, Dietrich Bonhoeffers and Martin Luther Kings—did not organize their lives around self-fulfillment and bucket lists. They, no doubt, found a sense of meaning in their heroic acts of self-sacrifice, but they did not do what they were doing in order to achieve that sense of meaning. They did—like my father and some of those kids from town—what they felt they had to do.

Dr. King taught that every life is marked by dimensions of length, breadth and height. Length refers to self-love, breadth to the community and care of others, and height to the transcendent, to something larger than oneself. Most would agree with Dr. King's prescription that self-fulfillment requires being able to relate yourself to something higher than the self. Traditionally, that something "higher" was code for God, but whatever the transcendent is, it demands obedience and the willingness to submerge and remold our desires.

Perhaps you relish running marathons. Perhaps you even think of your exercise regimen as a form of self-improvement. But if your "something higher" is, say, justice and equality, those ideals might behoove you to delegate some of the many hours spent pounding the track on tutoring kids at the youth center. Our desires should not be the ultimate arbiters of vocation. Sometimes we should do what we hate, or what most needs doing, and do it as best we can.

MAY 17, 2014

ON HUMAN NATURE

Evolution and Our Inner Conflict

—*Edward O. Wilson*

ARE HUMAN BEINGS INTRINSICALLY GOOD BUT CORRUPTIBLE BY
the forces of evil, or the reverse, innately sinful yet redeemable by
the forces of good? Are we built to pledge our lives to a group, even
to the risk of death, or the opposite, built to place ourselves and our
families above all else? Scientific evidence, a good part of it accu-
mulated during the past twenty years, suggests that we are all of
these things simultaneously. Each of us is inherently complicated.
We are all genetic chimeras, at once saints and sinners—not because
humanity has failed to reach some foreordained religious or ideological ideal but because of the way our species originated across
millions of years of biological evolution.

Don't get me wrong. I am not implying that we are driven by
instinct in the manner of animals. Yet in order to understand the
human condition, it is necessary to accept that we do have instincts
and will be wise to take into account our very distant ancestors, as far
back and in as fine a detail as possible. History is not enough to reach
this level of understanding. It stops at the dawn of literacy, where
it turns the rest of the story over to the detective work of archaeol-
ogy; in still deeper time the quest becomes paleontology. For the real
human story, history makes no sense without prehistory, and prehistory makes no sense without biology.

Within biology itself, the key to the mystery is the force that lifted
prehuman social behavior to the human level. The leading candidate

in my judgment is multilevel selection by which hereditary social behavior improves the competitive ability not of just individuals within groups but among groups as a whole. Its consequences can be plainly seen in the caste systems of ants, termites and other social insects. Between-group selection as a force operating in addition to between-individual selection simultaneously is not a new idea in biology. Charles Darwin correctly deduced its role, first in the insects and then in human beings—respectively in *On the Origin of Species* and *The Descent of Man*.

Even so, the reader should be warned that the revival of multi-level selection as the principal force of social evolution remains a hotly contested idea. Its opponents believe the principal force to be kin selection: when individuals favor kin (other than offspring), the evolution of altruistic behavior is favored. The loss suffered by the genes of the altruist are compensated by genes in the recipient made identical by common descent of the altruist and recipient. If the altruism thus created is strong enough, it can lead to advanced social behavior. This seems plausible, but in 2010 two mathematical biologists, Martin Nowak and Corina Tarnita, and I demonstrated that the mathematical foundations of the kin-selection theory are unsound, and that examples from nature thought to support kin-selection theory are better explained as products of multilevel selection.

A strong reaction from supporters of kin selection not surprisingly ensued, and soon afterward more than 130 of them famously signed on to protest our replacement of kin selection by multilevel selection, and most emphatically the key role given to group selection. But at no time have our mathematical and empirical arguments been refuted or even seriously challenged. Since that protest, the number of supporters of the multilevel-selection approach has grown, to the extent that a similarly long list of signatories could be obtained. But such exercises are futile: science is not advanced by polling. If it were, we would still be releasing phlogiston to burn logs and navigating the sky with geocentric maps.

I am convinced after years of research on the subject that multilevel selection, with a powerful role of group-to-group competition, has forged advanced social behavior—including that of humans, as I documented in my recent book *The Social Conquest of Earth*. In fact, it seems clear that so deeply ingrained are the evolutionary products of group-selected behaviors, so completely a part of the human condition, that we are prone to regard them as fixtures of nature, like air and water. They are instead idiosyncratic traits of our species. Among them is the intense, obsessive interest of people in other people, which begins in the first days of life as infants learn particular scents and sounds of the adults around them. Research psychologists have found that all normal humans are geniuses at reading the intentions of others, whereby they evaluate, gossip, proselytize, bond, cooperate and control. Each person, working his way back and forth through his social network, almost continuously reviews past experiences while imagining the consequences of future scenarios.

A second diagnostic hereditary peculiarity of human behavior is the overpowering instinctual urge to belong to groups in the first place. To be kept in solitude is to be kept in pain and put on the road to madness. A person's membership in his group—his tribe—is a large part of his identity. It also confers upon him to some degree or other a sense of superiority. When psychologists selected teams at random from a population of volunteers to compete in simple games, members of each team soon came to think of members of other teams as less able and trustworthy, even when the participants knew they had been selected at random.

All things being equal (fortunately things are seldom equal, not exactly), people prefer to be with others who look like them, speak the same dialect, and hold the same beliefs. An amplification of this evidently inborn predisposition leads with frightening ease to racism and religious bigotry.

It might be supposed that the human condition is so distinctive and came so late in the history of life on Earth as to suggest the hand of a divine creator. Yet in a critical sense the human achievement was not unique at all. Biologists have identified about two dozen evolutionary lines in the modern world fauna that attained advanced social life based on some degree of altruistic division of labor. Most arose in the insects. Several were independent origins, in marine shrimp, and three appeared among the mammals—that is, in two African mole rats, and us. All reached this level through the same narrow gateway: solitary individuals, or mated pairs, or small groups of individuals built nests and foraged from the nest for food with which they progressively raised their offspring to maturity.

Until about three million years ago, the ancestors of *Homo sapiens* were mostly vegetarians, and they most likely wandered in groups from site to site where fruit, tubers, and other vegetable food could be harvested. Their brains were only slightly larger than those of modern chimpanzees. By no later than half a million years ago, however, groups of the ancestral species *Homo erectus* were maintaining campsites with controlled fire—the equivalent of nests—from which they foraged and returned with food, including a substantial portion of meat. Their brain size had increased to midsize, between that of chimpanzees and modern *Homo sapiens*. The trend appears to have begun one to two million years previously, when the earlier prehuman ancestor *Homo habilis* turned increasingly to meat in its diet. With groups crowded together at a single site, and an advantage added by cooperative nest building and hunting, social intelligence grew, along with the centers of memory and reasoning in the prefrontal cortex.

Probably at this point, during the habiline period, a conflict ensued between individual-level selection, with individuals competing with other individuals in the same group, versus group-level selection, with competition among groups. The latter force promoted altruism and cooperation among all the group members. It led to group-wide morality and a sense of conscience and honor. The competitor between the two forces can be succinctly expressed as follows: within groups selfish individuals beat altruistic individuals, but groups of altruists beat groups of selfish individuals. Or, risking oversimplification, individual selection promoted sin, while group selection promoted virtue.

So it appeared that humans are forever conflicted by their prehistory of multilevel selection. They are suspended in unstable and constantly changing locations between the two extreme forces that created us. We are unlikely to yield completely to either force as an ideal solution to our social and political turmoil. To yield completely to the instinctual urgings born from individual selection would dissolve society. To surrender to the urgings from group selection would turn us into angelic robots—students of insects call them ants.

The eternal conflict is not God's test of humanity. It is not a machination of Satan. It is just the way things worked out. It might be the only way in the entire universe that human-level intelligence and social organization can evolve. We will find a way eventually to live with our inborn turmoil, and perhaps find pleasure in viewing it as a primary source of our creativity.

JUNE 24, 2012

Learning How to Die in the Anthropocene

—*Roy Scranton*

I.

DRIVING INTO IRAQ JUST AFTER THE 2003 INVASION FELT LIKE driving into the future. We convoyed all day, all night, past army checkpoints and burned-out tanks, till in the blue dawn Baghdad rose from the desert like a vision of hell: flames licked the bruised sky from the tops of refinery towers, cyclopean monuments bulged and leaned against the horizon, broken overpasses swooped and fell over ruined suburbs, bombed factories, and narrow ancient streets.

With "shock and awe," our military had unleashed the end of the world on a city of six million—a city about the same size as Houston or Washington. The infrastructure was totaled: water, power, traffic, markets and security fell to anarchy and local rule. The city's secular middle class was disappearing, squeezed out between gangsters, profiteers, fundamentalists and soldiers. The government was going down, walls were going up, tribal lines were being drawn, and brutal hierarchies were being savagely established.

I was a private in the United States Army. This strange, precarious world was my new home. If I survived.

Two and a half years later, safe and lazy back in Fort Sill, OK, I thought I had made it out. Then I watched on television as Hurricane Katrina hit New Orleans. This time it was the weather that brought shock and awe, but I saw the same chaos and urban collapse I'd seen in Baghdad, the same failure of planning and the same tide of anarchy. The 82nd Airborne hit the ground, took over strategic points and patrolled streets now under de facto martial law. My unit was put on alert to prepare for riot-control operations. The grim future I'd seen in Baghdad was coming home: not terrorism, not even WMDs, but a civilization in collapse, with a crippled infrastructure, unable to recuperate from shocks to its system.

And today, with recovery still going on more than a year after Sandy and many critics arguing that the Eastern Seaboard is no more prepared for a huge weather event than we were last November, it's clear that future's not going away.

This March, Admiral Samuel J. Locklear III, the commander of the United States Pacific Command, told security and foreign policy specialists in Cambridge, MA, that global climate change was the greatest threat the United States faced—more dangerous than terrorism, Chinese hackers, and North Korean nuclear missiles. Upheaval from increased temperatures, rising seas and radical destabilization "is probably the most likely thing that is going to happen," he said, ". . . that will cripple the security environment, probably more likely than the other scenarios we all often talk about."

Locklear's not alone. Tom Donilon, the national security adviser, said much the same thing in April, speaking to an audience at Columbia's new Center on Global Energy Policy. James Clapper, director of national intelligence, told the Senate in March that "extreme weather events (floods, droughts, heat waves) will increasingly disrupt food and energy markets, exacerbating state weakness, forcing human migrations, and triggering riots, civil disobedience, and vandalism."

On the civilian side, the World Bank's recent report, "Turn Down the Heat: Climate Extremes, Regional Impacts, and the Case for Resilience," offers a dire prognosis for the effects of global warming, which climatologists now predict will raise global temperatures by 3.6 degrees Fahrenheit within a generation and 7.2 degrees Fahrenheit within ninety years. Projections from researchers at the University of Hawaii find us dealing with "historically unprecedented" climates as soon as 2047. The climate scientist James Hansen, formerly with NASA, has argued that we face an "apocalyptic" future. This grim view is seconded by researchers worldwide, including Anders Levermann, Paul and Anne Ehrlich, Lonnie Thompson and many, many, many others.

This chorus of Jeremiahs predicts a radically transformed global climate forcing widespread upheaval—not possibly, not potentially, but *inevitably*. We have passed the point of no return. From the point of view of policy experts, climate scientists and national security officials, the question is no longer whether global warming exists or how we might stop it, but how we are going to deal with it.

II.

There's a word for this new era we live in: the Anthropocene. This term, taken up by geologists, pondered by intellectuals and discussed in the pages of publications such as the *Economist* and *The New York Times*, represents the idea that we have entered a new epoch in Earth's geological history, one characterized by the arrival of the human species as a geological force. The biologist Eugene F. Stoermer and the Nobel-Prize–winning chemist Paul Crutzen advanced the term in 2000, and it has steadily gained acceptance as evidence has increasingly mounted that the changes wrought by global warming will affect not just the world's climate and biological diversity, but its very geology—and not just for a few centuries, but for millenniums. The geophysicist David Archer's 2009 book, *The Long Thaw: How Humans Are Changing the Next 100,000 Years of Earth's Climate*, lays out a clear and concise argument for how huge concentrations of carbon dioxide in the atmosphere and melting ice will radically transform the planet, beyond freak storms and warmer summers, beyond any foreseeable future.

The Stratigraphy Commission of the Geological Society of London—the scientists responsible for pinning the "golden spikes" that demarcate geological epochs such as the Pliocene, Pleistocene, and Holocene—has adopted the Anthropocene as a term deserving further consideration, "significant on the scale of Earth history." Working groups are discussing what level of geological timescale it might be (an "epoch" like the Holocene, or merely an "age" like the Calabrian), and at what date we might say it began. The beginning of the Great Acceleration, in the middle of the twentieth century? The beginning of the Industrial Revolution, around 1800? The advent of agriculture?

The challenge the Anthropocene poses is a challenge not just to national security, to food and energy markets, or to our "way of life"—though these challenges are all real, profound, and inescapable. The greatest challenge the Anthropocene poses may be to our sense of what it means to be human. Within one hundred years— within three to five generations—we will face average temperatures seven degrees Fahrenheit higher than today, rising seas at least three to ten feet higher, and worldwide shifts in crop belts, growing seasons and population centers. Within a thousand years, unless we stop emitting greenhouse gases wholesale right now, humans will be living in a climate the Earth hasn't seen since the Pliocene, three million years ago, when oceans were seventy-five *feet* higher than they are today. We face the imminent collapse of the agricultural, shipping and energy networks upon which the global economy depends, a large-scale die-off in the biosphere that's already well on its way, and our own possible extinction. If *Homo sapiens* (or some genetically modified variant) survive the next millenniums, it will be survival in a world unrecognizably different from the one we have inhabited.

Geological timescales, civilization collapse and species extinction give rise to profound problems that humanities scholars and academic philosophers, with their taste for fine-grained analysis, esoteric debates and archival marginalia, might seem remarkably ill suited to address. After all, how will thinking about Kant help us trap carbon dioxide? Can arguments between object-oriented ontology and historical materialism protect honeybees from colony collapse disorder? Are ancient Greek philosophers, medieval theologians, and contemporary metaphysicians going to keep Bangladesh from being inundated by rising oceans?

Of course not. But the biggest problems the Anthropocene poses are precisely those that have always been at the root of humanistic and philosophical questioning: What does it mean to be human? and What does it mean to live? In the epoch of the Anthropocene, the question of individual mortality—What does *my life* mean in the face of death?—is universalized and framed in scales that boggle the imagination. What does human existence mean against 100,000 years of climate change? What does one life mean in the face of species death or the collapse of global civilization? How do we make meaningful choices in the shadow of our inevitable end?

These questions have no logical or empirical answers. They are philosophical problems *par excellence*. Many thinkers, including Cicero, Montaigne, Karl Jaspers, and The Stone's own Simon Critchley, have argued that studying philosophy is learning how to die. If that's true, then we have entered humanity's most philosophical age— for this is precisely the problem of the Anthropocene. The rub is that now we have to learn how to die not as individuals, but as a civilization.

III.

Learning how to die isn't easy. In Iraq, at the beginning, I was terrified by the idea. Baghdad seemed incredibly dangerous, even though statistically I was pretty safe. We got shot at and mortared, and IEDs laced every highway, but I had good armor, we had a great medic, and we were part of the most powerful military the world had ever seen. The odds were good I would come home. Maybe wounded, but probably alive. Every day I went out on mission, though, I looked down the barrel of the future and saw a dark, empty hole.

"For the soldier death is the future, the future his profession assigns him," wrote Simone Weil in her remarkable meditation on war, *The* Iliad *or the Poem of Force*. "Yet the idea of man's having death for a future is abhorrent to nature. Once the experience of war makes visible the possibility of death that lies locked up in each moment, our thoughts cannot travel from one day to the next without meeting death's face." That was the face I saw in the mirror, and its gaze nearly paralyzed me.

I found my way forward through an eighteenth-century samurai manual, Yamamoto Tsunetomo's *Hagakure*, which commanded, "Meditation on inevitable death should be performed daily." Instead of fearing my end, I owned it. Every morning, after doing maintenance on my Humvee, I'd imagine getting blown up by an IED, shot by a sniper, burned to death, run over by a tank, torn apart by dogs, captured and beheaded, and succumbing to dysentery. Then, before we rolled out through the gate, I'd tell myself that I didn't need to worry, because I was already dead. The only thing that mattered was that I did my best to make sure everyone else came back alive. "If by setting one's heart right every morning and evening, one is able to live as though his body were already dead," wrote Tsunetomo, "he gains freedom in the Way."

I got through my tour in Iraq one day at a time, meditating each morning on my inevitable end. When I left Iraq and came back Stateside, I thought I'd left that future behind. Then I saw it come home in the chaos that was unleashed after Katrina hit New Orleans. And then I saw it again when Sandy battered New York and New Jersey: government agencies failed to move quickly enough, and volunteer groups like Team Rubicon had to step in to manage disaster relief.

Now, when I look into our future—into the Anthropocene—I see water rising up to wash out Lower Manhattan. I see food riots, hurricanes, and climate refugees. I see 82nd Airborne soldiers shooting looters. I see grid failure, wrecked harbors, Fukushima waste, and plagues. I see Baghdad. I see the Rockaways. I see a strange, precarious world.

Our new home.

The human psyche naturally rebels against the idea of its end. Likewise, civilizations have throughout history marched blindly toward disaster, because humans are wired to believe that tomorrow will be much like today—it is unnatural for us to think that this way of life, this present moment, this order of things is not stable and permanent. Across the world today, our actions testify to our belief that we can go on like this forever, burning oil, poisoning the seas, killing off other species, pumping carbon into the air, ignoring the ominous silence of our coal mine canaries in favor of the unending robotic tweets of our new digital imaginarium. Yet the reality of global climate change is going to keep intruding on our fantasies of perpetual growth, permanent innovation and endless energy, just as the reality of mortality shocks our casual faith in permanence.

The biggest problem climate change poses isn't how the Department of Defense should plan for resource wars, or how we should put up seawalls to protect Alphabet City, or when we should evacuate Hoboken. It won't be addressed by buying a Prius, signing a treaty, or turning off the air-conditioning. The biggest problem we face is a philosophical one: understanding that this civilization is *already dead*. The sooner we confront this problem, and the sooner we realize there's nothing we can do to save ourselves, the sooner we can get down to the hard work of adapting, with mortal humility, to our new reality.

The choice is a clear one. We can continue acting as if tomorrow will be just like yesterday, growing less and less prepared for each new disaster as it comes, and more and more desperately invested in a life we can't sustain. Or we can learn to see each day as the death of what came before, freeing ourselves to deal with whatever problems the present offers without attachment or fear.

If we want to learn to live in the Anthropocene, we must first learn how to die.

NOVEMBER 10, 2013

Is Pure Altruism Possible?

—Judith Lichtenberg

WHO COULD DOUBT THE EXISTENCE OF ALTRUISM?
True, news stories of malice and greed abound. But all around us
we see evidence of human beings sacrificing themselves and doing
good for others. Remember Wesley Autrey? On January 2, 2007, Mr.
Autrey jumped down onto the tracks of a New York City subway platform as a train was approaching to save a man who had suffered a
seizure and fallen. A few months later the Virginia Tech professor
Liviu Librescu blocked the door to his classroom so his students
could escape the bullets of Seung-Hui Cho, who was on a rampage
that would leave thirty-two students and faculty members dead. In
so doing, Mr. Librescu gave his life.

Still, doubting altruism is easy, even when it seems at first glance
to be apparent. It's undeniable that people sometimes act in a way
that benefits others, but it may seem that they always get something
in return—at the very least, the satisfaction of having their desire
to help fulfilled. Students in introductory philosophy courses torture their professors with this reasoning. And its logic can seem
inexorable.

Contemporary discussions of altruism quickly turn to evolutionary explanations. Reciprocal altruism and kin selection are the two
main theories. According to reciprocal altruism, evolution favors
organisms that sacrifice their good for others in order to gain a favor
in return. Kin selection—the famous "selfish gene" theory popu-

larized by Richard Dawkins—says that an individual who behaves altruistically toward others who share its genes will tend to reproduce those genes. Organisms may be altruistic; genes are selfish. The feeling that loving your children more than yourself is hardwired lends plausibility to the theory of kin selection.

These evolutionary theories explain a puzzle: how organisms that sacrifice their own "reproductive fitness"—their ability to survive and reproduce—could possibly have evolved. But neither theory fully accounts for our ordinary understanding of altruism.

The defect of reciprocal altruism is clear. If a person acts to benefit another in the expectation that the favor will be returned, the natural response is, "That's not altruism!" Pure altruism, we think, requires a person to sacrifice for another without consideration of personal gain. Doing good for another person because something's in it for the doer is the very opposite of what we have in mind. Kin selection does better by allowing that organisms may genuinely sacrifice their interests for another, but it fails to explain why they sometimes do so for those with whom they share no genes, as Professor Librescu and Mr. Autrey did.

When we ask whether human beings are altruistic, we want to know about their motives or intentions. Biological altruism explains how unselfish behavior might have evolved, but as Frans de Waal suggested in his column in The Stone on Sunday, it implies nothing about the motives or intentions of the agent: after all, birds and bats and bees can act altruistically. This fact helps to explain why, despite these evolutionary theories, the view that people never intentionally act to benefit others except to obtain some good for themselves still possesses a powerful lure over our thinking.

The lure of this view—egoism—has two sources, one psychological, the other logical. Consider first the psychological. One reason people deny that altruism exists is that, looking inward, they doubt the purity of their own motives. We know that even when we appear to act unselfishly, other reasons for our behavior often rear their heads: the prospect of a future favor, the boost to reputation, or simply the good feeling that comes from appearing to act unselfishly. As

Kant and Freud observed, people's true motives may be hidden, even (or perhaps especially) from themselves. Even if we think we're acting solely to further another person's good, that might not be the real reason. (There might be no single "real reason"—actions can have multiple motives.)

So the psychological lure of egoism as a theory of human action is partly explained by a certain humility or skepticism people have about their own or others' motives. There's also a less flattering reason: denying the possibility of pure altruism provides a convenient excuse for selfish behavior. If "everybody is like that"—if everybody *must* be like that—we need not feel guilty about our own self-interested behavior or try to change it.

The logical lure of egoism is different: the view seems impossible to disprove. No matter how altruistic a person appears to be, it's possible to conceive of her motive in egoistic terms. On this way of looking at it, the guilt Mr. Autrey would have suffered had he ignored the man on the tracks made risking his life worth the gamble. The doctor who gives up a comfortable life to care for AIDS patients in a remote place does what she wants to do and therefore gets satisfaction from what only appears to be self-sacrifice. So, it seems, altruism is simply self-interest of a subtle kind.

The impossibility of disproving egoism may sound like a virtue of the theory, but, as philosophers of science know, it's really a fatal drawback. A theory that purports to tell us something about the world, as egoism does, should be falsifiable. Not false, of course, but capable of being tested and thus proved false. If every state of affairs is compatible with egoism, then egoism doesn't tell us anything distinctive about how things are.

A related reason for the lure of egoism, noted by Bishop Joseph Butler in the eighteenth century, concerns ambiguity in the concepts of desire and the satisfaction of desire. If people possess altruistic motives, then they sometimes act to benefit others without the prospect of gain to themselves. In other words, they desire the good of others for its own sake, not simply as a means to their own satisfaction. It's obvious that Professor Librescu desired that his students not die and acted accordingly to save their lives. He succeeded, so his desire was satisfied. But *he* was not satisfied—since he died in the attempt to save the students. From the fact that a person's desire is satisfied we can draw no conclusions about effects on his mental state or well-being.

Still, when our desires are satisfied, we normally experience satisfaction; we feel good when we do good. But that doesn't mean we do good only in order to get that "warm glow"—that our true incentives are self-interested (as economists tend to claim). Indeed, as de Waal argues, if we didn't desire the good of others for its own sake, then attaining it wouldn't produce the warm glow.

Common sense tells us that some people are more altruistic than others. Egoism's claim that these differences are illusory—that deep down, everybody acts only to further their own interests—contradicts our observations and deep-seated human practices of moral evaluation.

At the same time, we may notice that generous people don't necessarily suffer more or flourish less than those who are more self-interested. Altruists may be more content or fulfilled than selfish people. Nice guys don't always finish last.

But nor do they always finish first. The point is rather that the kind of altruism we ought to encourage, and probably the only kind with staying power, is satisfying to those who practice it. Studies of rescuers show that they don't believe their behavior is extraordinary; they feel they must do what they do, because it's just part of who they are. The same holds for more common, less newsworthy acts—working in soup kitchens, taking pets to people in nursing homes, helping strangers find their way, being neighborly. People who act in these ways believe that they ought to help others, but they also want to help because doing so affirms who they are and want to be and the kind of world they want to exist. As Professor Neera Badhwar has argued, their identity is tied up with their values, thus tying self-interest and altruism together. The correlation between doing good and feeling good is not inevitable—inevitability lands us again with that empty, unfalsifiable egoism—but it is more than incidental.

Altruists should not be confused with people who automatically sacrifice their own interests for others. We admire Paul Rusesabagina, the hotel manager who saved over one thousand Tutsis and Hutus during the 1994 Rwandan genocide; we admire health workers who give up comfortable lives to treat sick people in hard places. But we don't admire people who let others walk all over them; that amounts to lack of self-respect, not altruism.

Altruism is possible and altruism is real, although in healthy people it intertwines subtly with the well-being of the agent who does good. And this is crucial for seeing how to increase the amount of altruism in the world. Aristotle had it right in his *Nicomachean Ethics*: we have to raise people from their "very youth" and educate them "so as both to delight in and to be pained by the things that we ought."

OCTOBER 19, 2010

Moral Camouflage or Moral Monkeys?

—Peter Railton

Af, BEING SHOWN PROUDLY AROUND THE CAMPUS OF A PRES-
tigious American university built in gothic style, Bertrand Russell
is said to have exclaimed, "Remarkable. As near Oxford as monkeys
can make." Much earlier, Immanuel Kant had expressed a less ironic
amazement: "Two things fill the mind with ever new and increasing admiration and awe . . . the starry heavens above and the moral
law within." Today many who look at morality through a Darwinian
lens can't help but find a charming naïveté in Kant's thought. "Yes,
remarkable. As near morality as monkeys can make."

So the question is, just how near is that? Optimistic Darwinians
believe, near enough to be morality. But skeptical Darwinians won't
buy it. The great show we humans make of respect for moral principle they see as a civilized camouflage for an underlying, evolved
psychology of a quite different kind.

This skepticism is not, however, your great-grandfather's Social
Darwinism, which saw all creatures great and small as pitted against
one another in a life-or-death struggle to survive and reproduce—
"survival of the fittest." We now know that such a picture seriously
misrepresents both Darwin and the actual process of natural selection. Individuals come and go, but genes can persist for a thousand
generations or more. Individual plants and animals are the perish-
able vehicles that genetic material uses to make its way into the next
generation ("A chicken is an egg's way of making another egg"). From

this perspective, relatives, who share genes, are to that extent not really in *evolutionary* competition; no matter which one survives, the shared genes triumph. Such "inclusive fitness" predicts the survival not of selfish individuals but of "selfish" genes, which tend in the normal range of environments to give rise to individuals whose behavior tends to propel those genes into the future.

A place is thus made within Darwinian thought for such familiar phenomena as family members sacrificing for one another—helping when there is no prospect of payback, or being willing to risk life and limb to protect one's people or avenge harms done to them.

But what about unrelated individuals? "Sexual selection" occurs whenever one must attract a mate in order to reproduce. Well, what sorts of individuals are attractive partners? Henry Kissinger claimed that power is the ultimate aphrodisiac, but for animals who bear a small number of young over a lifetime, each requiring a long gestation and demanding a great deal of nurturance to thrive into maturity, potential mates who behave selfishly, uncaringly, and unreliably can lose their chance. And beyond mating, many social animals depend upon the cooperation of others for protection, foraging and hunting, or rearing the young. Here, too, power can attract partners, but so can a demonstrable tendency to behave cooperatively and share benefits and burdens fairly, even when this involves some personal sacrifice—what is sometimes called "reciprocal altruism." Baboons are notoriously hierarchical, but Joan Silk, a professor of anthropology at UCLA, and her colleagues recently reported a long-term study of baboons in which they found that among females, maintaining strong, equal, enduring social bonds—even when the individuals were not related—can promote individual longevity more effectively than gaining dominance rank, and can enhance the survival of progeny.

A picture thus emerges of selection for "proximal psychological mechanisms"—for example, individual dispositions like parental devotion, loyalty to family, trust and commitment among partners, generosity and gratitude among friends, courage in the face of enemies, intolerance of cheaters—that make individuals into good vehicles, from the gene's standpoint, for promoting the "distal goal" of enhanced inclusive fitness.

Why would human evolution have selected for such messy, emotionally entangling proximal psychological mechanisms, rather than produce yet more ideally opportunistic vehicles for the transmission of genes—individuals wearing a perfect camouflage of loyalty and reciprocity, but fine-tuned underneath to turn self-sacrifice or cooperation on or off exactly as needed? Because the same evolutionary processes would also be selecting for improved capacities to detect, preempt, and defend against such opportunistic tendencies in other individuals—just as evolution cannot produce a perfect immune system, since it is equally busily at work improving the effectiveness of viral invaders. Devotion, loyalty, honesty, empathy, gratitude, and a sense of fairness are credible signs of value as a partner or friend precisely *because* they are messy and emotionally entangling, and so cannot simply be turned on and off by the individual to capture each marginal advantage. And keep in mind the small scale of early human societies, and Abraham Lincoln's point about our power to deceive.

Why, then, aren't we *better*—more honest, more committed, more loyal? There will always be circumstances in which fooling some of the people some of the time is enough—for example, when society is unstable or individuals mobile. So we should expect a capacity for opportunism and betrayal to remain an important part of the mix that makes humans into monkeys worth writing novels about.

How close does all this take us to morality? Not all the way, certainly. An individual psychology primarily disposed to consider the interests of all equally, without fear or favor, even in the teeth of social ostracism, might be morally admirable but simply wouldn't cut it as a vehicle for reliable replication. Such *pure* altruism would not be favored in natural selection over an impure altruism that conferred benefits and took on burdens and risks more selectively—for "my kind" or "our kind." This puts us well beyond pure selfishness, but only as far as an impure *us*-ishness. Worse, us-ish individuals can be a greater threat than purely selfish ones, since they can gang up so effectively against those outside their group. Certainly greater atrocities have been committed in the name of "us vs. them" than "me vs. the world."

So, are the optimistic Darwinians wrong, and impartial morality beyond the reach of those monkeys we call humans? Does thoroughly logical evolutionary thinking force us to the conclusion that our love, loyalty, commitment, empathy, and concern for justice and fairness are always at bottom a mixture of selfish opportunism and us-ish clannishness? Indeed, is it only a sign of the effectiveness of the moral camouflage that we ourselves are so often taken in by it?

Speaking of what "thoroughly logical evolutionary thinking" might "force" us to conclude provides a clue to the answer. Think for a moment about science and logic themselves. Natural selection operates on a need-to-know basis. Between two individuals—one disposed to use scarce resources and finite capacities to seek out the most urgent and useful information and the other, heedless of immediate and personal concerns and disposed instead toward pure, disinterested inquiry, following logic wherever it might lead—it is clear which natural selection would tend to favor.

And yet, Darwinian skeptics about morality believe, humans somehow have managed to redeploy and leverage their limited, partial, human-scale psychologies to develop shared inquiry, experimental procedures, technologies and norms of logic and evidence that have resulted in genuine scientific knowledge and responsiveness to the force of logic. This distinctively human "cultural evolution" was centuries in the making, and overcoming partiality and bias remains a constant struggle, but the point is that these possibilities were not foreclosed by the imperfections and partiality of the faculties we inherited. As Wittgenstein observed, crude tools can be used to make refined tools. Monkeys, it turns out, can come surprisingly near to objective science.

We can see a similar cultural evolution in human law and morality—a centuries-long process of overcoming arbitrary distinctions, developing wider communities, and seeking more inclusive shared standards, such as the Geneva Conventions and the Universal Declaration of Humans Rights. Empathy might induce sympathy more readily when it is directed toward kith and kin, but we rely upon it to understand the thoughts and feelings of enemies and outsiders as well. And the human capacity for learning and following rules might have evolved to enable us to speak a native language or find our place in the social hierarchy, but it can be put into service understanding different languages and cultures, and developing more cosmopolitan or egalitarian norms that can be shared across our differences.

Within my own lifetime, I have seen dramatic changes in civil rights, women's rights, and gay rights. That's just one generation in evolutionary terms. Or consider the way that empathy and the pressure of consistency have led to widespread recognition that our fellow animals should receive humane treatment. Human culture, not natural selection, accomplished these changes, and yet it was natural selection that gave us the capacities that helped make them possible. We still must struggle continuously to see to it that our widened empathy is not lost, our sympathies engaged, our understandings enlarged, and our moral principles followed. But the point is that we have done this with our imperfect, partial, us-ish native endowment. Kant was right to be impressed. In our best moments, we can come surprisingly close to being moral monkeys.

JULY 18, 2010

How Should We Respond to "Evil"?

—Steven Paulikas

FOR A STUDENT OF EVIL, STEPHEN COLBERT'S EXCHANGE WITH Bill O'Reilly on *The Late Show* two days after the Orlando killings was an education. "This guy was evil," O'Reilly said of the gunman, Omar Mateen.

Colbert immediately asked, "What is the proper response to evil?"

"Destroy it," O'Reilly answered. "You don't contain evil, because you can't. You destroy evil. ISIS is evil, and Mateen is evil."

O'Reilly's attitude toward evil exemplifies the ethical justification for the most consequential American policy decisions of the past fifteen years—and, if we consent, for those that will be made in reaction to the Orlando massacre and others like it. Recent history and philosophy have taught that violence is the surest outcome of blithely ascribing the quality of evil to another. At best, this process may supplant the thing we brand evil for a time, but the notion that evil can be "destroyed" is an ethical version of a fool's errand. We have an opportunity now to reassess the politics of evil and to consider responses to it that would mitigate rather than amplify human suffering.

I was drawn to thought on evil as a seminarian trying to make sense of the intractable wars in Afghanistan and Iraq that framed my formation for the priesthood. I remembered when President George W. Bush described Iraq, Iran and North Korea as an "axis of evil" in his 2002 State of the Union address. Even now, the phrase evokes an instinctual sense of supernatural dread, which was precisely its purpose. As the presidential speechwriters David Frum and Michael Gerson were preparing the address, they tweaked the line from the slightly more benign "axis of hatred" to make it sound more "theological."

For most of Western intellectual history, the study of evil was reserved for theology. From Augustine and Aquinas to Luther and Calvin, Christian thinkers were preoccupied with the "problem of evil," or the question of how a good God could allow bad to exist in our world. When Immanuel Kant introduced the concept of a radical evil that exists outside the limits of reason and will, the eternal problem of evil was released from the church's exclusive grasp.

Perhaps because of its hybrid religious and secular credentials, our concept of evil exerts an almost mystical power over society's impulse to make order out of chaos and despair. As Susan Neiman writes in her landmark study, *Evil in Modern Thought*, "The problem of evil can be expressed in theological or secular terms, but it is fundamentally a problem about the intelligibility of the world as a whole."

Doubtless, Frum and Gerson were striving to answer the country's need for intelligibility amid the new and frightening sense of insecurity at the time. Yet as events unfolded, the axiomatic and quasi-theological assertion of evil pervading the entire Iraqi regime became the incontrovertible ethical framework for violent action.

As it turns out, there is a difference between good theology and bad theology—at least if we consider the exponential escalation of violence to be a bad thing. The almost 3,000 deaths in the Sept. 11 attacks were answered by an estimated 460,000 deaths in Iraq alone, including more American combatant deaths than civilians who died in the World Trade Center. Despite this high cost, evil is, if we accept a point on which O'Reilly actually agrees with President Obama, as plentiful in the region as it ever was and just as threatening to the United States.

As someone entrusted with a role of moral authority, I am deeply unsettled by this path from evil in political rhetoric to violence. Our inability to answer fundamental questions about the invocation of evil in our public discourse has only increased human suffering. It is imperative that we demand clarity in our common understanding of evil. How can we be sure something is evil and not simply opposed to our interests? Can evil ever fully be destroyed, and if not, is there no point at which we can cease our crusade against it? If evil is absolute, does one have an absolute right to use any means necessary to obliterate it?

These questions led me to the work of Paul Ricoeur, a prolific philosopher whose concerns grew, in part, from his contact with manifest evil in twentieth-century France. Ricoeur was orphaned when his father was killed in World War I. While serving in the French military, he was captured by the Germans in 1940 and spent five years as a prisoner of war. Like that of other European intellectual contemporaries whose lives were shaped by the unrelenting violence of their time, Ricoeur's work strives to create channels through which strangers and enemies can observe a common humanity in one another.

Ricoeur agrees with many other thinkers that evil is not a thing per se, but rather exists in a sort of black hole of thought, an aporia. This fact alone complicates arguments for the destruction of evil: how do you obliterate something that has no substance? For Ricoeur, we conceive of evil through the realm of myth, or grand narratives that express common human experience. Myth is not false; rather, it encapsulates truth about subjects like evil that cannot be perceived fully through reason alone. In this sense, "the axis of evil" is, arguably, a kind of myth, an explanation that makes sense of calamity in a world we think of as otherwise good and in which we can all participate.

Because evil exists beyond the limits of reason, what matters for Ricoeur is not that we identify evil, but that we respond to it appropriately. He rightly observes that the tragedy of evil is not the act committed, but the experience of the victim. Separating evil perpetrated from evil suffered shifts the concern from what or who is evil to the best possible action in the face of it, which according to him is "not a solution, but a *response*."

In the common conception, solutions to evil require retribution, and the most obvious way to achieve retribution is through violence. Responses, on the other hand, engender what Ricoeur calls "wisdom," an unwavering commitment to relieve and prevent suffering. Any violence used in a response to evil would, therefore, be focused on the alleviation of suffering rather than the attempt to stamp out evil where we think we see it.

We have ample evidence that our solutions to evil after Sept. 11 were unsuccessful. If the objective of our military intervention in the Middle East was to eradicate points on the axis of evil, our assertion of the continued presence of evil in the region points to a grand failure. What greater tool is at our disposal to destroy evil than the full power, skill and bravery of the military of the United States and its allies? If force alone were sufficient to destroy it, we already would have won the game of whack-a-mole we have been playing with evil for a decade and a half.

This knowledge is not deterring leaders from calling for more solutions rather than responses post-Orlando, even as evil is front and center in political discourse as almost never before. Defense Secretary Ash Carter announced plans for destroying the Islamic State's "parent tumor in Iraq and Syria" because the group "wants to spread its evil ideology and to plot or inspire attacks on Americans." Two days after the massacre in Orlando, Governor Rick Scott of Florida proposed retaliation against what he perceived to be the source of evil perpetrated against his state: "We're fed up. We want ISIS destroyed. Radical Islam does not belong here. If you believe in evil, we're gonna to do something about it."

President Obama's speech in Orlando, however, offered an intriguing glimpse into what a long-term response to evil might look like. Amid the usual call for the destruction of the Islamic State and Al Qaeda as retaliation for the week's "evil, hateful act" was a sincere focus on the experience of the victims—in other words, on evil suffered, not the evil perpetrated. He opened the speech with a long description of his meetings with families of the dead, linking their grief with that of the "American family." Perhaps almost eight years of an exhausting cat-and-mouse struggle with evil drone targets and surge enemies has given the president a Ricoeurian sense of wisdom in his final months in office. His successor would be wise indeed to note what he has learned.

JUNE 27, 2016

The Moral Logic of Survivor Guilt

—Nancy Sherman

I F THERE IS ONE THING WE HAVE LEARNED FROM RETURNING WAR veterans—especially those of the last decade—it's that the emotional reality of the soldier at home is often at odds with that of the civilian public they left behind. And while friends and families of return- ing service members may be experiencing gratefulness or relief this holiday, many of those they've welcomed home are likely struggling with other emotions.

High on that list of emotions is guilt. Soldiers often carry this burden home—survivor guilt being perhaps the kind most familiar to us. In war, standing here rather than there can save your life but cost a buddy his. It's flukish luck, but you feel responsible. The guilt begins an endless loop of counterfactuals—thoughts that you could have or should done otherwise, though in fact you did nothing wrong. The feelings are, of course, not restricted to the battlefield. But given the magnitude of loss in war, they hang heavy there and are perva- sive. And they raise the question of just how irrational those feelings are, and if they aren't, of what is the basis of their reasonableness.

Capt. Adrian Bonenberger, head of a unit in Afghanistan that James Dao and other journalists of *The New York Times* reported on in their series "A Year at War," pondered those questions recently as he thought about Specialist Jeremiah Pulaski, who was killed by police in the wake of a deadly bar fight shortly after he returned home. Back in Afghanistan, Pulaski had saved Bonenberger's life twice on one day, but when Pulaski needed help, Bonenberger couldn't be there for him: "When he was in trouble, he was alone," Captain Bonenberger said. "When we were in trouble, he was there for us. I know it's not rational or reasonable. There's nothing logical about it. But I feel responsible."

But how unreasonable is that feeling? Subjective guilt, associated with this sense of responsibility, is thought to be irrational because one feels guilty despite the fact that he knows he has done nothing wrong. Objective or rational guilt, by contrast—guilt that is "fitting" to one's actions—accurately tracks real wrongdoing or culpability: guilt is appropriate because one acted to deliberately harm someone, or could have prevented harm and did not. Blameworthiness, here, depends on the idea that a person could have done something other than he did. And so he is held responsible or accountable, by himself or others.

But as Bonenberger's remarks make clear, we often *take* responsibility in a way that goes beyond what we can reasonably be *held* responsible for. And we feel the guilt that comes with that sense of responsibility. Nietzsche is the modern philosopher who well understood this phenomenon: "Das schlechte Gewissen," (literally, "bad conscience")—his term for the consciousness of guilt where one has done no wrong, doesn't grow in the soil where we would most expect it, he argued, such as in prisons where there are actually "guilty" parties who should feel remorse for wrongdoing. In *The Genealogy of Morals*, he appeals to an earlier philosopher, Spinoza, for support: "The bite of conscience," writes Spinoza in the *Ethics*, has to do with an "offense" where "something has gone unexpectedly wrong." As Niezsche adds, it is not really a case of "I ought not to have done that."

But what then is it a case of? Part of the reasonableness of survivor guilt (and in a sense, its "fittingness") is that it tracks a moral significance that is broader than moral *action*. Who I am, in terms of my character and relationships, and not just what I do, matters morally. Of course, character is expressed in action, and when we don't "walk the walk," we are lacking; but it is also expressed in emotions and attitudes. Aristotle in his *Nicomachean Ethics* insists on the point: "virtue is concerned with emotions and actions;" to have good character is to "hit the mean" with respect to both. Moreover, many of the feelings that express character are not about what one has done or should have done, but rather about what one cares deeply about. Though Aristotle doesn't himself talk about guilt, it is the emotion that best expresses that conflict—the desire or obligation to help frustrated by the inability, through no fault of one's own, to do so. To not feel the guilt is to be numb to those pulls. It is that vulnerability, those pulls, that Boneneberger feels when he says he wasn't there for Pulaski when he needed him.

In many of the interviews I've conducted with soldiers over the years, feelings of guilt and responsibility tangle with feelings of having betrayed fellow soldiers. At stake is the duty to those soldiers, the imperative to hold intact the bond that enables them to fight for and with each other in the kind of "sacred band" that the ancients memorialized and that the Marine motto semper fidelis captures so well. But it is not just duty at work. It is love.

Service members, especially those higher in rank, routinely talk about unit members as "*my* soldiers," "*my* Marines," "*my* sailors." They are family members, their own children, of sorts, who have been entrusted to them. To fall short of unconditional care is experienced as a kind of perfidy, a failure to be faithful. Survivor guilt piles on the unconscious thought that luck is part of a zero-sum game. To have good luck is to deprive another of it. The anguish of guilt, its sheer pain, is a way of sharing some of the ill fate. It is a form of empathic distress.

Many philosophers have looked to other terms to define the feeling. What they have come up with is "agent-regret" (a term coined by the British philosopher Bernard Williams, but used by many others). The classic scenario is not so much one of good luck (as in survivor guilt), but of bad luck, typically having to do with accidents where again, there is little or no culpability for the harms caused. In these cases, people may be *causally* responsible for harm—they bring about the harm through their agency—but they are not morally responsible for what happened.

But to my ear, agent-regret is simply tone-deaf to how subjective guilt feels. Despite the insertion of "agent," it sounds as passive and flat as "regretting that the weather is bad." Or more tellingly, as removed from empathic distress as the message sent to the next of kin, after an official knock on the door: "The Secretary of Defense regrets to inform you that . . ."

Indeed, the soldiers I've talked to, involved in friendly fire accidents that took their comrades' lives, didn't feel regret for what happened, but raw, deep, unabashed guilt. And the guilt persisted long after they were formally investigated and ultimately exonerated. In one wrenching case in April 2003 in Iraq, the gun on a Bradley fighting vehicle misfired, blowing off most of the face of Private Joseph Mayek who was standing guard near the vehicle. The accident was ultimately traced to a faulty replacement battery that the commander in charge had authorized. When the Bradley's ignition was turned on, the replacement battery in the turret (a Marine battery rather than an Army one) failed to shut off current to the gun. Mayek, who was twenty, died.

The Army officer in charge, then Capt. John Prior, reconstructed the ghastly scene for me, and the failed attempts in the medic tent to save Mayek's life. He then turned to his feelings of responsibility: "I'm the one who placed the vehicles; I'm the one who set the security. As with most accidents, I'm not in jail right now. Clearly I wasn't egregiously responsible. But it is a comedy of errors. Any one of a dozen decisions made over the course of a two-month period and none of them really occurs to you at the time. Any one of those made differently may have saved his life. So I dealt with and still deal with the guilt of having cost him his life essentially. . . . There's probably not a day that doesn't go by that I don't think about it, at least fleetingly."

What Prior feels are feelings of guilt, and not simply regret that things didn't work out differently. He feels the awful weight of self-indictment, the empathy with the victim and survivors, and the need to make moral repair. If he didn't feel that, we would probably think less of him as a commander.

In his case, moral repair came through an empathic, painful connection with Mayek's mother. After the fratricide, Prior and his first sergeant wrote a letter to Mayek's mother. And for some time after, she replied with care packages to the company and with letters. "Oh it was terrible," said Prior. "The letters weren't just very matter of fact—here's what we did today; it was more like a mother writing to her son." Prior had become the son who was no longer. "It was her way of dealing with the grief," said Prior. "And so I had a responsibility to try to give back."

In all this we might say guilt, subjective guilt, has a redemptive side. It is a way that soldiers impose moral order on the chaos and awful randomness of war's violence. It is a way they humanize war for themselves, for their buddies, and for us as civilians, too.

But if that's all that is involved, it sounds too moralistic. It makes guilt appropriate or fitting because it's good for society. It is the way we all can deal with war. Maybe, instead, we want to say it is fitting because it is evolutionarily adaptive in the way that fear is. But again, this doesn't do justice to the phenomenon. The guilt that soldiers feel isn't just morally expedient or species-adaptive. It is fitting because it gets right certain moral (or evaluative) features of a soldier's world—that good soldiers depend on each other, come to love each other, and have duties to care and bring each other safely home. Philosophers, at least since the time of Kant, have called these "imperfect duties": even in the best circumstances, we can't perfectly fulfill them. And so, what duties to others need to make room for, even in a soldier's life of service and sacrifice, are duties to self, of self-forgiveness and self-empathy. These are a part of full moral repair.

JULY 3, 2011

How to Live Without Irony

—Christy Wampole

IF IRONY IS THE ETHOS OF OUR AGE—AND IT IS—THEN THE HIP-ster is our archetype of ironic living.

The hipster haunts every city street and university town. Manifesting a nostalgia for times he never lived himself, this contemporary urban harlequin appropriates outmoded fashions (the mustache, the tiny shorts), mechanisms (fixed-gear bicycles, portable record players) and hobbies (home brewing, playing trombone). He harvests awkwardness and self-consciousness. Before he makes any choice, he has proceeded through several stages of self-scrutiny. The hipster is a scholar of social forms, a student of cool. He studies relentlessly, foraging for what has yet to be found by the mainstream. He is a walking citation; his clothes refer to much more than themselves. He tries to negotiate the age-old problem of individuality, not with concepts, but with material things.

He is an easy target for mockery. However, scoffing at the hipster is only a diluted form of his own affliction. He is merely a symptom and the most extreme manifestation of ironic living. For many Americans born in the 1980s and 1990s—members of Generation Y, or Millennials—particularly middle-class Caucasians, irony is the primary mode with which daily life is dealt. One need only dwell in public space, virtual or concrete, to see how pervasive this phenomenon has become. Advertising, politics, fashion, television: almost every category of contemporary reality exhibits this will to irony.

Take, for example, an ad that calls itself an ad, makes fun of its own format, and attempts to lure its target market to laugh at and with it. It preemptively acknowledges its own failure to accomplish anything meaningful. No attack can be set against it, as it has already conquered itself. The ironic frame functions as a shield against criticism. The same goes for ironic living. Irony is the most self-defensive mode, as it allows a person to dodge responsibility for his or her choices, aesthetic and otherwise. To live ironically is to hide in public. It is flagrantly indirect, a form of subterfuge, which means etymologically to "secretly flee" (subter + fuge). Somehow, directness has become unbearable to us.

How did this happen? It stems in part from the belief that this generation has little to offer in terms of culture, that everything has already been done, or that serious commitment to any belief will eventually be subsumed by an opposing belief, rendering the first laughable at best and contemptible at worst. This kind of defensive living works as a pre-emptive surrender and takes the form of reaction rather than action.

Life in the Internet age has undoubtedly helped a certain ironic sensibility to flourish. An ethos can be disseminated quickly and widely through this medium. Our incapacity to deal with the things at hand is evident in our use of, and increasing reliance on, digital technology. Prioritizing what is remote over what is immediate, the virtual over the actual, we are absorbed in the public and private sphere by the little devices that take us elsewhere.

Furthermore, the nostalgia cycles have become so short that we even try to inject the present moment with sentimentality, for example, by using certain digital filters to "prewash" photos with an aura of historicity. Nostalgia needs time. One cannot accelerate meaningful remembrance.

While we have gained some skill sets (multitasking, technological savvy), other skills have suffered: the art of conversation, the art of looking at people, the art of being seen, the art of being present. Our conduct is no longer governed by subtlety, finesse, grace and attention, all qualities more esteemed in earlier decades. Inwardness and narcissism now hold sway.

Born in 1977, at the tail end of Generation X, I came of age in the 1990s, a decade that, bracketed neatly by two architectural crumblings—of the Berlin Wall in 1989 and the Twin Towers in 2001—now seems relatively irony-free. The grunge movement was serious in its aesthetics and its attitude, with a combative stance against authority, which the punk movement had also embraced. In my perhaps overnostalgic memory, feminism reached an unprecedented peak, environmentalist concerns gained widespread attention, questions of race were more openly addressed: all of these stirrings contained within them the same electricity and euphoria touching generations that witness a centennial or millennial changeover.

But Y2K came and went without disaster. We were hopeful throughout the '90s, but hope is such a vulnerable emotion; we needed a self-defense mechanism, for every generation has one. For Gen Xers, it was a kind of diligent apathy. We actively did not care. Our archetype was the slacker who slouched through life in plaid flannel, alone in his room, misunderstood. And when we were bored with not caring, we were vaguely angry and melancholic, eating antidepressants like they were candy.

From this vantage, the ironic clique appears simply too comfortable, too brainlessly compliant. Ironic living is a first-world problem. For the relatively well educated and financially secure, irony functions as a kind of credit card you never have to pay back. In other words, the hipster can frivolously invest in sham social capital without ever paying back one sincere dime. He doesn't own anything he possesses.

Obviously, hipsters (male or female) produce a distinct irritation in me, one that until recently I could not explain. They provoke me, I realized, because they are, despite the distance from which I observe them, an amplified version of me.

I, too, exhibit ironic tendencies. For example, I find it difficult to give sincere gifts. Instead, I often give what in the past would have been accepted only at a white elephant gift exchange: a kitschy painting from a thrift store, a coffee mug with flashy images of "Texas, the Lone Star State," plastic Mexican wrestler figures. Good for a chuckle in the moment, but worth little in the long term. Something about the responsibility of choosing a personal, meaningful gift for a friend feels too intimate, too momentous. I somehow cannot bear the thought of a friend disliking a gift I'd chosen with sincerity. The simple act of noticing my self-defensive behavior has made me think deeply about how potentially toxic ironic posturing could be.

First, it signals a deep aversion to risk. As a function of fear and preemptive shame, ironic living bespeaks cultural numbness, resignation and defeat. If life has become merely a clutter of kitsch objects, an endless series of sarcastic jokes and pop references, a competition to see who can care the least (or, at minimum, a performance of such a competition), it seems we've made a collective misstep. Could this be the cause of our emptiness and existential malaise? Or a symptom?

Throughout history, irony has served useful purposes, like providing a rhetorical outlet for unspoken societal tensions. But our contemporary ironic mode is somehow deeper; it has leaked from the realm of rhetoric into life itself. This ironic ethos can lead to a vacuity and vapidity of the individual and collective psyche. Historically, vacuums eventually have been filled by something—more often than not, a hazardous something. Fundamentalists are never ironists; dictators are never ironists; people who move things in the political landscape, regardless of the sides they choose, are never ironists.

Where can we find other examples of nonironic living? What does it look like? Nonironic models include very young children, elderly people, deeply religious people, people with severe mental or physical disabilities, people who have suffered, and those from economically or politically challenged places where seriousness is the governing state of mind. My friend Robert Pogue Harrison put it this way in a recent conversation: "Wherever the real imposes itself, it tends to dissipate the fogs of irony."

Observe a four-year-old child going through her daily life. You will not find the slightest bit of irony in her behavior. She has not, so to speak, taken on the veil of irony. She likes what she likes and declares it without dissimulation. She is not particularly conscious of the scrutiny of others. She does not hide behind indirect language. The most pure nonironic models in life, however, are to be found in nature: animals and plants are exempt from irony, which exists only where the human dwells.

What would it take to overcome the cultural pull of irony? Moving away from the ironic involves saying what you mean, meaning what you say, and considering seriousness and forthrightness as expressive possibilities, despite the inherent risks. It means undertaking the cultivation of sincerity, humility and self-effacement, and demoting the frivolous and the kitschy on our collective scale of values. It might also consist of an honest self-inventory.

Here is a start: Look around your living space. Do you surround yourself with things you really like or things you like only because they are absurd? Listen to your own speech. Ask yourself, Do I communicate primarily through inside jokes and pop culture references? What percentage of my speech is meaningful? How much hyperbolic language do I use? Do I feign indifference? Look at your clothes. What parts of your wardrobe could be described as costume-like, derivative or reminiscent of some specific style archetype (the secretary, the hobo, the flapper, yourself as a child)? In other words, do your clothes refer to something else or only to themselves? Do you attempt to look intentionally nerdy, awkward or ugly? In other words, is your style an antistyle? The most important question is, How would it feel to change yourself quietly, offline, without public display, from within?

Attempts to banish irony have come and gone in past decades. The loosely defined New Sincerity movements in the arts that have sprouted since the 1980s positioned themselves as responses to postmodern cynicism, detachment, and metareferentiality. (New Sincerity has recently been associated with the writing of David Foster Wallace, the films of Wes Anderson and the music of Cat Power.) But these attempts failed to stick, as evidenced by the new age of Deep Irony.

What will future generations make of this rampant sarcasm and unapologetic cultivation of silliness? Will we be satisfied to leave an archive filled with video clips of people doing stupid things? Is an ironic legacy even a legacy at all?

The ironic life is certainly a provisional answer to the problems of too much comfort, too much history and too many choices, but it is my firm conviction that this mode of living is not viable and conceals within it many social and political risks. For such a large segment of the population to forfeit its civic voice through the pattern of negation I've described is to siphon energy from the cultural reserves of the community at large. People may choose to continue hiding behind the ironic mantle, but this choice equals a surrender to commercial and political entities more than happy to act as parents for a self-infantilizing citizenry. So rather than scoffing at the hipster—a favorite hobby, especially of hipsters—determine whether the ashes of irony have settled on you as well. It takes little effort to dust them away.

NOVEMBER 17, 2012

Deluded Individualism

—Firmin DeBrabander

THERE IS A CURIOUS PASSAGE EARLY IN FREUD'S *EGO AND THE ID* where he remarks that the id behaves "as if" it were unconscious. The phrase is puzzling, but the meaning is clear: the id is the secret driver of our desires, the desires that animate our conscious life, but the ego does not recognize it as such. The ego—what we take to be our conscious, autonomous self—is ignorant to the agency of the id and sees itself in the driver seat instead. Freud offers the following metaphor: the ego is like a man on horseback, struggling to contain the powerful beast beneath; to the extent that the ego succeeds in guiding this beast, it's only by "transforming the id's will into action *as if* it were its own."

By Freud's account, conscious autonomy is a charade. "We are lived," as he puts it, and yet we don't see it as such. Indeed, Freud suggests that to be human is to rebel against that vision—the truth. We tend to see ourselves as self-determining, self-conscious agents in all that we decide and do, and we cling to that image. But why? Why do we resist the truth? Why do we wish—strain, strive against the grain of reality—to be autonomous individuals, and see ourselves as such?

Perhaps Freud is too cynical regarding conscious autonomy, but he is right to question our presumption to it. He is right to suggest that we typically—wrongly—ignore the extent to which we are determined by unknown forces and overestimate our self-control. The path to happiness for Freud, or some semblance of it in his stormy account of the psyche, involves accepting our basic condition. But why do we presume individual agency in the first place? Why do we insist on it stubbornly, irrationally, often recklessly?

I was reminded of Freud's paradox by a poignant article in the *Times* a few months back, which described a Republican-leaning district in Minnesota and its constituents' conflicted desire to be self-reliant ("Even Critics of Safety Net Increasingly Depend on It," February 11). The article cited a study from Dartmouth political science professor Dean Lacy, which revealed that, though Republicans call for deep cuts to the safety net, their districts rely more on government support than their Democratic counterparts.

In Chisago County, MN, the *Times'* reporters spoke with residents who supported the Tea Party and its proposed cuts to federal spending, even while they admitted they could not get by without government support. Tea Party aficionados, and many on the extreme right of the Republican Party for that matter, are typically characterized as self-sufficient middle-class folk, angry about sustaining the idle poor with their tax dollars. Chisago County revealed a different aspect of this anger: economically struggling Americans professing a robust individualism and self-determination, frustrated with their failures to achieve that ideal.

Why the stubborn insistence on self-determination, in spite of the facts? One might say there is something profoundly American in this. It's our fierce individualism shining through. Residents of Chisago County are clinging to notions of past self-reliance before the recession, before the welfare state. It's admirable in a way. Alternately, it evokes the delusional autonomy of Freud's poor ego.

These people, like many across the nation, rely on government assistance but pretend they don't. They even resent the government for their reliance. If they looked closely, though, they'd see that we are all thoroughly saturated with government assistance in this country: farm subsidies that lower food prices for us all, mortgage interest deductions that disproportionately favor the rich, federal mortgage guarantees that keep interest rates low, a bloated Department of Defense that sustains entire sectors of the economy and puts hundreds of thousands of people to work. We can hardly fathom the depth of our dependence on government and pretend we are bold individualists instead.

As we are in an election year, the persistence of this delusion has manifested itself politically, particularly as a foundation in the Republican Party ideology—from Ron Paul's insistence during the primaries that the government shouldn't intervene to help the uninsured even when they are deathly ill to Rick Santorum's maligning of public schools to Mitt Romney's selection of Paul Ryan as a running mate. There is no doubt that radical individualism will remain a central selling point of their campaign. Ryan's signature work, his proposal for the federal budget, calls for drastic cuts to Medicaid, Medicare, Pell grants and job-training programs, among others. To no surprise, as *The New Yorker* revealed in a recent profile of Ryan, the home district that supports him is boosted by considerable government largesse.

Of course the professed individualists have an easy time cutting services for the poor. But this is misguided. There are many counties across the nation that, like Chisago County, might feel insulated from the trials of the destitute. Perhaps this is because they are able to ignore the poverty in their midst, or because they are rather homogeneous and geographically removed from concentrations of poverty, like urban ghettos. But the fate of the middle-class counties and urban ghettos is entwined. When the poor are left to rot in their misery, the misery does not stay contained. It harms us all. The crime radiates, the misery offends, it debases the whole. Individuals, much less communities, cannot be insulated from it.

Thanks to a decades-long safety net, we have forgotten the trials of living without it. This is why, the historian Tony Judt argued, it's easy for some to speak fondly of a world without government: we can't fully imagine or recall what it's like. We can't really appreciate the horrors Upton Sinclair witnessed in the Chicago slaughterhouses before regulation, or the burden of living without Social Security and Medicare to look forward to. Thus, we can entertain nostalgia for a time when everyone pulled his own weight, bore his own risk, and was the master of his destiny. That time was a myth. But the notion of self-reliance is also a fallacy.

Spinoza greatly influenced Freud, and he adds a compelling insight we would do well to reckon with. Spinoza also questioned the human pretense to autonomy. Men believe themselves free, he said, merely because they are conscious of their volitions and appetites, but they are wholly determined. In fact, Spinoza claimed—to the horror of his contemporaries—that we are all just modes of one substance, "God or Nature" he called it, which is really the same thing. Individual actions are no such thing at all; they are expressions of another entity altogether, which acts through us unwittingly. To be human, according to Spinoza, is to be party to a confounding existential illusion—that human individuals are independent agents—which exacts a heavy emotional and political toll on us. It is the source of anxiety, envy, anger—all the passions that torment our psyche—and the violence that ensues. If we should come to see our nature as it truly is, if we should see that no "individuals" properly speaking exist at all, Spinoza maintained, it would greatly benefit humankind.

There is no such thing as a discrete individual, Spinoza points out. This is a fiction. The boundaries of "me" are fluid and blurred. We are all profoundly linked in countless ways we can hardly perceive. My decisions, choices, actions are inspired and motivated by others to no small extent. The passions, Spinoza argued, derive from seeing people as autonomous individuals responsible for all the objectionable actions that issue from them. Understanding the interrelated nature of everyone and everything is the key to diminishing the passions and the havoc they wreak.

In this, Spinoza and President Obama seem to concur: we're all in this together. We are not the sole authors of our destiny, each of us; our destinies are entangled—messily, unpredictably. Our cultural demands of individualism are too extreme. They are constitutionally irrational, Spinoza and Freud tell us, and their potential consequences are disastrous. Thanks to our safety net, we live in a society that affirms the dependence and interdependence of all. To that extent, it affirms a basic truth of our nature. We forsake it at our own peril.

AUGUST 18, 2012

ON MORALITY

The Dangers of Happiness

—Carl Cederström

W HENEVER WE TALK ABOUT HAPPINESS WE ALSO TALK ABOUT
something else: morality. We may not know what happiness itself
signifies, but we do know how it has been evoked historically—to set
out a template for a moral life. As we rush to make happiness the ultimate aim both for ourselves and society at large, we might want to
recall some of the wonderfully rich and depressingly contradictory
history of the concept. This might help us better understand our own
time and the moral values we subscribe to today.

In his book *Happiness: A History*, the historian Darrin M. McMahon
provides an account of how the notion was expressed and embraced
over time, going back to the birth of Western civilization, as many
such accounts do, in ancient Greece.

Aristotle, one of the first to pay significant attention to the topic,
thought that happiness consisted of being a good person. The happy
life, what the Greeks called eudaemonia, was one lived ethically,
guided by reason and dedicated to cultivating one's virtues. Soon
after, the Epicureans would connect happiness to pleasure. They
argued that a good life should be devoted to whatever brought pleasure. They were no hedonists, though, and preached a strict regulation of desire. To be happy, Epicurus himself said, he needed no
more than a barley cake and some water.

The Stoics gave no elevated status to pleasure, arguing that a person had the capacity to be happy no matter how daunting and pain-

ful the circumstances of life might be. Much later, Christianity, as preached and practiced throughout the Middle Ages, shunned pleasure altogether and regarded pain as the more useful path to, if not a happy life, then a sort of divine union in the afterlife. That desired state could not be attained in life on earth, but only as a gift from God, in heaven.

The Renaissance, though, brought happiness from heaven back to earth. It was not until the Enlightenment that it became a right—something that each and every person was able to pursue and attain. When Thomas Jefferson wrote in the Declaration of Independence that the pursuit of happiness was an unalienable right, he did not just intend to say that man should pursue pleasure, but that he should also have the right to acquire and possess property.

What we esteem today, in the rich West, has its own distinct flavor.

Contrary to the message of Christianity, according to which we abandon ourselves to achieve divine union, we are now asked to pursue union with ourselves. To be happy in a time when we prize authenticity and narcissism, we need to express our true inner self, get in touch with our deeper feelings, and follow the path set by ourselves.

We are also far from the Epicureans, who were famously reluctant to engage in physical activity. Today we pursue happiness by worshipping our bodies, building them up through long-distance running, punishing boot camps, ironman triathlons and kettlebell swinging.

And unlike the work-shy Greeks of antiquity, we are assumed to find happiness through work and by being productive. We are required to curate our market value, manage ourselves as corporations and live according to an entrepreneurial ethos. When no sin is greater than being unemployed and no vice more despised than laziness, happiness comes only to those who work hard, have the right attitude and struggle for self-improvement.

These are some of the moral values that seem to underlie happiness today: Be real, be strong, be productive—and most important, don't rely on other people to achieve these goals, because your fate is, of course, in your own hands.

This is a popular message, and has been for some time. It is drummed into the unemployed and poor who are led to believe that their misfortunes are symptoms of their inferior attitudes and inability to take ownership over their lives. They are, as Jeb Bush might claim, not working hard enough.

When happiness is recast as an individual choice, attitude becomes everything and circumstances are made irrelevant. Martin Seligman, the founder of positive psychology, has worked hard to spread this message, referring to studies that suggest that victims of car crashes are, on the whole, neither less nor more unhappy than lottery winners.

Even if we find such insights interesting or inspiring, they do not form a particularly helpful basis when we seek to make happiness the goal of politics. If we may all be equally happy, irrespective of our circumstances, then that would equip politicians like Mr. Bush with a convenient excuse to stop looking at structural issues like class, social and economic inequality or poverty.

It is tempting to see the Conservative British prime minister David Cameron's sudden interest in happiness in this light. When he decided a few years ago to initiate a so-called happiness index, he did so at the height of austerity, when public spending was being cut, and the "circumstances" were made worse for many people, especially those on benefits. As it happens, this survey was inspired by Mr. Seligman, producing an echo of the "circumstances make no difference" mantra.

When happiness has become championed and talked about incessantly, as it is today, the best we can hope for is that it raises other universal issues—like equality, justice, truth and ethics, which we desperately need to discuss. The worst that can happen—and this is unfortunately already underway—is that happiness becomes a Trojan horse used to normalize inequality and oppression. Poor people may then be sent to happiness courses to improve their attitudes, or assigned personal life coaches, as Paul Ryan once proposed in his bizarre anti-poverty plan.

"We believe that every American and in every community has a right to pursue happiness," Jeb Bush said in a speech delivered in Detroit in February, presenting his plan to address income inequality. "They have a right to rise."

Be wary. When politicians suggest that happiness be made the ultimate aim for society we should remember that they are probably not talking about happiness at all. They are talking about ideology: their own political agendas in disguise.

JULY 18, 2015

Are We Ready for a "Morality Pill"?

—Peter Singer and Agata Sagan

IN OCTOBER 2011, IN FOSHAN, CHINA, A TWO-YEAR-OLD GIRL WAS run over by a van. The driver did not stop. Over the next seven minutes, more than a dozen people walked or bicycled past the injured child. A second truck ran over her. Eventually, a woman pulled her to the side, and her mother arrived. The child died in a hospital. The entire scene was captured on video and caused an uproar when it was shown by a television station and posted online. A similar event occurred in London in 2004, as have others, far from the lens of a video camera.

Yet people can, and often do, behave in very different ways.

A news search for the words *hero saves* will routinely turn up stories of bystanders braving oncoming trains, swift currents and raging fires to save strangers from harm. Acts of extreme kindness, responsibility and compassion are, like their opposites, nearly universal.

Why are some people prepared to risk their lives to help a stranger when others won't even stop to dial an emergency number?

Scientists have been exploring questions like this for decades. In the 1960s and early '70s, famous experiments by Stanley Milgram and Philip Zimbardo suggested that most of us would, under specific circumstances, voluntarily do great harm to innocent people. During the same period, John Darley and C. Daniel Batson showed that even some seminary students on their way to give a lecture about the parable of the Good Samaritan would, if told that they were running late, walk past a stranger lying moaning beside the path. More recent research has told us a lot about what happens in the brain when people make moral decisions. But are we getting any closer to understanding what drives our moral behavior?

Here's what much of the discussion of all these experiments missed: some people did the right thing. A recent experiment (about which we have some ethical reservations) at the University of Chicago seems to shed new light on why.

Researchers there took two rats who shared a cage and trapped one of them in a tube that could be opened only from the outside. The free rat usually tried to open the door, eventually succeeding. Even when the free rats could eat up all of a quantity of chocolate before freeing the trapped rat, they mostly preferred to free their cage mate. The experimenters interpret their findings as demonstrating empathy in rats. But if that is the case, they have also demonstrated that individual rats vary, for only twenty-three of thirty rats freed their trapped companions.

The causes of the difference in their behavior must lie in the rats themselves. It seems plausible that humans, like rats, are spread along a continuum of readiness to help others. There has been considerable research on abnormal people, like psychopaths, but we need to know more about relatively stable differences (perhaps rooted in our genes) in the great majority of people as well.

Undoubtedly, situational factors can make a huge difference, and perhaps moral beliefs do as well, but if humans are just different in their predispositions to act morally, we also need to know more about these differences. Only then will we gain a proper understanding of our moral behavior, including why it varies so much from person to person and whether there is anything we can do about it.

If continuing brain research does in fact show biochemical differences between the brains of those who help others and the brains of those who do not, could this lead to a "morality pill"—a drug that makes us more likely to help? Given the many other studies linking biochemical conditions to mood and behavior, and the proliferation of drugs to modify them that have followed, the idea is not far-fetched. If so, would people choose to take it? Could criminals be given the option, as an alternative to prison, of a drug-releasing implant that would make them less likely to harm others? Might governments begin screening people to discover those most likely to commit crimes? Those who are at much greater risk of committing a crime might be offered the morality pill; if they refused, they might be required to wear a tracking device that would show where they had been at any given time, so that they would know that if they did commit a crime, they would be detected.

Fifty years ago, Anthony Burgess wrote *A Clockwork Orange*, a futuristic novel about a vicious gang leader who undergoes a procedure that makes him incapable of violence. Stanley Kubrick's 1971 movie version sparked a discussion in which many argued that we could never be justified in depriving someone of his free will, no matter how gruesome the violence that would thereby be prevented. No doubt any proposal to develop a morality pill would encounter the same objection.

But if our brain's chemistry does affect our moral behavior, the question of whether that balance is set in a natural way or by medical intervention will make no difference in how freely we act. If there are already biochemical differences between us that can be used to predict how ethically we will act, then either such differences are compatible with free will or they are evidence that at least as far as some of our ethical actions are concerned, none of us have ever had free will anyway. In any case, whether or not we have free will, we may soon face new choices about the ways in which we are willing to influence behavior for the better.

JANUARY 28, 2012

Why Our Children Don't Think There Are Moral Facts

—Justin P. McBrayer

WHAT WOULD YOU SAY IF YOU FOUND OUT THAT OUR PUBLIC schools were teaching children that it is not true that it's wrong to kill people for fun or cheat on tests? Would you be surprised?

I was. As a philosopher, I already knew that many college-aged students don't believe in moral facts. While there are no national surveys quantifying this phenomenon, philosophy professors with whom I have spoken suggest that the overwhelming majority of college freshmen in their classrooms view moral claims as mere opinions that are not true or are true only relative to a culture.

What I didn't know was where this attitude came from. Given the presence of moral relativism in some academic circles, some people might naturally assume that philosophers themselves are to blame. But they aren't. There are historical examples of philosophers who endorse a kind of moral relativism, dating back at least to Protagoras who declared that "man is the measure of all things," and several who deny that there are any moral facts whatsoever. But such creatures are rare. Besides, if students are already showing up to college with this view of morality, it's very unlikely that it's the result of what professional philosophers are teaching. So where is the view coming from?

A few weeks ago, I learned that students are exposed to this sort of thinking well before crossing the threshold of higher education. When I went to visit my son's second grade open house, I found a troubling pair of signs hanging over the bulletin board. They read:

Fact: Something that is true about a subject
and can be tested or proven.

Opinion: What someone thinks, feels, or believes.

Hoping that this set of definitions was a one-off mistake, I went home and Googled "fact vs. opinion." The definitions I found online were substantially the same as the one in my son's classroom. As it turns out, the Common Core standards used by a majority of K-12 programs in the country require that students be able to "distinguish among fact, opinion, and reasoned judgment in a text." And the Common Core institute provides a helpful page full of links to definitions, lesson plans and quizzes to ensure that students can tell the difference between facts and opinions.

So what's wrong with this distinction and how does it undermine the view that there are objective moral facts?

First, the definition of a fact waffles between truth and proof—two obviously different features. Things can be true even if no one can prove them. For example, it could be true that there is life elsewhere in the universe even though no one can prove it. Conversely, many of the things we once "proved" turned out to be false. For example, many people once thought that the earth was flat. It's a mistake to confuse truth (a feature of the world) with proof (a feature of our mental lives). Furthermore, if proof is required for facts, then facts become person-relative. Something might be a fact for me if I can prove it but not a fact for you if you can't. In that case, $E=MC^2$ is a fact for a physicist but not for me.

But second, and worse, students are taught that claims are *either* facts or opinions. They are given quizzes in which they must sort claims into one camp or the other but not both. But if a fact is something that is true and an opinion is something that is believed, then many claims will obviously be both. For example, I asked my son about this distinction after his open house. He confidently explained that facts were things that were true whereas opinions are things that are believed. We then had this conversation:

Me: "I believe that George Washington was the first president. Is that a fact or an opinion?"

Him: "It's a fact."

Me: "But I believe it, and you said that what someone believes is an opinion."

Him: "Yeah, but it's true."

Me: "So it's both a fact and an opinion?"

The blank stare on his face said it all.

How does the dichotomy between fact and opinion relate to morality? I learned the answer to this question only after I investigated my son's homework (and other examples of assignments online). Kids are asked to sort facts from opinions and, without fail, *every* value claim is labeled as an opinion. Here's a little test devised from questions available on fact vs. opinion worksheets online: are the following facts or opinions?

- *Copying homework assignments is wrong.*

- *Cursing in school is inappropriate behavior.*

- *All men are created equal.*

- *It is worth sacrificing some personal liberties to protect our country from terrorism.*

- *It is wrong for people under the age of 21 to drink alcohol.*

- *Vegetarians are healthier than people who eat meat.*

- *Drug dealers belong in prison.*

The answer? In each case, the worksheets categorize these claims as opinions. The explanation on offer is that each of these claims is a value claim and value claims are not facts. This is repeated ad nauseum: any claim with good, right, wrong, etc. is not a fact.

In summary, our public schools teach students that all claims are either facts or opinions and that all value and moral claims fall into the latter camp. The punchline: there are no moral facts. And if there are no moral facts, then there are no moral truths.

The inconsistency in this curriculum is obvious. For example, at the outset of the school year, my son brought home a list of student rights and responsibilities. Had he already read the lesson on fact vs. opinion, he might have noted that the supposed rights of other students were based on no more than opinions. According to the school's curriculum, it certainly wasn't *true* that his classmates deserved to be treated a particular way—that would make it a fact. Similarly, it wasn't really true that he had any responsibilities—that would be to make a value claim a truth. It should not be a surprise that there is rampant cheating on college campuses: If we've taught our students for 12 years that there is no fact of the matter as to whether cheating is wrong, we can't very well blame them for doing so later on.

Indeed, in the world beyond grade school, where adults must exercise their moral knowledge and reasoning to conduct themselves in the society, the stakes are greater. There, consistency demands that we acknowledge the existence of moral facts. If it's not true that it's wrong to murder a cartoonist with whom one disagrees, then how can we be outraged? If there are no truths about what is good or valuable or right, how can we prosecute people for crimes against humanity? If it's not true that all humans are created equal, then why vote for any political system that doesn't benefit you over others?

Our schools do amazing things with our children. And they are, in a way, teaching moral standards when they ask students to treat one another humanely and to do their schoolwork with academic integrity. But at the same time, the curriculum sets our children up for doublethink. They are told that there are no moral facts in one breath even as the next tells them how they ought to behave.

We can do better. Our children deserve a consistent intellectual foundation. Facts are things that are true. Opinions are things we believe. Some of our beliefs are true. Others are not. Some of our beliefs are backed by evidence. Others are not. Value claims are like any other claims: either true or false, evidenced or not. The hard work lies not in recognizing that at least some moral claims are true but in carefully thinking through our evidence for which of the many competing moral claims is correct. That's a hard thing to do. But we can't sidestep the responsibilities that come with being human just because it's hard.

That would be wrong.

MARCH 2, 2015

Morals Without God?

—Frans de Waal

I WAS BORN IN DEN BOSCH, THE CITY AFTER WHICH HIERONYMUS Bosch named himself. This obviously does not make me an expert on the Dutch painter, but having grown up with his statue on the market square, I have always been fond of his imagery, his symbolism and how it relates to humanity's place in the universe. This remains relevant today since Bosch depicts a society under a waning influence of God.

His famous triptych with naked figures frolicking around—*The Garden of Earthly Delights*—seems a tribute to paradisaical innocence. The tableau is far too happy and relaxed to fit the interpretation of depravity and sin advanced by puritan experts. It represents humanity free from guilt and shame either before the Fall or without any Fall at all. For a primatologist, like myself, the nudity, references to sex and fertility, the plentiful birds and fruits and the moving about in groups are thoroughly familiar and hardly require a religious or moral interpretation. Bosch seems to have depicted humanity in its natural state, while reserving his moralistic outlook for the right-hand panel of the triptych in which he punishes *not* the frolickers from the middle panel but monks, nuns, gluttons, gamblers, warriors and drunkards.

Five centuries later, we remain embroiled in debates about the role of religion in society. As in Bosch's days, the central theme is morality. Can we envision a world without God? Would this world be good? Don't think for one moment that the current battle lines between biology and fundamentalist Christianity turn around evidence. One has to be pretty immune to data to doubt evolution, which is why books and documentaries aimed at convincing the skeptics are a waste of effort. They are helpful for those prepared to listen but fail to reach their target audience. The debate is less about the truth than about how to handle it. For those who believe that morality comes straight from God the creator, acceptance of evolution would open a moral abyss.

OUR VAUNTED FRONTAL LOBE

Echoing this view, Reverend Al Sharpton opined in a recent videotaped debate, "If there is no order to the universe, and therefore some being, some force that ordered it, then who determines what is right or wrong? There is nothing immoral if there's nothing in charge." Similarly, I have heard people echo Dostoevsky's Ivan Karamazov, exclaiming that "if there is no God, I am free to rape my neighbor!"

Perhaps it is just me, but I am wary of anyone whose belief system is the only thing standing between them and repulsive behavior. Why not assume that our humanity, including the self-control needed for livable societies, is built into us? Does anyone truly believe that our ancestors lacked social norms before they had religion? Did they never assist others in need or complain about an unfair deal? Humans must have worried about the functioning of their communities well before the current religions arose, which is only a few thousand years ago. Not that religion is irrelevant—I will get to this—but it is an add-on rather than the wellspring of morality.

Deep down, creationists realize they will never win factual arguments with science. This is why they have construed their own science-like universe, known as Intelligent Design, and eagerly jump on every tidbit of information that seems to go their way. The most recent opportunity arose with the Hauser affair. A Harvard colleague, Marc Hauser, has been accused of eight counts of scientific misconduct, including making up his own data. Since Hauser studied primate behavior and wrote about morality, Christian websites were eager to claim that "all that people like Hauser are left with are unsubstantiated propositions that are contradicted by millennia of human experience" (Chuck Colson, September 8, 2010). A major newspaper asked, "Would it be such a bad thing if Hausergate resulted in some intellectual humility among the new scientists of morality?" (Eric Felten, August 27, 2010). Even a linguist could not resist this occasion to reaffirm the gap between human and animal by warning against "naive evolutionary presuppositions."

These are rearguard battles, however. Whether creationists jump on this scientific scandal or linguists and psychologists keep selling human exceptionalism does not really matter. Fraud has occurred in many fields of science, from epidemiology to physics, all of which are still around. In the field of cognition, the march toward continuity between human and animal has been inexorable—one misconduct case won't make a difference. True, humanity never runs out of claims of what sets it apart, but it is a rare uniqueness claim that holds up for over a decade. This is why we don't hear anymore that only humans make tools, imitate, think ahead, have culture, are self-aware or adopt another's point of view.

If we consider our species without letting ourselves be blinded by the technical advances of the last few millennia, we see a creature of flesh and blood with a brain that, albeit three times larger than a chimpanzee's, doesn't contain any new parts. Even our vaunted prefrontal cortex turns out to be of typical size: recent neuron-counting techniques classify the human brain as a linearly scaled-up monkey brain. No one doubts the superiority of our intellect, but we have no basic wants or needs that are not also present in our close relatives. I interact on a daily basis with monkeys and apes, which just like us strive for power, enjoy sex, want security and affection, kill over territory and value trust and cooperation. Yes, we use cell phones and fly airplanes, but our psychological makeup remains that of a social primate. Even the posturing and deal-making among the alpha males in Washington is nothing out of the ordinary.

THE PLEASURE OF GIVING

Charles Darwin was interested in how morality fits the human-animal continuum, proposing in *The Descent of Man*, "Any animal whatever, endowed with well-marked social instincts . . . would inevitably acquire a moral sense or conscience, as soon as its intellectual powers had become as well developed . . . as in man."

Unfortunately, modern popularizers have strayed from these insights. Like Robert Wright in *The Moral Animal*, they argue that true moral tendencies cannot exist—not in humans and even less in other animals—since nature is 100 percent selfish. Morality is just a thin veneer over a cauldron of nasty tendencies. Dubbing this position "veneer theory" (similar to Peter Railton's "moral camouflage"), I have fought it ever since my 1996 book *Good Natured*. Instead of blaming atrocious behavior on our biology ("We're acting like animals!"), while claiming our noble traits for ourselves, why not view the entire package as a product of evolution? Fortunately, there has been a resurgence of the Darwinian view that morality grew out of the social instincts. Psychologists stress the intuitive way we arrive at moral judgments while activating emotional brain areas, and economists and anthropologists have shown humanity to be far more cooperative, altruistic, and fair than predicted by self-interest models. Similarly, the latest experiments in primatology reveal that our close relatives will do each other favors even if there's nothing in it for themselves.

Chimpanzees and bonobos will voluntarily open a door to offer a companion access to food, even if they lose part of it in the process. And capuchin monkeys are prepared to seek rewards for others, such as when we place two of them side by side, while one of them barters with us with differently colored tokens. One token is "selfish," and the other "prosocial." If the bartering monkey selects the selfish token, it receives a small piece of apple for returning it, but its partner gets nothing. The prosocial token, on the other hand, rewards both monkeys. Most monkeys develop an overwhelming preference for the prosocial token, which preference is not due to fear of repercussions, because dominant monkeys (who have least to fear) are the most generous.

Even though altruistic behavior evolved for the advantages it confers, this does not make it selfishly motivated. Future benefits rarely figure in the minds of animals. For example, animals engage in sex without knowing its reproductive consequences, and even humans had to develop the morning-after pill. This is because sexual motivation is unconcerned with the reason why sex exists. The same is true for the altruistic impulse, which is unconcerned with evolutionary consequences. It is this disconnect between evolution and motivation that befuddled the veneer theorists and made them reduce everything to selfishness. The most quoted line of their bleak literature says it all: "Scratch an 'altruist,' and watch a 'hypocrite' bleed."

It is not only humans who are capable of genuine altruism; other animals are, too. I see it every day. An old female, Peony, spends her days outdoors with other chimpanzees at the Yerkes Primate Center's field station. On bad days, when her arthritis is flaring up, she has trouble walking and climbing, but other females help her out. For example, Peony is huffing and puffing to get up into the climbing frame in which several apes have gathered for a grooming session. An unrelated younger female moves behind her, placing both hands on her ample behind, and pushes her up with quite a bit of effort until Peony has joined the rest.

We have also seen Peony getting up and slowly moving toward the water spigot, which is at quite a distance. Younger females sometimes run ahead of her, take in some water, then return to Peony and give it to her. At first, we had no idea what was going on, since all we saw was one female placing her mouth close to Peony's, but after a while the pattern became clear: Peony would open her mouth wide, and the younger female would spit a jet of water into it.

Such observations fit the emerging field of animal empathy, which deals not only with primates, but also with canines, elephants, even rodents. A typical example is how chimpanzees console distressed parties, hugging and kissing them, which behavior is so predictable that scientists have analyzed thousands of cases. Mammals are sensitive to each other's emotions and react to others in need. The whole reason people fill their homes with furry carnivores and not with, say, iguanas and turtles, is because mammals offer something no reptile ever will. They give affection, they want affection, and they respond to our emotions the way we do to theirs.

Mammals may derive pleasure from helping others in the same way that humans feel good doing good. Nature often equips life's essentials—sex, eating, nursing—with built-in gratification. One study found that pleasure centers in the human brain light up when we give to charity. This is of course no reason to call such behavior "selfish" as it would make the word totally meaningless. A selfish individual has no trouble walking away from another in need. Someone is drowning: let him drown. Someone cries: let her cry. These are truly selfish reactions, which are quite different from empathic ones. Yes, we experience a "warm glow," and perhaps some other animals do as well, but since this glow reaches us *via* the other, and *only* via the other, the helping is genuinely other-oriented.

BOTTOM-UP MORALITY

A few years ago Sarah Brosnan and I demonstrated that primates will happily perform a task for cucumber slices until they see others getting grapes, which taste so much better. The cucumber eaters become agitated, throw down their measly veggies and go on strike. A perfectly fine food has become unpalatable as a result of seeing a companion with something better.

We called it *inequity aversion*, a topic since investigated in other animals, including dogs. A dog will repeatedly perform a trick without rewards but refuse as soon as another dog gets pieces of sausage for the same trick. Recently, Sarah reported an unexpected twist to the inequity issue, however. While testing pairs of chimps, she found that also the one who gets the *better* deal occasionally refuses. It is as if they are satisfied only if both get the same. We seem to be getting close to a sense of fairness.

Such findings have implications for human morality. According to most philosophers, we reason ourselves toward a moral position. Even if we do not invoke God, it is still a top-down process of us formulating the principles and then imposing those on human conduct. But would it be realistic to ask people to be considerate of others if we had not already a natural inclination to be so? Would it make sense to appeal to fairness and justice in the absence of powerful reactions to their absence? Imagine the cognitive burden if every decision we took needed to be vetted against handed-down principles. Instead, I am a firm believer in the Humean position that reason is the slave of the passions. We started out with moral sentiments and intuitions, which is also where we find the greatest continuity with other primates. Rather than having developed morality from scratch, we received a huge helping hand from our background as social animals.

At the same time, however, I am reluctant to call a chimpanzee a "moral being." This is because sentiments do not suffice. We strive for a logically coherent system and have debates about how the death penalty fits arguments for the sanctity of life, or whether an unchosen sexual orientation can be wrong. These debates are uniquely human. We have no evidence that other animals judge the appropriateness of actions that do not affect themselves. The great pioneer of morality research, the Finn Edward Westermarck, explained what makes the moral emotions special: "Moral emotions are disconnected from one's immediate situation: they deal with good and bad at a more abstract, disinterested level." This is what sets human morality apart: a move toward universal standards combined with an elaborate system of justification, monitoring and punishment.

At this point, religion comes in. Think of the narrative support for compassion, such as the Parable of the Good Samaritan, or the challenge to fairness, such as the Parable of the Workers in the Vineyard, with its famous conclusion "The last will be first, and the first will be last." Add to this an almost Skinnerian fondness of reward and punishment—from the virgins to be met in heaven to the hellfire that awaits sinners—and the exploitation of our desire to be "praiseworthy," as Adam Smith called it. Humans are so sensitive to public opinion that we only need to see a picture of two eyes glued to the wall to respond with good behavior, which explains the image in some religions of an all-seeing eye to symbolize an omniscient God.

THE ATHEIST DILEMMA

Over the past few years, we have gotten used to a strident atheism arguing that God is not great (Christopher Hitchens) or a delusion (Richard Dawkins). The New Atheists call themselves "brights," thus hinting that believers are not so bright. They urge trust in science and want to root ethics in a naturalistic worldview.

While I do consider religious institutions and their representatives—popes, bishops, megapreachers, ayatollahs and rabbis—fair game for criticism, what good could come from insulting individuals who find value in religion? And more pertinently, what alternative does science have to offer? Science is not in the business of spelling out the meaning of life and even less in telling us how to live our lives. We scientists are good at finding out why things are the way they are, or how things work, and I do believe that biology can help us understand what kind of animals we are and why our morality looks the way it does. But to go from there to offering moral guidance seems a stretch.

Even the staunchest atheist growing up in Western society cannot avoid having absorbed the basic tenets of Christian morality. Our societies are steeped in it: everything we have accomplished over the centuries, even science, developed either hand in hand with or in opposition to religion, but never separately. It is impossible to know what morality would look like without religion. It would require a visit to a human culture that is not now and never was religious. That such cultures do not exist should give us pause.

Bosch struggled with the same issue—not with being an atheist, which was not an option, but science's place in society. The little figures in his paintings with inverted funnels on their heads or the buildings in the form of flasks, distillation bottles, and furnaces reference chemical equipment. Alchemy was gaining ground yet mixed with the occult and full of charlatans and quacks, which Bosch depicted with great humor in front of gullible audiences. Alchemy turned into science when it liberated itself from these influences and developed self-correcting procedures to deal with flawed or fabricated data. But science's contribution to a moral society, if any, remains a question mark.

Other primates have of course none of these problems, but even they strive for a certain kind of society. For example, female chimpanzees have been seen to drag reluctant males toward each other to make up after a fight, removing weapons from their hands, and high-ranking males regularly act as impartial arbiters to settle disputes in the community. I take these hints of *community concern* as yet another sign that the building blocks of morality are older than humanity, and that we do not need God to explain how we got where we are today. On the other hand, what would happen if we were able to excise religion from society? I doubt that science and the naturalistic worldview could fill the void and become an inspiration for the good. Any framework we develop to advocate a certain moral outlook is bound to produce its own list of principles, its own prophets, and attract its own devoted followers so that it will soon look like any old religion.

OCTOBER 17, 2010

The Dangers of Certainty:
A Lesson From Auschwitz

—*Simon Critchley*

As a kid in England, I watched a lot of television. There weren't any books in our house, not even the Bible. TV was therefore pretty important, omnipresent actually. Of course, most of what it delivered was garbage. But in 1973, the BBC aired an extraordinary documentary series called *The Ascent of Man*, hosted by one Dr. Jacob Bronowski in thirteen hour-long episodes. Each episode was what he called an "essay" and involved some exotic and elaborate locations, but the presentation was never flashy and consisted mostly of Dr. Bronowski speaking directly and deliberately to the camera.

Dr. Bronowski (he was always referred to as "Dr." and I can't think of him with any other, more familiar moniker) died forty years ago this year, at the relatively young age of sixty-six. He was a Polish-born British mathematician who wrote a number of highly regarded books on science, but who was equally at home in the world of literature. He wrote his own poetry as well as a book on William Blake.

He was a slight, lively, lovely man. Because it was the early '70s, some of his fashion choices were bewilderingly pastel, especially his socks, though on some occasions he sported a racy leather box jacket. He often smiled as he spoke, not out of conceit or because he lived in California (which, incidentally, he did, working at the Salk Institute in San Diego), but out of a sheer, greedy joy at explaining what he thought was important. But there was a genuine humility in his demeanor that made him utterly likable.

The Ascent of Man (admittedly a little sexist now—great men abound, but there are apparently few great women) deliberately inverted the title of Darwin's 1871 book. It was not an account of human biological evolution, but cultural evolution—from the origins of human life in the Rift Valley to the shifts from hunter/gatherer societies to nomadism and then settlement and civilization, from agriculture and metallurgy to the rise and fall of empires: Assyria, Egypt, Rome.

Bronowski presented everything with great gusto, but with a depth that never sacrificed clarity and which was never condescending. The tone of the programs was rigorous yet permissive, playful yet precise, and always urgent, open and exploratory. I remember in particular the programs on the trial of Galileo, Darwin's hesitancy about publishing his theory of evolution, and the dizzying consequences of Einstein's theory of relativity. Some of it was difficult for a thirteen-year-old to understand, but I remember being absolutely riveted.

The ascent of man was secured through scientific creativity. But unlike many of his more glossy and glib contemporary epigones, Dr. Bronowski was never reductive in his commitment to science. Scientific activity was always linked to artistic creation. For Bronowski, science and art were two neighboring mighty rivers that flowed from a common source: the human imagination. Newton and Shakespeare, Darwin and Coleridge, Einstein and Braque: all were interdependent facets of the human mind and constituted what was best and most noble about the human adventure.

For most of the series, Dr. Bronowski's account of human development was a relentlessly optimistic one. Then, in the eleventh episode, called "Knowledge or Certainty," the mood changed to something more somber. Let me try and recount what has stuck in my memory for all these years.

He began the show with the words, "One aim of the physical sciences has been to give an actual picture of the material world. One achievement of physics in the twentieth century has been to show

that such an aim is unattainable." For Dr. Bronowski, there was no
absolute knowledge and anyone who claims it—whether a scientist, a
politician or a religious believer—opens the door to tragedy. All scientific information is imperfect and we have to treat it with humility.
Such, for him, was the human condition.

This is the condition for what we can know, but it is also, crucially, a moral lesson. It is the lesson of twentieth-century painting
from cubism onward, but also that of quantum physics. All we can
do is to push deeper and deeper into better approximations of an
ever-evasive reality. The goal of complete understanding seems to
recede as we approach it.

There is no God's-Eye view, Dr. Bronowski insisted, and the people who claim that there is and that they possess it are not just wrong,
they are morally pernicious. Errors are inextricably bound up with
pursuit of human knowledge, which requires not just mathematical
calculation but insight, interpretation and a personal act of judgment
for which we are *responsible*. The emphasis on the moral responsibility of knowledge was essential for all of Dr. Bronowski's work. The
acquisition of knowledge entails a responsibility for the integrity of
what we are as ethical creatures.

Dr. Bronowski's eleventh essay took him to the ancient university city of Göttingen in Germany, to explain the genesis of Werner
Heisenberg's uncertainty principle in the hugely creative milieu
that surrounded the physicist Max Born in the 1920s. Dr. Bronowski
insisted that the principle of uncertainty was a misnomer, because it
gives the impression that in science (and outside of it) we are always
uncertain. But this is wrong. Knowledge is precise, but that precision
is confined within a certain *toleration* of uncertainty. Heisenberg's
insight is that the electron is a particle that yields only limited information; its speed and position are confined by the tolerance of Max
Planck's quantum, the basic element of matter.

Dr. Bronowski thought that the uncertainty principle should
therefore be called the principle of tolerance. Pursuing knowledge
means accepting uncertainty. Heisenberg's principle has the consequence that no physical events can ultimately be described with

absolute certainty or with "zero tolerance," as it were. The more we know, the less certain we are.

In the everyday world, we do not just accept a lack of ultimate exactitude with a melancholic shrug, but we constantly employ such inexactitude in our relations with other people. Our relations with others also require a principle of tolerance. We encounter other people across a gray area of negotiation and approximation. Such is the business of listening and the back and forth of conversation and social interaction.

For Dr. Bronowski, the moral consequence of knowledge is that we must never judge others on the basis of some absolute, godlike conception of certainty. All knowledge, all information that passes between human beings, can be exchanged only within what we might call "a play of tolerance," whether in science, literature, politics or religion. As he eloquently put it, "Human knowledge is personal and responsible, an unending adventure at the edge of uncertainty."

The relationship between humans and nature and humans and other humans can take place only within a certain play of tolerance. Insisting on certainty, by contrast, leads ineluctably to arrogance and dogma based on ignorance.

At this point, in the final minutes of the show, the scene suddenly shifts to Auschwitz, where many members of Bronowski's family were murdered. He then delivers this soliloqy:

> It's said that science will dehumanize people and turn them into numbers. That is false, tragically false. Look for yourself. This is the concentration camp and crematorium at Auschwitz. This is where people were turned into numbers. Into this pond were flushed the ashes of some four million people. And that was not done by gas. It was done by arrogance. It was done by dogma. It was done by ignorance. When people believe that they have absolute knowledge, with no test in reality, this is how they behave. This is what men do when they aspire to the knowledge of gods.
>
> Science is a very human form of knowledge. We are always at the brink of the known, we always feel forward for what is to be

hoped. Every judgment in science stands on the edge of error, and is personal. Science is a tribute to what we can know although we are fallible. In the end the words were said by Oliver Cromwell: "I beseech you, in the bowels of Christ, think it possible you may be mistaken."

I owe it as a scientist to my friend Leo Szilard, I owe it as a human being to the many members of my family who died at Auschwitz, to stand here by the pond as a survivor and a witness. We have to cure ourselves of the itch for absolute knowledge and power. We have to close the distance between the push-button order and the human act. We have to touch people.

It is an extraordinary and moving moment. Bronowski dips his hand into the muddy water of a pond which contained the remains of his family members and the members of countless other families. All victims of the same hatred: the hatred of the other human being. By contrast, he says—just before the camera hauntingly cuts to slow motion—"We have to touch people."

The play of tolerance opposes the principle of monstrous certainty that is endemic to fascism and, sadly, not just fascism but all the various faces of fundamentalism. When we think we have certainty, when we aspire to the knowledge of the gods, then Auschwitz can happen and can repeat itself. Arguably, it has repeated itself in the genocidal certainties of past decades.

The pursuit of scientific knowledge is as personal an act as lifting a paintbrush or writing a poem, and they are both profoundly human. If the human condition is defined by limitedness, then this is a glorious fact because it is a moral limitedness rooted in a faith in the power of the imagination, our sense of responsibility and our acceptance of our fallibility. We always have to acknowledge that we might be mistaken. When we forget that, then we forget ourselves and the worst can happen.

In 1945, nearly three decades before *The Ascent of Man*, Dr. Bronowski—who was a close friend of the Hungarian physicist Leo Szilard, the reluctant father of the atomic bomb—visited Nagasaki to help assess the damage there. It convinced him to discontinue his work for British military research with which he had been engaged extensively during the Second World War. From that time onward, he focused on the relations between science and human values. When someone said to Szilard in Bronowski's company that the bombing of Hiroshima and Nagasaki was science's tragedy, Szilard replied firmly that this was wrong: it was a human tragedy.

Such was Dr. Bronowski's lesson for a thirteen-year-old boy some forty years ago. Being slightly old school, I treated myself last Christmas to a DVD deluxe boxed set of *The Ascent of Man*. I am currently watching it with my ten-year-old son. Admittedly, it is not really much competition for *Candy Crush* and his sundry other video games, but he is showing an interest. Or at least he is tolerating my enthusiasm. And of course beginning to learn such toleration is the whole point.

FEBRUARY 2, 2014

Confessions of an Ex-Moralist

—*Joel Marks*

T HE DAY I BECAME AN ATHEIST WAS THE DAY I REALIZED I HAD been a believer.

Up until then I had numbered myself among the "secular ethicists." Plato's *Euthyphro* had convinced me, as it had so many other philosophers, that religion is not needed for morality. Socrates puts the point characteristically in the form of a question: "Do the gods love something because it is pious, or is something pious because the gods love it?" To believe the latter would be to allow that any act whatever might turn out to be the "pious" or right thing to do, provided only that one of the gods (of Olympus), or the God of Genesis and Job in one of his moods, "loved" or willed it. Yet if God commanded that we kill our innocent child in cold blood, would we not resist the rightness of this act?

This would seem to be the modern, sane view of the matter. We have an intuitive sense of right and wrong that trumps even the commands of God. We have the ability to judge that God is good or bad. Therefore, even if God did not exist, we could fend for ourselves in matters of conscience. Ethics, not divine revelation, is the guide to life. That is indeed the clarion call of the New Atheists. As the philosopher Louise Antony puts it in the introduction to a recent collection of philosophers' essays, *Philosophers without Gods: Meditations on Atheism and the Secular Life*, "Another charge routinely leveled at atheists is that we have no moral values. The essays in this volume

should serve to roundly refute this. Every writer in this volume ada-
mantly affirms the objectivity of right and wrong."

But I don't. Not any longer. Yet I once devoted my professional life
to studying ethics in the spirit of Anthony's book. The task seemed
squarely on our human shoulders to figure out how to act on particular occasions and how to live in general. Yes, there were deep problems to unravel, but they were subject to rational resolution. Most
of my thinking concerned the dispute between the moral doctrine
known as consequentialism and so-called deontological ethics: Is
it the outcome of our actions that determines their moral value, or,
alternatively, the quality of the act itself? For example, is a lie that
leads to something good thereby permissible, perhaps even obligatory, or would it be forbidden simply in virtue of being a lie? This
kind of inquiry is known as normative ethics.

Then there is another kind of motive for doing ethics, more practical in nature. So-called applied ethics seeks to find answers for the
pressing moral problems of the day. Can abortion ever be justified?
Capital punishment? Euthanasia? War? In my case the plight of nonhuman animals at human hands became the great preoccupation. I
could think of no greater atrocity than the confinement and slaughter of untold billions of innocent creatures for sustenance that can be
provided through other, more humane diets.

In my most recent published book, I defended a particular moral
theory—my own version of deontological ethics—and then "applied"
that theory to defend a particular moral claim: that other animals
have an inherent right not to be eaten or otherwise used by humans.
Oddly enough, it was as I crossed the final *t* and dotted the final *i* of
that monograph that I underwent what I call my anti-epiphany.

A friend had been explaining to me the nature of her belief in
God. At one point she likened divinity to the beauty of a sunset:
the quality lay not in the sunset but in her relation to the sunset. I
thought to myself, "Ah, if that is what she means, then I could believe
in *that* kind of God. For when I think about the universe, I am filled
with awe and wonder; if that feeling is God, then I am a believer."

But then it hit me: Is not morality like this God? In other words, could I believe that, say, the wrongness of a lie was any more intrinsic to an intentionally deceptive utterance than beauty was to a sunset or wonderfulness to the universe? Does it not make far more sense to suppose that all of these phenomena arise in my breast, that they are the responses of a particular sensibility to otherwise valueless events and entities?

So someone else might respond completely differently from me, such that for him or her, the lie was permissible, the sunset banal, the universe nothing but atoms and the void. Yet that prospect was so alien to my conception of morality that it was tantamount to there being no morality at all. For essential to morality is that its norms apply with equal legitimacy to everyone; moral relativism, it has always seemed to me, is an oxymoron. Hence I saw no escape from moral nihilism.

The dominoes continued to fall. I had thought I was a secularist because I conceived of right and wrong as standing on their own two feet, without prop or crutch from God. We should do the right thing because it is the right thing to do, period. *But this was a God, too.* It was the Godless God of secular morality, which commanded without commander—whose ways were thus even more mysterious than the God I did not believe in, who at least had the intelligible motive of rewarding us for doing what he wanted.

And what is more, I had known this. At some level of my being there had been the awareness, but I had brushed it aside. I had therefore lived in a semiconscious state of self-delusion—what Sartre might have called bad faith. But in my case this was also a pun, for my bad faith was precisely *the belief that I lacked faith in a divinity.*

In the three years since my anti-epiphany I have attempted to assess these surprising revelations and their implications for my life and work. I found myself in the thick of metaethics, which looks at the nature of morality, including whether there even is such a thing as right and wrong. I myself had ignored the latter issue for most of my career, since, if there was one thing I knew in this entire universe, it was that some things are morally wrong. It is wrong to toss male chicks, alive and conscious, into a meat grinder, as happens in the egg industry. It is wrong to scorn homosexuals and deny them civil rights. It is wrong to massacre people in death camps. All of these things have met with general approval in one society or another. And yet I knew in my soul, with all of my conviction, with a passion, that they were wrong, wrong, wrong. I knew this with more certainty than I knew that the earth is round.

But suddenly I knew it no more. I was not merely skeptical or agnostic about it; I had come to believe, and do still, that these things are not wrong. But neither are they right; nor are they permissible. The entire set of moral attributions is out the window. Think of this analogy: A tribe of people lives on an isolated island. They have no formal governmental institutions of any kind. In particular they have no legislature. Therefore in that society it would make no sense to say that someone had done something "illegal." But neither would anything be "legal." The entire set of legal categories would be inapplicable. In just this way I now view moral categories.

Certainly I am not the first to have had thoughts like these, and today the philosopher Richard Garner in particular is a soul mate. Nor has there been a shortage of alternative conceptions of morality to the one I held. But the personal experiment of excluding all moral concepts and language from my thinking, feeling and actions has proved so workable and attractive, I am convinced that anyone who gives it a fair shot would likely find it to his liking.

One interesting discovery has been that there are fewer practical differences between moralism and amoralism than might have been expected. It seems to me that what could broadly be called desire has been the moving force of humanity, no matter how we might have window-dressed it with moral talk. By desire I do not mean sexual craving, or even only selfish wanting. I use the term generally to refer to whatever motivates us, which ranges from selfishness to altruism and everything in between and at right angles. Mother Teresa was acting as much from desire as was the Marquis de Sade. But the sort of desire that now concerns me most is what we would want if we were absolutely convinced that there is no such thing as moral right and wrong. I think the most likely answer is this: pretty much the same as what we want now.

For instance, I used to think that animal agriculture was wrong. Now I will call a spade a spade and declare simply that I very much dislike it and want it to stop. Has this lessened my commitment to ending it? I do not find that to be the case at all. Does this lessen my ability to bring others around to sharing my desires, and hence diminish the prospects of ending animal agriculture? On the contrary, I find myself in a far better position than before to change minds—and, what is more important, hearts. For to argue that people who use animals for food and other purposes are doing something terribly wrong is hardly the way to win them over. That is more likely to elicit their defensive resistance.

Instead I now focus on conveying information: about the state of affairs on factory farms and elsewhere, the environmental devastation that results and, especially, the sentient, intelligent, gentle and noble natures of the animals who are being brutalized and slaughtered. It is also important to spread knowledge of alternatives, like how to adopt a healthy and appetizing vegan diet. If such efforts will not cause people to alter their eating and buying habits, support the passage of various laws and so forth, I don't know what will.

So nothing has changed, and everything has changed. For while my desires are the same, my manner of trying to implement them has altered radically. I now acknowledge that I cannot count on either God or morality to back up my personal preferences or clinch the case in any argument. I am simply no longer in the business of trying to derive an *ought* from an *is*. I must accept that other people sometimes have opposed preferences, even when we are agreed on all the relevant facts and are reasoning correctly.

My outlook has therefore become more practical: I desire to influence the world in such a way that my desires have a greater likelihood of being realized. This implies being an active citizen. But there is still plenty of room for the sorts of activities and engagements that characterize the life of a philosophical ethicist. For one thing, I retain my strong preference for honest dialectical dealings in a context of mutual respect. It's just that I am no longer giving premises in moral arguments; rather, I am offering considerations to help us figure out what to do. I am not attempting to justify anything; I am trying to motivate informed and reflective choices.

In the process my own desires are likely to undergo further change as well, in the direction of greater compassion and respect, I would anticipate—and not only for the victims of the attitudes, behaviors and policies I don't like, but also for their perpetrators. But this won't be because a god, a supernatural law or even my conscience told me I must, I ought, I have an obligation. Instead I will be moved by my head and my heart. Morality has nothing to do with it.

AUGUST 21, 2011

The Maze of Moral Relativism

—Paul Boghossian

Relativism about morality has come to play an increasingly important role in contemporary culture. To many thoughtful people, and especially to those who are unwilling to derive their morality from a religion, it appears unavoidable. Where would absolute facts about right and wrong come from, they reason, if there is no supreme being to decree them? We should reject moral absolutes, even as we keep our moral convictions, allowing that there can be right and wrong relative to this or that moral code, but no right and wrong per se. (See, for example, Stanley Fish's 2001 op-ed, "Condemnation Without Absolutes.")[1]

Is it plausible to respond to the rejection of absolute moral facts with a relativistic view of morality? Why should our response not be a more extreme, nihilistic one, according to which we stop using normative terms like *right* and *wrong* altogether, be it in their absolutist or relativist guises?

Relativism is not always a coherent way of responding to the rejection of a certain class of facts. When we decided that there were no such things as witches, we didn't become relativists about witches. Rather, we just gave up witch talk altogether, except by way of characterizing the attitudes of people (such as those in Salem) who mistakenly believed that the world contained witches, or by way of characterizing what it is that children find it fun to pretend to be on Halloween. We became what we may call "eliminativists" about witches.

On the other hand, when Einstein taught us, in his special theory of relativity, that there was no such thing as the absolute simultaneity of two events, the recommended outcome was that we become relativists about simultaneity, allowing that there is such a thing as "simultaneity relative to a (spatio-temporal) frame of reference," but not simultaneity as such.

What's the difference between the witch case and the simultaneity case? Why did the latter rejection lead to relativism, but the former to eliminativism?

In the simultaneity case, Einstein showed that while the world does not contain simultaneity as such, it does contain its relativistic cousin—simultaneity relative to a frame of reference—a property that plays something like the same sort of role as classical simultaneity did in our theory of the world.

By contrast, in the witch case, once we give up on witches, there is no relativistic cousin that plays anything like the role that witches were supposed to play. The property, that two events may have, of "being simultaneous relative to frame of reference F" is recognizably a kind of simultaneity. But the property of "being a witch according to a belief system T" is not a kind of witch, but a kind of content (the content of belief system T): it's a way of characterizing what belief system T says, not a way of characterizing the world.

Now, the question is whether the moral case is more like that of simultaneity or more like that of witches? When we reject absolute moral facts, is moral relativism the correct outcome or is it moral eliminativism (nihilism)?

The answer, as we have seen, depends on whether there are relativistic cousins of "right" and "wrong" that can play something like the same role that absolute "right" and "wrong" play.

It is hard to see what those could be.

What's essential to "right" and "wrong" is that they are *normative* terms, terms that are used to say how things ought to be, in contrast with how things actually are. But what relativistic cousin of "right" and "wrong" could play anything like such a normative role?

Most moral relativists say that moral right and wrong are to be relativized to a community's "moral code." According to some such codes, eating beef is permissible; according to others, it is an abomination and must never be allowed. The relativist proposal is that we must never talk simply about what's right or wrong, but only about what's "right or wrong relative to a particular moral code."

The trouble is that while "Eating beef is wrong" is clearly a normative statement, "Eating beef is wrong relative to the moral code of the Hindus" is just a descriptive remark that carries no normative import whatsoever. It's just a way of characterizing what is claimed by a particular moral code, that of the Hindus. We can see this from the fact that anyone, regardless of their views about eating beef, can agree that eating beef is wrong relative to the moral code of the Hindus.

So, it looks as though the moral case is more like the witch case than the simultaneity case: there are no relativistic cousins of "right" and "wrong." Denial of moral absolutism leads not to relativism, but to nihilism.[2]

There is no halfway house called "moral relativism" in which we continue to use normative vocabulary with the stipulation that it is to be understood as relativized to particular moral codes. If there are no absolute facts about morality, "right" and "wrong" would have to join "witch" in the dustbin of failed concepts.

The argument is significant because it shows that we should not rush to give up on absolute moral facts, mysterious as they can sometimes seem, for the world might seem even more mysterious without any normative vocabulary whatsoever.

One might be suspicious of my argument against moral relativism. Aren't we familiar with some normative domains—such as that of etiquette—about which we are all relativists? Surely, no one in their right minds would think that there is some absolute fact of the matter about whether we ought to slurp our noodles while eating.

If we are dining at Buckingham Palace, we ought not to slurp, since our hosts would consider it offensive, and we ought not, other things being equal, offend our hosts. On the other hand, if we are dining in Xian, China, we ought to slurp, since in Xian slurping is considered to be a sign that we are enjoying our meal, and our hosts would consider it offensive if we didn't slurp, and we ought not, other things being equal, offend our hosts.

But if relativism is coherent in the case of etiquette, why couldn't we claim that morality is relative in the same way?

The reason is that our relativism about etiquette does not actually dispense with all absolute moral facts. Rather, we are relativists about etiquette in the sense that, with respect to a restricted range of issues (such as table manners and greetings), we take the correct absolute norm to be "we ought not, other things being equal, offend our hosts."

This norm is absolute and applies to everyone and at all times. Its relativistic flavor comes from the fact that, with respect to that limited range of behaviors (table manners and greetings, but not, say, the abuse of children for fun), it advocates varying one's behavior with local convention.

In other words, the relativism of etiquette depends on the existence of absolute moral norms. Since etiquette does not dispense with absolute moral facts, one cannot hope to use it as a model for moral relativism.

Suppose we take this point on board, though, and admit that there have to be some absolute moral facts. Why couldn't they all be like the facts involved in etiquette? Why couldn't they all say that, with respect to any morally relevant question, what we ought to do depends on what the local conventions are?

The trouble with this approach is that once we have admitted that there are some absolute moral facts, it is hard to see why we shouldn't think that there are many—as many as common sense and ordinary reasoning appear to warrant. Having given up on the purity of a thoroughgoing antiabsolutism, we would now be in the business of trying to figure out what absolute moral facts there are. To do that, we would need to employ our usual mix of argument, intuition and experience. And what argument, intuition and experience tell us is that whether we should slurp our noodles depends on what the local conventions are, but whether we should abuse children for fun does not.

A would-be relativist about morality needs to decide whether his view grants the existence of some absolute moral facts, or whether it is to be a pure relativism, free of any commitment to absolutes. The latter position, I have argued, is mere nihilism, whereas the former leads us straight out of relativism and back into the quest for the moral absolutes.

None of this is to deny that there are hard cases where it is not easy to see what the correct answer to a moral question is. It is merely to emphasize that there appears to be no good alternative to thinking that, when we are in a muddle about what the answer to a hard moral question is, we are in a muddle about what the absolutely correct answer is.

JULY 24, 2011

1. Pinning a precise philosophical position on someone, especially a nonphilosopher, is always tricky, because people tend to give nonequivalent formulations of what they take to be the same view. Fish, for example, after saying that his view is that "there can be no independent standards for determining which of many rival interpretations of an event is the true one," which sounds appropriately relativistic, ends up claiming that all he means to defend is "the practice of putting yourself in your adversary's shoes, not in order to wear them as your own but in order to have some understanding (far short of approval) of why someone else might want to wear them." The latter, though, is just the recommendation of empathetic understanding and is, of course, both good counsel and perfectly consistent with the endorsement of moral absolutes.

Another view with which moral relativism is sometimes conflated is the view that the right thing to do can depend on the circumstances. There is no question that the right thing to do can depend on the circumstances, even on an absolutist view. Whether you should help someone in need can depend on what your circumstances are, what their circumstances are, and so forth. What makes a view relativistic is its holding that the right thing to do depends not just on the circumstances, but on what the person (or his community) takes to be the right thing to do, on their moral code.

In this column, I am only concerned with those who wish to deny that there are any absolute moral truths in this sense. If that is not your view, then you are not the target of this particular discussion.

2. Some philosophers may think that they can evade this problem by casting the relativism in terms of a relativized truth predicate rather than a relativized moral predicate. But as I have explained elsewhere, the problem of the loss of normative content recurs in that setting.

Can Moral Disputes Be Resolved?

—Alex Rosenberg

MORAL DISPUTES SEEM INTRACTABLE—MORE INTRACTABLE
than other disputes. Take an example of a moral position that most
of us would consider obvious: Honor killing is wrong. But honor killing has its supporters. Anyone who suggests that we can compromise
with its supporters on the matter misunderstands the nature of this
type of disagreement. It's absolute. One party has to be right. Us. So
why can't we convince those who hold the opposite view?

With some exceptions, political disputes are not like this. When
people disagree about politics, they often agree about ends, but disagree about means to attain them. Republicans and Democrats may
differ on, say, health care policy, but share goals—a healthy American population. They differ on fiscal policy but agree on the goal of
economic growth for the nation. Of course, this is often a matter of
degree. Political disputes can have moral aspects, too. The two sides
in the debate over abortion rights, for instance, clearly don't agree on
the ends. There is an ethical disagreement at the heart of this debate.
It is safe to say that the more ethical a political dispute is, the more
heated and intractable it is likely to become.

Honor killing is the execution of one's own family member, often
a woman, who is seen to have brought disgrace to the family. It is a
practice most of us find absolutely wrong, no matter the goal—in this
case, restoring dignity to the family. The fact that it is a practice long
sanctioned in other cultures does not matter to us. Meanwhile, those

who approve of or carry out honor killings reject our condemnation, and most likely see it as a moral lapse of ours.

What makes moral disagreements so intractable? Ethics shouldn't be as hard as rocket science.

Can religion help? It might seem that if morality is a matter of obeying divine commands, we could make short work of moral disagreement, if only we knew which was the true faith. Of course, we don't. But 2,300 years ago Plato showed that appeals to God's wisdom, no matter which faith, is irrelevant to what makes for moral rightness.

His argument was simple. Take for example, "Honor killing is wrong." Now ask, is our condemnation of honor killing right because God commands us to do so? Or does God command us to oppose it because it's morally right? It can't be a coincidence that it's right and that he chose it for us. So, which is it: right because God choose it, or chosen by God because right? Most people think it's the latter. But then whatever it is that makes honor killing wrong, it must be something about honor killing itself, not simply God's having chosen to prohibit it. So, even if we accept that God chose the right morality for us, we are still in the dark about what makes it the right one.

So religion may tend to enforce a certain morality, but it certainly can't show it's right.

What about reason?

Many philosophers have argued that rational beings can reason their way to the right answers in morality. Kant and Mill both tried to do this, but ended up building incompatible moral theories by reasoning from two quite different starting points.

Mill founded his concept of morality on the feeling of pleasure, which he held is the only thing everyone seeks for itself alone. Therefore, it had to be the intrinsic good, and morality is a matter of trying to maximize its quantity. The trouble with this argument was obvious from the start: just because we all seek pleasure for its own sake doesn't make it morally valuable.

Kant started with our consciousness of freedom and reasoned to moral principles that any autonomous rational agent logically must endorse for him or herself. Alas, no one has ever converted Kant's convoluted prose into a clear argument that all can agree is a convincing reason for any moral rule. In spite of the complexity of Kant's argument, the resulting moral rule, his famous "categorical imperative" sounds little different from "The Golden Rule." Neither is likely to settle the honor killing dispute.

A few philosophers claimed that we have a moral sense that perceives the moral rightness or wrongness of things directly and immediately. This theory might be worth taking seriously if morality were like mathematics. Mathematicians all agree that we know with certainty a large number of mathematical truths. Since experiment and observation could never be the source of such certainty, we (or at least mathematicians) must have some other way of knowing mathematical truths—a mathematical sense that directly perceives them. For this argument to work in ethics, there would have to be little or no ethical disagreement to begin with. Since many moral disagreements seem intractable even among experts, the hypothesis that we are equipped to know moral truths directly is very difficult to sustain.

Still another way of attempting to justify moral judgments goes back to Aristotle: What is morally right is what virtuous people do. We can see what is morally right by observing how virtuous people behave. The very existence of honor killing reflects the problems this approach faces. The practices one culture identifies as vicious are virtues in other cultures. And there is no culture-free point from which to adjudicate such disagreements about what counts as a virtue.

In recent years some thinkers have argued that the foundations of morality are given by what science, especially evolutionary biology, shows us about the conditions of human flourishing. These philosophers, social psychologists and evolutionary anthropologists argue that there was strong selection for a core set of moral norms that are so widespread they are absent only in psychopaths. Their lack of a moral sense, they assert, is the result of brain damage—neurological conditions caused by genetic mutation and/or environmental damage.

The trouble with this argument is clear: first, Mother Nature selects only for traits that lead to more offspring. But there is nothing particularly moral about having more children than someone else. Even if some set of norms we all share were conducive to having more offspring, this wouldn't in any way underwrite them as the morally right ones. Second, as we know only too well, Darwinian processes, whether biological or cultural, sometimes select for norms we absolutely reject as immoral.

THIS SHORT TOUR OF the history of ethical theorizing might make one pessimistic about the very possibility of resolving ethical disputes. The pessimism is part of what has led to meta-ethics, a subdiscipline of philosophy that may shed light on why moral disputes are so intractable. Instead of trying to figure out which moral claims are right and which are wrong, meta-ethics starts by examining the meaning of ethical claims in general. If we can agree on their meanings, we may be able to figure out under what conditions they are right or wrong.

One thing to notice is that, despite appearances, moral claims like "honor killing is wrong" are not good candidates for being simply true or false statements. They are more like disguised imperatives: "Though shalt not engage in honor killing!" Another difference some meta-ethicists argue for is that when we really endorse a claim as morally right, we are prepared to act on it. Moral claims motivate in a way factual claims don't.

If believing moral claims motivates in a way factual claims don't, this may be because they express emotions that can spur actions: positive ones like admiration in the case of moral praise; negative ones like anger in the case of moral blame. It is hard to deny that morality at least harnesses our emotions. That is in part what makes moral disagreement often so heated and so intractable. But is the connection closer? "Sentimentalists," following David Hume, argue that because they express our emotions (or sentiments), moral claims are like other reports of our sensations. "The sky is blue" reports a fact about the subjective sensation light rays produce in us. Hume and the meta-ethicists who followed him argue that ethical statements express our emotional responses to the actions of others.

The notion that moral judgments are not just true or false claims about human conduct helps explain the failure of ethical theories as far back as Aristotle's. These theories started out on the wrong foot, by treating morality and immorality as intrinsic to the actions themselves, instead of our responses to them.

Factoring human emotions into moral judgment explains much about them. Why they are held so strongly, why different cultures that shape human emotional responses have such different moral norms, even why people treat abstract ethical disagreement by others as a moral flaw. And most of all, this meta-ethical theory helps us understand why such disputes are sometimes intractable.

Meta-ethics has begun to make use of findings in cognitive social psychology, and in neuroscience, to help understand the nature of ethical claims. For example, we now have a good brain imaging data that shows why a person's moral judgments in the so-called trolley problems change as a result of even slight changes in the way the problem is described. The differences are to be found in distinct brain networks that generate different emotional responses.

These conclusions encourage tolerance of ethical differences and an appropriate diffidence about our own moral judgments. But they also make it harder to condemn honor killing or even more extreme or violent actions. If "honor killing is wrong" reports our emotional horror at the practice, and not its objective wrongness, then even worse moral catastrophes will be hard to condemn.

Many people will not find this a satisfactory outcome. They will hope to show that even if moral judgments are expressions of our emotions, nevertheless at least some among these attitudes are objective, right, correct, well justified. But if we can't find objective grounds for our emotional response to honor killing, our condemnation of it might turn out to just be cultural prejudice.

JULY 13, 2015

Moral Dispute or Cultural Difference?

—Carol Rovane

T HE WORD "RELATIVISM" TENDS TO GENERATE STRONG REAC-
tions. This is odd, given that the word is not generally used with a
clear and agreed upon meaning. I want to offer a specific proposal
about what it means, with a view to navigating the following "real-
world" problem, discussed by Alex Rosenberg here at The Stone in
July: What should we do when we face what are often described as
irresolvable moral disagreements?

In a disagreement, two parties affirm and deny the same thing;
because the parties contradict each other, they cannot both be right;
because they cannot both be right, there is something *to be resolved*
between them by figuring out which of them is mistaken; a disagreement remains *unresolved* so long as both parties continue to think the
other is mistaken; it is *irresolvable* when there is no method by which
to resolve it.

Are there any such irresolvable disagreements?

A moral relativist will most likely argue that moral disputes
are irresolvable because moral beliefs are not strictly true or false,
because there are no facts in the world that would make them
so—no moral facts. Therefore, such "truth" they may be said to
have is grounded in subjective elements—states of mind such as
our desires and emotions. Since these subjective elements will vary
among persons and cultures, they may generate conflicts that no
possible appeal to objective facts could ever resolve.

Because the term "moral relativism" is closely associated with this subjectivist picture of morality, it elicits understandable hostility. How can we earnestly hold our moral commitments if we give up on the aspiration to objectivity regarding morals, to getting them right rather than wrong?

I think there is another way to understand what moral relativism involves, which does not require us to give up our aspiration to objectivity. Let me use an example.

Imagine me to be a middle-aged woman of middle-class origin who grew up in middle America. I went to college, graduated, then went on to get a master's degree in business, after which I worked on Wall Street and made a lot of money—so much that I retired early. I never married or had children, which was a source of regret to my parents. But they are proud of me. We are all committed to the ideals of liberal individualism, and agree that each of us is responsible for his or her own life, financially and otherwise.

Shortly after retirement, I decide to travel, and during a visit to a rural village in the Punjab I meet a woman my age named Anjali. The main facts of her life are: her parents arranged her marriage when she was a very young girl, she was married in her early teens and since then she has had many children. She is already a grandmother. Her life has been organized entirely around family responsibilities.

Initially, Anjali finds my decision not to marry or have children repugnant, especially since my parents clearly wished it. She tells me, through an interpreter, that we are all morally obliged to defer to our parents' wishes. I initially take myself to have a moral disagreement with her, for I believe that I was not morally obliged to defer to my parents' wish that I marry and have children.

Many Westerners may think this moral disagreement can easily be resolved in my favor: I have done no wrong in seeking my fortune, and Anjali should be allowed a right to do the same. But this Western attitude overlooks an important fact: it does not generally lie within human power to re-make a whole culture at will.

In her actual cultural circumstances, it isn't an option for Anjali to set off to seek her fortune on her own, apart from her family network, any more than it is an option for me to take up the various traditional duties that befall females in extended families in rural Punjab. Owing to these differences in our cultural circumstances, Anjali and I need very different moral truths to live by, in order to navigate the specific moral options that we face. Does this mean that she and I are bound to live by conflicting values—that we face an irresoluble moral disagreement, about whether it is morally obligatory to defer to our parents' wishes?

No. When Anjali recognizes her moral obligation to defer to her parents' wishes, she conceives it as one among many special duties that she bears to her parents, which sit alongside other special duties to other members of her extended family, all of which go by the name *katarvya*. When I deny that I have any moral obligation to defer to my parents' wishes, I am not thinking of *katarvya*, and in fact before I got to know Anjali I had no conception of *katarvya* at all. I was thinking in terms of the sorts of obligations that are recognized within the framework of liberal individualism; I was not violating my parents' rights when I fashioned my life plan according to my own wishes rather than theirs. So Anjali and I never really *contradicted* each other concerning what we owe our parents. She had been affirming that she owes her parents the special duties of *katarvya*, while I had been denying that my parents' rights include dictating my major life decisions.

What we really confront here, then, is a kind of *difference* which is not a disagreement. We come to see that we are each *right* to live by our respective moral beliefs, due to the way in which they speak to our respective circumstances, and the specific moral issues that arise within them. Yet although we each come to regard the other's moral beliefs as *true*, neither of us adopts the other's moral beliefs for herself, as truths to live by. When this occurs, we have occasion to adopt a distinctively relativist stance, which is a stance of *disengagement* rather than disagreement. As we learn about one anothers' moral beliefs, we do not thereby gain any moral insight into how we should live our own moral lives, and nor do we try to instruct others about how they should live theirs.

The moral relativism I am proposing makes sense of this situation by concluding that while moral truths hold objectively, they do not hold universally, only locally. If Anjali and I require different moral beliefs to live by, this shows that we live in different moral worlds, in which different moral truths hold.

This conception of moral relativism is not without its problems. It seems more plausible for some cases, such as the one I just gave, than for others. Take, for example, such practices as sati (widow burning), female genital mutilation and honor killing. Our immediate response is likely to be: We deem these practices *wrong*; they must be stopped, preferably by *convincing* those who participate in them that they are wrong. If we cannot convince them, then we take ourselves to face irresoluble moral disagreements, in the face of which we should remain true to our moral beliefs, by continuing to insist that the practices are wrong, and opposing them by all the usual means available in a polity—legislation, state intervention, etc.

The response I just described is essentially anti-relativist. And note that it opposes relativism on *both* of the conceptions I have been discussing. It insists that the parties to a disagreement cannot both be right, that there are objective matters to be right or wrong about. It also insists that we should not disengage from those who morally differ from us, but should retain a sense of disagreement with them, by putting forward the moral truths by which we live as universal truths that hold for everyone.

But before we reject moral relativism, we should explore one other possibility. While the relativist does want to say, in a general way, that people with moral differences probably are responding to very different cultural circumstances, she does not have to say that those who participate in the specific practices of sati, female genital mutilation and honor killing are right to do so. She may also say that they are wrong *by their own standards*. For there may be local moral truths, which hold in the very cultural conditions in which those practices have arisen, in the light of which they are wrong. If that is so, then the participants in these practices misunderstand what their own moral principles entail. This is one perfectly plausible way of understanding how American society came to realize that it was wrong to give only white males full civil rights. And it would be a particularly parochial form of self-congratulation to say that what was true of America is not feasible for other societies.

Of course, it is conceivable that there are no local truths in the light of which sati, female genital mutilation and honor killing would count as wrong. But, the point is, *only then*—that is, only if there are no local truths that stand in tension with these practices—would the moral relativist have to conclude that our moral differences over them are like the case I described above about Anjali and me, in the respect that both parties are actually *right*.

Moral relativism, as I propose understanding it, calls for an exploratory approach to encounters with moral difference. It discourages us from taking the appearance of irresoluble moral disagreements at face value, without first exploring the possibility that the parties might not actually be disagreeing, but addressing quite different moral circumstances, for which they need quite different moral truths to live by. If we arrived at this relativist conclusion, which gives up on the universality of moral truth, we would not then abandon the idea of moral objectivity. It is still possible for the parties involved to be in error, insofar as they misunderstand their own moral principles.

NOVEMBER 23, 2015

ON RELIGION

Navigating Past Nihilism

—Sean D. Kelly

"NIHILISM STANDS AT THE DOOR," WROTE NIETZSCHE. "WHENCE comes this uncanniest of all guests?" The year was 1885 or 1886, and Nietzsche was writing in a notebook whose contents were not intended for publication. The discussion of nihilism—the sense that it is no longer obvious what our most fundamental commitments are, or what matters in a life of distinction and worth, the sense that the world is an abyss of meaning rather than its God-given preserve— finds no sustained treatment in the works that Nietzsche prepared for publication during his lifetime. But a few years earlier, in 1882, the German philosopher had already published a possible answer to the question of nihilism's ultimate source. "God is dead," Nietzsche wrote in a famous passage from *The Gay Science*. "God remains dead. And we have killed him."

There is much debate about the meaning of Nietzsche's famous claim, and I will not attempt to settle that scholarly dispute here. But at least one of the things that Nietzsche could have meant is that the social role that the Judeo-Christian God plays in our culture is radically different from the one he has traditionally played in prior epochs of the West. For it used to be the case in the European Middle Ages, for example, that the mainstream of society was grounded so firmly in its Christian beliefs that someone who did not share those beliefs could therefore not be taken seriously as living an even potentially admirable life. Indeed, a life outside the church was not only execrable but condemnable, and in certain periods of European history it invited a close encounter with a burning pyre.

Whatever role religion plays in our society today, it is not this one. For today's religious believers feel strong social pressure to admit that someone who doesn't share their religious belief might nevertheless be living a life worthy of their admiration. That is not to say that every religious believer accepts this constraint. But to the extent that they do not, then society now rightly condemns them as dangerous religious fanatics rather than sanctioning them as scions of the church or mosque. God is dead, therefore, in a very particular sense. He no longer plays his traditional social role of organizing us around a commitment to a single right way to live. Nihilism is one state a culture may reach when it no longer has a unique and agreed-upon social ground.

The twentieth century saw an onslaught of literary depictions of the nihilistic state. The story had both positive and negative sides. On the positive end, when it is no longer clear in a culture what its most basic commitments are, when the structure of a worthwhile and well-lived life is no longer agreed upon and taken for granted, then a new sense of freedom may open up. Ways of living life that had earlier been marginalized or demonized may now achieve recognition or even be held up and celebrated. Social mobility—for African-Americans, gays, women, workers, people with disabilities or others who had been held down by the traditional culture—may finally become a possibility. The exploration and articulation of these new possibilities for living a life was found in such great twentieth-century figures as Martin Luther King Jr., Simone de Beauvoir, Studs Terkel and many others.

But there is a downside to the freedom of nihilism as well, and the people living in the culture may experience this in a variety of ways. Without any clear and agreed-upon sense for what to be aiming at in a life, people may experience the paralyzing type of indecision depicted by T. S. Eliot in his famously vacillating character Prufrock; or they may feel, like the characters in a Samuel Beckett play, as though they are continuously waiting for something to become clear in their lives before they can get on with living them; or they may feel the kind of "stomach level sadness" that David Foster Wallace described, a sadness that drives them to distract themselves by any number of entertainments, addictions, competitions or arbitrary goals, each of which leaves them feeling emptier than the last. The threat of nihilism is the threat that freedom from the constraint of agreed-upon norms opens up new possibilities in the culture only through its fundamentally destabilizing force.

There may be parts of the culture where this destabilizing force is not felt. The *Times'* David Brooks argued recently, for example, in a column discussing Jonathan Franzen's novel *Freedom*, that Franzen's depiction of America as a society of lost and fumbling souls tells us "more about America's literary culture than about America itself." The suburban life full of "quiet desperation," according to Brooks, is a literary trope that has taken on a life of its own. It fails to recognize the happiness, and even fulfillment, that is found in the everyday engagements with religion, work, ethnic heritage, military service and any of the other pursuits in life that are "potentially lofty and ennobling."

There is something right about Brooks's observation, but he leaves the crucial question unasked. Has Brooks's happy, suburban life revealed a new kind of contentment, a happiness that is possible even after the death of God? Or is the happy suburban world Brooks describes simply self-deceived in its happiness, failing to face up to the effects of the destabilizing force that Franzen and his literary compatriots feel? I won't pretend to claim which of these options actually prevails in the suburbs today, but let me try at least to lay them out.

Consider the options in reverse order. To begin with, perhaps the writers and poets whom Brooks questions have actually noticed something that the rest of us are ignoring or covering up. This is what Nietzsche himself thought. "I have come too early," he wrote. "God is dead; but given the way of men, there may still be caves for thousands of years in which his shadow will be shown." On this account there really is no agreement in the culture about what constitutes a well-lived life; God is dead in this particular sense. But many people carry on in God's shadow nevertheless; they take the life at which they are aiming to be one that is justifiable universally. In this case the happiness that Brooks identifies in the suburbs is not genuine happiness but self-deceit.

What would such a self-deceiving life look like? It would be a matter not only of finding meaning in one's everyday engagements, but of clinging to the meanings those engagements offer as if they were universal and absolute. Take the case of religion, for example. One can imagine a happy suburban member of a religious congregation who, in addition to finding fulfillment for herself in her lofty and ennobling religious pursuits, experiences the aspiration to this kind of fulfillment as one demanded of all other human beings as well. Indeed, one can imagine that the kind of fulfillment she experiences through her own religious commitments *depends upon* her experiencing those commitments as universal and therefore depends upon her experiencing those people not living in the fold of her church as somehow living depleted or unfulfilled lives. I suppose this is not an impossible case. But if this is the kind of fulfillment one achieves through one's happy suburban religious pursuit, then in our culture today it is self-deception at best and fanaticism at worst. For it stands in constant tension with the demand in the culture to recognize that those who don't share your religious commitments might nevertheless be living admirable lives. There is therefore a kind of happiness in a suburban life like this. But its continuation depends upon deceiving oneself about the role that any kind of religious commitment can now play in grounding the meanings for a life.

But there is another option available. Perhaps Nietzsche was wrong about how long it would take for the news of God's death to reach the ears of men. Perhaps he was wrong, in other words, about how long it would take before the happiness to which we can imagine aspiring would no longer need to aim at universal validity in order for us to feel satisfied by it. In this case the happiness of the suburbs would be consistent with the death of God, but it would be a radically different kind of happiness from that which the Judeo-Christian epoch of Western history sustained.

Herman Melville seems to have articulated and hoped for this kind of possibility. Writing thirty years before Nietzsche, in his great novel *Moby-Dick*, the canonical American author encourages us to "lower the conceit of attainable felicity"; to find happiness and meaning, in other words, not in some universal religious account of the order of the universe that holds for everyone at all times, but rather in the local and small-scale commitments that animate a life well-lived. The meaning that one finds in a life dedicated to "the wife, the heart, the bed, the table, the saddle, the fire-side, the country"—these are genuine meanings. They are, in other words, completely sufficient to hold off the threat of nihilism, the threat that life will dissolve into a sequence of meaningless events. But they are nothing like the kind of universal meanings for which the monotheistic tradition of Christianity had hoped. Indeed, when taken up in the appropriate way, the commitments that animate the meanings in one person's life—to family, say, or work, or country, or even local religious community—become completely consistent with the possibility that someone else with radically different commitments might nevertheless be living in a way that deserves one's admiration.

The new possibility that Melville hoped for, therefore, is a life that steers happily between two dangers: the monotheistic aspiration to universal validity, which leads to a culture of fanaticism and self-deceit, and the atheistic descent into nihilism, which leads to a culture of purposelessness and angst. To give a name to Melville's new possibility—a name with an appropriately rich range of historical resonances—we could call it polytheism. Not every life is worth living from the polytheistic point of view—there are lots of lives that don't inspire one's admiration. But there are nevertheless many different lives of worth, and there is no single principle or source or meaning in virtue of which one properly admires them all.

Melville himself seems to have recognized that the presence of many gods—many distinct and incommensurate good ways of life— was a possibility our own American culture could and should be aiming at. The death of God therefore, in Melville's inspiring picture, leads not to a culture overtaken by meaninglessness but to a culture directed by a rich sense for many new possible and incommensurate meanings. Such a nation would have to be "highly cultured and poetical," according to Melville. It would have to take seriously, in other words, its sense of itself as having grown out of a rich history that needs to be preserved and celebrated, but also a history that needs to be reappropriated for an even richer future. Indeed, Melville's own novel could be the founding text for such a culture. Though the details of that story will have to wait for another day, I can at least leave you with Melville's own cryptic, but inspirational comment on this possibility. "If hereafter any highly cultured, poetical nation," he writes, "shall lure back to their birthright, the merry May-day gods of old; and livingly enthrone them again in the now egotistical sky; on the now unhaunted hill; then be sure, exalted to Jove's high seat, the great Sperm Whale shall lord it."

DECEMBER 5, 2010

Does It Matter Whether God Exists?

—Gary Gutting

DISCUSSIONS OF RELIGION ARE TYPICALLY ABOUT GOD. ATHEists reject religion because they don't believe in God; Jews, Christians and Muslims take belief in God as fundamental to their religious commitment. The philosopher John Gray, however, has recently been arguing that belief in God should have little or nothing to do with religion. He points out that in many cases—for instance, "polytheism, Hinduism and Buddhism, Daoism and Shinto, many strands of Judaism and some Christian and Muslim traditions"—belief is of little or no importance. Rather, "practice—ritual, meditation, a way of life—is what counts." He goes on to say that "it's only religious fundamentalists and ignorant rationalists who think the myths we live by are literal truths" and that "what we believe doesn't in the end matter very much. What matters is how we live."

The obvious response to Gray is that it all depends on what you hope to find in a religion. If your hope is simply for guidance and assistance in leading a fulfilling life here on earth, a "way of living" without firm beliefs in any supernatural being may well be all you need. But many religions, including mainline versions of Christianity and Islam, promise much more. They promise ultimate salvation. If we are faithful to their teachings, they say, we will be safe from final annihilation when we die and will be happy eternally in our life after death.

If our hope is for salvation in this sense—and for many that is the main point of religion—then this hope depends on certain religious beliefs being true. In particular, for the main theistic religions, it depends on there being a God who is good enough to desire our salvation and powerful enough to achieve it.

But here we come to a point that is generally overlooked in debates about theism, which center on whether there is reason to believe in God, understood as all-good and all-powerful. Suppose that the existence of such a God could be decisively established. Suppose, for example, we were to be entirely convinced that a version of the ontological argument, which claims to show that the very idea of an all-perfect being requires that such a being exist, is sound. We would then be entirely certain that there is a being of supreme power and goodness. But what would this imply about our chances for eternal salvation?

On reflection, very little. Granted, we would know that our salvation was possible: an all-powerful being could bring it about. But would we have any reason to think that God would in fact do this? Well, how could an all-good being not desire our salvation? The problem is that an all-good being needs to take account of the entire universe, not just us.

Here, discussions of the problem of evil become crucial. An all-good being, even with maximal power, may have to allow considerable local evils for the sake of the overall good of the universe; some evils may be necessary for the sake of avoiding even worse evils. We have no way of knowing whether we humans might be the victims of this necessity.

Of course, an all-good God would do everything possible to minimize the evil we suffer, but for all we know that minimum might have to include our annihilation or eternal suffering. We might hope that any evil we endure will at least be offset by an equal or greater amount of good for us, but there can be no guarantee. As defenders of theism often point out, the freedom of moral agents may be an immense good, worth God's tolerating horrendous wrongdoing. Perhaps God in his omniscience knows that the good of allowing some higher type of beings to destroy our eternal happiness outweighs the good of that happiness. Perhaps, for example, their destroying our happiness is an unavoidable step in the moral drama leading to their salvation and eternal happiness.

My point here reflects the two-edged character of religious responses to the problem of evil. The only plausible answer to the question, "How could an all-good and all-powerful God allow immense evils?" is that such a God may well have knowledge beyond our understanding. As David Hume suggested in his *Dialogues Concerning Natural Religion*, the problem of evil is solved only by an appeal to our own ignorance. (There are powerful formulations of this approach by philosophers called "skeptical theists.")

Such an appeal may save us from the apparent contradiction of evil in a world created by an all-good God. But it also severely limits our judgments about what an all-good God would do. It may seem to us that if we live as we should, God will ensure our salvation. But it also seems, from our limited viewpoint, that God would not permit things like the Holocaust or the death of innocent children from painful diseases. Once we appeal to the gap between our limited knowledge and God's omniscience, we cannot move from what we *think* God will do to what he *will* in fact do. So the fact that we think an all-good God would ensure our salvation does not support the conclusion that, all things considered, he will in fact do so.

It follows, then, that even a decisive proof that there is an all-good, all-powerful God cannot assure us that we are ultimately safe. Even if we insist on a religion that goes beyond John Gray's beliefless way of living, belief that there is a God leaves us far short of what we hope for from religion.

Many believers will agree. Their confidence in salvation, they say, comes not from philosophical arguments but from their personal contact with God, either through individual experience or a religious tradition. But what can such contact provide concretely? At best, certainty that there is a very powerful being who promises to save us. But there may well be—and many religions insist that there are—very powerful beings (demons or devils) intent on leading us away from salvation. How could we possibly know that the power we are in contact with is not deceiving us?

The inevitable response is that an all-good God would not permit such a thing. But that takes us back to the previous difficulty: there is no reason to think that we are good judges of what God is likely to permit. God may have to allow us to be deceived to prevent even greater evils.

We can, of course, simply will to believe that we are not being deceived. But that amounts to blind faith, not assured hope. If that doesn't satisfy us, we need to find a better response to the problem of evil than an appeal to our ignorance. Failing that, we may need to reconsider John Gray's idea of religion with little or no belief.

MARCH 22, 2012

Good Minus God

—Louise M. Antony

I WAS HEARTENED TO LEARN RECENTLY THAT ATHEISTS ARE NO longer the most reviled group in the United States: according to the political scientists Robert Putnam and David Campbell, we've been overtaken by the Tea Party. But even as I was high-fiving my fellow apostates ("We're number two! We're number two!"), I was wondering anew: Why do so many people dislike atheists?

I gather that many people believe that atheism implies nihilism—that rejecting God means rejecting morality. A person who denies God, they reason, must be, if not actively evil, at least indifferent to considerations of right and wrong. After all, doesn't the dictionary list *wicked* as a synonym for *godless*? And isn't it true, as Dostoevsky said, that "if God is dead, everything is permitted"?

Well, actually—no, it's not. (And for the record, Dostoevsky never said it was.) Atheism does not entail that anything goes.

Admittedly, some atheists *are* nihilists. (Unfortunately, they're the ones who get the most press.) But such atheists' repudiation of morality stems more from an antecedent cynicism about ethics than from any philosophical view about the divine. According to these nihilistic atheists, "morality" is just part of a fairy tale we tell each other in order to keep our innate, bestial selfishness (mostly) under control. Belief in objective "oughts" and "ought nots," they say, must fall away once we realize that there is no universal enforcer to dish out rewards and punishments in the afterlife. We're left with pure self-interest, more or less enlightened.

This is a Hobbesian view: in the state of nature "the notions of right and wrong, justice and injustice have no place. Where there is no common power, there is no law: where no law, no injustice." But no atheist has to agree with this account of morality, and lots of us do not. We "moralistic atheists" do not see right and wrong as artifacts of a divine protection racket. Rather, we find moral value to be immanent in the natural world, arising from the vulnerabilities of sentient beings and from the capacities of rational beings to recognize and to respond to those vulnerabilities and capacities in others.

This view of the basis of morality is hardly incompatible with religious belief. Indeed, anyone who believes that God made human beings in his image believes something like this—that there is a moral dimension of things, and that it is in our ability to apprehend it that we resemble the divine. Accordingly, many theists, like many atheists, believe that moral value is inherent in morally valuable things. Things don't become morally valuable because God prefers them; God prefers them because they are morally valuable. At least this is what I was taught as a girl, growing up Catholic: that we could see that God was good because of the things he commands us to do. If helping the poor were not a good thing on its own, it wouldn't be much to God's credit that he makes charity a duty.

It may surprise some people to learn that theists ever take this position, but it shouldn't. This position is not only consistent with belief in God, it is, I contend, a *more* pious position than its opposite. It is only if morality is independent of God that we can make moral sense out of religious worship. It is only if morality is independent of God that any person can have a *moral* basis for adhering to God's commands.

Let me explain why. First let's take a cold, hard look at the consequences of pinning morality to the existence of God. Consider the following moral judgments—judgments that seem to me to be obviously true:

- *It is wrong to drive people from their homes or to kill them because you want their land.*

- *It is wrong to enslave people.*

- *It is wrong to torture prisoners of war.*

- *Anyone who witnesses genocide, or enslavement, or torture is morally required to try to stop it.*

To say that morality depends on the existence of God is to say that none of these specific moral judgments is true unless God exists. That seems to me to be a remarkable claim. If God turned out not to exist, then slavery would be OK? There'd be nothing wrong with torture? The pain of another human being would mean nothing?

Think now about our personal relations—how we love our parents, our children, our life partners, our friends. To say that the moral worth of these individuals depends on the existence of God is to say that these people are, in themselves, worth nothing—that the concern we feel for their well-being has no more ethical significance than the concern some people feel for their boats or their cars. It is to say that the historical connections we value—the traits of character and personality that we love—all count for nothing in themselves. Other people warrant our concern only because they are valued by someone else—in this case, God. (Imagine telling a child, "You are not inherently lovable. I love you only because I love your father, and it is my duty to love anything he loves.")

What could make anyone think such things? Ironically, I think the answer is the same picture of morality that lies behind atheistic nihilism. It's the view that the only kind of "obligation" there could possibly be is the kind that is disciplined by promise of reward or threat of punishment. Such a view cannot find or comprehend any value inherent in the nature of things, value that could warrant particular attitudes and behavior on the part of anyone who can apprehend it. For someone who thinks that another being's pain is not in itself a reason to give aid, or that the welfare of a loved one is not on its own enough to justify sacrifice, it is only the Divine Sovereign that stands between us and—as Hobbes put it—the war of "all against all."

This will seem a harsh judgment on the many theists who subscribe to what is called divine command theory—the view that what is morally good is constituted by what God commands. Defenders of DCT will say that their theory explains a variety of things about morality that nontheistic accounts of moral value cannot, and that it should be preferred for that reason. For example, they will say that atheists cannot explain the objectivity of morality—how there could be moral truths that are independent of any human being's attitudes, will, or knowledge and how moral truths could hold universally. It is true that DCT would explain these things. If God exists, then he exists independently of human beings and their attitudes, and so his commands do, too. If we didn't invent God, then we didn't invent his commands, and hence didn't invent morality. We can be ignorant of God's will, and hence mistaken about what is morally good. Because God is omnipresent, his commands apply to all people at all times and in all places.

That's all fine. It would follow from DCT that moral facts are objective. The problem is that it wouldn't follow that they are *moral*. Commands issued by a tyrant would have all the same features. For DCT to explain morality, it must also explain what makes God good.

The problem I'm pointing to is an ancient one, discussed by Plato. In his dialogue *Euthyphro*, the eponymous character tries to explain his conception of piety to Socrates: "The pious acts," Euthyphro says, "are those which are loved by the gods." But Socrates finds this definition ambiguous and asks Euthyphro, "Are the pious acts pious because they are loved by the gods, or are the pious acts loved by the gods because they are pious?"

What's the difference? Well, if the first reading is correct, then it's the god's loving those particular acts that *makes* them count as pious acts, that *grounds* their piousness. "Pious," on this alternative, is just shorthand for "something the gods love." *Whatever* the gods happen to love, bingo—that's pious. If the gods change their preferences on a whim—and they did, if Homer knew his stuff—then the things that are pious change right along with them. In contrast, on the second reading, pious acts are presumed to have a distinctive, substantive property in common, a property in virtue of which the gods love them, a property that *explains why* the gods love them.

Translated into contemporary terms, the question Socrates is asking is this: Are morally good actions morally good simply *in virtue* of God's favoring them? Or does God favor them because they are— independently of his favoring them—morally good? DCT picks the first option; it says that it's the mere fact that God favors them that makes morally good things morally good.

Theories that endorse the second option—let's call any such theory a "divine independence theory" (DIT)—contend, on the contrary, that the goodness of an action is a feature that is independent of, and antecedent to, God's willing it. God could have commanded either this action or its opposite, but in fact, he commands only the good one.

Both DCT and DIT entail a perfect correspondence between the class of actions God commands and the class of actions that are good (or rather, they do so on the assumption that God is perfectly benevolent). The two theories differ, however, on what accounts for this congruence. DCT says that it is God's command that explains why the good acts are "good"—it becomes true *merely by definition* that God commands "good" actions. "Goodness," on this view, becomes an empty honorific, with no independent content. To say that God chooses the good is like saying that the prime meridian is at zero degrees longitude, or that in baseball, three strikes make an out. DIT, on the other hand, says that it is a substantive property of the acts—their goodness—that explains why God commanded them. Indeed, it says that God's goodness consists in his choosing all and only the good. DIT presumes that we have an independent grasp of moral goodness, and that it is because of that that we can properly appreciate the goodness of God.

DCT is arguably even more radical and bizarre than the Hobbesian nihilism I discussed earlier. On the nihilistic view, there is no pretense that a sovereign's power would generate moral obligation—the view is rather that "morality" is an illusion. But DCT insists both that there is such a thing as moral goodness and that it is defined by what God commands. This makes for really appalling consequences from an intuitive, moral point of view. DCT entails that anything at all could be "good" or "right" or "wrong." If God were to command you to eat your children, then it would be "right" to eat your children. The consequences are also appalling from a religious point of view. If all "moral" means is "commanded by God," then we cannot have what we would otherwise have thought of as moral reasons for obeying him. We might have prudential reasons for doing so, self-interested reasons for doing so. God is extremely powerful and so can make us suffer if we disobey him, but the same can be said of tyrants, and we have no moral obligation (speaking now in ordinary terms) to obey tyrants. (We might even have a moral obligation to disobey tyrants.) The same goes for worshipping God. We might find it in our interest to flatter or placate such a powerful person, but there could be no way in which God was deserving of praise or tribute.

This is the sense in which I think that it is a more pious position to hold that morality is independent of the existence of God. If the term *good* is not just an empty epithet that we attach to the Creator, whoever or whatever that turns out to be, then it must be that the facts about what is good are independent of the other facts about God. If "good" is to have normative force, it must be something that we can understand independently of what is commanded by a powerful omnipresent being.

So what about atheism? What I think all this means is that the capacity to be moved by the moral dimension of things has nothing to do with one's theological beliefs. The most reliable allies in any moral struggle will be those who respond to the ethically significant aspects of life, whether or not they conceive these things in religious terms. You do not lose morality by giving up God; neither do you necessarily find it by finding him.

I want to close by conceding that there are things one loses in giving up God, and they are not insignificant. Most importantly, you lose the guarantee of redemption. Suppose that you do something morally terrible, something for which you cannot make amends, something, perhaps, for which no human being could ever be expected to forgive you. I imagine that the promise made by many religions, that God will forgive you if you are truly sorry, is a thought that would bring enormous comfort and relief. You cannot have that if you are an atheist. In consequence, you must live your life and make your choices with the knowledge that every choice you make contributes, in one way or another, to the only value your life can have.

Some people think that if atheism were true, human choices would be insignificant. I think just the opposite—they would become surpassingly important.

DECEMBER 18, 2011

Pascal's Wager 2.0

—Gary Gutting

O NE BENEFIT OF TEACHING INTRODUCTORY PHILOSOPHY TO undergraduates is that it lets you talk about philosophy with eager and intelligent people who do not come with predispositions formed by years of technical study. This semester, preparing for a philosophy seminar with first-year honors students at Notre Dame, I reread with fresh eyes one of philosophy's best-known arguments for belief in God—Pascal's wager.

The argument, made by the 17th-century French mathematician and philosopher Blaise Pascal, holds that believing in God is a good bet at any odds, since the possible payoff—eternal happiness—far outweighs any costs of believing—even of believing in a God who does not exist.

Most discussions of Pascal's wager take it as a peculiar if not perverse calculation of self-interest. As Pascal puts it: "If you win, you win everything; if you lose, you lose nothing." Taken this way, the argument seems morally suspect; William James noted that those who engaged in such egotistic reasoning might be among the first that God would exclude from heaven. In considering it again, I found what I think may be a more fruitful way of developing the wager argument.

The wager requires a choice between believing and not believing. But there are two ways of not believing. I can either deny that God exists or doubt that God exists. Discussions of the wager usually follow Pascal and lump these two together in the single option of not believing in God. They don't distinguish denying from doubting because both are ways of not believing. The argument then is about whether believing is a better option than not believing. My formulation of the argument will focus instead on the choice between denying and doubting God.

Denial of God means that I simply close the door on the hope that there is something beyond the natural world; doubt may keep that door open. I say "may" because doubt can express indifference to what is doubted. I don't know and I don't care whether there is an even number of stars or whether there are planets made of purple rock. Indifferent doubt is the practical equivalent of denial, since both refuse to take a given belief as a viable possibility—neither sees it as what William James called a "live option." But doubt may also be open to and even desirous of what it doubts. I may doubt that I will ever understand and appreciate Pierre Boulez's music, but still hope that I someday will.

I propose to reformulate Pascal's wager as urging those who doubt God's existence to embrace a doubt of desire rather than a doubt of indifference. This means, first, that they should hope—and therefore desire—that they might find a higher meaning and value to their existence by making contact with a beneficent power beyond the natural world. There's no need to further specify the nature of this power in terms, say, of the teachings of a particular religion.

The argument begins by noting that we could be much happier by making appropriate contact with such a power. The next question is whether there are paths we can take that have some prospect of achieving this contact. Many people, including some of the most upright, intelligent and informed, have claimed that there are such paths. These include not just rituals and good deeds but also private spiritual exercises of prayer, meditation and even philosophical speculation. A person's specific choices would depend on individual inclinations and capacities.

So far, then, we have good reason to expect much greater happiness if there is a beneficent power we could contact, and we know of paths that might lead to that contact. The only remaining question is whether there are negative effects of seeking God that would offset the possible (but perhaps very improbable) value of contact with God.

Unlike the traditional versions, this wager does not require believing that there is a God. So the standard drawbacks of self-deception or insincerity don't arise. The wager calls for some manner of spiritual commitment, but there is no demand for belief, either immediately or eventually. The commitment is, rather, to what I have called religious agnosticism: serious involvement with religious teachings and practices, in hope for a truth that I do not have and may never attain. Further, religious agnosticism does not mean that I renounce all claims to other knowledge. I may well have strong commitments to scientific, philosophical and ethical truths that place significant constraints on the religious approaches I find appropriate. Religious agnosticism demands only that I reject atheism, which excludes the hope for something beyond the natural world knowable by science.

Religious agnosticism may accept the ethical value of a religious way of living and even endorse religious ideas as a viable basis for understanding various aspects of human existence. But the ethical value is a matter of my own judgment, independent of religious authority. And the understanding may be only a partial illumination that does not establish the ultimate truth of the ideas that provide it, as, for example, both Dante and Proust help us understand the human condition, despite their conflicting intellectual frameworks. None of this will interfere with a commitment to intellectual honesty.

But perhaps a "serious involvement" with religion will require giving up other humanly fulfilling activities to make room for religious thought and action. Given a low likelihood of attaining a "higher" form of happiness, it may make more sense to seek only the "worldly" satisfactions that are more certain, even if less profound. But we can decide for ourselves how much worldly satisfaction is worth giving up for the sake of possible greater spiritual happiness. And, it may well turn out that religious activities such as meditation and charitable works have their own significant measure of worldly satisfaction. Given all this, what basis is there for refusing the wager?

I don't see this new wager as merely a way of nudging atheists and indifferent agnostics onto a religious path. It's also important for those who are committed to a religious community to realize that such commitment doesn't require believing the teachings of that community. It's enough to see those teachings—and the practices connected with them—as a good starting point for an inquiry into their truth. We should also realize that the real truth of a religion may be quite different from its official "self-understanding" of this truth. A living religion should have room both for believers at rest with its official teachings and for nonbelievers (religious agnostics) who see these teachings as a promising beginning in their search for the truth.

I don't claim that my version of the wager argument is a faithful explication of what Pascal had in mind. It is, rather, an adaptation of the argument to our intellectual context, where doubt rather than belief is becoming the default position on religion. But I do think that this version avoids the standard objections to the usual interpretations of the wager argument. It does not require belief and isn't an attempt to trick God into sending us to heaven. It merely calls us to follow a path that has some chance of leading us to an immensely important truth.

SEPTEMBER 28, 2015

The Sacred and the Humane

—*Anat Biletzki*

Hᴜᴍᴀɴ ʀɪɢʜᴛs ᴀʀᴇ ᴀʟʟ ᴛʜᴇ ʀᴀɢᴇ. Tʜᴇʏ ʜᴀᴠᴇ ʙᴇᴄᴏᴍᴇ, ᴄᴜʀ-
rently, a very popular arena for both political activism and rampant
discourse. Human rights, as we all know, are the rights humans
are due simply by virtue of being human. But there is nothing simple here, since both "human" and "rights" are concepts in need of
investigation.

One deep philosophical issue that invigorates debates in human
rights is the question of their foundation and justification, the question Where do human rights come from, and what grounds them?
There are two essentially different approaches to answering that
question—the religious way and the secular, or philosophical, way.
Writing in *The New York Times Magazine* in 1993 ("Life Is Sacred:
That's the Easy Part"), Ronald Dworkin put this very succinctly: "We
almost all accept . . . that human life in all its forms is *sacred*—that it
has intrinsic and objective value quite apart from any value it might
have to the person whose life it is. For some of us, this is a matter of
religious faith; for others, of secular but deep philosophical belief."
A good representative of the first camp is the religious historian and
educator R. H. Tawney: "The essence of all morality is this: to believe
that every human being is of infinite importance, and therefore that
no consideration of expediency can justify the oppression of one by
another. But to believe this it is necessary to believe in God."

The second, nonreligious grounding of human rights is harder to give voice to by a single representative since there is a multiplicity of distinct, nonreligious groundings of human rights. But think again of Dworkin's words. We all accept, he says, that human life is *sacred*. By using that word—sacred—he seems to have already put the ball in the religious field. And that field, the field of the sacred as opposed to the mundane, plays a straightforward game, claiming that the only possible answer to the question of the foundations of human rights is the religious answer. Only by positing a divine creator of everything (including human beings) can we give a satisfactory account of the sacredness of human beings, of why we "deserve" or "are entitled" to something that derives from our being just that—sacred human beings.

On this view, any highfalutin philosophical concept that is called upon to be a comparable base for human rights is no more than a religious foundation clothed in secular garb; it is really just God by any other name. Thus, in a recent book, *The Idea of Human Rights*, Michael Perry is unequivocal about the worthlessness of the secular bunch: "There is, finally, no intelligible (much less persuasive) secular version of the conviction that every human being is sacred; the only intelligible versions are religious." Think of conspicuous elements in the vocabulary of human rights, the notions of "dignity," "inviolable," "end in himself," and the like. Although we try to give them meaning and standing without a turn to religious essence, these terms hold no secular water according to thinkers like Perry. There can be no human dignity, no inviolable person, no end in herself without the supposition of the human as sacred, and therefore as a godly creation.

There is, however, no philosophically robust reason to accept this claim. True, the religious answer is straightforward and clear-cut. True, philosophical theorizing on the foundations of human rights in particular, and morality in general, may be complex, or nuanced, or even convoluted. True, the word *sacred* carries religious connotations. But that could just be a manner of speaking—and dignity and inviolability certainly do not need to be tied down to the sacred.

Aristotelian virtue and natural justice or the Kantian categorical imperative (arising from reason, of course) offer philosophical bases for morality at large. Theories of human needs, human interests and human agency provide analytical foundations for the idea of human rights. And then there is Hart's one natural right (the equal right to be free), Gewirth's turn to human action and logic, Sen and Nussbaum's talk of basic human capabilities, and oh-so-many others, all affording *humanistic* starting points for the human dignity at the base of human rights that need nary a wink at religion. There is also a legitimate and, to my mind, strong critique of the individualism guiding the *liberal* idea of human rights that enjoins us to rethink our mantras regarding the autonomous self who is the "human." That these are intricate and sometimes problematic, that they might be in tension with, even contradict, each other, that we must do considerable analytic and philosophical work in their explication does not cancel out their equal profundity—equal to religion, that is—in justifying human rights.

What difference does it make? Beyond the theoretical discussions on human rights—What grounds them *theoretically*? What justifies them *theoretically*? What legal implications do they carry *theoretically*?—there is the "so what?" question. Why do we care, or why should we care, if the practice of human rights is born of religious or secular motivation?

Take a look at how we work on the ground, so to speak; look at how we do human rights, for example, in Israel-Palestine. When Rabbi Arik Ascherman, the leader of Rabbis for Human Rights in Israel, squats in the mud trying to stop soldiers who have come to set a blockade around a village or fights settlers who have come to uproot olive trees (as he has done so often, in villages like Yanoun and Jamain and Biddu, in the last decade) along with me (from B'Tselem—the Information Center for Human Rights in the Occupied Territories), or a group of secular kids from Anarchists against the Wall, or people from the Israeli Committee against House Demolitions—and he does this on a Friday afternoon, knowing full well that he might be courting religious transgression should the Sabbath arrive—does it matter that his reasons for doing so spring from his faith while the anarchists' derive from their secular political worldview and B'Tselem's and ICAHD's from secular international human rights law? The end product, the human rights *activity*, is similar, even identical; but the reason, the intention, the motivation for it are distinctly different. Does that matter?

I think it does. I dare say that religion, even when indirectly in the service of human rights, is not really working for human rights. Although there is recognition of the human as sacred, it is not the concept of *rights* that propels the religious person. For him, the human status of sacredness draws from divine creation and directive, from man (and woman) having been created in God's image, and therefore has nothing to do with a human right. As Jack Donnelly says in *Universal Human Rights in Theory and Practice*, " 'Traditional' societies . . . typically have had elaborate systems of duties . . . conceptions of justice, political legitimacy, and human flourishing that sought to realize human dignity, flourishing, or well-being entirely independent of human rights. These institutions and practices are alternative to, rather than different formulations of, human rights."

The question, we have seen, is what functions as the source of moral authority, assuming that "human rights" are morally based. Hilary Putnam, in *Jewish Philosophy as a Guide to Life*, says it beautifully: "Every human being should experience him/herself as commanded to be available to the neediness, the suffering, the vulnerability of the other person." But notice Putnam's terminology: "commanded." Who commands us? The question boils down to who or what is the source of moral authority—God or the human being, religion or ethics? I want to say that that makes a great difference. And I want to ask, If we—the religious person and the secular person—end up engaging in the same activity and also, more so, do it by thinking of ourselves as available to another's neediness, why does it make a difference?

The problem arises not when we act together, but rather when we don't. Or put differently, when we act together, the problem stays in the realm of theory, providing fodder for the philosophical game of human rights. It is when we disagree—about abortion, about capital punishment, about settling occupied lands—that the religious authority must vacate the arena of human rights. This is not to say that all religious people hold the same views on these issues or that secular persons are always in agreement (although opinion polls, for whatever they are worth, point to far more unity of thought on the religious side). It is rather that an internal, secular debate on issues that pertain to human rights is structurally and essentially different from the debate between the two camps. In the latter, the authority that is conscripted to "command" us on the religious side is God, while on the secular side it is the human, with her claim to reason, her proclivity to emotion, and her capacity for compassion. In a sense, that is no commandment at all. It is a turn to the human, and a (perhaps axiomatic, perhaps even dogmatic) posit of human dignity, that turns the engine of human rights, leaving us open to discussion, disagreement, and questioning without ever deserting that first posit. The parallel turn to God puts our actions under his command; if he commands a violation of human rights, then so be it. There is no meaning to human *rights* under divine commandment. A deep acceptance of divine authority—and that is what true religion demands—entails a renunciation of human rights if God so wills. Had God's angel failed to call out, "Abraham! Abraham!" Abraham would have slain Isaac.

THERE MIGHT SEEM to be a dogmatic antireligiosity arising from my reluctance to admit religion as a legitimate player in the human rights game. I have been using *religion* all along in, you might say, a very conservative, traditional way. Philosophers of religion and anthropologists have opened up the study of religion to recognize a variety of religious *experience*, religion as a *form of life*, religion as a *cultural* framework, religion as a system of *symbols*, a religious *phenomenology*, etc. Adopting a certain view on religion or a specific definition of religion is hugely pertinent to how one sees human rights functioning in a religious context. Let me, then, make explicit the definition of religion at the root of my unrest: religion is a system of myth and ritual; it is a communal system of propositional attitudes—beliefs, hopes, fears, desires—that are related to super-human agents. This very common definition (recently recognized in academic circles as that of the "Dartmouth School"), along with several essential terms (*myth, ritual, communal, propositional*), asserts the unconditional "superhuman agents,"—that is, God(s)—that are necessary for the divorce I espouse between religion and human rights. Other perceptions of religion that are "God-less" would not, perhaps, suffer the same fate.

And, you may say, what about the wonder of religion, the majestic awe that encompasses the religious person when confronted by a spiritual revelation that motivates and "regulates for in all his life"? (This was Ludwig Wittgenstein's "definition" of religion.) Can secular morals live up to that type of enchantment? Is there not something about secular rationalism that conduces rather to skepticism, fallibility and indifference than to the kind of awesome respect for the sacred human being that comes with religion? Here I have no choice than to turn to dogmatism—call it Kantian dogmatism: "Two things fill the mind with ever new and increasing admiration and awe, the more often and steadily we reflect upon them: the starry heavens above me and the moral law within me." For some, the physics that runs the natural world and the ethics that provide for our moral sense are seen to be more ordinary than religious experience. I, on the other hand, can think of nothing more awe inspiring than humanity and its fragility and its resilience.

JULY 17, 2011

Why God Is a Moral Issue

—Michael Ruse

T HE NEW ATHEISTS ARE NOT A COMFORTABLE GROUP OF PEOPLE.
They have scornful contempt for those with whom they differ—that
includes religious believers, agnostics and other atheists who don't
share their vehement brand of nonbelief. They are self-confident to
a degree that seems designed to irritate. And they have an ignorance
of anything beyond their fields to an extent remarkable even in modern academia. They also have a moral passion unknown outside the
pages of the Old Testament. For that, we can forgive much.

When asked in Ireland a few years ago about the abuse of children by priests, Richard Dawkins—who, along with Sam Harris and
the late Christopher Hitchens, is among the best known of the New
Atheists—responded that he was more concerned about bringing a
child up Catholic in the first place. You don't say something like that
seriously—and Dawkins is always serious—without a deep sense that
something is dreadfully morally wrong. The whole system is rotten,
this stance shouts, and corrupting to the core.

Now at one level you can understand the feelings. Religious belief
and disputes have certainly propelled amoral behavior—in Northern Ireland during the Troubles, for example, or on 9/11, or more
recently in the horrific murders of the Charlie Hebdo staff in Paris.
It is hard not to see the hand of religion in things like this and to
regret that people can be thus motivated to be so cruel to their fellow
human beings. The sadism of shooting someone in the back so they

will never walk again because they are a Catholic not a Protestant—or any such variation—is nauseating.

The New Atheists are not the first to feel this way. One can go back to the Greeks (and especially to the dialogues of Plato) to find those who argued in a similar fashion. And certainly in the thought and writings of others throughout history—Diderot in the eighteenth century, or Robert Ingersoll in the nineteenth, or Bertrand Russell in the twentieth—we find the same sort of moral passion.

What is truly striking is that atheists of Dawkins's stripe don't just say that believing in God is an intellectual mistake. They also claim that it's morally wrong to believe in the existence of God or gods.

You might think there is something a little funny here. The basic question is not about religion in all its diversity and complexity. It's about whether God exists. Either God (let us stay for convenience with one God, the God of theism) exists or God does not exist. Belief in God, seen this way, is not a moral matter. Whether two plus two equals four is not a moral question: It does. You should believe it. End of argument. Same with God.

The trouble is that the God question is not so easily solved as the mathematical one—and this, as we'll see, is what leads to moral issues. There are arguments going both ways. Take one positive case for a moment, the "argument from design."

This is a pretty remarkable state of affairs that we have here—planets, suns, organisms, humans and so forth. Why is there any of it? Why is there something rather than nothing? This question is not about the Big Bang or if anything went before. It is about the very fact of existence. One doesn't expect something like this, with its astounding interdependency and innumerable complex parts functioning in service of the whole, to just happen.

The existence of consciousness, or sentience, can be seen in the same way. Brain science has thrown a lot of light on the way we think, but the very fact of thinking is a puzzle. And the problem is that there doesn't seem to be a lot of progress forward. We know a lot about how conscious states are correlated with brain states, but this tells us nothing about how consciousness as we experience it could be a brain state.

Can such a wonderful universe be entirely without point?

Is everything we humans do—heroic sacrifices like Sophie Scholl of the White Rose group going bravely to her death for distributing pamphlets against Hitler and the war or the marches on Selma— nothing but a cosmic game? But then you start to look at the other side.

According to many monotheistic religions, God is supposed to be both all loving and all powerful. If so, why does he/she allow human suffering? For war, starvation or painful diseases to exist? And more to the point, perhaps, why does he allow the abuse of children by members of the clergy of his/her own religion, whether they be Catholic priests, Jewish rabbis, Muslim clerics or Protestant pastors?

There are other modes of objection: If the Christian God is absolute how could such an astonishing variety of alternative beliefs flourish? Why does the Pope believe one thing and the Dalai Lama believe something completely different? Not just a bit different—like the variations in belief between Jews and Catholics—but completely different. Calvinists say that we have a "sensus divinitatis"—a kind of direct Skype to God—that needs no justification but that lets us know without argument that God exists and is good. But why then doesn't the Dalai Lama know this? The Calvinist might answer that his sense is clouded by original sin. But does one really think that the Dalai Lama is befogged by original sin in a way that a televangelist in Florida is not? Surely no one could be quite this insensitive.

This is only a small sample of what is going on in the minds of atheists. Yes, there are good reasons to think that there is more than meets the eye. But no, the Christian and other theistic solutions are simply not adequate. So, if there are so many problems with theistic belief, why do people continue to take it seriously?

The truth is that many don't. In parts of the world where people are allowed and encouraged to take these things seriously and to think them through, people increasingly find that they can do without the God factor. It is in places where one is being indoctrinated from childhood and bullied in adulthood that people continue with God belief.

There is also a feeling that when people are given the chance to decide for themselves and still stay religious it is for the wrong reasons. The evidence is against it, so why do it? Because you are afraid of death or into wish fulfillment or some such thing. I suspect we can all speak to this to some extent.

When I was thirteen and had just gone off to boarding school, my thirty-three-year-old mother died suddenly. I have spent my whole life wanting just one last hour of conversation with her. But that is no good reason to believe in God and the afterlife. To behave this way is to be like someone who buys a lottery ticket with their last pennies and thinks they will win. This sort of irrational behavior is not worthy of a human being.

You might say that you still cannot deny that there might be something, of an order we cannot conceive. The biologist J. B. S. Haldane said, "My own suspicion is that the Universe is not only queerer than we suppose, but queerer than we can suppose." Perhaps so and I would not be surprised if a lot of people go along with this. That, however, is no reason to believe in Christianity or Judaism or any of the other religions. Even more, it seems morally repugnant to accept—if not rejoice in—living in a world ruled by the God of religions.

This is what motivated nonbelievers down through the ages. It is what motivated John Stuart Mill to say, when he rejected the Christian doctrine of a good God, "I will call no being good who is not what I mean when I apply that epithet to my fellow creatures; and if such a creature can sentence me to hell for not so calling him, to hell I will go."

The moral repugnance is only increased when we see the self-deception and indoctrination that leads people to accept such astounding claims on such paltry evidence. Here it is worth recalling the Victorian philosopher and mathematician W. K. Clifford's admonition: "It is wrong always, everywhere, and for anyone, to believe anything upon insufficient evidence." That universal claim may be too strong. But too often religious believers seem oblivious to Clifford's admonition and accept things with way too little evidence.

That I much suspect is what motivates the New Atheists and in fact expresses the deepest and most powerful moral objection to theism.

The Rigor of Love

—Simon Critchley

CAN THE EXPERIENCE OF FAITH BE SHARED BY THOSE UNABLE to believe in the existence of a transcendent God? Might there be a faith of the faithless?

For a non-Christian, such as myself, but one out of sympathy with the triumphal evangelical atheism of the age, the core commandment of Christian faith has always been a source of both fascinated intrigue and perplexity. What is the status and force of that deceptively simple five-word command "you shall love your neighbor"? With Gary Gutting's wise counsel on the relation between philosophy and faith still ringing in our ears, I'd like to explore the possible meaning of these words through a reflection on a hugely important and influential philosopher not yet even mentioned so far in The Stone: Søren Kierkegaard (1813–55).

In the conclusion to *Works of Love* (1847)—which some consider the central work in Kierkegaard's extensive and often pseudonymous authorship—he ponders the nature of the commandment of love that he has been wrestling with throughout the book. He stresses the strenuousness and, in the word most repeated in these pages, the *rigor* of love. As such, Christian love is not, as many nonbelievers contend, some sort of "coddling love," which spares believers any particular effort. Such love can be characterized as "pleasant days or delightful days without self-made cares." This easy and fanciful idea of love reduces Christianity to "a second childhood" and renders faith infantile.

Kierkegaard then introduces the concept of "the Christian like-for-like," which is the central and decisive category of *Works of Love*. The latter is introduced by distinguishing it from what Kierkegaard calls "the Jewish like-for-like," by which he means "an eye for an eye, a tooth for a tooth": namely, a conception of obligation based on the equality and reciprocity of self and other. Although, as a cursory reading of Franz Rosenzweig's *The Star of Redemption*—one of the great works of German-Jewish thought—could easily show, this is a stereotypical and limited picture of Judaism, Kierkegaard's point is that Christian love cannot be reduced to what he calls the "worldly" conception of love where you do unto others what others do unto you and no more. The Christian like-for-like brackets out the question of what others may owe to me and instead "makes every relationship to other human beings into a God-relationship."

This move coincides with a shift from the external to the inward. Although the Christian, for Kierkegaard, "must remain in the world and the relationships of earthly life allotted to him," he or she views those relationships from the standpoint of inwardness—that is, mediated through the relationship to God. As Kierkegaard puts it emphatically in part 1 of *Works of Love*,

> Worldly wisdom thinks that love is a relationship between man and man. Christianity teaches that love is a relationship between: man-God-man, that is, that God is the middle term.

The rigor of Christianity is a conception of love based on radical inequality—namely, the absolute difference between the human and the divine. This is how Kierkegaard interprets Jesus's words from the Sermon on the Mount, "Why do you see the speck that is in your brother's eye, but do not notice the log that is in your own eye?" (Matthew 7:3). The log in my own eye does not permit me to *judge* the speck in the other's. Rather, I should abstain from any judgment of what others might or might not do. To judge others is to view matters from the standpoint of externality rather than inwardness. It is arrogance and impertinence. What others owe to me is none of my business.

This is why it is very hard to be Christian. And maybe there are not as many true Christians around as one might have thought. Kierkegaard writes, "Christianly understood you have absolutely nothing to do with what others do to you." "Essentially," he continues, "you have only to do with yourself before God." Once again, the move to inwardness does not turn human beings away from the world; it is rather "a new version of what other men call reality, this is reality."

The address of Kierkegaard's writing has a specific direction: the second person singular, *you*. He tells the story from the Gospels (versions appear in Matthew and Luke) of the Roman centurion in Capernaum who approached Jesus and asked him to cure his servant or boy, the sense is ambiguous, "sick with the palsy, grievously tormented" (Matthew 8:6). After Jesus said that he would visit the boy, the centurion confessed that, as a representative of the occupying imperial authority with soldiers under his command, he did not feel worthy that Jesus should enter his house. When Jesus heard this, he declared that he had not experienced a person of such great faith in the whole of Israel. He added, and this is the line that interests Kierkegaard, "Be it done for you, as you believed."

This story reveals the essential insecurity of faith. Kierkegaard writes that it does not belong to Christian doctrine to vouchsafe that you—"precisely *you*," as he emphasizes—have faith. If someone were to say, "It is absolutely certain that I have faith because I have been baptized in the church and follow its rituals and ordinances," then Kierkegaard would reply, "Be it done for you, as you believed." The point of the story is that the centurion, although he was not baptized as a Christian, nonetheless believed. As Kierkegaard writes, "In his faith, *the* Gospel is first *a* gospel." The New Testament Greek for *gospel* is *euaggelion*, which can mean good tidings but can also be thought of as the act of proclamation or pledging. On this view, faith is a proclamation or pledge that brings the inward subject of faith into being over against an external everydayness. Such a proclamation is as true for the non-Christian as for the Christian. Indeed, it is arguably *more* true for the non-Christian, because their faith is not supported by the supposed guarantee of baptism, creedal dogma, regular church attendance or some notion that virtue will be rewarded with happiness if not here on earth, then in the afterlife. Thus, paradoxically, non-Christian faith might be said to reveal the true nature of the faith that Christ sought to proclaim. Even—and indeed especially— those who are denominationally faithless can have an experience of faith. If faith needs to be underpinned by some sort of doctrinal security, then inwardness becomes externalized and the strenuous rigor of faith evaporates.

What sort of certainty, then, is the experience of faith? Kierkegaard writes, and again the second-person singular direction of address should be noted, "It is eternally certain that it will be done for you as you believe, but the certainty of faith, or the certainty that *you, you in particular*, believe, you must win at every moment with God's help, consequently not in some external way" (emphasis mine).

Kierkegaard insists—and one feels here the force of his polemic against the irreligious, essentially secular order of so-called Christendom, in his case what he saw as the pseudo-Christianity of the Danish National Church—that no pastor or priest has the right to say that one has faith or not according to doctrines like baptism and the like. To proclaim faith is to abandon such external or worldly guarantees. Faith has the character of a continuous "striving . . . in which you get occasion to be tried every day." This is why faith and the commandment of love that it seeks to sustain is not law. It has no coercive, external force. As Rosenzweig writes, "The commandment of love can only proceed from the mouth of the lover." He goes on to contrast this with law, "which reckons with times, with a future, with duration." By contrast, the commandment of love "knows only the moment; it awaits the result in the very moment of its promulgation." The commandment of love is mild and merciful, but, as Kierkegaard insists, "there is rigor in it." We might say love is that disciplined act of absolute spiritual daring that eviscerates the old self of externality so something new and inward can come into being.

As Kierkagaard puts it earlier in *Works of Love*, citing Paul, "Owe no one anything, except to love one another" (Romans 13:8). It sounds simple. But what is implicit in this minimal-sounding command is a conception of love as an experience of infinite debt—a debt that it is impossible to repay: "When a man is gripped by love, he feels that this is like being in infinite debt." To be is to be in debt—I owe, therefore I am.

If sin is the theological name for the essential ontological indebtedness of the self, then love is the experience of a countermovement to sin that is orientated around a demand that exceeds the capacity or ability of the self. Love is shaped in relation to what, in my parlance, can be called an infinite demand. Kierkegaard writes, and the double emphasis on the "moment" that finds an echo in Rosenzweig should be noted, "God's relationship to a human being is the infinitizing at every moment of that which at every moment is in a man." Withdrawn into inwardness and solitude ("If you have never been solitary, you have never discovered that God exists," Kierkegaard writes), each and every word and action of the self resounds through the infinite demand of God.

At this point, in the penultimate paragraph of *Works of Love* Kierkegaard shifts to auditory imagery. God is a vast echo chamber where each sound, "the slightest sound," is duplicated and resounds back loudly into the subject's ears. God is nothing more than the name for the *repetition* of each word that the subject utters. But it is a repetition that resounds with "the intensification of infinity." In what Kierkegaard calls "the urban confusion" of external life, it is nigh impossible to hear this repetitive echo of the infinite demand. This is why the bracketing out of externality is essential: "externality is too dense a body for resonance, and the sensual ear is too hard-of-hearing to catch the eternal's repetition." We need to cultivate the inner or inward ear that infinitizes the words and actions of the self. As Kierkegaard makes clear, what he is counseling is not "to sit in the anxiety of death, day in and day out, listening for the repetition of the eternal." What is rather being called for is a rigorous and activist conception of faith that proclaims itself into being at each instant without guarantee or security and that abides with the infinite demand of love.

Faith is not a like-for-like relationship of equals, but the asymmetry of the like-to-unlike. It is a subjective strength that only finds its power to act through an admission of weakness. Faith is an enactment of the self in relation to an infinite demand that both exceeds my power and yet requires all my power. Such an experience of faith is not only shared by those who are faithless from a creedal or denominational perspective, but can—in my view—be had by them in an exemplary manner. Like the Roman centurion of whom Kierkegaard writes, it is perhaps the faithless who can best sustain the rigor of faith without requiring security, guarantees and rewards: "Be it done for you, as you believed."

AUGUST 8, 2010

God Is a Question, Not an Answer

—William Irwin

Near end of Albert Camus's existentialist novel *The Stranger*, Meursault, the protagonist, is visited by a priest who offers him comfort in the face of his impending execution. Meursault, who has not cared about anything up to this point, wants none of it. He is an atheist in a foxhole. He certainly has not been a strident atheist, but he claims to have no time for the priest and his talk of God. For him, God is not the answer.

Some seventy years later, Kamel Daoud, in his 2013 novel *The Meursault Investigation*, picks up the thread of Camus's story. In one scene late in that novel, an imam hounds Harun, the brother of the unnamed Arab who was killed in *The Stranger*. In response, Harun gives a litany of his own impieties, culminating in the declaration that "God is a question, not an answer." Harun's declaration resonates with me as a teacher and student of philosophy. The question is permanent; answers are temporary. I live in the question.

Any honest atheist must admit that he has his doubts, that occasionally he thinks he might be wrong, that there could be a God after all—if not the God of the Judeo-Christian tradition, then a God of some kind. Nathaniel Hawthorne said of Herman Melville, "He can neither believe, nor be comfortable in his unbelief; and he is too honest and courageous not to try to do one or the other." Dwelling in a state of doubt, uncertainty and openness about the existence of God marks an honest approach to the question.

There is no easy answer. Indeed, the question may be fundamentally unanswerable. Still, there are potentially unpleasant consequences that can arise from decisions or conclusions, and one must take responsibility for them.

Anyone who does not occasionally worry that he may be a fraud almost certainly is. Nor does the worry absolve one from the charge; one may still be a fraud, just one who rightly worries about it on occasion. Likewise, anyone who does not occasionally worry that she is wrong about the existence or nonexistence of God most likely has a fraudulent belief. Worry can make the belief or unbelief genuine, but it cannot make it correct.

People who claim certainty about God worry me, both those who believe and those who don't believe. They do not really listen to the other side of conversations, and they are too ready to impose their views on others. It is impossible to be certain about God.

Bertrand Russell was once asked what he would say to God if it turned out there was one and he met him at judgment. Russell's reply: "You gave us insufficient evidence." Even believers can appreciate Russell's response. God does not make it easy. God, if he exists, is "dues absconditus," the hidden God. He does not show himself unambiguously to all people, and people disagree about his existence. We should all feel and express humility in the face of the question even if we think the odds are tilted heavily in favor of a particular answer. Indeed, the open-minded search for truth can unite believers and nonbelievers.

In a previous essay in The Stone, Gary Gutting re-conceived Pascal's wager. Rather than consider it as a bet on whether God exists, which has tremendous consequences on one side and relatively trivial consequences on the other, we should consider it as a bet on whether to embrace a "doubt of indifference" or a "doubt of desire." A doubt of indifference is simply a matter of not caring, and it has no clear benefits. By contrast, a doubt of desire approaches the question with the hope that a higher power could be found that would provide greater meaning and value to human existence. As Gutting sees it, the choice is obvious.

Of course, nonbelievers will object that there are various secular alternatives for finding meaning and value in life. Additionally, there is an assumption built into Pascal's wager that we are talking about the God of the Judeo-Christian tradition. Nonbelievers may see no reason to favor that particular deity. So Gutting's "doubt of desire" needs to be more explicitly conceived as an openness to the question in which the nonbeliever explores what various religious traditions have to offer. The nonbeliever might embrace the ethical teachings of Christianity, the yogic practices of Hinduism, the meditative techniques of Zen Buddhism, or any of the vast array of teachings and practices that the world's religions have to offer. Such embrace may lead the nonbeliever to belief in God, or it may not.

This proposal should be taken in the other direction as well: There should be no dogmatic belief. The believer should concede that she does not know with certainty that God exists. There is no faith without doubt. The Trappist monk Thomas Merton wrote that faith "is a decision, a judgment that is fully and deliberately taken in the light of a truth that cannot be proven—it is not merely the acceptance of a decision that has been made by somebody else."

Indeed, belief without doubt would not be required by an all-loving God, and it should not be worn as a badge of honor. As nonbelievers should have a doubt of desire, so, too believers should have a faith inflected by doubt. Such doubt can enliven belief by putting it at risk and compelling it to renew itself, taking it from the mundane to the transcendent, as when a Christian takes the leap of faith to believe in the resurrection.

We can all exist along a continuum of doubt. Some of us will approach religious certainty at one extreme and others will approach atheistic certainty at the other extreme. Many of us will slide back and forth over time.

What is important is the common ground of the question, not an answer. Surely, we can respect anyone who approaches the question honestly and with an open mind. Ecumenical and interfaith religious dialogue has increased substantially in our age. We can and should expand that dialogue to include atheists and agnostics, to recognize our common humanity and to stop seeing one another as enemy combatants in a spiritual or intellectual war. Rather than seeking the security of an answer, perhaps we should collectively celebrate the uncertainty of the question.

This is not to say that we should cease attempts to convince others of our views. Far from it. We should try to unsettle others as we remain open to being unsettled ourselves. In a spirit of tolerance and intellectual humility, we should see ourselves as partners in a continuing conversation, addressing an enduring question.

MARCH 26, 2016

What's Wrong with Blasphemy?

—*Andrew F. March*

Suppose there had not been a single riot in response to the now infamous video "The Innocence of Muslims." Not a single car burned, not a single embassy breached, not a single human being physically hurt. Would the makers of this risible little clip have done anything wrong? If so, to whom, and why?

These questions are now at the center of an international debate. President Obama himself touched on the issue in his speech to the United Nations General Assembly this month (September 2012), in which he directly addressed the violent reaction in the Muslim world to the "crude and disgusting video." But does philosophy have anything to say to the view that many people have that there is something about this kind of speech itself—not just its harm to public order or its adding of insult to the injury of imperialism and war—that should not be uttered or produced?

Obviously, we think this about many other kinds of speech. Most of us think that it is wrong for white people to use the "n-word." (Use it? I can't even bring myself to *mention* it.) Personally, I would feel a shiver of guilt and shame if that word crossed my mind as a thought about another person. And it's not hard to account for that feeling. It is a word that is intimately associated with a chain of some of humanity's greatest historical evils—the trans-Atlantic slave trade, the practice of chattel slavery and countless legal, social and psychological practices aiming at the effective dehumanization of persons of black African origin. To perpetuate it publicly is to harm other persons, and this matters objectively even if I don't personally, subjectively care about the persons in question. But my feelings about this word are even deeper than this: I don't even want to participate in the history that produced it and its meaning by letting it grow roots in my own mind.

This word is just an archetype to fix our thoughts. I feel that way about a lot of other words, even if nothing can quite rise to the level of emotion as that one. I can account in a very similar way for my disgust at similar epithets that seek to target for exclusion, suffering and disrespect gays, Jews, Arabs, Muslims, women and others. The suffering and disadvantage of humans matters, and I am doing nothing important in the world when I use such an epithet without considering the well-being of other humans. Even when it should be legal to do so, I have good—often decisive—reasons for not using such speech.

Can the same be said not about epithets but about speech that mocks, insults or tells lies about things that others hold sacred, whether they be texts, human prophets or physical objects? What reasons do we have to censor ourselves (something we do all the time, and often for very good reasons) in how we speak about things other people hold sacred?

Most secular philosophical approaches to the morality of speech about the sacred are going to begin with three starting points:

- *Human beings have very strong interests in being free to express themselves.*

- *The "sacred" is an object of human construction and thus the fact that something is called "sacred" is insufficient itself to explain why all humans ought to respect it.*

- *Respect is owed to persons but not everything they value or venerate, even if other persons themselves do not uphold such a difference between their selves and their attachments.*

These three premises make it hard for some common arguments about speech and the sacred to fully persuade. Here are six I find to be common.

1. *Blasphemy transgresses a boundary and violates the sacred.*

From the perspective of the religious, this is the greatest harm in blasphemy. In Islamic law, for example, both God and the Prophet Muhammad not only have value for the believers but also have interests and rights themselves. But what reason does this give others not to violate the sacred if they do not agree that x or y is sacred or has such awesome value? No reason at all.

2. *We should respect whatever people regard as "sacred" or treat as religious.*

I have no objection to this as one principle of the morality of speech. Certainly, the fact that x is called "sacred" by someone else should give me some reason to rethink what I am about to say. But there are two obvious problems here: (a) this gives other persons wide latitude to claim a veto over my speech by calling "sacred" things I find anything but—the American flag, David Miscavige, Mormon underpants—and (b) it is so easy to think of examples where I am doing valuable and important things in speaking that outweigh the otherwise regrettable fact that others are injured or pained as an unintended consequence of my speech.

3. *People are deeply hurt and injured by violations of the sacred or objects of love.*

This matters. The pain of others always matters. But pain alone cannot explain the totality of our moral relationships. People are pained by all kinds of things. People attach themselves to all kinds of histories, symbols and institutions. Pain is sometimes deserved.

At the very least, it is sometimes a reasonable cost to bear for other things we value. The religious know this better than most of us.

4. Blasphemy is dangerous.

The great Thomas Hobbes went so far as to declare insults to be a violation of natural law, even before we enter the social contract. He would not have been surprised at the reaction to the Danish cartoons, the "Innocence of Muslims" film or any bar fight: "Any sign of hatred and contempt is more provocative of quarrels and fighting than anything else, so that most men prefer to lose their peace and even lives rather than suffer insult." So, yes, the fact that an offensive word will contribute to an outbreak of violence is a very good reason not to utter it, often a decisive and sufficient reason. The problem is, what kind of reason? If we think that our words were reasonable and not meant to provoke and we still censor ourselves, we are acting out of prudence or fear, and in a way treating the other as irrational. Aren't humans capable of more inspiring terms of association than mutual fear?

5. Blasphemy is hate speech.

There is no question that many in the West today use speech about Muhammad and "Islam" as cover for expressing hatred toward Muslims. They know that if they are talking about "religion," they can deny they are talking about persons. Many people doing this—from Geert Wilders to those behind "Innocence of Muslims"—are indeed hatemongers. But we should avoid the all-too-common conclusion that because much speech about Muhammad is de facto barely coded hate speech about Muslims (and much of it is), *all* such speech is. Many believers will in good faith testify that no one who expresses hatred for Islam's doctrines and prophet can respect them as persons. I believe them. But from a secular moral perspective, there is no way to completely eliminate the gap between whatever qualities or value we imagine all humans to have and the many valuable attachments and beliefs actual humans are made of. After all, many religious thinkers will say that they despise secular materialism or atheism and yet still respect the misguided humans enslaved to those doctrines. I believe them then, too.

6. *Blasphemy disrupts social harmony.*

This is a different argument from the one that blasphemy is dangerous. Let us return to the "n-word." A plausible case can be made that the widespread public use of this word does more than offend, harm or intimidate African-Americans. It harms a certain kind of public good that many Americans are striving hard to attain—the public good of a society where people feel safe, valued and at home in their social home. There is a way in which *all* Americans are the victims of such speech; for I as a white American have an interest in an America where my sense of belonging is not achieved at the expense of others. In Europe and North America today, lots of public blasphemy about Islam (especially in visual form) performs this function. It serves to tell Muslims, "We don't trust you, we don't like you, and it's your job to change." All we have to do is remember speech about Catholicism in this country until quite recently. Cartoons of Catholic bishops as crocodiles coming to devour potentially Protestant children were much worse than an assault on the institution of the bishopric or a theological disputation about where Christ's ecclesia is embodied. It was Protestant nativism directed at Catholics as persons, not only as believers.

For all the instinctive talk about the need for "respect for religion" or "sensitivity toward the sacred," this I think is what most people find most troubling about everything from the "Innocence of Muslims" to the (much worse) "Muslim Rage" *Newsweek* cover of last week. And I agree. But there are at least two caveats: (a) it leaves us with the conclusion that there is absolutely nothing wrong with the blasphemous content of such speech per se (nothing about Catholic bishops or the Prophet Muhammad that should never be maligned), and (b) we have to explain what kinds of social relationships we are obligated to care for in this way. Yes, I have an obligation not to make my Scientologist neighbor feel unwelcome . . . but Tom Cruise? Bombs away.

WHAT I HAVE TRIED to argue is that none of these common arguments alone gives us sufficient reason to refrain from blasphemous speech merely because it is blasphemous, the way that I do feel I have more than sufficient reason to never use (and to try to never think) then n-word. But that doesn't mean that none of the aforementioned were reasons not to violate what others hold sacred. They were reasons, just ones that might be outweighed by the value of the things I want to say.

So are we left with some crude felicific arithmetic: (amount of emotional pain) - (value of blasphemous speech uttered) = net morality of this or that utterance? I think there is something more to be said here.

We all too often speak about the harms of speech either in abstract terms (the speech is wrong) or in attribute-sensitive terms (one should not be mocked for this). But what is missing here is the sense of *relational duties* that so many of us feel. The view that one just says whatever one wishes regardless of the company one is keeping is not virtuous honesty or moral heroism, but a kind of moral autism. The content of speech is just one element of its morality; the recipient is another.

While certain aspects of morality ought to apply without regard for the identity of other persons and any relationships I may have with them, many other aspects of morality are precisely relational. I care about specific persons and my relationship with them. This increases the costs to my own conscience, moral costs, in saying things that I otherwise think are worth saying. There are lots of things I would normally say that I do not say to or around specific people. This is sometimes because I am scared of them, or scared of experiencing social awkwardness. Other times it is because I care about them and our relationship. They matter to me, and our relationship is a good worth sacrificing for. This is why we don't tell lies, or do tell lies, to certain people.

Could the morality of blasphemy be something like this? No—there is no abstract, relation-independent wrong in mocking someone else's prophet, even to the extent that I think there is wrong in using speech like the n-word. Instead, given the awareness of the impact such speech on others whom you might care about might have (even if you think it is wrong or silly for such speech to impact them in this way), the value you place on these relationships alters your moral judgment about such speech. The emotional world of someone about whom you care, or with whom you have a social relationship about which you care, matters to you when you speak.

Now, this is not a shortcut to merely condemning blasphemy. I may continue to judge my friends to be oversensitive, or my speech to be so important as to outweigh their emotional pain. And, of course, fellow citizens do not usually matter as much to me as people in my day-to-day life. And distant strangers matter still less. But, nonetheless, I think there is something for philosophy to encourage us to think about beyond the recycled clichés that emerge on all sides each time some new utterance creates an international crisis. At the very least, it encourages us to see conflicts over such speech not only as a conflict between the value of free speech and the value of sensitivity, but also in terms of social and political relationships that we have some obligation to care for.

SEPTEMBER 25, 2012

ON GOVERNMENT

Questions for Free-Market Moralists

—Amia Srinivasan

IN 1971 JOHN RAWLS PUBLISHED A *THEORY OF JUSTICE*, THE MOST
significant articulation and defense of political liberalism of the
twentieth century. Rawls proposed that the structure of a just society
was the one that a group of rational actors would come up with if they
were operating behind a "veil of ignorance"—that is, provided they
had no prior knowledge what their gender, age, wealth, talents, ethnicity and education would be in the imagined society. Since no one
would know in advance where in society they would end up, rational
agents would select a society in which everyone was guaranteed basic
rights, including equality of opportunity. Since genuine (rather than
"on paper") equality of opportunity requires substantial access to
resources—shelter, medical care, education—Rawls's rational actors
would also make their society a redistributive one, ensuring a decent
standard of life for everyone.

In 1974, Robert Nozick countered with *Anarchy, State, and Utopia*. He argued that a just society was simply one that resulted from
an unfettered free market—and that the only legitimate function of
the state was to ensure the workings of the free market by enforcing
contracts and protecting citizens against violence, theft and fraud.
(The seemingly redistributive policy of making people pay for such
a "night watchman" state, Nozick argued, was in fact nonredistribu-
tive, since such a state would arise naturally through free bargain-
ing.) If one person—Nozick uses the example of Wilt Chamberlain,

the great basketball player—is able to produce a good or service that is in high demand and others freely pay him for that good or service, then he is entitled to his riches. Any attempt to "redistribute" his wealth, so long as it is earned through free market exchange, is, Nozick says, "forced labor."

Rawls and Nozick represent the two poles of mainstream Western political discourse: welfare liberalism and laissez-faire liberalism, respectively. (It's hardly a wide ideological spectrum, but that's the mainstream for you.) On the whole, Western societies are still more Rawlsian than Nozickian: they tend to have social welfare systems and redistribute wealth through taxation. But since the 1970s, they have become steadily more Nozickian. Such creeping changes as the erosion of the welfare state, the privatization of the public sphere and increased protections for corporations go along with a moral worldview according to which the free market is the embodiment of justice. This rise in Nozickian thinking coincides with a dramatic increase in economic inequality in the United States over the past five decades—the top 1 percent of Americans saw their income multiply by 275 percent in the period from 1979 to 2007, while the middle 60 percent of Americans saw only a 40 percent increase. If the operations of the free market are always moral—the concrete realization of the principle that you get no more and no less than what you deserve—then there's nothing in principle wrong with tremendous inequality.

The current economic crisis is no exception to the trend toward Nozickian market moralizing. In the recent debates in the Senate and House of Representatives about food stamps—received by one out of six Americans, about two-thirds of them children, disabled or elderly—Republicans made their case for slashing food subsidies largely about fairness. As Senator Jeff Sessions, Republican, of Alabama, said in his speech, "This is more than just a financial issue. It is a moral issue as well."

The Harvard economist N. Gregory Mankiw recently published a draft of a paper titled "Defending the One Percent." In it he rehearses (but, oddly, does not cite) Nozick's argument for the right of the wealthy to keep their money, referring to the moral principle of "just deserts" as what makes distribution by the market essentially ethical. And in a recent issue of *Forbes*, the Ayn Rand apostle Harry Binswanger proposed that those earning over one million dollars should be exempt from paying taxes, and the highest earner each year should be awarded a medal of honor—as a reward (and incentive) for producing so much market value. Again, Binswanger explained that "the real issue is not financial, but moral."

The Nozickian outlook is often represented as moral common sense. But is it? Here I pose four questions for anyone inclined to accept Nozick's argument that a just society is simply one in which the free market operates unfettered. Each question targets one of the premises or implications of Nozick's argument. If you're going to buy Nozick's argument, you must say yes to all four. But doing so isn't as easy as it might first appear.

1. *Is any exchange between two people in the absence of direct physical compulsion by one party against the other (or the threat thereof) necessarily free?*

If you say yes, then you think that people can never be coerced into action by circumstances that do not involve the direct physical compulsion of another person. Suppose a woman and her children are starving, and the only way she can feed her family, apart from theft, is to prostitute herself or to sell her organs. Since she undertakes these acts of exchange not because of direct physical coercion by another, but only because she is compelled by hunger and a lack of alternatives, they are free.

2. *Is any free (not physically compelled) exchange morally permissible?*

If you say yes, then you think that any free exchange can't be exploitative and thus immoral. Suppose that I inherited from my rich parents a large plot of vacant land, and that you are my poor, landless neighbor. I offer you the following deal. You can work the land, doing all the hard labor of tilling, sowing, irrigating, and harvesting. I'll pay you $1 a day for a year. After that, I'll sell the crop for $50,000. You decide this is your best available option and so take the deal. Since you consent to this exchange, it is morally permissible.

3. Are people entitled to all they are able, and only what they are able, to get through free exchange?

If you say yes, you think that what people are entitled to is largely a matter of luck. Why? First, because only a tiny minority of the population is lucky enough to inherit wealth from their parents. (A fact lost on Mitt Romney, who famously advised America's youth to "take a shot, go for it, take a risk . . . borrow money if you have to from your parents, start a business.") Since giving money to your kids is just another example of free exchange, the accumulation of wealth and privilege in the hands of the few is morally permissible. Second, people's capacities to produce goods and services in demand on the market is largely a function of the lottery of their birth: their genetic predispositions, their parents' education, the amount of race- and sex-based discrimination to which they're subjected, their access to health care and good education.

It's also a function of what the market happens to value at a particular time. Van Gogh, William Blake, Edgar Allan Poe, Vermeer, Melville, and Schubert all died broke. If you're a good Nozickian, you think they weren't entitled to anything more.

4. Are people under no obligation to do anything they don't freely want to do or freely commit themselves to doing?

If you say yes, then you think the only moral requirements are the ones we freely bring on ourselves—say, by making promises or contracts. Suppose I'm walking to the library and see a man drowning in the river. I decide that the pleasure I would get from saving his life wouldn't exceed the cost of getting wet and the delay. So I walk on by. Since I made no contract with the man, I am under no obligation to save him.

MOST OF US, I suspect, will find it difficult to say yes to all four of these questions. (Even Nozick, in *Anarchy, State, and Utopia*, found it hard to say yes to question 3.) In philosophical terms, we have a *reductio ad absurdum*. The Nozickian view implies what, from the perspective of common sense morality, is absurd: that a desperate person who sells her organs or body does so freely, that it's permissible to pay someone a paltry sum while profiting hugely off their labor, that people are entitled to get rich because of accidents of birth, that you're within your rights to walk by a drowning man. Thus Nozick's view must be wrong: justice is not simply the unfettered exercise of the free market. Free market "morality" isn't anything of the sort.

Some might object that these are extreme cases, and that all they show is that the market, to be fully moral, needs some tweaking. But to concede that there is more to freedom than consent, that there is such a thing as nonviolent exploitation, that people shouldn't be rewarded and punished for accidents of birth, that we have moral obligations that extend beyond those we contractually incur—this is to concede that the entire Nozickian edifice is structurally unsound. The proponent of free market morality has lost his foundations.

Why worry about the morally pernicious implications of Nozickianism? After all, I said that most Western societies remain Rawlsian in their organization, even if they are growing more Nozickian in their ideology. In the United States for example, there are legal prohibitions on what people can sell, a safety net to help those who suffer from really bad luck, and a civic ethos that prevents us from letting people drown. The first answer is, of course, that the material reality is being rapidly shaped by the ideology, as recent debates about welfare in the United States demonstrate.

The second is that most Western societies hardly constitute a Rawlsian utopia. People might be legally prohibited from selling their organs, but that doesn't remedy the desperate circumstances that might compel them to do so. The law does not stop people from falling into poverty traps of borrowing and debt, from being exploited by debt settlement companies promising to help them escape those traps, or losing their homes after buying mortgages they can't afford to pay back. And there is certainly no prohibition against the mind-numbing and often humiliating menial work that poor people do in exchange for paltry wages from hugely rich companies. A swiftly eroding welfare state might offer the thinnest of safety nets to those who fall on hard times, but it does nothing to address the lack of social mobility caused by the dramatic rise in inequality. And while it might be thought poor form to walk by a drowning man, letting children go hungry is considered not only permissible, but as Senator Sessions said, "a moral issue." These facts might be not quite as ethically outraging as walking past a drowning man, but they, too, grate against our commonsense notions of fairness.

Rejecting the Nozickian worldview requires us to reflect on what justice really demands, rather than accepting the conventional wisdom that the market can take care of morality for us. If you remain a steadfast Nozickian, you have the option of biting the bullet (as philosophers like to say) and embracing the counterintuitive implications of your view. This would be at least more consistent than what we have today: an ideology that parades as moral common sense.

OCTOBER 20, 2013

Is Our Patriotism Moral?

—*Gary Gutting*

To MY MIND, THE FOURTH OF JULY HAS A LOT GOING FOR IT COM-pared with other holidays: great food without a lot of work, warm weather, no presents, and fireworks. And in our house, at least, there's the special moment when we read out loud the Declaration of Independence and follow with a toast (American sparkling wine, of course), "To the United States of America!" And I have to force back tears of pride at being an American.

This is my own distinctive experience of what we call "patriotism," and I suspect that many Americans experience something similar and acknowledge it in their own ways. Amid the frequent confusion, frustration and anger of our political disagreements, patriotism—a deep-seated love of our country—remains something that has the potential to bring us together, particularly at times of national crisis or triumph.

But within my own particular intellectual tribe of philosophers, patriotism is often regarded as a "problem," an emotion that many find hard to defend as morally appropriate. Of course, many Americans are uneasy with, even repelled by, certain expressions of patriotism—perhaps the obligatory flag pins of politicians, the inanity of "freedom fries," the suggestion in the revised Pledge of Allegiance that atheists aren't patriotic, or even readings of the Declaration of Independence. But the philosophical problem of patriotism is not about whether or not certain expressions of patriotism are appropriate; it is about the moral defensibility of the attitude as such.

At the beginning of Plato's *Republic*, Socrates asks what justice (doing the morally right thing) is, and Polemarchus replies that it's helping your friends and harming your enemies. That was the answer among the ancient Greeks as well as many other traditional societies. Moral behavior was the way you treated those in your "in-group," as opposed to outsiders.

Socrates questioned this ethical exclusivism, thus beginning a centuries-long argument that, by modern times, led most major moral philosophers (for example, Mill and Kant) to conclude that morality required an impartial, universal viewpoint that treated all human beings as equals. In other words, the "in-group" for morality is not any particular social group (family, city, nation) but humankind as a whole. This universal moral viewpoint seems to reject patriotism for "cosmopolitanism"—the view perhaps first formulated by Diogenes, who, when asked where he came from, replied that he was a citizen of the world.

Certainly, patriotism can take an explicitly amoral form: "My country, right or wrong." But even strong traditional patriots can accept moral limits on the means we use to advance the cause of our country. They may agree, for example, that it's wrong to threaten Canada with nuclear annihilation to obtain a more favorable trade agreement.

But the moral problem for patriotism arises at a deeper level. Suppose the question is not about blatantly immoral means but simply about whether our country should flourish at the expense of another. Suppose, for example, that at some point Saudi Arabia, now allied with China, threatened to curtail our access to its oil, thereby significantly reducing our productivity and tipping the balance of world economic power to China. Imagine an American president who declined to oppose this action because he had concluded that, from a disinterested moral viewpoint, it was better for mankind as a whole. Even if we admired such a response, it's hard to think that it would express patriotic regard for the United States.

Should we therefore conclude that patriotism is ultimately at odds with a moral viewpoint? There remains the option of denying that morality has the universal, all-inclusive nature modern philosophers think it has. Alasdair MacIntyre, for example, argues that morality is rooted in the life of a specific real community—a village, a city, a nation, with its idiosyncratic customs and history—and that, therefore, adherence to morality requires loyalty to such a community. Patriotism, on this view, is essential for living a morally good life. MacIntyre's argument (in his Lindley Lecture, "Is Patriotism a Virtue?") has provided the most powerful contemporary defense of a full-blooded patriotism.

It may seem, then, that we must either accept modern universalist ethics and reject patriotism as a basic moral virtue or accept patriotism along with MacIntyre's traditional localist morality. But perhaps, at least in the American context, there is a way of avoiding the dilemma.

For what is the animating ideal of American patriotism if not the freedom of all persons, not just its own citizens? This is apparent in our Declaration, which bases its case for independence on the principle that government exist to "secure the rights" of "life, liberty and the pursuit of happiness" to which all persons are equally entitled. This principle is the avowed purpose of all our actions as a nation, and we may read our history as the story of our successes and failures in carrying out this principle. America, then, is the paradox of a local historical project that aims at universal liberation. Through this project, we have a way of combining traditional patriotism with universal morality.

This project has had many failures, most often when we forget that the freedom of a nation must always grow from its own historical roots. We cannot simply wage a war that rips up those roots and then transplant shoots from our own stock (American-style capitalism, political parties, our popular culture). We have also often forgotten that the liberation of our own citizens is by no means complete. But none of this alters the fact that our governments have often worked and our soldiers died not just for our own freedom but for the freedom of all nations.

We are a MacIntyrean community that is still trying to live out a modern morality that seeks the freedom of everyone. I love America because I still believe that this sublime project is possible.

The Irrationality of Natural Life Sentences

—Jennifer Lackey

I'VE BEEN TEACHING PHILOSOPHY FOR FIFTEEN YEARS, AND WHILE I've had some very memorable experiences along the way, I knew early on that my current seminar would be unique. The course itself is on values, and each Monday for nearly three hours my students debate—in an often lively and engaging manner—issues ranging from the existence of universal moral truths to the permissibility of torture and the death penalty. In fact, a few weeks ago, there was a complaint about the level of noise coming from my classroom. The reason for the noise? The utilitarians were rather loudly arguing to the Kantians that sacrificing one of their classmates to prevent the Paris attacks would clearly have been justified.

The complaint resulted in a guard being stationed in the doorway of my classroom to ensure that there wasn't "a security threat," followed by some breath-holding as I waited to see if I would, once again, be removed from the building. You see, the course I'm teaching is at Stateville Correctional Center—a maximum-security men's prison in a suburb of Chicago—where raised voices aren't typically the result of intense philosophical debate about normative ethical theories. Yet, the room felt no more in need of a guard than do my classes at Northwestern.

In some respects, this is a striking fact. Just about all of my students at Stateville have been convicted of at least one murder; some have assaulted staff members, and others have spent over a decade in solitary confinement. Some are former gang members, and others were on death row—neighbors with John Wayne Gacy—for almost half of their lives.

In other respects, however, this is not at all surprising. The most obvious is that some end up at Stateville for reasons that are disconnected from culpability—coerced confessions, poor counsel, a racist jury, and so on. But even where these external forces are largely absent, the fact that my classroom seems indistinguishable from those at an elite university turns out not to be that shocking. And here's the simple, yet crucially important reason: People can change, often in profoundly transformative ways.

SUCH TRANSFORMATIONS CAN BE seen most clearly by considering the two ends of the spectrum of life. On the early side, it is often noted that the prefrontal cortex of the brains of adolescents is still developing, and so they are more likely than adults to act on impulse, engage in dangerous or risky behavior, and misread social cues and emotions. This raises a host of questions about the level of responsibility that juveniles bear for their crimes and the appropriate punishments that should be handed out to them. If the underdeveloped brains of adolescents at least partly explain their criminal behavior, then holding them fully responsible for their actions, and punishing them as adults, seems wildly off the mark.

On the later side of the spectrum, only 1 percent of serious crime is committed by people over the age of sixty. According to Jonathan Turley, a professor of public interest law at George Washington University: "Everyone agrees on what is the most reliable predictor of recidivism: age. As people get older, they statistically become less dangerous." Turley refers to this period as "criminal menopause," a phenomenon that raises serious questions about the rationale for incarcerating the elderly. Still, researchers project that the elderly prison population in the United States will be over 400,000 in 2030, compared with 8,853 in 1981.

At the early end of the spectrum of life, then, there is the possibility that prisoners *might change*; at the later end, there is the reality that they *have changed*. Both facts bump up against natural life sentences. A sentence of "natural life" means that there are no parole hearings, no credit for time served, no possibility of release. Short of a successful appeal or an executive pardon, such a sentence means that the convicted will, in no uncertain terms, die behind bars.

MANY TYPES OF ARGUMENTS have been leveled against natural life sentences. Economic ones focus on the ballooning costs of mass incarceration and the toll this takes on government budgets, especially as the age and medical expenses of prisoners rapidly increase. Legal ones ask whether such sentences are cruel and unusual and therefore violate the Eighth Amendment, particularly for juveniles. Social arguments ask whether natural life sentences discourage reform by providing no incentive for rehabilitation. Moral concerns are grounded in the dignity and rights of prisoners, while psychological objections call attention to the myriad causes of deviant behavior and their responsiveness to appropriate treatment.

But one argument that is surprisingly absent from these conversations is an *epistemic* one that has to do with *us*. For natural life sentences say to all involved that there is no possible piece of information that could be learned between sentencing and death that could bear in any way on the punishment the convicted is said to deserve, short of what might ground an appeal. Nothing. So no matter how much a juvenile is transformed behind bars, and no matter how unrecognizable an elderly prisoner is from his earlier self, this is utterly irrelevant to whether they should be incarcerated. Our absence of knowledge about the future, our ignorance of what is to come, our lack of a crystal ball, is in no way a barrier to determining now what someone's life ought to be like decades from now.

Moreover, prisoners aren't the only ones who can change: victims and their families can come to see the convicted as being worthy of forgiveness and a second chance, and public attitudes can evolve, moving away from a zealous "war on crime" approach to one that sees much criminal activity as the result of broader social problems that call for reform. Even if we set aside the other arguments against natural life sentences—economic, legal, moral and so on—the question I want to ask here is this: how is it *rational* to screen off the relevance of this information? How, that is, is it rational to say today that there can be no possible evidence in the future that could bear on the punishment that a decades-from-now prisoner deserves?

In any other domain, it would obviously be irrational to make a high-stakes decision about the rest of another person's life that not only rules out the possibility of ever considering additional evidence, but is also meant to be absolutely final.

If I were given the option to heavily invest in one, and only one, career for my fifteen-year-old based only on her current beliefs, preferences, and character, I would refuse without hesitation. A lot can change in a decade, especially during the critical transition between adolescence and adulthood. Even choices that we expect to significantly constrain our future selves, such as marriage, can be revisited in light of new evidence. This is precisely why divorce is legal. Yet natural life sentences stand out as a glaring exception: They permit binding, life-altering decisions to be made in a state of radical *epistemic impoverishment*.

Of course, when punishment is connected with rehabilitation, it's undeniable that information about changes, especially among prisoners, is relevant. But this is also true for all but the crudest forms of retributive justice. It's a commonplace that information about a person's mental states bears on the punishment deserved, regardless of its consequences. When considering punishments, including at parole hearings, we are often highly sensitive to whether the wrongdoer appreciates the wrongness of the act, feels remorse, and is committed to not being a repeat offender.

Compare two students known to have cheated: The first fully acknowledges that looking at her notes during an exam was wrong, is clearly contrite, and promises to never do so again; the second flagrantly and steadfastly lies about it and shows no evidence that he won't cheat again. It is fairly standard for the second student's punishment to be harsher than the first's.

But if we take two students with such different mental states regarding cheating as deserving of different sanctions, why would we not regard two stages of the same person—one at nineteen and another at forty-nine—with radically different attitudes toward his crime, as deserving of different punishments? Current selves and future selves can vary from one another no less than two altogether distinct people do.

NOTICE THAT NOTHING IN the epistemic argument here suggests that no prisoners should, in fact, spend the rest of their natural lives behind bars. Instead, the point is that rationality requires that we leave the epistemic door open to acquiring new information. Put bluntly, the argument says that it is irrational for the possibility of parole to be taken off the table at the outset of any sentence.

If Hume is right that "a wise man proportions his belief to the evidence," then our beliefs about the punishment a person deserves at any given time need to be sensitive to the evidence available at that time. But if we screen off huge amounts of potentially relevant information decades before the beliefs about what a prisoner deserves are even formed, then it is impossible for them to be proportioned to the evidence.

Nearly all of my students at Stateville are serving natural life sentences. At least a handful of them have been incarcerated since they were teenagers, one since he was fourteen. While I didn't know any of their decades-earlier selves, their current selves are some of the most extraordinary students I've had in my fifteen years of teaching. They are painters and poets, mentors and authors, researchers and advocates. They breathe new life into philosophical questions I've been asking for the entirety of my career. And yet we tell these men that who they are now and what they have accomplished matters so little to how they ought to be treated that we won't even bother to consider it. Rationality demands that we do better.

Spinoza's Vision of Freedom, and Ours

—Steven Nadler

Baruch Spinoza, the seventeenth-century Dutch thinker, may be among the more enigmatic (and mythologized) philosophers in Western thought, but he also remains one of the most relevant, to his time and to ours. He was an eloquent proponent of a secular, democratic society, and was the strongest advocate for freedom and tolerance in the early modern period. The ultimate goal of his *Theological-Political Treatise*—published anonymously to great alarm in 1670, when it was called by one of its many critics "a book forged in hell by the devil himself"—is enshrined both in the book's subtitle and in the argument of its final chapter: to show that the "freedom of philosophizing" not only *can* be granted "without detriment to public peace, to piety, and to the right of the sovereign, but also that it must be granted if these are to be preserved."

Spinoza was incited to write the *Treatise* when he recognized that the Dutch Republic, and his own province of Holland in particular, was wavering from its uncommonly liberal and relatively tolerant traditions. He feared that with the rising political influence in the 1660s of the more orthodox and narrow-minded elements in the Dutch Reformed Church, and the willingness of civil authorities to placate the preachers by acting against works they deemed "irreligious," "licentious" and "subversive," the nearly two decades–long period of the "True Freedom" was coming to an end. The *Treatise* is both a personally angry book—a friend of Spinoza's, the author of a radical treatise, had recently been thrown in prison, where he soon died—and a very public plea to the Dutch Republic not to betray the political, legal and religious principles that made its flourishing possible.

In this work, Spinoza approaches the issue of individual liberty from several perspectives. To begin with, there is the question of belief, and especially the state's tolerance of the beliefs of its citizens. Spinoza argues that all individuals are to be absolutely free and unimpeded in their beliefs, by right and in fact. "It is impossible for the mind to be completely under another's control; for no one is able to transfer to another his natural right or faculty to reason freely and to form his own judgment on any matters whatsoever, nor can he be compelled to do so."

For this reason, any effort on the government's part to rule over the beliefs and opinions of citizens is bound to fail, and will ultimately serve to undermine its own authority. A sovereign is certainly free to try and limit what people think, but the result of such a policy, Spinoza predicts, would be only to create resentment and opposition to its rule.

It can be argued that the state's tolerance of individual belief is not a difficult issue. As Spinoza points out, it is "impossible" for a person's mind to be under another's control, and this is a necessary reality that any government must accept. The more difficult case, the true test of a regime's commitment to toleration, concerns the liberty of citizens to express those beliefs, either in speech or in writing. And here Spinoza goes further than anyone else of his time: "Utter failure," he says, "will attend any attempt in a commonwealth to force men to speak only as prescribed by the sovereign despite their different and opposing opinions . . . The most tyrannical government will be one where the individual is denied the freedom to express and to communicate to others what he thinks, and a moderate government is one where this freedom is granted to every man."

Spinoza has a number of compelling arguments for the freedom of expression. One is based both on the natural right (or natural power) of citizens to speak as they desire, as well as on the apparent fact that (as in the case of belief per se) it would be self-defeating for a government to try to restrain that freedom. No matter what laws are enacted against speech and other means of expression, citizens will continue to say what they believe (because they can), only now they will do so in secret. The result of the suppression of freedom is, once again, resentment and a weakening of the bonds that unite subjects to their government. In Spinoza's view, intolerant laws lead ultimately to anger, revenge and sedition. The attempt to enforce them is a "great danger to the state." (This would certainly have been the lesson gleaned from recent history, as the Dutch revolt originated in the repressive measures that the Spanish crown imposed on its northern territories in the sixteenth century.)

Spinoza also argues for freedom of expression on utilitarian grounds—that it is necessary for the discovery of truth, economic progress, and the growth of creativity. Without an open marketplace of ideas, science, philosophy and other disciplines are stifled in their development, to the technological, fiscal and even aesthetic detriment of society. As Spinoza puts it, "This freedom [of expressing one's ideas] is of the first importance in fostering the sciences and the arts, for it is only those whose judgment is free and unbiased who can attain success in these fields."

Spinoza's extraordinary views on freedom have never been more relevant. In 2010, for example, the United States Supreme Court declared constitutional a law that, among other things, criminalized certain kinds of speech. The speech in question need not be extremely and imminently threatening to anyone or pose "a clear and present danger" (to use Justice Oliver Wendell Holmes's phrase). It may involve no incitement to action or violence whatsoever; indeed, it can be an exhortation to *nonviolence*. In a troubling 6–3 decision, *Holder v. Humanitarian Law Project*, the Court, acceding to most of the arguments presented by President Obama's attorney general, Eric Holder, upheld a federal law which makes it a crime to provide support for a foreign group designated by the State Department as a "terrorist organization," even if the "help" one provides involves only peaceful and legal advice, including speech encouraging that organization to adopt nonviolent means for resolving conflicts and educating it in the means to do so. (The United States, of course, is not alone among Western nations in restricting freedom of expression. Just this week, France—fresh from outlawing the wearing of veils by Muslim women, and in a mirror image of Turkey's criminalizing the public affirmation of the Armenian genocide—made it illegal to deny, in print or public speech, officially recognized genocides.)

For Spinoza, by contrast, there is to be no criminalization of ideas in the well-ordered state. *Libertas philosophandi*, the freedom of philosophizing, must be upheld for the sake of a healthy, secure and peaceful commonwealth and material and intellectual progress.

Now Spinoza does not support *absolute* freedom of speech. He explicitly states that the expression of "seditious" ideas is *not* to be tolerated by the sovereign. There is to be no protection for speech that advocates the overthrow of the government, disobedience to its laws or harm to fellow citizens. The people are free to argue for the repeal of laws that they find unreasonable and oppressive, but they must do so peacefully and through rational argument; and if their argument fails to persuade the sovereign to change the law, then that must be the end of the matter. What they may not do is "stir up popular hatred against [the sovereign or his representatives]."

Absolutists about the freedom of speech will be troubled by these caveats on Spinoza's part, and rightly so. After all, who is to decide what kind of speech counts as seditious? May not the government declare to be seditious simply those views with which it disagrees or that it finds contrary to its policies? Spinoza, presumably to allay such concerns, does offer a definition of "seditious political beliefs" as those that "*immediately* have the effect of annulling the covenant whereby everyone has surrendered his right to act just as he thinks fit" (my emphasis). The salient feature of such opinions is "the action that is implicit therein"—that is, they are more or less verbal incitements to act against the government and thus they are directly contrary to the tacit social contract of citizenship.

What is important is that Spinoza draws the line, albeit a somewhat hazy one, between ideas and action. The government, he insists, has every right to outlaw certain kinds of actions. As the party responsible for the public welfare, the sovereign must have absolute and exclusive power to monitor and legislatively control what people may or may not do. But Spinoza explicitly does not include ideas, even the *expression* of ideas, under the category of "action." As individuals emerged from a state of nature to become citizens through the social contract, "it was only the right to act as he thought fit that each man surrendered, and not his right to reason and judge."

In the penultimate paragraph of the *Treatise*, Spinoza insists that "the state can pursue no safer course than to regard piety and religion as consisting solely in the exercise of charity and just dealing, and that the right of the sovereign, both in religious and secular spheres, should be restricted to men's actions, with everyone being allowed to think what he will and to say what he thinks." There is no reason to think that Spinoza believed that this remarkable and unprecedented principle of toleration and liberty was to be qualified according to who was speaking, the ideas being expressed (with the noted exception of explicit calls for sedition), or the audience being addressed.

I cited the case of *Holder v. Humanitarian Law Project* not to make a constitutional point—I leave it to legal scholars to determine whether or not the Supreme Court's decision represents a betrayal of our country's highest ideals—but rather to underscore the continuing value of Spinoza's philosophical one.

Well before John Stuart Mill, Spinoza had the acuity to recognize that the unfettered freedom of expression is in the state's own best interest. In this post-9/11 world, there is a temptation to believe that "homeland security" is better secured by the suppression of certain liberties than their free exercise. This includes a tendency by justices to interpret existing laws in restrictive ways and efforts by lawmakers to create new limitations, as well as a willingness among the populace, "for the sake of peace and security," to acquiesce in this. We seem ready not only to engage in a higher degree of self-censorship, but also to accept a loosening of legal protections against prior restraint (whether in print publications or the dissemination of information via the Internet), unwarranted surveillance, unreasonable search and seizure, and other intrusive measures. Spinoza, long ago, recognized the danger in such thinking, both for individuals and for the polity at large. He saw that there was no need to make a trade-off between political and social well-being and the freedom of expression; on the contrary, the former depends on the latter.

FEBRUARY 5, 2012

If War Can Have Ethics, Wall Street Can, Too

—Nathaniel B. Davis

NEARLY A DECADE AFTER ONE OF THE MOST DEVASTATING financial collapses in modern history, Wall Street appears as corrupt as ever. Evidence is not hard to come by—most recently, the Wells Fargo scandal, in which employees of the company, spurred by perverse incentive structures, opened two million fraudulent accounts in their customer's names. The bank had put intense pressure on employees to meet sales goals; some employees who reported the wrongdoing were fired, along with 5,300 more, after the scandal broke. All this is but one reminder of how far major actors in the economy have strayed from any reasonable standard of moral behavior.

Despite the recent urging of high-profile figures like Pope Francis and Senator Bernie Sanders to establish a "moral economy," we have not. Free-market advocates hold fast to justifications that amount to variations on the "invisible hand" theory of Adam Smith—that the economy is not a moral space, but one that relies on a free and fair market, self-interested (as opposed to selfish) actors and amoral (as opposed to immoral) calculation to arrive at the most efficient and innovative outcomes. The invisible hand of the market must be allowed to act; placing moral limits on the economy, they argue, would hinder this flourishing.

To some, the unbridled force and overarching goal to be pursued is the efficiency of the market, even to the detriment of society, transforming market theory into a sort of divine scripture, to be faithfully followed. The suggestion of a moral economy is decried for the inefficiencies that moral limits would place on behavior in the market. It is as if society exists to serve the market, not the other way around.

The pursuit of a comparative advantage in the market has come to justify nearly any behavior and its consequences. The result of this approach in the United States is already well-known—a staggering level of economic inequality and widespread, devastating effects on millions of citizens struggling against this tide.

Hedge funds and investment banks utilize high-speed trading to place the individual investor at an insurmountable disadvantage. Multinational corporations pump money into political campaigns to influence tax policies that allow them to skirt paying taxes. The mega-wealthy deploy a small army of accountants and attorneys to hide their assets. Slavish devotion to market theories serves as a convenient rational justification for some to take selfish actions they know to be wrong or questionable.

In short, the amoral economy envisioned by free market theory is a fantasy, a theoretical construct that has never really existed in practice. It has been overwhelmed by immoral actors who have turned it into an immoral space, tipping the playing field to their advantage.

So what is to be done? Can the economy be transformed from an immoral space into a *moral* space?

Some progress on this question can be made by examining how we have chosen to navigate an even more perilous manifestation of the human condition: war. The economy, like war, creates winners and losers, makes heroes of those who seize opportunities and victims of those caught between forces beyond their control, and can transform the fortunes of society for better or ill. Yet, unlike war, the economy has no foundational morality. Instead it leaves critical moral judgments with real consequences in the tenuous hands of self-interested economic actors whose guiding light is the maximization of their own benefit, without consideration for the effects on others.

The Prussian military theorist Carl von Clausewitz warned of "total war" as a theoretical construct in which, by rationally following the escalations of war to their conclusion, war outstrips its strategic logic and becomes irrational, therefore requiring limits in practice. Without limits, Clausewitz argued, theory could be misused to justify and rationalize the unjust and irrational. Unless war is bounded by a higher societal purpose and tempered by what Clausewitz referred to as "the spirit of the age," it threatens to become its own raison d'être, an irrational end in itself.

In war, immoral action may provide the combatant with a comparative advantage, but it also stains society and humanity in ways that we have collectively deemed to be unacceptable.

Humanity has tried to limit war on moral terms since Cicero first outlined the Just War Ethic, an effort that continues to this day. In war, the reversion to barbarism can be tempting in the heat of battle, and as passions and hatreds rise between peoples. However, even here, humanity has managed to place moral limits.

In the modern world, the Just War Ethic may seem like a distant abstraction; but its effects influence the relationship between war and society in profound ways. Michael Walzer, perhaps the most influential living philosopher of just war theories, articulated the importance of seeking to establish moral principles there: "War is the hardest place: if comprehensive and consistent moral judgments are possible there, they are possible everywhere."

The Just War Ethic provides the foundational principles on which the laws of war have been constructed; when policy makers seek to justify the use of force, they employ the language of the Just War Ethic; they speak in terms of the principles of just cause, last resort, necessity, proportionality and the reasonable prospects of success. Although often overshadowed by the horrors of war, the principles of the Just War Ethic do limit war's worst excesses by underpinning the discourse, decisions, behaviors and accountability related to war.

Of course, the Just War Ethic suffers from a problem: the normative ideal in this case is the absence of war, yet the reality of war precludes that ideal. Therefore, any applied ethics of war are by definition morally flawed. The question for the ethicist then is this: Is it more ethical to make continued (and often ignored) normative pronouncements against the existence of war, or to engage with the temporal reality of war with ethics that seek to limit the cases in which war is undertaken, to moderate its effects, and to guide it toward the normative goal, with the understanding that this goal is not immediately or fully achievable? Obviously, advocates of the Just War Ethic, myself included, come to the latter conclusion.

The question is not one of moral perfection, but of moral improvement. It is a step in the right direction.

If we can seek to regulate war in terms of morality, there is no reason such morality cannot be equally applied to the economy, as Walzer indicates. When faced with illegal or immoral orders, it is the duty of professional soldiers to refuse such orders. When such a refusal occurs, it is followed by thorough investigations, and potentially courts-martial or war crimes prosecutions for those who issue such orders. In the case of the former Wells Fargo employees, the opposite occurred. Imagine the moral and societal hazard if the military permitted such retaliation against those who reported illegal and immoral behaviors.

The principles of a moral economy would seek to curb the market's more harmful excesses while preserving its societal benefit. Developing fair and just principles to guide a more moral understanding of capitalism may provide a pathway to a more equitable distribution of income and wealth, one that creates more perfect outcomes for society at large.

While the immoral economy has provided advantages to some, it has also stained society and humanity in ways that we are beginning to collectively deem to be unacceptable. The task then is to develop and implement principles of a moral economy which serves the greater good of society.

In a "just" economy, venture capitalists would consider the collateral damage (layoffs, defaulted retirements, etc.) that may result from their actions in the same way that military commanders must consider whether the use of a certain weapon in proximity to civilians would be discriminate and proportional. Chief executives would begin to care for their employees and their families the same way that professional military commanders care for their troops and their families. The promise of these outcomes, and society's growing dissatisfaction with the current reality, makes this a conversation worth having.

Some might argue that we already have laws and regulations to perform these functions, but these have, at times spectacularly, failed to maintain the market as a truly neutral, free, and fair space. In a theoretical sense, law should approximate the normative ideal in the real world. Yet, in economic thought we have no normative ideal, no foundational morality. We have economic ideals derived from market theory, but these are not tempered by a coherent set of ethical ideals, allowing the market's worst excesses, and resulting in many of the morally troubling outcomes produced by the economy. We need better laws and regulations, but first we must establish a foundational morality to guide their development.

To demand moral perfection or to succumb in the face of seeming futility is to turn our backs on what can be achieved by acknowledging both the ideal and the limits of reality. Applied ethics guide our interactions in the world as it exists while nudging us incrementally closer to the normative ideal and the world we seek to create.

War is inherently unjust, but the Just War Ethic has made it more just. The economy is not moral, but a foundational ethics of the economy could make it more moral. The product of such ethics would be decidedly imperfect, but it would be better than no ethics at all.

The views expressed in this article are those of the author and do not reflect the official policy or position of the United States Military Academy, Department of the Army, Department of Defense or the United States government.

OCTOBER 3, 2016

The Moral Hazard of Drones

—*John Kaag and Sarah Kreps*

As the debate on the morality of the United States' use of unmanned aerial vehicles (UAVs, also known as drones) has intensified in recent weeks, several news and opinion articles have appeared in the media. Two, in particular, both published this month, reflect the current ethical divide on the issue. A feature article in *Esquire* by Tom Junod censured the "Lethal Presidency of Barack Obama" for the administration's policy of targeted killings of suspected militants; another, "The Moral Case for Drones," a news analysis by the *Times'* Scott Shane, gathered opinions from experts that implicitly commended the administration for replacing Dresden-style strategic bombing with highly precise attacks that minimize collateral damage.

Amid this discussion, we suggest that an allegory might be helpful to illustrate some of the many moral perils of drone use that have been overlooked. It shows that our attempts to avoid obvious ethical pitfalls of actions like firebombing may leave us vulnerable to other, more subtle, moral dangers.

While drones have become the weapons of our age, the moral dilemma that drone warfare presents is not new. In fact, it is very, very old:

Once upon a time, in a quiet corner of the Middle East, there lived a shepherd named Gyges. Despite the hardships in his life, Gyges was relatively satisfied with his meager existence. Then, one day, he found a ring buried in a nearby cave.

This was no ordinary ring; it rendered its wearer invisible. With this new power, Gyges became increasingly dissatisfied with his simple life. Before long, he seduced the queen of the land and began to plot the overthrow of her husband. One evening, Gyges placed the ring on his finger, sneaked into the royal palace, and murdered the king.

In his *Republic*, Plato recounts this tale but does not tell us the details of the murder. Still, we can rest assured that, like any violent death, it was not a pleasant affair. However, the story ends well, at least for Gyges. He marries the queen and assumes the position of king.

This story, which is as old as Western ethics itself, is meant to elicit a particular moral response from us: disgust. So why do we find Plato's story so appalling?

Maybe it's the way that the story replaces moral justification with practical efficiency: Gyges's being able to commit murder without getting caught, without any real difficulty, does not mean he is justified in doing so. (Expediency is not necessarily a virtue.)

Maybe it's the way that Gyges's ring obscures his moral culpability: it's difficult to blame a person you can't see and even harder to bring them to justice.

Maybe it's that Gyges is successful in his plot: a wicked act not only goes unpunished but is rewarded.

Maybe it's the nagging sense that any kingdom based on such deception could not be a just one: What else might happen in such a kingdom under the cover of darkness?

Our disgust with Gyges could be traced to any one of these concerns, or to all of them.

One might argue that the myth of Gyges is a suitable allegory to describe the combatants who have attacked and killed American civilians and troops in the last ten years. A shepherd from the Middle East discovers that he has the power of invisibility, the power to strike a fatal blow against a more powerful adversary, the power to do so without getting caught, the power to benefit from his deception. These, after all, are the tactics of terrorism.

But the myth of Gyges is really a story about modern counterterrorism, not terrorism.

We believe a stronger comparison can be made between the myth and the moral dangers of employing precision-guided munitions and drone technologies to target suspected terrorists. What is distinctive about the tale of Gyges is the ease with which he can commit murder and get away scot-free. The technological advantage provided by the ring ends up serving as the justification of its use.

Terrorists, whatever the moral value of their deeds, may be found and punished; as humans they are subject to retribution, whether it be corporal or legal. They may lose or sacrifice their lives. They may, in fact, be killed in the middle of the night by a drone. Because remote-controlled machines cannot suffer these consequences, and the humans who operate them do so at a great distance, the myth of Gyges is more a parable of modern counterterrorism than it is about terrorism.

Only recently has the use of drones begun to touch on questions of morality. Perhaps it's because the answers to these questions appear self-evident. What could be wrong with the use of unmanned aerial vehicles? After all, they limit the cost of war, in terms of both blood and treasure. The US troops who operate them can maintain safer standoff positions in Eastern Europe or at home. And armed with precision-guided munitions, these drones are said to limit collateral damage. In 2009, Leon Panetta, who was then the director of the Central Intelligence Agency, said UAVs are "very precise and very limited in terms of collateral damage . . . the only game in town in terms of confronting or trying to disrupt the al Qaeda leadership." What could be wrong with all this?

Quite a bit, it turns out.

Return, for a minute, to the moral disgust that Gyges evokes in us. Gyges also risked very little in attacking the king. The success of his mission was almost assured, thanks to the technological advantage of his ring. Gyges could sneak past the king's guards unscathed, so he did not need to kill anyone he did not intend on killing. These are the facts of the matter.

What we find unsettling here is the idea that these facts could be confused for moral justification. Philosophers find this confusion particularly abhorrent and guard against it with the only weapon they have: a distinction. The "fact-value distinction" holds that statements of fact should never be confused with statements of value. More strongly put, this distinction means that statements of fact do not even *imply* statements of value. "Can" does not imply "ought." To say that we *can* target individuals without incurring troop casualties does not imply that we *ought* to.

This seems so obvious. But, as Peter W. Singer noted earlier this year in the *Times*, when the Obama administration was asked why continued US military strikes in the Middle East did not consti-tute a violation of the 1973 War Powers Resolution, it responded that such activities did not "involve the presence of U.S. ground troops, U.S. casualties or a serious threat thereof." The justification of these strikes rested solely on their ease. The Ring of Gyges has the power to obscure the obvious.

This issue has all the hallmarks of what economists and phi-losophers call a "moral hazard"—a situation in which greater risks are taken by individuals who are able to avoid shouldering the cost associated with these risks. It thus seems wise, if not convenient, to underscore several ethical points if we are to avoid our own "Gyges moment."

First, we might remember Marx's comment that "the windmill gives you a society with the feudal lord; the steam engine gives you one with the industrial capitalist." And precision-guided munitions and drones give you a society with perpetual asymmetric wars.

The creation of technology is a value-laden enterprise. It cre-ates the material conditions of culture and society and therefore its creation should be regarded as always already moral and political in nature. However, technology itself (the physical stuff of robotic war-fare) is neither smart nor dumb, moral nor immoral. It can be used more or less precisely, but precision and efficiency are not inherently morally good. Imagine a very skilled dentist who painlessly removes the wrong tooth. Imagine a drone equipped with a precision-guided munition that kills a completely innocent person but spares the people who live in his or her neighborhood. The use of impressive technologies does not grant one impressive moral insight. Indeed, as Gyges demonstrates, the opposite can be the case.

Second, assassination and targeted killings have always been in the repertoires of military planners, but never in the history of warfare have they been so cheap and easy. The relatively low number of troop casualties for a military that has turned to drones means that there is relatively little domestic blowback against these wars. The United States and its allies have created the material conditions whereby these wars can carry on indefinitely. The noncombatant casualty rates in populations that are attacked by drones are slow and steady, but they add up. That the casualty rates are relatively low by historical standards—this is no Dresden—is undoubtedly a good thing, but it may allow the international media to overlook pesky little facts like the slow accretion of foreign casualties.

Third, the impressive expediency and accuracy in drone targeting may also allow policy makers and strategists to become lax in their moral decision making about who exactly should be targeted. Consider the stark contrast between the ambiguous language used to define legitimate targets and the specific technical means a military uses to neutralize these targets. The terms *terrorist*, *enemy combatant* and *contingent threat* are extremely vague and do very little to articulate the legitimacy of military targets. In contrast, the technical capabilities of weapon systems define and "paint" these targets with ever-greater definition. As weaponry becomes more precise, the language of warfare has become more ambiguous.

This ambiguity has, for example, altered the discourse surrounding the issue of collateral damage. There are two very different definitions of collateral damage, and these definitions affect the truth of the following statement: "Drone warfare and precision-guided munitions limit collateral damage." One definition views collateral damage as the inadvertent destruction of property and persons in a given attack. In other words, collateral damage refers to "stuff we don't mean to blow up." Another definition characterizes collateral damage as objects or individuals "that would not be lawful military targets in the circumstances ruling at the time." In other words, collateral damage refers to "the good guys." Since 1998, this is the definition that has been used. What is the difference between these definitions?

The first is a description of technical capabilities (being able to hit x while not hitting y); the second is a normative and indeed legal judgment about who is and is not innocent (and therefore who is a legitimate target and who is not). The first is a matter of fact, the second a matter of value. There is an important difference between these statements, and they should not be confused.

Fourth, questions of combatant status should be the subject of judicial review and moral scrutiny. Instead, if these questions are asked at all, they are answered as if they were mere matters of fact, unilaterally, behind closed doors, rather than through transparent due process. That moral reasoning has become even more slippery of late, as the American government has implied that all military-aged males in a strike area are legitimate targets: a "guilt by association" designation.

Finally, as the strategic repertoires of modern militaries expand to include drones and precision-guided munitions, it is not at all clear that having more choices leads strategists to make better and more-informed ones. In asking, "Is More Choice Better than Less?" the philosopher Gerald Dworkin once argued that the answer is "not always." In the words of Kierkegaard, "In possibility everything is possible. Hence in possibility one can go astray in all possible ways."

Some might object that these guidelines set unrealistically high expectations on military strategists and policy makers. They would probably be right. But no one—except Gyges—said that being ethical was easy.

JULY 22, 2012

Reasons for Reason

—Michael P. Lynch

THE VOCAL DISMISSALS OF EVOLUTION FROM RICK PERRY, THE Republican governor of Texas, during his 2012 presidential campaign and his confident assertion that "God is how we got here" reflect an obvious divide in our culture. In one sense, that divide is just over the facts: Some of us believe God created human beings just as they are now, others of us don't. But underneath this divide is a deeper one. Really divisive disagreements are typically not just over the facts. They are also about the best way to support our views of the facts. Call this a disagreement in epistemic principle. Our epistemic principles tell us what is rational to believe, what sources of information to trust. Thus, while a few people may agree with Perry because they really think that the scientific evidence supports creationism, I suspect that for most people, scientific evidence (or its lack) has nothing to do with it. Their belief in creationism is instead a reflection of a deeply held epistemic principle: that, at least on some topics, scripture is a more reliable source of information than science. For others, including myself, this is never the case.

Disagreements like this give rise to an unnerving question: How do we rationally defend our most fundamental epistemic principles? Like many of the best philosophical mysteries, this is a problem that can seem both unanswerable and yet extremely important to solve.

The ancient Greek skeptics were the first to show why the problem is so difficult to solve. Every one of our beliefs is produced by some method or source, be it humble (like memory) or complex (like technologically assisted science). But why think our methods, whatever they are, are trustworthy or reliable for getting at the truth? If I challenge one of your methods, you can't just appeal to the same method to show that it is reliable. That would be circular. And appealing to another method won't help either—for unless *that* method can be shown to be reliable, using it to determine the reliability of the first method answers nothing. So you end up either continuing on in the same vein—pointlessly citing reasons for methods and methods for reasons forever—or arguing in circles, or granting that your method is groundless. Any way you go, it seems you must admit you can give no reason for trusting your methods, and hence can give no reason to defend your most fundamental epistemic principles.

This skeptical argument is disturbing because it seems to suggest that in the end, all "rational" explanations end up grounding out on something arbitrary. It all just comes down to what you happen to believe, what you feel in your gut, your faith. Human beings have historically found this to be a very seductive idea, in part because it is liberating. It levels the playing field, intellectually speaking. After all, if all reasons are grounded on something arbitrary, then no one's principles rest on any firmer foundation than anyone else's. It seems to give us the freedom to go with any epistemic principle we choose.

Many people who are committed to the core epistemic principles of science—say, that observation and experiment should be trusted over appeals to scripture—are inclined to shrug this worry off. Why, they ask, should I care about convincing people who don't understand the obvious fact that science is always the better method for knowing about matters like the origin of life on this planet? Again, epistemic principles tell us what is rational. So anyone who doubts my basic epistemic principles is going to appear to *me* as someone who doubts the rules of rationality. So, why should I care about what they think? It's not as if they'll be able to recognize my (good) reasons anyway, and to me, *their* "reasons" will not be legitimate.

But what counts as "legitimate"? There's the rub. A legitimate challenge is presumably a rational challenge. Disagreements over epistemic principles are disagreements over which methods and sources to trust. And there we have the problem. We can't decide on what counts as a legitimate reason to doubt my epistemic principles unless we've already settled on our principles—and that is the very issue in question. The problem that skepticism about reason raises is not about whether I have good evidence by my principles for my principles. Presumably I do. The problem is whether I can give a more objective defense of them. That is, whether I can give reasons for them that can be appreciated from what Hume called a "common point of view"—reasons that can "move some universal principle of the human frame, and touch a string, to which all mankind have an accord and symphony."

I think that we ignore this problem—the problem of defending our epistemic principles from a common point of view—at our peril. It is not that I think we should come up with a list of bullet points to convince people to employ scientific reason in public discourse. That would be a waste of time. Nor is my point that it is *politically* stupid to dismiss other people's viewpoints in a democratic society. (Although it is. You don't help your message by displaying a haughty indifference to others' challenges.) My point is that defending some of our epistemic principles, our faith in reason, is required by some of our other principles. Hume's point, in alluding to what he also sometimes called "the principle of humanity" was that the ideal of civility requires us to find common currency with those with whom we must discuss practical matters. More recent political philosophers like Rawls and Habermas have seen this ideal as a key component of a functioning liberal democracy. In this view, democracies aren't simply organizing a struggle for power between competing interests; democratic politics isn't war by other means. Democracies are, or should be, spaces of reasons.

So one reason we should take the project of defending our epistemic principles seriously is that the ideal of civility demands it. But there is also another, even deeper, reason. We need to justify our epistemic principles from a common point of view because we need shared epistemic principles in order to even have a common point of view. Without a common background of standards against which we measure what counts as a reliable source of information, or a reliable method of inquiry, and what doesn't, we won't be able *to agree on the facts*, let alone values. Indeed, this is precisely the situation we seem to be headed toward in the United States. We live isolated in our separate bubbles of information culled from sources that only reinforce our prejudices and never challenge our basic assumptions. No wonder that—as in the debates over evolution or what to include in textbooks illustrate—we so often fail to reach agreement over the history and physical structure of the world itself. No wonder joint action grinds to a halt. When you can't agree on your principles of evidence and rationality, you can't agree on the facts. And if you can't agree on the facts, you can hardly agree on what to do in the face of the facts.

Put simply, we need an epistemic common currency because we often have to decide, jointly, what to do in the face of disagreement. Sometimes we can accomplish this, in a democratic society, by voting. But we can't decide every issue that way, and we certainly can't decide on our epistemic principles—which methods and sources are *actually* rationally worthy of trust—by voting. We need some forms of common currency before we get to the voting booth. And that is one reason we need to resist skepticism about reason: we need to be able to give reasons for why some standards of reasons—some epistemic principles—should be part of that currency and some not.

Yet this very fact—the fact that a civil democratic society requires a common currency of shared epistemic principles—should give us hope that we can answer the skeptical challenge. Even if, as the skeptic says, we can't defend the truth of our principles without circularity, we might still be able to show that some are better than others. Observation and experiment, for example, aren't just good because they are reliable means to the truth. They are valuable because almost everyone can appeal to them. They have roots in our natural instincts, as Hume might have said. If so, then perhaps we can hope to give reasons for our epistemic principles. Such reasons will be "merely" practical, but reasons—reasons for reason, as it were—all the same.

OCTOBER 2, 2011

ON CITIZENSHIP

The Morality of Migration

—Seyla Benhabib

I<small>N ANNOUNCING THE DEPARTMENT OF HOMELAND SECURITY'S</small> policy directive on June 15 stating that undocumented migrant youths who meet certain conditions would no longer be deported, President Obama said that "It was the right thing to do." What he did not say was whether he meant "the right thing" legally or morally.

Obviously, he considered the action to be legal, even though this invocation of his administration's power drew strong criticism from many, including Supreme Court Justice Antonin Scalia. But the president's grounds for believing it moral were much less clear.

This should come as no surprise: the morality and politics of migration are among the most divisive issues in much of the world. In the United States, discussions of immigration flow seamlessly into matters of national security, employment levels, the health of the American economy, and threats to a presumptive American national identity and way of life. Much the same is true in Europe. Not a week goes by without a story of refugees from Africa or Asia perishing while trying to arrive at the shores of the European Union.

Nor are such developments restricted to the resource-rich countries of the Northern Hemisphere. The United Arab Emirates, Kuwait, Singapore, Israel and Jordan are countries with the *highest percentage share* of migrants among their total population, while the United States, the Russian Federation, Germany, Saudi Arabia, Canada and France lead in the *actual number* of international migrants. Migrations are now global, challenging many societies in many parts of the world.

Whereas from 1910 to 2012, the world's population increased slightly more than fourfold, from 1.6 billion to more than 7 billion, the number of people living in countries other than their own as migrants increased nearly sevenfold, from roughly 33 million to more than 200 million.

Migrations pit two moral and legal principles, foundational to the modern state system, against each other. On one hand, the human right of individuals to move across borders whether for economic, personal or professional reasons or to seek asylum and refuge is guaranteed by Articles 13 and 14 of the 1948 Universal Declaration of Human Rights. On the other hand, Article 21 of the declaration recognizes a basic right to self-government, stipulating that "the will of the people shall be the basis of the authority of government." Under the current regime of states, that fundamental right includes control over borders as well as determining *who* is to be a citizen as distinguished from a resident or an alien.

The international system straddles these dual principles but it has not been able to reconcile them. The irony of global developments is that while state sovereignty in economic, military, and technological domains is eroded and national borders have become more porous, they are still policed to keep out aliens and intruders. The migrant's body has become the symbolic site upon which such contradictions are enacted.

Why not advocate a "world without borders" then? From a moral point of view, no child *deserves* to be born on one side of the border rather than another, and it is deeply antithetical to our moral principles to punish individuals for what they cannot help being or doing. Punishment implies responsibility and accountability for one's actions and choices; clearly, children who through their parents' choices end up on one side of the border rather than another cannot be penalized for these choices.

A strong advocate of the right to self-government might retort that rewarding certain children for the wrongs committed by their parents, in this case illegal immigration, by legalizing undocumented youths is illogical as well as immoral and that "the right thing to do" would be to deport *all* undocumented migrants—parents and children alike. Apart from the sheer impracticality of this solution, its advocates seem to consider undocumented "original entry" into a country as the analog of "original sin" that no amount of subsequent behavior and atonement can alter.

But such punitive rigor unfairly conflates the messy and often inadvertent reasons that lead one to become an undocumented migrant with no criminal intent to break the law.

If conditions in a person's native country so endanger his life and well-being and he becomes willing to risk illegality in order to survive, his right to survival, from a moral point of view, carries as much weight as does the new country's claim to control borders against migrants. Immanuel Kant, therefore, called the moral claim to seek refuge or respite in the lands of another, a "universal right of hospitality," provided that the intentions of the foreigner upon arriving on foreign lands were peaceful. Such a right, he argued, belonged to each human being placed on this planet who had to share the earth with others.

Even though morally the right to hospitality is an individual right, the socioeconomic and cultural causes of migrations are for the most part collective. Migrations occur because of economic, environmental, cultural and historical "push" and "pull" factors. "We are here," say migrants, "because in effect you were there." "We did not cross the border; the border crossed us."

We do have special obligations to our neighbors, as opposed to moral obligations to humanity at large, if, for example, our economy has devastated theirs; if our industrial output has led to environmental harm or if our drug dependency has encouraged the formation of transnational drug cartels.

These claims of interdependence require a third moral principle—

in addition to the right of universal hospitality and the right to self-government—to be brought into consideration: *associative obligations* among peoples arising through historical factors.

States cannot ignore such associative obligations. Migration policies, though they are often couched in nation-centric terms, always have transnational causes and consequences. It is impossible to address Mexican migration into the United States, for example, without considering the decades-long dependency of the rich California agricultural fields upon the often undocumented and unorganized labor of Mexican workers, some of whose children have now grown up to become "Dreamers" (so named after the Development, Relief, and Education for Alien Minors Act introduced to Congress in 2001). Among the three million students who graduate from United States high schools, 65,000 are undocumented.

The United States owes these young people a special duty of hospitality, not only because we, as a society, have benefited from the circumstances under which their parents entered this country, but also because they have formed strong affiliations with this society through being our friends, students, neighbors and coworkers. In a liberal-democratic society the path to citizenship must follow along these associative ties through which an individual shows him or herself to be capable and worthy of citizenship.

Migratory movements are sites of imperfect justice in that they bring into play the individual right to freedom of movement, the universal right to hospitality and the right of collectives to self-government as well as specific associative moral obligations. These rights cannot always be easily reconciled. Furthermore, international law does not as yet recognize a "human right to citizenship" for migrants, and considers this a sovereign prerogative of individual states. Nonetheless, the responsible politician is the one who acts with a lucid understanding of the necessity to balance these principles rather than giving in to a punitive rigorism that would deny, in Thomas Jefferson's words, "the right which nature has given to all men of departing from [and I would add, from joining with] the country in which choice, not chance has placed them" (1774).

Whether or not President Obama considered all these moral aspects of the matter, his handling of this issue shows that he acted as a "responsible politician," and not opportunistically as some of his critics charged. It was "the right thing to do."

JULY 29, 2012

What Do We Owe Each Other?

—Aaron James Wendland

T HE THOUSANDS OF REFUGEES WHO CONTINUE TO ARRIVE IN Europe each day face barriers: not only physical barriers—walls, fences, barbed wire—but an even deeper resistance, in the nationalism and xenophobia bubbling up across the Continent.

A handful of recent events—Islamic State attacks in Istanbul, Paris and elsewhere, as well as the mass assault of women in Cologne, Germany, on New Year's Eve—continue to feed a deep-seated and often irrational fear of the "other." And then there is the debate about refugees coming to the United States, where a nationalist sentiment has also emerged, often in the rhetoric of certain presidential candidates.

Now, in Germany and elsewhere, doors are closing. But what are the potential consequences of this resistance to outsiders, to those in need? Is it justified? Do we owe the suffering and dispossessed something more, if we are to call ourselves ethical beings?

Few philosophers confronted questions like these more directly than Emmanuel Levinas. Born into a Jewish family in Kaunas, Lithuania, in 1906, Levinas moved to France in 1923 and studied philosophy in Germany under Edmund Husserl and Martin Heidegger in the late 1920s. Levinas made a name for himself in the 1930s as one of the first interpreters and defenders of Husserl's and Heidegger's phenomenology in France, but his commitment to and understanding of phenomenology's often arcane search for the meaning of being was transformed during the Second World War. Levinas was drafted into the French Army in 1939. He was taken prisoner by the Nazis in 1940. And while his status as an officer saved him from being sent to the concentration camps, all the members of his immediate family were killed by the Nazis for their Jewish faith and ancestry.

After the war, Levinas's abiding concern was to describe the concrete source of ethical relations between human beings: our ability to respond to the wants and needs of others.

The epigraph to Levinas's *Otherwise Than Being* reads: "To the memory of those who were closest among the six million assassinated by the National Socialists, and of the millions upon millions of all confessions and all nations, victims of the same hatred of the other man, the same anti-semitism." The book that follows is a profound meditation on the essence of exclusion. It is also an uncompromising account of a basic hospitality that constitutes our humanity. And Levinas's extensive body of work has much to teach us about the nature and danger of nationalism as well as the necessity of welcoming and protecting vulnerable human beings.

Nationalism is the result of identification and differentiation and it follows from the similarities and differences we see between ourselves and others. As an American, you share the same upbringing with many of your fellow citizens. Your background is different than that of most Britons or Italians. And it is partially by recognizing the traits you share with Americans and then distinguishing them from citizens of other states that you develop your sense of identity. But as we know from history, this identity building, taken to extremes, can often lead to horrible things.

Levinas traces the roots of virulent nationalism to the sharp distinctions we draw between "same" and "other." And while identification and differentiation enables the formation of personal identity, it can also result in hostility when the traits we use to distinguish ourselves from others are totalized and taken as absolute. "Totalization" occurs when members of one group take a feature of another group to be both definitive of that group and all members in it. Generalizations like "Americans are outgoing," "Brits are reserved" and "Italians are passionate" are often unfairly applied to individual Americans, Britons or Italians. And negative stereotypes such as "Jews are greedy," "Blacks are dangerous" and "Muslims are terrorists" have a history of leading to unjust aggression against members of those communities. In each of these examples, we reduce others to a simple or single category that distinguishes "them" from "us" in an absolute way. And this reduction often produces an allergic reaction to others; a reaction exemplified by the rush to build fences around Europe to keep Afghan, Iraqi and Syrian refugees out.

Levinas's antihistamine for our allergic reactions involves three things: an appeal to the "infinity" in human beings, a detailed description of face-to-face encounters and an account of a basic hospitality that constitutes humanity.

Infinity is Levinas's technical term for the idea that other people are always more than our categories can capture. You may be a British Anglican from the Midlands, but you're much more than that. You are a father, a son and a husband. You have black hair, blue eyes and a graying beard. You have political opinions and controversial beliefs about the beginning of the world. And so on, ad infinitum.

Similarly, a Syrian refugee may be Muslim, but she's much more than that! She is a mother, a daughter and a wife. She has black hair, brown eyes and a sharp jaw-line. She has political opinions and controversial beliefs about the beginning of the world. And so on, ad infinitum. By calling attention to this infinity in human beings, Levinas was trying to show us that our identifications and differentiations always fail as adequate descriptions of others. And he aims to interrupt our totalizing and xenophobic tendencies by indicating the irreducible humanity of other human beings.

Concretely, the irreducible humanity of other human beings is found in the face. Faces confront us directly and immediately and they refuse typologies. Levinas indicates the irreducibility of others by speaking of God's presence in the face, but his account of the face also illustrates another aspect of human beings: vulnerability. The face is naked, exposed, and open to attack. It is hungry and thirsty. And it seeks protection and nourishment. Levinas invokes the stranger, the widow and the orphan as examples of deprivation. We could also add asylum seekers and embattled exiles as acute cases of suffering. However, Levinas's general account of vulnerability shows us how hospitality in the face of another's need constitutes individual human beings and bespeaks a humanity that precedes and is more fundamental than the establishment of all national boundaries.

Hospitality, according to Levinas, involves curtailing our enjoyment of the world when confronted with another's wants. It is exemplified by the act of welcoming another into our home and sharing our possessions. Welcoming and sharing with others determines who and what we are as specific human beings. Levinas expresses this idea in a discussion of subjectivity in which the self is described as a host and hostage to others. We are hosts to others because welcoming them into our world is a precondition for a relation of identification and differentiation between us. And we are hostages because our personal identity is determined by how we respond to the demands others place upon us.

For instance, your identity as an Italian high school teacher is achieved with your recognition and response to the fact that others want an education. Likewise, a Syrian man's status as a trafficker of refugees is possible via his recognition and response to an exile's need for safe passage across the sea. With these examples we discover that our place in a distinct human community is based on our ability to respond to the wants and needs of others. Yet Levinas shows us that hospitality not only determines our identities in specific communities but is also the mark of humanity—hospitality is the basis of human community as such.

The existence of distinct human communities presupposes our ability to welcome and share our property with others. "To recognize the other," Levinas wrote in *Totality and Infinity*, "is to come to him across the world of possessed things, but at the same time to estab-

lish, by gift, community and universality." Once our enjoyment of
the world has been questioned by another's need, hospitality estab-
lishes human community in the act of giving and with the creation
of a common tongue. Language, Levinas wrote in his work, is universal because it is the very passage from the individual to the general, because it offers things that are mine to the other. To speak is
to make the world common, to create commonplaces. Language does
not refer to the generality of concepts, but lays the foundations for
a possession in common. It abolishes the inalienable property of
enjoyment. The world in discourse is no longer what it is in separation, in the being at home with oneself where everything is given to
me; it is what I give: the communicable, the thought, the universal.

While the creation of a common tongue is the basis of human community, language also allows us to label others and thus explicitly
identify and distinguish our selves from them. This facilitates our
tendency to overlook a face in need and see a "Syrian" or "Muslim"
that is not like me. The foundation of a human community also raises
the question of "other others" whereby any face-to-face encounter
may be interrupted by the face of another. We are asked, in other
words, to share our possessions with *all* human beings. Levinas sees
this request as an infinite but impossible responsibility, since we
could give what we have to anyone, but we do not have enough to give
to all. In the face of this impossible responsibility we require justice:
the systematic organization and distribution of resources amongst
human beings. And from here we are not far from the formation of
nation states with rigid identities and physical boundaries and the
barbed-wire resistance with which we began.

Although we seem to have come full circle, Levinas has taught
us that our responsibility for others is the foundation of all human
communities, and that the very possibility of living in a meaningful
human world is based on our ability to give what we can to others.
And since welcoming and sharing are the foundation upon which
all communities are formed, no amount of inhospitable nationalism
can be consistently defended when confronted with the suffering of

other human beings. "In the relationship between same and other, my welcoming of the other is," as Levinas puts it, "the *ultimate* fact." It is the hospitality of humanity, or a peace prior to all hostility. And in this primary peace, in this basic welcoming of refugees, Levinas reminds us that "things figure not as what one *builds* but as what one *gives*."

JANUARY 18, 2016

Can Refugees Have Human Rights?

—Omri Boehm

BERLIN—THE PUBLIC DISCUSSION SURROUNDING THE REFUGEE crisis has been saturated in recent weeks with allusions to Germany's past. Joachim Gauck, the president of Germany, set the tone in late August when he spoke of "Dunkeldeutschland vs. Helles Deutschland"—Dark Germany vs. Bright Germany—the subtext was old Nazi Germany vs. the new Democratic one; and a front-page headline of the German weekly *Die Zeit* from September speaks for itself: "Wie 1989" ("Like 1989"). What perhaps does deserve comment is that all direct 1989 allusions are indirect allusions to 1933.

International media shared similar historical sensibilities. In September *The New York Times* reported that "the treatment of the migrants" evoked "memories of Europe's darkest hour," and the Israeli daily *Yediot Aharonot* used the headline "Again on the Platform" on its front-page, pointing out that some of the train stations in which the refugees now assemble are the same ones from which Jews had been deported or sent to camps.

Up to a point, such historical allusions are not only natural, but also adequate. After all, Germany's Asylum Law was itself constructed with a nod to past persecutions, as National Socialist politics forced millions of Europeans, Jews and others, to seek asylum overseas. Nevertheless, extensive attention to Germany's fascist past in this context can also be misleading. To understand the political background of the refugee crisis, we must turn our gaze elsewhere;

in fact, in the opposite direction. The crisis at hand confronts us with a predicament of modern political thought—modern liberalism even. It is a problem that we have successfully repressed but that now returns with a vengeance, namely the inadequacy of the lingo of human rights.

Consider this proposition:

> *We hold these truths to be self-evident, that all men are created equal, that they are endowed by their Creator with certain unalienable Rights, that among these are Life, Liberty and the Pursuit of Happiness.*

Why do we believe in the existence of these "self-evident" truths? According to the Declaration of Independence, our inalienable human rights were given to us by our "Creator"—earlier in the text the founding fathers had appealed to the "station" given to us by "God's Nature"—but from the perspective of modern political science this appeal to God is, of course, futile. Germany's Basic Law refrains from turning to God as a grounding principle, but it does so in a characteristically modern way—that is by deceiving itself that simply disregarding the Almighty would be sufficient to achieving secular humanist ideals.

The truth is that we have never managed to vouch for human rights in sensible modern terms. One common strategy has been to appeal to nature rather than to God—on this view, human beings have inalienable *natural* rights—but in order to accept this alternative one must ascribe to nature qualities that science tells us it doesn't have. (Blind evolution, the source of anything we might call human nature, certainly cannot be the source of normatively binding inalienable rights.)

A more promising alternative has been to follow Kant in appealing to reason instead of nature or God; that is to claim that the rights of humanity are grounded in our capacity for rational deliberation. However, in order to uphold this position one must defend a metaphysical conception of reason—an account of rationality that transcends its reduction back to blind naturalistic explanations—and while Kant himself indeed defended such a metaphysics, current political thinking prides itself for being "post-metaphysical." John Rawls's dominant formulation of justice is famously "political, not metaphysical," and the eminent German philosopher Jürgen Habermas recently reaffirmed his early slogan, according to which "we have no alternative to post-metaphysical thinking."

While it may well be true that we do not have such an alternative, it is also true, to speak with Kant, that "every theory of justice must . . . contain a metaphysics, and without the theory of justice there is no theory of the state." We're trying to make room for the refugees somewhere between Habermas's proposition and Kant's. Modern political thinkers can meaningfully speak of the state as an instrument for defending the *interests* of its *citizens*. When they speak of the state as defending justice, or universal human rights, they are missing the necessary concepts.

Consequently, it has been more comfortable in the present context to appeal, consciously or not, to the *extra* commitments generated by the German past. This evades the more general, but urgent question of the refugees' actual political claim. Here lies a subtle but pernicious fallacy: While it is true that German history generates special commitments to human rights, the problem is precisely that we do not know how to think of these rights in political terms.

At no moment was the inadequacy of our language clearer than in Angela Merkel's recent summer news conference. "Universal citizen rights," she said, "have so far been closely connected with Europe and its history"; fail to answer to the refugees, she continued, "and this close connection with universal citizen rights will be destroyed." If the chancellor wanted to address the refugees, she should have probably said human, not citizen, rights. What she did say was all that she could politically vouch for, but it wasn't relevant to the refugees whose standing is precisely of noncitizens. Subconsciously, Merkel must have been struggling with her reduction of humans to citizens, for she repeatedly insisted on prefacing "citizen rights" with the adjective "universal." But "universal citizen rights" is in fact a contradiction in terms: universality is a property of the set of all humans, whereas the exclusive set of citizens is one to which the refugees do not belong.

Unfortunately, we cannot blame Angela Merkel. The fact that her contradictory reference to universal citizen-rights went virtually unnoticed is a sign that we have all managed to internalize the reduction of humans into citizens. That's the reduction with which Europe is now facing the refugees.

Most of the time, this quandary is easily contained. "We" are all citizens of states; "our" rights are protected, so the metaphysical confusion remains an academic problem (in the derogatory sense of the term). But, clearly, under some circumstances an academic metaphysical question can make a comeback as an urgent political one.

In a short article from 1943, "We Refugees," Hannah Arendt warned that the one fate more dangerous in the world than being a Jew is being a human being. "If we should start telling the truth that we are nothing but Jews," she wrote, "it would mean that we expose ourselves to the fate of human beings who . . . are nothing but human beings." It is impossible to imagine a stance more dangerous than this, "since we actually live in a world in which human beings as such have ceased to exist for quite a while."

Her response to the situation is best captured by a term she coined, "the right to have rights," and reflections on the topic have been footnotes to Arendt ever since. But Arendt knew well that the "right to have rights" can only be an articulation of the problem, not the statement of a solution, which would require to think beyond the horizon of familiar political thinking. Among other things, it is likely that this knowledge encouraged Arendt's break with the Zionist movement. Whereas she wanted to address the Jewish refugee crisis by learning to address the Jewish refugees as humans, Zionism preferred to fall back on the old political categories—to secure the Jews' rights by making them citizens of their own nation state.

That we still haven't found the adequate political categories to address human beings is clear from *Die Zeit*'s aforementioned headline, "Like 1989." This headline's function, I suppose, was to convey something about the historical weight of the situation, and to point out that in order to deal with it Germany would have to change. However, in order to properly address the refugees Germany would have to undergo a change whose dynamics are exactly *unlike* those of 1989. The reunification of Germany did not challenge existing political categories. On the contrary, as a reunification not just of east and west but of nation and state it was much more a reaffirmation of the familiar politics. Therefore, despite its historical momentous magnitude, there was nothing in Germany's reunification to embarrass political thinking—as the present crisis now does—by exposing our inability to address the rights of those who are nothing but human.

Arguably, in order to address the refugee crisis not only would Germany have to change, but so would political philosophy itself.

OCTOBER 19, 2015

Dependents of the State

—Amia Srinivasan

O F ALL THE SINS TO WHICH AN AMERICAN CAN SUCCUMB, THE worst may be dependence on the state.

Think back for a moment to the two biggest missteps in the 2012 presidential election: Mitt Romney's dismissal of the "47 percent" of people "dependent on the government," and President Obama's "you didn't build that," intended to remind American business owners that their success wasn't all due to smarts and hard work, but also to the roads and bridges built by others, the government-sponsored research that produced the Internet and the "unbelievable American system we have that allowed you to thrive." Both statements came off as stinging insults directed at large groups of voters, and both were seen as tactical disasters.

Conservatives champion an ethos of hard work and self-reliance, and insist—heroically ignoring the evidence—that people's life chances are determined by the exercise of those virtues. Liberals, meanwhile, counter the accusation that their policies encourage dependence by calling the social welfare system a "safety net," there only to provide a "leg up" to people who have "fallen on hard times." Unlike gay marriage or abortion, issues that divide left from right, everyone, no matter where they lie on the American political spectrum, loathes and fears state dependence. If dependence isn't a moral failing to be punished, it's an addictive substance off which people must be weaned.

Like so many politically important notions, the concept of "state dependence" purports to do no more than describe the way things are but contains within it a powerful and suspect moral judgment. What is it for one thing to depend on another? Put most simply, x depends on y when it's the case that x wouldn't exist if y didn't exist. More subtly, x depends on y when it's the case that x wouldn't be in the state it is in without y's being in the state it is in. Americans who collect food stamps, Medicaid, unemployment insurance or welfare checks are said to be dependent on the state because the lives they lead would be different (indeed, worse) if the state did not provide these services—at least without their working harder and longer. Despite the symbolic resonance of Ronald Reagan's fictitious "welfare queen," most of the people who rely on means-tested social services either cannot work, have been recently laid off thanks to the economic downturn, or are already working in poorly paid, immiserating jobs. Of the 32 million American children currently being raised in low-income families—families who cannot afford to meet their basic needs—nearly half have parents who are in full-time, year-round jobs.

But if the poor are dependent on the state, so, too, are America's rich. The extraordinary accumulation of wealth enjoyed by the socioeconomic elite—in 2007, the richest 1 percent of Americans accounted for about 24 percent of all income—simply wouldn't be possible if the United States wasn't organized as it is. Just about every aspect of America's economic and legal infrastructure—the laissez-faire governance of the markets; a convoluted tax structure that has hedge fund managers paying less than their office cleaners; the promise of state intervention when banks go belly-up; the legal protections afforded to corporations as if they were people; the enormous subsidies given to corporations (in total, about 50 percent more than social services spending); electoral funding practices that allow the wealthy to buy influence in government—allows the rich to stay rich and get richer. In primitive societies, people can accumulate only as much stuff as they can physically gather and hold on to. It's only in "advanced" societies that the state provides the means to socioeconomic domination by a tiny minority. "The poverty of our century is unlike that of any other," the writer John Berger said about the twentieth century, though he might equally have said it of this one: "It is not, as poverty was before, the result of natural scarcity, but of a set of priorities imposed upon the rest of the world by the rich."

The irony isn't only that the poor are condemned for being dependent on the state while the rich are not. It's also that the rich get so much more out of their dependence on the state than the poor. Without the support of the state, poor people's quality of life would certainly drop, but only by degrees: their lives would go from bad to worse. Take the state's assistance away from the rich, however, and their lives would take a serious plunge in comfort. No wonder rich people are on the whole conservative: the most ferocious defenders of the status quo are usually those who are most dependent on the system.

So, the question should not be why Americans loathe and fear dependence on the state, but rather, why do Americans loathe and fear some forms of state dependence but not others? Why is state dependence condemned when evinced by the poor, but tolerated, even unrecognized, when enjoyed by the rich? What justifies this double standard?

Here's one possible answer. While the rich are dependent on the state, the state is in turn dependent on them. The elite might enjoy levels of comfort and prosperity that the majority can scarcely imagine, but it's no more than they deserve: they are, after all, the "job creators," the engines of economic growth. The poor, by contrast, are just a drag on the system.

Even if it were granted that some sort of market-driven economy is in the public interest (or, to adapt Churchill's quip about democracy, that it is the worst option except for all the rest), the case would remain to be made that the sort of market-driven economy we have in the United States serves that interest. Indeed, this case would be especially difficult to argue at a time when we are living with the effects of an economic recession caused by the wealthiest among us, the cost of which is being paid largely by the poor and middle classes—in the loss of their homes and jobs, but also in the form of tax-dollar-driven bank bailouts. The orthodoxy is that inequality is the necessary price of economic growth, but research strongly suggests that inequality of income causes economic instability and slows overall growth, and that the rapid rise in inequality in the last few decades is to blame for the current economic recession.

The case for our current arrangements is still harder to make once one acknowledges the argument, put forward by Richard G. Wilkinson and Kate Pickett in their book *The Spirit Level*, that economic inequality has a negative multiplier effect, making poor people in very unequal societies like the United States' worse off—in terms of mortality, education, imprisonment rates, social mobility and so on—than they would be in more equal societies, even if they were just as poor. In other words, when the rich get richer, it doesn't just make them better off: it makes everyone else worse off.

Neither will it help anyone trying to make the case for the American way to compare the United States with other developed nations, where the average citizen is healthier, happier, better educated and enjoys more social mobility. Here we have a real-life chance to apply the political philosopher John Rawls's test for a just society, what he called the "veil of ignorance." If you didn't know what kind of person you were going to be—your gender, family circumstances, ethnicity—which of the developed nations would you choose to be born into? Would you be hoping to have a home, a job and good medical care? Would you like to be able to clothe, feed and educate your children someday? In that case you'd be foolish to pick the United States. You'd be better off choosing Norway, or any one of a number of countries that have better evened the balance between rich and poor state dependence with higher taxes and greater investment in social services.

Here's another answer one might give when asked why we should tolerate state dependence on the part of the rich but not of the poor: the rich earn the benefits they accrue from the state, while the poor get something for nothing. Sure, the rich might have needed the state's help to get rich, but they have also had to work for their success; the poor can just sit back and wait for the welfare check to arrive. But this is to ignore the fact that most rich Americans didn't earn their wealth: they were given it, either directly through inheritance from their parents, or only slightly less directly through their access to elite secondary and higher education.

Despite the sustaining myth of American meritocracy, one of the most significant determinants of where a child will end up on the socioeconomic ladder is which rung his or her parents occupied. (This reminds me of a story I heard from a fellow philosopher, Jason Stanley, about a guy he met in a bar, who explained that he had lost his job in the economic downturn but that he had pulled himself up by his own bootstraps and relaunched his career as an entrepreneur. If he could do it, he said, anyone could. It turned out that he got his start-up capital from his father, a venture capitalist.) While middle-class and rich children no doubt have to burn the midnight oil to get into Harvard and Yale, they mostly end up at those places because of the huge advantages that wealth confers in the context of a failing public education system. Liberals and conservatives alike pin their hopes on education as the "great leveler," but the data tells us that the American education system magnifies the advantages of wealth and the disadvantages of poverty. The unearned advantages enjoyed by the children of rich parents dwarf the sums given to welfare recipients.

To claim that the rich earn what they have also ignores the fact that most of the people who depend on social services do work—only they work for their poverty rather than their wealth. Many of them depend on the state because the jobs available to them—the ones produced by the much-vaunted job creators—don't pay enough to allow them to live. Thus welfare payments to the poor effectively operate as yet another kind of corporate subsidy, making up for the difference between the increasing cost of living and declining real wages. California taxpayers alone pay $86 million annually to subsidize Walmart via state assistance to its employees and their children.

America's socioeconomic elite has been successful in part because it has been allowed to get away with the argument that its success has nothing to do with the state: with a little elbow grease, the rich seem to say, the poor can be just like them. And the poor may all be too ready to agree. "Socialism never took root in America," John Steinbeck said, "because the poor see themselves not as an exploited proletariat but as temporarily embarrassed millionaires." It's a myth dear to the American psyche, the myth that Obama tried to pierce when he insisted that "you didn't build that." And while Obama might have retained the presidency, Romney and his ideological comrades have won, it seems, the long fight against "state dependence."

The tax bill passed by Congress just in time to avert the "fiscal cliff," making the Bush tax cuts permanent for households under the $450,000 threshold, will cost the government $3.6 trillion over the next decade, as compared with the $4.5 trillion it would have cost if the Bush tax cuts had stayed in place. That isn't a lot in savings—and isn't enough to allow the government to continue funding social services at current levels. In the short term, America's rich, those earning above $450,000, will see their tax bills increase. But in the long term, it's America's poor who will be paying. Under the terms of the latest deal, the poor will enjoy a temporary extension on refundable tax credits; at the same time, the Bush-era estate tax cut, which will cost about $375 billion over the next decade as compared with the Clinton-era estate tax policy and will benefit only millionaires and their children, was made permanent. Now the once unthinkable sequester will almost surely go into effect on March 1, bringing $85 billion in budget cuts. The Democrats are scrambling to replace some of the most drastic of those spending cuts—to primary and secondary education, vaccination programs, medical research and environmental protection—with increased taxes on the rich, but the Republicans aren't budging. The sequester will almost certainly come into force by the end of this week and is estimated to cost 700,000 jobs. Meanwhile, of the 47 percent that Romney lambasted for not paying taxes and scrounging off the state, 7,000 are millionaires.

We are all dependents of the state, not just the poor, and it's certainly not the poor who benefit most from their dependence. The question isn't who is dependent on the state but whether the current political settlement treats everyone with fairness and dignity: whether the odds are stacked in particular people's favor, whether some are able to prosper only at the expense of others, whether everyone has an equal opportunity to make a decent human life. That we may not like the answers to these questions is the very reason we should ask them.

FEBRUARY 26, 2013

Is Voting Out of Self-Interest Wrong?

—*Gary Gutting*

IT IS A STAPLE OF AMERICAN POLITICS TO CRITICIZE THOSE WHO vote simply out of their own self-interest. Democrats often denounce the superrich for supporting candidates who promise to lower their taxes; Republicans frequently say workers opposed to free trade put their job security over the nation's economic health. In particular, it's easy to think of elections as primarily a clash between conflicting economic interests.

But political scientists disagree. True, the richer you are the more likely you are to vote Republican, and the poorer you are the more likely you are to vote Democratic. But in the last presidential election, more than 40 percent of those with incomes over $200,000 a year voted Democratic, and more than 30 percent with incomes under $25,000 voted Republican. Political ideology was a much stronger factor than economic self-interest. Independent of income, 87 percent of those falling into the category "steadfast conservatives" voted Republican in 2012, while 90 percent of "solid liberals" voted Democratic. (But this election's focus on middle-class wage losses might increase self-interested voting.)

The statistical issue, however, is only about what factors have the most influence on political behavior. People do, nonetheless, often vote out of self-interest. My question is when, if ever, is it *right* to vote simply for the sake of your own self-interest?

Some philosophers argue that self-interested voting is always wrong and that we should vote instead for what we see as best for society as a whole (the "common good"). There may be cases where my self-interest happens to coincide with the common good. A tax cut or a minimum wage from which I profit may be good for the economy as a whole. But it's naïve to think that's true of every tax deduction and credit that serves a personal or corporate self-interest. It's tempting, therefore, to think that I'm wrong to vote my self-interest when it's opposed to the common good.

But what about the poor who vote for welfare programs that benefit them? Such programs may also benefit society as a whole, but there's no reason to think they always will. Suppose the benefits to the poor will be more than offset by losses for those who are better off. Might it still be right for the poor to try to better their lot? Here we need to distinguish between what people *want* and what they *need*. Suppose, for example, the poor are seeking adequate medical care, funded by a surtax on incomes over a million dollars. It seems clear that in such a case the poor would be right to vote for their self-interest.

But what about the rich? Would it be morally wrong for them to vote against the surtax out of self-interest? We might well answer yes on the grounds that the rich have a duty to help provide the poor with health care if the cost is equivalent to giving up a few meals at fancy restaurants. But can we generalize to the claim that we must always meet others' needs at the expense of satisfying our wants? Such a general principle seems to confuse an ethical obligation with an ethical ideal. It might be *admirable* to always make such sacrifices, but does it make sense to say that we are always morally *obliged* to do so? The issue is similar to that raised by Peter Singer's suggestion that we are ethically required to give up everything except what we need for a minimally decent life and donate our excess income to save those who would otherwise starve to death. In both cases, we may think, we should refuse to make heroic virtue a moral obligation.

Still, we surely have some obligation to give up what we don't need, in order to help those in serious need. Here we might distinguish between modest luxuries—those that might generally be considered rewards for work or business success—and excessive luxuries, which exceed any sensible standard of what we somehow deserve. The idea would be that we are always obligated to sacrifice excessive, but not modest, luxuries to others' needs.

This distinction may provide an answer in principle to the general question of when we must subordinate our self-interest to the needs of others. But it's hard to see it providing much practical guidance. The problem is that almost all of us are likely to see our luxuries as modest compared with the indulgences of those who are *really* rich. A couple who vacation in Europe twice a year and routinely dine at Michelin-starred restaurants may think little of their luxuries when they compare them with those who own private jets, have multiple homes or even own tropical islands. Given degrees of excess that far exceed our own, the dictates of morality have little chance of standing up to our capacity for self-deception.

So far I've been talking about preferring self-interest to others' needs. But there may even be a case for voting out of self-interest when there is no question of anyone's needs. Suppose you vote for government funding of a museum of contemporary art simply because you would enjoy visiting it. Is this ethically wrong? Once again, you might claim that the museum would in fact benefit the community as a whole, since more and more people would come to enjoy art they'd previously had no exposure to, or found repugnant.

But suppose in fact people would not come to enjoy the art, and on the whole there would be a higher level of unhappiness because of the museum. Why should your vote be determined by what a bunch of philistines would think? It might seem that I could rightly vote for my own self-interest when I have good reason to think that others should share that interest, even if I know they won't.

It seems that, contrary to what many think, self-interested voting is sometimes ethically justified. But the question of whether we can be morally justified in putting our own interests over the interests of others—and if so, when—needs a lot more thought. I invite readers to share their own answers to this question, and look forward to reading comments that shed further light on the issue.

MARCH 31, 2016

ON VIOLENCE

Philosophizing with Guns

—Simone Gubler

IN A MATTER OF MONTHS, THE OFFICES, LIBRARIES AND CLASS-
rooms where I work, study and teach at the University of Texas at
Austin will become "concealed carry zones"—areas in which people
with concealed handgun licenses may carry their weapons. The
"campus carry" bill that brought about this situation represents
a fiftieth anniversary gift of sorts from Texas state legislators. For
when the law comes into effect on August 1, it will be fifty years to the
day since a heavily armed young man ascended the clock tower on
campus and shot forty-five people, killing fourteen of them, in the
first mass shooting at an American college.

Following the signing of the bill into law last June, university
administrators began to carve my daily environment into armed and
unarmed zones: Guns in classrooms? *Yes.* Guns at sporting events?
No. Appalled by this spectacle, I proceeded to do the two things that
I have been trained to do as a philosopher: I debated with my colleagues and I wrote a critical essay. Then, having had my little scream
into the abyss, I experienced a period of peace.

But now, as August 1 approaches, I find myself drawn back to the
problems, both practical and philosophical, that are posed by campus carry. It seems to me that if we care about the future of American education, we must inquire after those things of value that stand
at risk on armed campuses. The campus carry bill is, after all, not a

peculiarly Texan piece of legislation. It has precedent in other states and, given the political climate, may be emulated elsewhere.

Much of the debate around campus carry has focused on physical risk—on the enhanced likelihood of suicide, domestic violence, assault or accidental discharge. Indeed, it was advice concerning the risk of accidental discharge that persuaded university administrators that it would be better to have students wear their guns into classrooms than to have them deposit them in lockers outside. The working group assigned by the president of our university with the task of providing recommendations about the implementation of campus carry determined that: "A policy that increases the number of instances in which a handgun must be stored multiplies the danger of an accidental discharge." So now, people who cannot be trusted to safely transfer their weapons to lockers will instead carry them into spaces of learning.

In order to assess the physical risks of campus carry, we must rely on quantitative studies. But as philosophers, my colleagues and I can speak to some of the less explicit threats that campus carry poses by turning to our own long tradition of the *qualitative* study of violence and its role in human affairs. Consider the classroom, for example. What happens to it when its occupants suspect that someone has brought a gun inside? Campus carry poses a threat to the classroom as a space of discourse and learning even if no concealed carrier ever discharges their gun.

In general, we do not feel apprehension about the presence of strong people in spaces reserved for intellectual debate (although we might in other contexts—a boxing ring, say, or a darkened alley), but we do feel apprehension about the presence of a gun. This is because the gun is not there to contribute to the debate. It exists primarily as a tool for killing and maiming. Its presence tacitly relates the threat of physical harm.

But the gun in the classroom also communicates the dehumanizing attitude to other human beings that belongs to the use of violence. For the use of violence, and of the weapons of violence, is associated with an attitude under which human beings figure as *mere* means, and not as ends in themselves—as inherently valuable. Adapting Simone Weil's characterization of force in her essay, "The Illiad, or the Poem of Force": violence is "that x that turns anybody subjected to it into a thing." When I strap on my gun and head into a public space, I alter the quality of that space. I introduce an object that conveys an attitude in which people figure as things—as obstacles to be overcome, as items to be manipulated, as potential corpses. A gun is an object that carries with it a sense and a potency that is public and that affects those around it, regardless of its wearer's intentions.

We live, as the philosopher Richard Bernstein has observed, in what might be called "The Age of Violence," immersed in a soup of real and fantastic violent imagery. And it is difficult under these conditions of cultural saturation to forswear the correctives that violence appears to offer to itself. But when we arm ourselves and enter a classroom, we prefigure others and ourselves in terms of force, as "things"—and not as equals in speech and thought. And we thereby endanger the humanist values that (along with a fair helping of *verbal* conflict) characterize the conduct of scholarly life at its best.

In addition to these relatively abstract considerations, there remains a need for more concrete philosophical work concerning campus carry—situated work that draws on gender, race and labor theory. We need to ask: What bodies are at greatest risk? What disproportionate harms might the law visit on people of color? What sorts of psychological and physical threats can employees be subjected to in the workplace? And what is the significance of this law for academic freedom?

Finally, those of us who teach on armed campuses will need to confront pedagogical problems. As a philosopher, I work with questions that are challenging, controversial and even upsetting. As a teacher of philosophy, I try to animate these questions for students, and to provide them with the critical tools to pursue independent inquiry.

A few weeks ago, I read Albert Camus's novel *The Stranger* with my students, and we considered the question of suicide—of whether life is worth living. This is an important question (*the* important question, if we are to believe Camus), but it is one that demands sensitive treatment. It is my worst fear that, one day, when teaching problems like these, I will have a Young Werther on my hands. And, to my mind, the normalization of guns on campus enhances the probability of this event. So what are we to do if we want to be responsible teachers?

Perhaps we should abandon the big, morally important questions. Perhaps, when teaching Existentialism, we should steer clear of any material dealing with the meaningfulness or meaninglessness of existence. And perhaps, when we teach contemporary moral issues, we should avoid discussing abortion, race and gun rights. Such a retreat is not inconceivable. In a slideshow on campus carry, prepared by the Faculty Senate at the University of Houston, professors were counseled to "be careful in discussing sensitive topics; to drop certain topics from curriculum; [to] not 'go there' if you sense anger. . . ."

Of course, if we resolve that the most responsible thing to do under campus carry is to avoid topics that are likely to elicit strong feeling, then there is little point in continuing with the academic practice of philosophy. But before we do away with philosophy altogether, let us decide whether there is anything that we can or should do to resist the wider adoption of campus carry policies. And let us resolve, where resistance is unsuccessful, to think carefully about what needs to be done to protect the practice of philosophical inquiry, and our students, from harm.

APRIL 11, 2016

A Crack in the Stoic's Armor

—*Nancy Sherman*

IN A REMARKABLY PRESCIENT MOMENT IN SEPTEMBER 1965, JAMES B. Stockdale, then a senior navy pilot shot down over Vietnam, muttered to himself as he parachuted into enemy hands, "Five years down there at least. I'm leaving behind the world of technology and entering the world of Epictetus." As a departing graduate student at Stanford, Stockdale received a gift of Epictetus's famous *Enchiridion*, a first-century Stoic handbook. The text looked esoteric, but in his long nights aboard the USS *Ticonderoga*, he found himself memorizing its content. Little did he know then that Stoic tonics would become his salvation for seven and a half years as the senior prisoner of war, held under brutal conditions by the North Vietnamese at Hoa Lo prison, the Hanoi Hilton.

Epictetus, who was a slave around the time of Nero, wrote, "Our thoughts are up to us, and our impulses, desires, and aversions—in short, whatever is our doing. . . . Of things that are outside your control, say they are nothing to you."

With these words, Stockdale drew a stripe between what he could and could not control. But he never lost the sense that what he could control was what mattered most and that his survival, even when tortured and in solitary confinement for four years, required constant refortification of his will.

Stockdale's resilience is legendary in the military. And it remains a living example, too, for philosophers, of how you might put into practice ancient Stoic consolations. But for many in the military, taking up Stoic armor comes at a heavy cost.

The Stoic doctrine is essentially about reducing vulnerability. And it starts off where Aristotle leaves off. Aristotle insists that happiness depends to some degree on chance and prosperity. Though the primary component of happiness is virtue—and that, a matter of one's own discipline and effort—realizing virtue in the world goes beyond one's effort. Actions that succeed and relationships that endure and are reciprocal depend upon more than one's own goodness. For the Stoics, this makes happiness far too dicey a matter. And so in their revision, virtue, and virtue alone, is sufficient for happiness. Virtue itself becomes purified, based on reason only, and shorn of ordinary emotions, like fear and grief, that cling to objects beyond our control.

In the military, even those who have never laid eyes on a page of Epictetus, still live as if they have. To suck it up is to move beyond grieving and keep fighting; it is to stare death down in a death-saturated place; it is to face one more deployment after two or three or four already. It is hard to imagine a popular philosophy better suited to deprivation and constant subjection to stressors.

And yet in the more than thirty interviews I conducted with soldiers who have returned from the long current wars, what I heard was the wish to let go of the Stoic armor. They wanted to feel and process the loss. They wanted to register the complex inner moral landscape of war by finding some measure of empathy with their own emotions. One retired army major put it flatly to me, "I've been sucking it up for twenty-five years, and I'm tired of it." For some, like this officer, the war after the war is unrelenting. It is about psychological trauma and multiple suicide attempts, exacerbated by his own sense of shame in not being the Stoic warrior that he thought he could and should be. He went to war to prove himself but came home emasculated.

Still we oversimplify grossly if we view all returning warriors through the lens of pathology and post-traumatic stress. Many soldiers wrestle with what they have seen and done in uniform, even when their conflicts don't rise to the level of acute or chronic psychological trauma. And they feel guilt and shame even when they do no wrong by war's best standards. Some anguish about having interrogated detainees not by torture, but the proper way, by slowly and deliberately building intimacy only in order to exploit it. Others feel shame for going to war with a sense of revenge and for then feeling its venom well up when a sniper guns down their buddy and their own survival depends on the raw desire for payback. They worry that their triumph in coming home alive is a betrayal of battle buddies who didn't make it. And then once home, they worry that their real family is back on the battlefield, and they feel guilt for what feels like a misplaced intimacy.

These feelings of guilt and shame are ubiquitous in war. They are not just responses to committing atrocities or war crimes. They are the feelings good soldiers bear, in part as testament to their moral humanity. And they are feelings critical to shaping soldiers' future lives as civilians. Yet these are feelings blocked off by idealized notions of Stoic purity and strength that leave little room for moral conflict and its painful residue.

One of the more compelling stories I heard was from a former army interrogator, Will Quinn, who had been at Abu Ghraib as part of the "clean-up" act a year after the torture scandal. This young interrogator had not engaged in torture or "enhanced" interrogation techniques: he did not subject detainees to waterboarding, or prolonged stress positions, or extreme sleep or sensory deprivation. Still, what he did do did not sit well with his civilian sensibilities. In one incident that especially bothered him, he showed a detainee a picture of a friend killed by American soldiers in order to get identification of the body. The detainee broke down. Will told me, "When I was going in, I was excited by the prospect of seeing his reaction, because it would make me feel good to know that the bad guy got killed. It was a sense of victory, a bit like Osama Bin Laden being killed. But when you encounter others for whom the death of a friend is a deeply personal loss, you have to humanize the experience."

He offered a striking analogy for what it felt like to be the interrogator he once was: Entering the interrogation cell was a bit like going into a mass with Gregorian chants sung in Latin. It takes place, he said, "in a different universe. . . . War, too, takes place in a different time and space." In essence, he was describing dissociation, or for the Stoics, what amounts to detachment from certain objects so they cannot affect you. Yet for this young interrogator detachment was not ultimately a viable solution: "I know I am the same person who was doing those things. And that's what tears at your soul."

Cicero, a great translator and transmitter of the earliest Greek Stoic texts, records a similar inner struggle. After the loss of his daughter Tullia in childbirth, he turned to Stoicism to assuage his grief. But ultimately he could not accept its terms: "It is not within our power to forget or gloss over circumstances which we believe to be evil. . . . They tear at us, buffet us, goad us, scorch us, stifle us— and you tell us to forget about them?"

Put in the context of today's wars, this could just as easily be a soldier's narrative about the need to put on Stoic armor and the need to take it off.

MAY 30, 2010

Who Needs a Gun?

—Gary Gutting

IN SEPTEMBER, THE NAVY YARD; IN NOVEMBER, A RACIALLY fraught shooting in Michigan and a proposed stand-your-ground law in Ohio; now the first anniversary of the Newtown massacre—there's no avoiding the brutal reality of guns in America. Once again, we feel the need to say something, but we know the old arguments will get us nowhere. What's the point of another impassioned plea or a new subtlety of constitutional law or further complex analyses of statistical data?

Our discussions typically start from the right to own a gun, go on to ask how, if at all, that right should be limited, and wind up with intractable disputes about the balance between the right and the harm that can come from exercising it. I suggest that we could make more progress if each of us asked a more direct and personal question: Should I own a gun?

A gun is a tool, and we choose tools based on their function. The primary function of a gun is to kill or injure people or animals. In the case of people, the only reason I might have to shoot them—or threaten to do so—is that they are immediately threatening serious harm. So a first question about owning a gun is whether I'm likely to be in a position to need one to protect human life. A closely related question is whether, if I were in such a position, the gun would be available and I would be able to use it effectively.

Unless you live in (or frequent) dangerous neighborhoods or have family or friends likely to threaten you, it's very unlikely that you'll need a gun for self-defense. Further, counterbalancing any such need is the fact that guns are dangerous. If I have one loaded and readily accessible in an emergency (and what good is it if I don't?), then there's a nonnegligible chance that it will lead to great harm. A gun at hand can easily push a family quarrel, a wave of depression or a child's curiosity in a fatal direction.

Even when a gun makes sense in principle as a means of self-defense, it may do more harm than good if I'm not trained to use it well. I may panic and shoot a family member coming home late, fumble around and allow an unarmed burglar to take my gun, have a cleaning or loading accident. The NRA rightly sets high standards for gun safety. If those unable or unwilling to meet these standards gave up their guns, there might well be a lot fewer gun owners.

Guns do have uses other than defense against attackers. There may, for example, still be a few people who actually need to hunt to feed their families. But most hunting now is recreational and does not require keeping weapons at home. Hunters and their families would be much safer if the guns and ammunition were securely stored away from their homes and available only to those with licenses during the appropriate season. Target shooting, likewise, does not require keeping guns at home.

Finally, there's the idea that citizens need guns so they can, if need be, oppose the force of a repressive government. Those who think there are current (or likely future) government actions in this country that would require armed resistance are living a paranoid fantasy. The idea that armed American citizens could stand up to our military is beyond fantasy.

Once we balance the potential harms and goods, most of us—including many current gun owners—don't have a good reason to keep guns in their homes. This conclusion follows quite apart from whether we have a right to own guns or what restrictions should be put on this right. Also, the conclusion derives from what makes sense for each of us as individuals and so doesn't require support from contested interpretations of statistical data.

I entirely realize that this line of thought will not convince the most impassioned gun supporters, who see owning guns as fundamental to their way of life. But about 70 million Americans own guns and only about 4 million belong to the NRA, which must include a large number of the most impassioned. So there's reason to think that many gun owners would be open to reconsidering the dangers their weapons pose. Also, almost 30 percent of gun owners don't think that guns make a household safer, and only 48 percent cite protection (rather than hunting, target shooting, etc.) as their main reason for having a gun.

It's one thing to be horrified at gun violence. It's something else to see it as a meaningful threat to your own existence. Our periodic shock at mass shootings and gang wars has little effect on our gun culture because most people don't see guns as a particular threat to them. This is why opposition to gun violence has lacked the intense personal commitment of those who see guns as essential to their safety—or even their self-identity.

I'm not suggesting that opponents of gun violence abandon political action. We need to make it harder to buy guns (through background checks, waiting periods, etc.) both for those with criminal intentions and for law-abiding citizens who have no real need. But on the most basic level, much of our deadly violence occurs because we so often have guns readily available. Their mere presence makes suicide, domestic violence and accidents more likely. The fewer people with guns at hand, the less gun violence.

It's easier to get people to see that they don't want something than that they don't have a right to it. Focusing on the need rather than the right to own a gun, many may well conclude that for them a gun is more a danger than a protection. Those fewer guns will make for a safer country.

DECEMBER 10, 2013

The Freedom of an Armed Society

—Firmin DeBrabander

THE NIGHT OF THE SHOOTINGS AT SANDY HOOK ELEMENTARY School in Newtown, CT, I was in the car with my wife and children, working out details for our eldest son's twelfth birthday the following Sunday—convening a group of friends at a showing of the film *The Hobbit*. The memory of the Aurora movie theater massacre was fresh in his mind, so he was concerned that it not be a late-night showing. At that moment, like so many families, my wife and I were weighing whether to turn on the radio and expose our children to coverage of the school shootings in Connecticut. We did. The car was silent in the face of the flood of gory details. When the story was over, there was a long, thoughtful pause in the back of the car. Then my eldest son asked if he could be homeschooled.

That incident brought home to me what I have always suspected but found difficult to articulate: an armed society—especially as we prosecute it at the moment in this country—is the opposite of a civil society.

The Newtown shootings occurred at a peculiar time in gun rights history in this nation. On one hand, since the mid-1970s, fewer households each year on average have had a gun. Gun control advocates should be cheered by that news, but it is eclipsed by a flurry of contrary developments. As has been well publicized, gun sales have steadily risen over the past few years and spiked with each of Obama's election victories.

Furthermore, of the weapons that proliferate among the armed public, an increasing number are high caliber weapons (the weapon of choice in the goriest shootings in recent years). Then there is the legal landscape, which looks bleak for the gun control crowd.

Every state except for Illinois has a law allowing the carrying of concealed weapons—and just last week, a federal court struck down Illinois's ban. States are now lining up to allow guns on college campuses. In September, Colorado joined four other states in such a move, and statehouses across the country are preparing similar legislation. And of course, there was Oklahoma's ominous open carry law approved by voters this election day—the fifteenth of its kind, in fact—which, as the name suggests, allows those with a special permit to carry weapons in the open, with a holster on their hip.

Individual gun ownership—and gun violence—has long been a distinctive feature of American society, setting us apart from the other industrialized democracies of the world. Recent legislative developments, however, are progressively bringing guns out of the private domain, with the ultimate aim of enshrining them in public life. Indeed, the NRA strives for a day when the open carry of powerful weapons might be normal, a fixture even, of any visit to the coffee shop or grocery store—or classroom.

As NRA president Wayne LaPierre expressed in a recent statement on the organization's website, more guns equal more safety, by their account. A favorite gun rights saying is "An armed society is a polite society." If we allow ever more people to be armed, at any time, in any place, this will provide a powerful deterrent to potential criminals. Or if more citizens were armed—like principals and teachers in the classroom, for example—they could halt senseless shootings ahead of time, or at least early on, and save society a lot of heartache and bloodshed.

As ever more people are armed in public, however—even brandishing weapons on the street—this is no longer recognizable as a civil society. Freedom is vanished at that point.

And yet, gun rights advocates famously maintain that individual gun ownership, even of high caliber weapons, is the defining mark of our freedom as such, and the ultimate guarantee of our enduring liberty. Deeper reflection on their argument exposes basic fallacies.

In her book *The Human Condition*, the philosopher Hannah Arendt states that "violence is mute." According to Arendt, speech dominates and distinguishes the polis, the highest form of human association, which is devoted to the freedom and equality of its component members. Violence—and the threat of it—is a prepolitical manner of communication and control, characteristic of undemocratic organizations and hierarchical relationships. For the ancient Athenians who practiced an incipient, albeit limited form of democracy (one that we surely aim to surpass), violence was characteristic of the master-slave relationship, not that of free citizens.

Arendt offers two points that are salient to our thinking about guns: For one, they insert a hierarchy of some kind, but fundamental nonetheless, and thereby undermine equality. But furthermore, guns pose a monumental challenge to freedom, and in particular, the liberty that is the hallmark of any democracy worthy of the name—that is, freedom of speech. Guns do communicate, after all, but in a way that is contrary to free speech aspirations: for, guns chasten speech.

This becomes clear if only you pry a little more deeply into the NRA's logic behind an armed society. An armed society is polite, by their thinking, precisely because guns would compel everyone to tamp down eccentric behavior and refrain from actions that might seem threatening. The suggestion is that guns liberally interspersed throughout society would cause us all to walk gingerly—not make any sudden, unexpected moves—and watch what we say, how we act, whom we might offend.

As our Constitution provides, however, liberty entails precisely the freedom to be reckless, within limits, also the freedom to insult and offend as the case may be. The Supreme Court has repeatedly upheld our right to experiment in offensive language and ideas, and in some cases, offensive action and speech. Such experimentation is inherent to our freedom as such. But guns by their nature do not mix with this experiment—they don't mix with taking offense. They are combustible ingredients in assembly and speech.

I often think of the armed protestor who showed up to one of the famously raucous town hall hearings on Obamacare in the summer of 2009. The media was very worked up over this man, who bore a sign that invoked a famous quote of Thomas Jefferson, accusing the president of tyranny. But no one engaged him at the protest; no one dared approach him even, for discussion or debate—though this was a town hall meeting, intended for just such purposes. Such is the effect of guns on speech—and assembly. Like it or not, they transform the bearer and end the conversation in some fundamental way. They announce that the conversation is not completely unbounded, unfettered and free; there is or can be a limit to negotiation and debate—definitively.

The very power and possibility of free speech and assembly rests on their nonviolence. The power of the Occupy Wall Street movement, as well as the Arab Spring protests, stemmed precisely from their nonviolent nature. This power was made evident by the ferocity of government response to the Occupy movement. Occupy protestors across the country were increasingly confronted by police in military-style garb and affect.

Imagine what this would have looked like had the protestors been armed: in the face of the New York Police Department assault on Zuccotti Park, there might have been armed insurrection in the streets. The nonviolent nature of protest in this country ensures that it can occur.

Gun rights advocates also argue that guns provide the ultimate insurance of our freedom, insofar as they are the final deterrent against encroaching centralized government, and an executive branch run amok with power. Any suggestion of limiting guns rights is greeted by ominous warnings that this is a move of expansive, would-be despotic government. It has been the means by which gun rights advocates withstand even the most seemingly rational gun control measures. An assault weapons ban, smaller ammunition clips for guns, longer background checks on gun purchases—these are all measures centralized government wants, they claim, in order to exert control over us and ultimately impose its arbitrary will. I have often suspected, however, that contrary to holding centralized authority in check, broad individual gun ownership gives the powers-that-be exactly what they want.

After all, a population of privately armed citizens is one that is increasingly fragmented, and vulnerable as a result. Private gun ownership invites retreat into extreme individualism—I heard numerous calls for homeschooling in the wake of the Newtown shootings—and nourishes the illusion that I can be my own police, or military, as the case may be. The NRA would have each of us steeled for impending government aggression, but it goes without saying that individually armed citizens are no match for government force. The NRA argues against that interpretation of the Second Amendment that privileges armed militias over individuals, and yet it seems clear that armed militias, at least in theory, would provide a superior check on autocratic government.

As Michel Foucault pointed out in his detailed study of the mechanisms of power, nothing suits power so well as extreme individualism. In fact, he explains, political and corporate interests aim at nothing less than "individualization," since it is far easier to manipulate a collection of discrete and increasingly independent individuals than a community. Guns undermine just that—community. Their pervasive, open presence would sow apprehension, suspicion, mistrust and fear—all emotions that are corrosive of community and civic cooperation. To that extent, then, guns give license to autocratic government.

Our gun culture promotes a fatal slide into extreme individualism. It fosters a society of atomistic individuals, isolated before power—and one another—and in the aftermath of shootings such as at Newtown, paralyzed with fear. That is not freedom, but quite its opposite. And as the Occupy movement makes clear, also the demonstrators that precipitated regime change in Egypt and Myanmar last year, assembled masses don't require guns to exercise and secure their freedom and wield world-changing political force. Arendt and Foucault reveal that power does not lie in armed individuals, but in assembly—and everything conducive to that.

Is American Nonviolence Possible?

—*Todd May*

The choice is not between violence and nonviolence but between nonviolence and nonexistence.

—MARTIN LUTHER KING JR.

WE ARE STEEPED IN VIOLENCE.

This past week was, of course, a searing reminder: Monday's bombing at the Boston Marathon and the ensuing manhunt that ended on Friday with the death of one suspect and the capture of another, his brother, dominated the news. But there were other troubling, if less traumatic, reminders, too. On Tuesday, a 577-page report by the Constitution Project concluded that the United States had engaged in torture after the September 11 attacks. On Wednesday, a turning point in the heated national debate on gun control was reached when the United States Senate dropped consideration of some minimal restrictions on the sale and distribution of guns. Looming above all this is the painful memory of the mass killing at Sandy Hook Elementary School.

Now is as good a time as any to reflect on our responses to the many recent horrors that seem to have engulfed us, and to consider whether we can hope to move from an ethos of violence to one of nonviolence. Facing ourselves squarely at this difficult moment might provide a better lesson for the future than allowing ourselves to once again give in to blind fury.

We might begin by asking the question, *Who are we now?*

Clearly, we are a violent country. Our murder rate is three to five times that of most other industrialized countries. The massacres that regularly take place here are predictable in their occurrence, if not in their time and place. Moreover, and more telling, our response to violence is typically more violence. We display our might—or what is left of it—abroad in order to address perceived injustices or a threat to our interests. We still have not rid ourselves of the death penalty, a fact that fills those in other countries with disbelief. Many of us, in response to the mindless gun violence around us, prescribe more guns as the solution, as the Republicans sought to do during the gun debate. And we torture people. It is as though, in thinking that the world responds only to violence, we reveal ourselves rather than the world.

Why is this? How has the United States become so saturated in slaughter?

There are, of course, many reasons, but three stand out, one of which is deep and long-standing and the others are of more recent vintage. The deep reason lies in our competitive individualism. Americans are proud of our individualism, and indeed it is not entirely a curse. To believe that one has a responsibility to create oneself rather than relying on others for sustenance has its virtues. No doubt many of the advances—scientific, technological and artistic—that have emerged from the United States have their roots in the striving of individuals whose belief in themselves bolstered their commitment to their work. However, the dark side of this individualism is a wariness of others and a rejection of the social solidarity characteristic of countries like Denmark, Sweden, New Zealand and, at least to some extent, France. We make it, if we do make it, but we do so alone. Our neighboring citizens are not so much our fellows as our competitors.

The second reason is the decline of our ability to control events in the world. We might date this decline from our military failure in Vietnam, or, if we prefer, more recently to the debacle in Iraq. In any event, it is clear that the United States cannot impose its will as it did during much of the twentieth century. We live in a different world now, and this makes many of us insecure. We long for a world more cooperative with our wishes than the one we now live in. Our insecurity, in turn, reinforces our desire to control, which reinforces violence. If we cannot control events in the world, this must be a result not of our impotence or the complexity of the world's problems but of our unwillingness to "man up." And so we tell ourselves fairy tales about what would have happened if we had committed to victory in Vietnam or bombed one or another country back to the Stone Age.

The third reason is economic. The welfare state has been in decline for more than thirty years now. The embrace of classical liberalism or neoliberalism erodes social solidarity. Each of us is an investor, seeking the best return on our money, our energies, our relationships, indeed our lives. We no longer count on government, which is often perceived as the enemy. And we no longer have obligations to those with whom we share the country, or the planet. It is up to each of us to take our freedom and use it wisely. Those who do not are not unlucky or impoverished. They are simply imprudent.

Competitive individualism, insecurity, neoliberalism: the triad undergirding our penchant for violence. This, as much as anything else, is the current exceptionalism of America. Others are not our partners, nor even our colleagues. They are our competitors or our enemies. They are hardly to be recognized, much less embraced. They are to be vanquished.

What would the alternative, nonviolence, look like? And what does it require of us?

We must understand first that nonviolence is not passivity. It is instead creative activity. That activity takes place within particular limits. To put the point a bit simply, those limits are the recognition of others as fellow human beings, even when they are our adversaries. That recognition does not require that we acquiesce to the demands of others when we disagree. Rather, it requires that our action, even when it coerces the other (as boycotts, strikes, sit-ins and human blockades often do), does not aim to destroy that other in his or her humanity. It requires that we recognize others as fellow human beings, even when they are on the other side of the barricades.

This recognition limits what we can do, but at the same time it forces us to be inventive. No longer is it a matter of bringing superior firepower to bear. Now we must think more rigorously about how to respond, how to make our voices heard and our aims prevail. In a way it is like writing a Shakespearean sonnet, where the fourteen-line structure and iambic pentameter require thoughtful and creative work rather than immediate and overwhelming response.

To recognize someone's humanity is, in perhaps the most important way, to recognize him or her as an equal. Each of us, nonviolence teaches, carries our humanity within us. That humanity cannot always be appealed to. In some cases, as with the tragedy at Sandy Hook, it can even become nearly irrelevant. However, in all but the most extreme cases nonviolence summons us to recognize that humanity even when it cannot serve as the basis for negotiation or resolution. It demands that we who act do so with a firm gaze upon the face of the other. It demands the acknowledgment that we are all fragile beings, nexuses of hope and fear, children of some mother, and perhaps parents to others: that is, no more and no less than fellow human beings in a world fraught with imponderables.

Can we do this? Are we capable at this moment of taking on the mantle of nonviolence?

The lessons are already there in our history. The civil rights movement is perhaps the most shining example of nonviolence in our human legacy. After 9/11, after Hurricane Katrina and Hurricane Sandy, and now, in the immediate on-the-ground responses to the Boston bombing, Americans pulled together with those they did not know in order to restore the web of our common existence. We are indeed violent, but we have shown flashes of nonviolence—that is to say moments where our competitive individualism, our insecurity, our desire for the highest return on our investment of time and money has been trumped by the vividness of the likeness of others. Granted, these are only moments.

They have not lasted. But they teach us that when it comes to nonviolent relations with others, we are not entirely bereft.

What would it require for these lessons to become sedimented in our collective soul? There is much work to be done. We must begin to see our fellow human beings as precisely that: fellows. They need not be friends, but they must be counted as worthy of our respect, bearers of dignity in their own right. Those who struggle must no longer be seen as failures but more often as unlucky, and perhaps worthy of our extending a hand. Those who come to our shores, whatever our policy toward them, must be seen as human beings seeking to stitch together a decent life rather than as mere parasites upon our riches. Those who are unhealthy must be seen as more than drains upon our taxes but instead as peers that, but for good fortune, might have been us.

None of this requires that we allow others to abdicate responsibility for their lives. Nor does it require that we refuse, when no other means are available, to defend ourselves with force. Instead it calls upon us to recognize that we, too, have a responsibility to more than our own security and contentment. It commands us to look *to* ourselves and *at* others before we start casting stones.

Would this end all senseless killing? No, it would not. Would it substitute for the limits on guns that are so urgently needed? Of course not. While the recently rejected limits on guns, however timid, might have provided a first public step toward the recognition of the requirements of our situation, our task would remain: to create a culture where violence is seen not as the first option but as the last, one that would allow us to gaze upon the breadth of space that lies between an unjust act and a violent response.

The philosopher Immanuel Kant said that the core of morality lay in treating others not simply as means but also as ends in themselves. Nonviolence teaches us nothing more than this. It is a simple lesson, if difficult to practice—especially so at a moment like this when our rage and grief are still raw. But it is a lesson that has become buried under our ideology and our circumstances. We need to learn it anew.

Learning this lesson will not bring back the life of Martin Richard, Krystle Campbell or the other murdered victims in Boston. It will not return to health those who were injured on that day. It won't bring back Trayvon Martin or the children of Sandy Hook. But it will, perhaps, point the way toward a future where, instead of recalling yet more victims of violence in anger and with vows of retribution, we find ourselves with fewer victims to recall.

APRIL 21, 2013

ON RACE

Walking While Black in the "White Gaze"

—*George Yancy*

I.

"*M*AN, *I ALMOST BLEW YOU AWAY!*"

Those were the terrifying words of a white police officer—one of those who policed black bodies in low-income areas in North Philadelphia in the late 1970s—who caught sight of me carrying the new telescope my mother had just purchased for me.

"I thought you had a weapon," he said.

The words made me tremble and pause; I felt the sort of bodily stress and deep existential anguish that no teenager should have to endure.

This officer had already inherited those poisonous assumptions and bodily perceptual practices that make up what I call the "white gaze." He had already come to "see" the black male body as different, deviant, ersatz. He failed to conceive, or perhaps could not conceive, that a black teenage boy living in the Richard Allen Project Homes for very low-income families would own a telescope and enjoyed looking at the moons of Jupiter and the rings of Saturn.

A black boy carrying a telescope wasn't conceivable—unless he had stolen it—given the white racist horizons within which my black body was policed as dangerous. To the officer, I was something (not some*one*) patently foolish, perhaps monstrous or even fictional. My telescope, for him, *was* a weapon.

In retrospect, I can see the headlines: "Black Boy Shot and Killed while Searching the Cosmos."

That was more than thirty years ago. Only last week, our actual headlines were full of reflections on the fiftieth anniversary of the 1963 March on Washington, Rev. Dr. Martin Luther King's "I Have a Dream" speech, and President Obama's own speech at the steps of the Lincoln Memorial to commemorate it fifty years on. As the many accounts from that long-ago day will tell you, much has changed for the better. But some things—those perhaps more deeply embedded in the American psyche—haven't. In fact, we should recall a speech given by Malcolm X in 1964 in which he said, "For the 20 million of us in America who are of African descent, it is not an American dream; it's an American nightmare."

II.

Despite the ringing tones of Obama's Lincoln Memorial speech, I find myself still often thinking of a more informal and somber talk he gave. And despite the inspirational and ethical force of Dr. King and his work, I'm still thinking about someone who might be considered old news already: Trayvon Martin.

In his now much-quoted White House briefing several weeks ago, not long after the verdict in the trial of George Zimmerman, the president expressed his awareness of the ever-present danger of death for those who inhabit black bodies. "You know, when Trayvon Martin was first shot, I said that this could have been my son," he said. "Another way of saying that is Trayvon Martin could have been me thirty-five years ago." I wait for the day when a white president will say, "There is no way that I could have experienced what Trayvon Martin did (and other black people do) because I'm white and through white privilege I am immune to systematic racial profiling."

Obama also talked about how black men in this country know what it is like to be followed while shopping and how black men have had the experience of "walking across the street and hearing the locks click on the doors of cars." I have had this experience on many occasions as whites catch sight of me walking past their cars: *Click, click, click, click.* Those clicks can be deafening. There are times when I want to become their boogeyman. I want to pull open the car door and shout, "Surprise! You've just been carjacked by a fantasy of your own creation. Now get out of the car."

The president's words, perhaps consigned to a long-ago news cycle now, remain powerful: they validate experiences that blacks have undergone in their everyday lives. Obama's voice resonates with those philosophical voices (Frantz Fanon, for example) that have long attempted to describe the lived interiority of racial experiences. He has also deployed the power of narrative autobiography, which is a significant conceptual tool used insightfully by critical race theorists to discern the clarity and existential and social gravity of what it means to experience white racism. As a black president, he has given voice to the epistemic violence that blacks often face as they are stereotyped and profiled within the context of quotidian social spaces.

III.

David Hume claimed that to be black was to be "like a parrot who speaks a few words plainly." And Immanuel Kant maintained that to be "black from head to foot" was "clear proof" that what *any* black person says is stupid. In his *Notes on the State of Virginia*, Thomas Jefferson wrote, "In imagination they [Negroes] are dull, tasteless and anomalous," and inferior. In the first American edition of the *Encyclopædia Britannica* (1798), the term Negro was defined as someone who is cruel, impudent, revengeful, treacherous, nasty, idle, dishonest, a liar and given to stealing.

My point here is to say that the white gaze is global and historically mobile. And its origins, while from Europe, are deeply seated in the making of America.

Black bodies in America continue to be reduced to their surfaces and to stereotypes that are constricting and false, that often force those black bodies to move through social spaces in ways that put white people at ease. We fear that our black bodies incite an accusation. We move in ways that help us to survive the procrustean gazes of white people. We dread that those who see us might feel the irrational fear to stand their ground rather than "finding common ground," a reference that was made by Bernice King as she spoke about the legacy of her father at the steps of the Lincoln Memorial.

The white gaze is also hegemonic, historically grounded in material relations of white power: it was deemed disrespectful for a black person to violate the white gaze by looking directly into the eyes of someone white. The white gaze is also ethically solipsistic: within it only whites have the capacity of making valid moral judgments.

Even with the unprecedented White House briefing, our national discourse regarding Trayvon Martin and questions of race have failed to produce a critical and historically conscious discourse that sheds light on what it means to be black in an antiblack America. If historical precedent says anything, this failure will only continue. Trayvon Martin, like so many black boys and men, was under surveillance (etymologically, "to keep watch"). Little did he know that on February 26, 2012, he would enter a space of social control and bodily policing, a kind of Benthamian panoptic nightmare that would truncate his being as suspicious—a space where he was, paradoxically, both invisible and yet hypervisible.

"I am invisible, understand, simply because people [in this case white people] refuse to see me." Trayvon was invisible to Zimmerman; he was not seen as the black child that he was, trying to make it back home with Skittles and an iced tea. He was not seen as having done nothing wrong, as one who dreams and hopes.

As black, Trayvon was already known and rendered invisible. His childhood and humanity were already criminalized as part of a white racist narrative about black male bodies. Trayvon needed no introduction: "Look, the black; the criminal!"

IV.

Many have argued that the site of violence occurred upon the confrontation between Trayvon and Zimmerman. Yet, the violence began with Zimmerman's nonemergency dispatch call, a call that was racially assaultive in its discourse, one that used the tropes of antiblack racism. Note, Zimmerman said, "There's a real suspicious guy." He also said, "This guy looks like he's up to no good or he's on drugs or something." When asked by the dispatcher, he said, within seconds, that "he looks black." Asked what he is wearing, Zimmerman says, "A dark hoodie, like a gray hoodie." Later, Zimmerman said that "now he's coming toward me. He's got his hands in his waistband." And then, "And he's a black male." But what does it mean to be "a real suspicious guy"? What does it mean to look like one is "up to no good"? Zimmerman does not give any details, nothing to buttress the validity of his narration. Keep in mind that Zimmerman is in his vehicle as he provides his narration to the dispatcher. As "the looker," it is *not* Zimmerman who is in danger; rather, it is Trayvon Martin, "the looked at," who is the target of suspicion and possible violence.

After all, it is Trayvon Martin who is wearing the hoodie, a piece of "racialized" attire that apparently signifies black criminality. Zimmerman later said, "Something's wrong with him. Yep, he's coming to check me out," and, "He's got something in his hands." Zimmerman also said, "I don't know what his deal is." A black young male with "something" in his hands, wearing a hoodie, looking suspicious, and perhaps on drugs, and there being "something wrong with him" is a racist narrative of fear and frenzy. The history of white supremacy underwrites this interpretation. Within this context of *discursive violence*, Zimmerman was guilty of an act of aggression against Trayvon Martin, even before the trigger was pulled. Before his physical death, Trayvon Martin was rendered "socially dead" under the weight of Zimmerman's racist stereotypes. Zimmerman's aggression was enacted through his gaze, through the act of profiling, through his discourse and through his warped reconstruction of an innocent black boy that instigates white fear.

V.

What does it say about America when to be black is the ontological crime, a crime of simply being?

Perhaps the religious studies scholar Bill Hart is correct: "To be a black man is to be marked for death." Or as the political philosopher Joy James argues, "Blackness as evil [is] destined for eradication." Perhaps this is why when writing about the death of his young black son, the social theorist W. E. B. Du Bois said, "All that day and all that night there sat an awful gladness in my heart—nay, blame me not if I see the world thus darkly through the Veil—and my soul whispers ever to me saying, 'Not dead, not dead, but escaped; not bond, but free.'"

Trayvon Martin was killed walking while black. As the protector of all things "gated," of all things standing on the precipice of being endangered by black male bodies, Zimmerman created the conditions upon which he *had no grounds to stand on*. Indeed, through his racist stereotypes and his pursuit of Trayvon, he created the conditions that belied the applicability of the stand-your-ground law and created a situation where Trayvon was killed. This is the narrative that ought to have been told by the attorneys for the family of Trayvon Martin. It is part of the narrative that Obama brilliantly told, one of black bodies being racially policed and having suffered a unique history of racist vitriol in this country.

Yet it is one that is perhaps too late, one already rendered mute and inconsequential by the verdict of "not guilty."

SEPTEMBER 1, 2013

Race, Truth and Our Two Realities

—*Chris Lebron*

T HE CORRESPONDENCE THEORY OF TRUTH NO LONGER REIGNS
supreme in philosophical circles when it comes to the study of
knowledge and judgment. But it remains handy for everyday people, especially citizens. That theory says, simply, a proposal is true
if it corresponds to an observation in the world. Not a bad way to
go when people are trying to figure out the stuff of democratic living. After a week in which we have seen the unwarranted killing
by police of two black men—Philando Castile in Minnesota and
Alton Sterling in Louisiana—I'd like to think the correspondence
theory of truth would get all Americans on the same page. But this
has consistently failed to be the case. Maybe we can figure out
why together.

So, I say: In America, black lives don't matter. You say: That is
false. I respond, implicitly invoking the correspondence theory of
truth: Just look at the rate at which blacks are killed by the police and
the rate at which police officers are exculpated. You respond with a
number of points: the justice system works; black kill one another
at tragic rates; the people killed sometimes had questionable back-
grounds; if the officer pulled his weapon (for it's almost always a man
who does the shooting), he had a reason related to enforcing the law,
and we must respect that. After I claim that black lives don't matter
in America and you respond with any of the above, one idea becomes

clear: We are no longer talking about the same thing. At this point I realize the mistake I've made.

When I claim that black lives don't matter in America, I mean to say something that to my mind is abundantly clear. Here's how it works. We live in a liberal democracy that is founded on the sanctity of liberty. This implies that fairness is essential; indeed, that proposition is often explicitly at the heart of many democratic debates. The very idea of democracy reaches back to ancient Greece and is the foundation for our deepest principles concerning human rights. We believe that democracies are superior to other systems of government largely because they intrinsically respect the rights of the men and women who live in them.

I must then take into account the history of racial dominance in this country—the centuries of slavery; the decades of Jim Crow; the continuation of systemic racial inequality in wealth, jobs, education and public services. Then there are the deaths—the body count at the hands of the police that ticks these days almost as regularly as a national clock. I take all of these basic observations together and my considered position is that the claim that black lives don't matter in America corresponds to the facts.

I then offer you this claim. But then it all goes wrong. You say I am not right, that I am not speaking the truth.

Where does the problem lie? The fiction writer George Saunders, considering not race relations but the divide between the political left and right, wrote in *The New Yorker* recently: "Not only do our two subcountries reason differently; they draw upon non-intersecting data sets and access entirely different mythological systems." But our case is different. The distance between the left and right is represented by ideology and self-interest. While ideology and self-interest have something to do with our differences on racial truth, it crucially has more to do with the moment at which my experience enlivens my perception of how the racial past makes the racial present and how your experience leaves race in the past and renders the present as something unrecognizable to me but comforting to you.

Here's one way of making sense of the misfire between us. You are with me when I am making my general comments about America's foundational aspects. You are likely still with me on the observations about slavery. You may begin to edge away from our shared space of critical judgment somewhere around Jim Crow, but the horrors of lynching may persuade you to stay. The place, or the time rather, I mostly likely lose you is 1964. In your mind, our celebrated Martin Luther King Jr. made the world right in helping to usher in the era of formal equality when he cornered Lyndon B. Johnson into pushing for the Civil Rights Act of 1964.

In your mind, that moment introduced a new world order in which blacks could no longer be victims. The law had set them free and listed the bad things that people could no longer do. Moreover, it said that those people would be held responsible for the bad things they did. Thus, even if bad things happened to black people, the law would settle all accounts; therefore, no one could ever claim again that blacks were at the special mercy of racism. You, at this point, are sure that my proposition cannot be true since it fails to correspond.

As I said, I see the mistake I've made, but it's not in my construction of the truth. It is in presuming that you and I were ever speaking about the same thing. And the reason we weren't speaking about the same thing is that we were not looking in the same direction; thus, our basis for correspondence is mismatched.

The direction I was looking toward was the internal life of a black person in America. The very real anxieties and fears we have in whether our ambitions are as secure as any other American's. Whether our opportunities are equal. Whether our health care is of sufficient quality. Whether our college degrees are of equal worth. Whether our spouses will make it home from the grocery store. Whether our children will one day counsel a parent that everything will be O.K. while someone is slumped over in the car seat in front of her, bleeding to death after being shot by a police officer.

You were looking in an altogether different direction. You were looking in the direction of your own innocence. Though you bought a house in an entirely segregated neighborhood, it's not your fault the schools are better where you live. Though you have only one black friend, it's not your fault because your friends are your co-workers and your company or university is doing poorly on diversity. Though it's a shame that this black man or woman died (pick one, any one), it's not your fault that the police officer you pay with your tax dollars and who is sworn to protect you did so at the expense of an unnecessary killing.

And none of these are your fault because that day in 1964 made it all right—the law said what could not happen, and thus, it must not be happening. Your sense of America is predicated on the assumption of a reliable and stable democratic system. We cannot possibly speak about the same thing given these conditions.

That is a problem. A core idea of democratic life is consensus citizens coming to a wide agreement on contentious issues. Americans disagree on all kinds of issues, but this one, whether black lives matter, is genuinely special and momentous. We have the facts: systemic racial inequality and rampant police-perpetrated killings. Then we have the observation of those facts seen from our distinct perspectives. Everything depends on you and I not only agreeing in our judgment but also taking up the proper positions to get genuine buy-in for the sake of justice. If you insist on standing where you do while I stand where I stand, there will never be agreement that black lives don't matter in America.

The terrible events Thursday night in Dallas, where five police officers were slain by a sniper at a rally to protest police shootings, has complicated things still more, as do the charged and sometimes violent protests still arising in cities around the country. From where I stand—and maybe here we can stand together—I see once again that violence tragically begets violence, and that if America had faced its history of racial violence many decades ago, maybe even a few years ago when Eric Garner was seen by millions of Americans being strangled by a police officer on YouTube, we'd all be better for it today. If America had decided that black lives do matter when it had the chance, the cycle of violence that has robbed us and threatens to continue to rob us of precious lives could have been broken.

One reason the correspondence theory of truth has lost favor among professional philosophers is that we can't always rely on our senses to corroborate facts. But we've seen the videos. The difference between you and me isn't a matter of error, but of will.

JULY 11, 2016

Getting Past the Outrage on Race

—Gary Gutting

GEORGE YANCY'S RECENT PASSIONATE RESPONSE IN THE STONE to Trayvon Martin's killing—and the equally passionate comments on his response—vividly present the seemingly intractable conflict such cases always evoke. There seems to be a sense in which each side is right, but no way to find common ground on which to move discussion forward. This is because, quite apart from the facts of the case, Trayvon Martin immediately became a symbol for two apparently opposing moral judgments. I will suggest, however, that both these judgments derive from the same underlying injustice—one at the heart of the historic March on Washington fifty years ago and highlighted in the Rev. Dr. Martin Luther King Jr.'s speech on that occasion.

Trayvon Martin was, for the black community, a symbol of every young black male, each with vivid memories of averted faces, abrupt street crossings, clicking car locks and insulting police searches. As we move up the socioeconomic scale, the memories extend to attractive job openings that suddenly disappear when a black man applies, to blacks interviewed just to prove that a company tried, and even to a president some still hate for his color. It's understandable that Trayvon Martin serves as a concrete emblem of the utterly unacceptable abuse, even today, of young black men.

But for others this young black man became a symbol of other disturbing realities—that, for example, those most likely to drop out of school, belong to gangs and commit violent crimes are those who "look like" Trayvon Martin. For them—however mistakenly—his case evokes the disturbing amount of antisocial behavior among young black males.

Trayvon Martin's killing focused our national discussion because Americans made him a concrete model of opposing moral judgments about the plight of young black men. Is it because of their own lack of values and self-discipline, or to the vicious prejudice against them? Given either of these judgments, many conclude that we need more laws—against discrimination if you are in one camp, and against violent crime if you are in the other—and stronger penalties to solve our racial problems.

There may be some sense to more legislation, but after many years of both "getting tough on crime" and passing civil rights acts, we may be scraping the bottom of the legal barrel. In any case, underlying the partial truths of the two moral pictures, there is a deeper issue. We need to recognize that our continuing problems about race are essentially rooted in a fundamental injustice of our economic system.

This is a point that Martin Luther King Jr. made in his "I Have a Dream" speech, one rightly emphasized by a number of commentators on the anniversary of that speech, including President Obama and Joseph Stiglitz. Dr. King made the point in a striking image at the beginning of his speech. "The Negro is not free," he said, because he "lives on a lonely island of poverty in the midst of a vast sea of material prosperity." In 2011, for 28 percent of African-Americans, the island was still there, the source of both images of Trayvon Martin.

The poverty is not an accident. Our free-enterprise system generates enough wealth to eliminate Dr. King's island. But we primarily direct the system toward individuals' freedom to amass personal wealth. Big winners beget big losers, and a result is a socioeconomic underclass deprived of the basic goods necessary for a fulfilling human life: adequate food, housing, health care and education, as well as meaningful and secure employment. (Another Opinionator series, The Great Divide, examines such inequalities in detail each week.)

People should be allowed to pursue their happiness in the competitive market. But it makes no sense to require people to compete in the market for basic goods. Those who lack such goods have little chance of winning them in competition with those who already have them. This is what leads to an underclass exhibiting the antisocial behavior condemned by one picture of young black men and the object of the prejudice condemned by the other picture.

We need to move from outrage over the existence of an underclass to serious policy discussions about economic justice, with the first issue being whether our current capitalist system is inevitably unjust. If it is, is there a feasible way of reforming or even replacing it? If it is not, what methods does it offer for eliminating the injustice?

It is easy—and true—to say that a society as wealthy as ours should be able to keep people from being unhappy because they do not have enough to eat, have no safe place to live, have no access to good education and medical care, or cannot find a job. But this doesn't tell us how—if at all—to do what needs to be done. My point here is just that saying it can't be done expresses not realism but despair. Unless we work for this fundamental justice, then we must reconcile ourselves to a society with a permanent underclass, a class that, given our history, will almost surely be racially defined. Then the bitter conflict between the two pictures of this class will never end, because the injustice that creates it will last forever. Dr. King's island will never disappear, and there will always be another Trayvon Martin.

SEPTEMBER 11, 2013

Philosophy's Western Bias

—Justin E. H. Smith

THERE IS MUCH TALK IN ACADEMIC PHILOSOPHY ABOUT THE NEED
to open up the discipline to so-called non-Western traditions and
perspectives, both through changes to the curriculum and also
within the demographics of philosophy departments themselves.
These two aspects are seen as connected: it is thought that greater
representation of non-Western philosophy will help to bring about
greater diversity among the women and men who make up the philosophical community.

When I teach classical Indian philosophy, or advocate teaching it,
for example, I often hear in response that doing so provides a service
to the university community, and to the student body, insofar as it
enhances the diversity of the philosophy curriculum and makes the
curriculum representative of a wider portion of the student body. But
what I'm teaching are topics such as fifth-century Indian theories of
logical inference, or the concept of qualitative atomism in classical
Buddhism: material that is sufficiently obscure that no student, of
any background, should be expected at the outset to recognize him-
or herself in it.

The goal of reflecting the diversity of our own society by expand-
ing the curriculum to include non-European traditions has so far
been a tremendous failure. And it has failed for at least two reasons. One is that non-Western philosophy is typically represented
in philosophy curricula in a merely token way. Western philosophy

is always the unmarked category, the standard in relation to which non-Western philosophy provides a useful contrast.

Non-Western philosophy is not approached on its own terms, and thus philosophy remains, implicitly and by default, Western. Second, non-Western philosophy, when it does appear in curricula, is treated in a methodologically and philosophically unsound way: it is crudely supposed to be wholly indigenous to the cultures that produce it and to be fundamentally different than Western philosophy in areas like its valuation of reason or its dependence on myth and religion. In this way, non-Western philosophy remains fundamentally "other."

One good way to begin to correct this problem would be to stop describing it as "non-Western," but instead to be explicit about which geographical region, or which tradition, we are discussing: Kashmir Shaivism, for example, or Chinese Mohist logic, just as we would speak of German Aristotelian Scholasticism or American Pragmatism, without, ordinarily, bothering to specify that these are both "Western." Imagine, for comparison, the righteous vigor with which we would condemn the academic subfield of agricultural history if 95 percent of all the research in this field were devoted to irrigation techniques in Southeast Asia, while the remaining 5 percent was required to package itself as the study of "non-Southeast Asian irrigation techniques." This sounds absurd, and it is, but it really is no more so than when the small minority of scholars who work on, say, Indian or Chinese philosophy are obligated to present their research as having something to do with "non-Western philosophy" for the simple reason that it does not come from Northwest Eurasia.

An alternative approach to the history of philosophy—one that takes the aim of opening up the discipline seriously—would treat both Western and non-Western philosophy as the regional inflections of a global phenomenon.

When we say "West," we mean, ordinarily, Europe, along with its recent extension into North America. Europe is, literally, a peninsula of Eurasia, comparable roughly in size, cultural diversity and civilizational antiquity to the Indian subcontinent. Certain significant things happened first in Europe rather than elsewhere, such as industrialization; other important things first appeared outside of Europe, such as movable type. Now it is, of course, very difficult to define "philosophy," but if we think of it broadly as systematic reflection on the nature of reality and on humanity's place in that reality, then it is clear that Europe can make no special claim to be the home of philosophy.

What Europe does claim is a certain tradition reaching back to Greek antiquity. But even that claim is in question. The "Greek miracle" is in the end only a historiographical artifact, a result of our habit of beginning our histories when and where we do, for there was always influence from neighboring civilizations. But whatever the complexities of the world in which Plato wrote, it is at least true that the subsequent tradition that would come to be called "Western" or "European"—with, of course, a long detour through Islamic Spain, North Africa, Persia and Central Asia, without which the Greek tradition would surely have died out—really does constitute, as Alfred North Whitehead put it, a "series of footnotes to Plato." Seen from this perspective, the only reason to take European philosophy as the default tradition for our curricula is that it just happens to be, for contingent historical reasons, *our* tradition.

But nearly every subject taught in Western universities developed in large part out of the Western intellectual tradition, yet this legacy has not prevented any discipline other than philosophy from aspiring to an objective, global and, I dare say, scientific perspective on its object of study, free of the idea that the European instance of it is something special in the history of humanity.

Now, a large part of the difficulty of thinking of Western philosophy as one tradition among others has to do with the fact that many if not most of its practitioners reject the idea that what they do is essentially bound to the discipline's past. Philosophy is conceived on the model of the sciences, which are indeed free to ignore disproven theories from long ago, and thus to ignore not just, say, ancient China but early modern Europe as well. In this respect the history of ancient Chinese philosophy is doubly peripheral, not just because of Eurocentrism, but also because of presentism, a lack of interest in history in general. This stems from the fact that philosophy, modeling itself after the sciences, believes it is closer to the truth than it was in the past, and that if a theory is not true, there is little reason to spend much time on it.

I will not argue against this view of philosophy here. But I will point out that it does make the current situation of philosophy, when considered from a global perspective, fairly difficult to comprehend. Chinese and American polymer researchers speak exactly the same language when they are doing their job, and there was never any danger that A. Q. Khan's development of Pakistan's nuclear program would be slowed down by cultural differences in the understanding of uranium enrichment. With philosophy, however, it is plainly a different story.

In the developing world in particular, the version of philosophy put forward—be it French or Anglo-American in character, or entirely homegrown—has very much to do with the country's broader project of national identity construction. In Iran, Islamic philosophy is given priority; in Turkey, at least until recently, there was scarcely any mention of local or regional traditions in the university philosophy curriculum, but only a fervent devotion to a vision of philosophy principally concerned with analysis of the language and methodology of science. Now one can't say—or at least I'm not prepared to say—that Iran is doing things wrong, as one might if they were to teach medieval Islamic alchemy in their chemistry departments. The difference is that philosophy is simply not like science; it is much more intricately wrapped up in cultural legacies (some have argued that science is just another cultural practice, too, but I'm not prepared to say that either). Much of the difficulty of taking a rigorous and serious approach to the teaching and study of non-Western philosophy in Western philosophy departments is that many philosophers remain attached to the article of faith that philosophy is something independent of culture.

G. W. Leibniz, writing in the early eighteenth century on the future course of Sino-European relations, suggested evocatively that "the commerce of light," which is to say of illumination, or knowledge, always piggybacks on the commerce of goods. Indeed, the past two thousand years reveal a fairly close correspondence between the global centers of economic activity and the centers of intellectual production. Most tellingly, Europe becomes the principal locus of philosophical and scientific activity only when it comes to dominate the global economy through the conquest of the New World and the consequent shifting of the economic center of the world from Asia to Europe.

It is no secret that the center is shifting once again, this time toward the Pacific. A bit of historical perspective makes it easy to see that this shift will have consequences for our understanding of what philosophy is, and of who gets to define the set of questions with which it is concerned.

The West has an extremely rich philosophical tradition—one of the two or three richest, in fact—and it is eminently worthy of preservation and transmission to future generations. But its richness has always been a result of its place as a node in a global network through which ideas and things are always flowing. This was true in 500 BC and is no less true today. Increasingly, moreover, this interconnectedness is something that is not only of interest to the antiquarian trivia collector who can't wait to tell you where the printing press really comes from. It is fast becoming the defining fact about our geopolitical reality. In this reality, Western academic philosophy will likely come to appear utterly parochial in the coming years if it does not find a way to approach non-Western traditions that is much more rigorous and respectful than the tokenism that reigns at present.

JUNE 3, 2012

Dear White America

—*George Yancy*

DEAR WHITE AMERICA,

I have a weighty request. As you read this letter, I want you to listen with love, a sort of love that demands that you look at parts of yourself that might cause pain and terror, as James Baldwin would say. Did you hear that? You may have missed it. I repeat: *I want you to listen with love*. Well, at least try.

We don't talk much about the urgency of love these days, especially within the public sphere. Much of our discourse these days is about revenge, name calling, hate, and divisiveness. I have yet to hear it from our presidential hopefuls, or our political pundits. I don't mean the Hollywood type of love, but the scary kind, the kind that risks not being reciprocated, the kind that refuses to flee in the face of danger. To make it a bit easier for you, I've decided to model, as best as I can, what I'm asking of you. Let me demonstrate the vulnerability that I wish you to show. As a child of Socrates, James Baldwin and Audre Lorde, let me speak the truth, refuse to err on the side of caution.

This letter is a gift for you. Bear in mind, though, that some gifts can be heavy to bear. You don't have to accept it; there is no obligation. I give it freely, believing that many of you will throw the gift back in my face, saying that I wrongly accuse you, that I am too sensitive, that I'm a race hustler, and that I blame white people (you) for everything.

I have read many of your comments. I have even received some hate mail. In this letter, I ask you to look deep, to look into your souls with silence, to quiet that voice that will speak to you of your white "innocence." So, as you read this letter, take a deep breath. Make a space for my voice in the deepest part of your psyche. Try to listen, to practice being silent. There are times when you must quiet your own voice to hear from or about those who suffer in ways that you do not.

What if I told you that I'm sexist? Well, I am. Yes. I said it and I mean just that. I have watched my male students squirm in their seats when I've asked them to identify and talk about their sexism. There are few men, I suspect, who would say that they are sexist, and even fewer would admit that their sexism actually oppresses women. Certainly not publicly, as I've just done. No taking it back now.

To make things worse, I'm an academic, a philosopher. I'm supposed to be one of the "enlightened" ones. Surely, we are beyond being sexists. Some, who may genuinely care about my career, will say that I'm being too risky, that I am jeopardizing my academic livelihood. Some might even say that as a black male, who has already been stereotyped as a "crotch-grabbing, sexual fiend," that I'm at risk of reinforcing that stereotype. (Let's be real, that racist stereotype has been around for centuries; it is already part of white America's imaginary landscape.)

Yet, I refuse to remain a prisoner of the lies that we men like to tell ourselves—that we are beyond the messiness of sexism and male patriarchy, that we don't oppress women. Let me clarify. This doesn't mean that I intentionally hate women or that I desire to oppress them. It means that despite my best intentions, I perpetuate sexism every day of my life. Please don't take this as a confession for which I'm seeking forgiveness. Confessions can be easy, especially when we know that forgiveness is immediately forthcoming.

As a sexist, I have failed women. I have failed to speak out when I should have. I have failed to engage critically and extensively their pain and suffering in my writing. I have failed to transcend the rigidity of gender roles in my own life. I have failed to challenge those poisonous assumptions that women are "inferior" to men or to speak out loudly in the company of male philosophers who believe that feminist philosophy is just a nonphilosophical fad. I have been complicit with, and have allowed myself to be seduced by, a country that makes billions of dollars from sexually objectifying women, from pornography, commercials, video games, to Hollywood movies. I am not innocent.

I have been fed a poisonous diet of images that fragment women into mere body parts. I have also been complicit with a dominant male narrative that says that women enjoy being treated like sexual toys. In our collective male imagination, women are "things" to be used for our visual and physical titillation. And even as I know how poisonous and false these sexist assumptions are, I am often ambushed by my own hidden sexism. I continue to see women through the male gaze that belies my best intentions not to sexually objectify them. Our collective male erotic feelings and fantasies are complicit in the degradation of women. And we must be mindful that not all women endure sexual degradation in the same way.

I recognize how my being a sexist has a differential impact on black women and women of color who are not only victims of racism, but also sexism, *my sexism*. For example, black women and women of color not only suffer from sexual objectification, but the ways in which they are objectified is linked to how they are racially depicted, some as "exotic" and others as "hyper-sexual." You see, the complicity, the responsibility, the pain that I cause runs deep. And, get this. I refuse to seek shelter; I refuse to live a lie. So, every day of my life I fight against the dominant male narrative, choosing to see women as subjects, not objects. But even as I fight, there are moments of failure. Just because I fight against sexism does not give me clean hands, as it were, at the end of the day; I continue to falter, and I continue to oppress. And even though the ways in which I oppress women is unintentional, this does not free me of being responsible.

If you are white, and you are reading this letter, I ask that you don't run to seek shelter from your own racism. Don't hide from your responsibility. Rather, begin, right now, to practice being vulnerable. Being neither a "good" white person nor a liberal white person will get you off the proverbial hook. I consider myself to be a decent human being. Yet, I'm sexist. Take another deep breath. I ask that you try to be "un-sutured." If that term brings to mind a state of pain, open flesh, it is meant to do so. After all, it is painful to let go of your "white innocence," to use this letter as a mirror, one that refuses to show you what you want to see, one that demands that you look at the lies that you tell yourself so that you don't feel the weight of responsibility for those who live under the yoke of whiteness, your whiteness.

I can see your anger. I can see that this letter is being misunderstood. This letter is not asking you to feel bad about yourself, to wallow in guilt. That is too easy. I'm asking for you to tarry, to linger, with the ways in which you perpetuate a racist society, the ways in which you are racist. I'm now daring you to face a racist history which, paraphrasing Baldwin, has placed you where you are and that has formed your own racism. Again, in the spirit of Baldwin, I am asking you to enter into battle with your white self. I'm asking that you open yourself up; to speak to, to admit to, the racist poison that is inside of you.

Again, take a deep breath. Don't tell me about how many black friends you have. Don't tell me that you are married to someone of color. Don't tell me that you voted for Obama. Don't tell me that *I'm* the racist. Don't tell me that you don't see color. Don't tell me that I'm blaming whites for everything. To do so is to hide yet again. You may have never used the N-word in your life, you may hate the KKK, but that does not mean that you don't harbor racism and benefit from racism. After all, you are part of a system that allows you to walk into stores where you are not followed, where you get to go for a bank loan and your skin does not count against you, where you don't need to engage in "the talk" that black people and people of color must tell their children when they are confronted by white police officers.

As you reap comfort from being white, we suffer for being black and people of color. But your comfort is linked to our pain and suffering. Just as my comfort in being male is linked to the suffering of women, which makes me sexist, so, too, you are racist. That is the gift that I want you to accept, to embrace. It is a form of knowledge that is taboo. Imagine the impact that the acceptance of this gift might have on you and the world.

Take another deep breath. I know that there are those who will write to me in the comment section with boiling anger, sarcasm, disbelief, denial. There are those who will say, "Yancy is just an angry black man." There are others who will say, "Why isn't Yancy telling black people to be honest about the violence in their own black neighborhoods?" Or, "How can Yancy say that all white people are racists?" If you are saying these things, then you've already failed to listen. I come with a gift. You're already rejecting the gift that I have to offer. This letter is about *you*. Don't change the conversation. I assure you that so many black people suffering from poverty and joblessness, which is linked to high levels of crime, are painfully aware of the existential toll that they have had to face because they are black and, as Baldwin adds, "*for no other reason.*"

Some of your white brothers and sisters have made this leap. The legal scholar Stephanie M. Wildman, has written, "I simply believe that no matter how hard I work at not being racist, I still am. Because part of racism is systemic, I benefit from the privilege that I am struggling to see." And the journalism professor Robert Jensen: "I like to think I have changed, even though I routinely trip over the lingering effects of that internalized racism and the institutional racism around me. Every time I walk into a store at the same time as a black man and the security guard follows him and leaves me alone to shop, I am benefiting from white privilege."

What I'm asking is that you first accept the racism within yourself, accept all of the truth about what it means for you to be white in a society that was created for you. I'm asking for you to trace the binds that tie you to forms of domination that you would rather not see. When you walk into the world, you can walk with assurance; you have already signed a contract, so to speak, that guarantees you a certain form of social safety.

Baldwin argues for a form of love that is "a state of being, or state of grace—not in the infantile American sense of being made happy but in the tough and universal sense of quest and daring and growth." Most of my days, I'm engaged in a personal and societal battle against sexism. So many times, I fail. And so many times, I'm complicit. But I refuse to hide behind that mirror that lies to me about my "non-sexist nobility." Baldwin says, "Love takes off the masks that we fear we cannot live without and know we cannot live within." In my heart, I'm done with the mask of sexism, though I'm tempted every day to wear it. And, there are times when it still gets the better of me.

White America, are you prepared to be at war with yourself, your white identity, your white power, your white privilege? Are you prepared to show me a white self that love has unmasked? I'm asking for love in return for a gift; in fact, I'm hoping that this gift might help you to see yourself in ways that you have not seen before. Of course, the history of white supremacy in America belies this gesture of black gift-giving, this gesture of non-sentimental love. Martin Luther King Jr. was murdered even as he loved.

Perhaps the language of this letter will encourage a split—not a split between black and white, but a fissure in your understanding, a space for loving a Trayvon Martin, Eric Garner, Tamir Rice, Aiyana Jones, Sandra Bland, Laquan McDonald and others. I'm suggesting a form of love that enables you to see the role that you play (even despite your anti-racist actions) in a *system* that continues to value black lives on the cheap.

Take one more deep breath. I have another gift.

If you have young children, before you fall off to sleep tonight, I want you to hold your child. Touch your child's face. Smell your child's hair. Count the fingers on your child's hand. See the miracle that is your child. And then, with as much vision as you can muster, I want you to imagine that your child is black.

In peace,

George Yancy

DECEMBER 24, 2015

Of Cannibals, Kings and Culture:
The Problem of Ethnocentricity

—Adam Etinson

In August of 1563, Michel de Montaigne, the famous French essayist, was introduced to three Brazilian cannibals who were visiting Rouen, France, at the invitation of King Charles the Ninth. The three men had never before left Brazil, had just been subjected to a long interrogation by the king (who was thirteen years old at the time), and if they had not already contracted some dangerous European illness, they were surely undergoing a rather severe case of culture shock. Despite this, they still had enough poise to lucidly respond to Montaigne's questions about what they thought of their new surroundings.

The observations shared by the native Brazilians have a certain comical quality. Because they looked on French society with such fresh eyes, their observations make the familiar seem absurd. But they are also morally revealing. First, the Brazilians expressed surprise that "so many tall, bearded men, all strong and well armed" (i.e., the king's guards) were willing to take orders from a small child: something that would have been unthinkable in their own society. And second, the Brazilians were shocked by the severe inequality of French citizens, commenting on how some men "were gorged to the full with things of every sort" while others "were beggars at their doors, emaciated with hunger and poverty." Since the Brazilians saw all human beings "as halves of one another . . . they found it strange that these poverty-stricken halves should suffer such injustice, and that they did not take the others by the throat or set fire to their houses."

Montaigne records these observations in an essay entitled, "Des cannibals." Well ahead of its time, the essay challenges the haughty denigration of cannibals that was so common among Montaigne's contemporaries, but not by arguing that cannibalism itself is a morally acceptable practice. Instead, Montaigne makes the more provocative claim that, as barbaric as these Brazilian cannibals may be, they are not nearly as barbaric as sixteenth-century Europeans themselves. To make his case, Montaigne cites various evidence: the wholesome simplicity and basic nobility of native Brazilian life; the fact that some European forms of punishment—which involved feeding people to dogs and pigs while they were still alive—were decidedly more horrendous than the native Brazilian practice of eating one's enemies after they are dead; and the humane, egalitarian character of the Brazilians' moral sensibility, which was on display in their recorded observations.

The fact that, despite all this, sixteenth-century Western Europeans remained so deeply convinced of their own moral and intellectual superiority was, to Montaigne, evidence of a more general phenomenon. He writes,

> *We all call barbarous anything that is contrary to our own habits. Indeed we seem to have no other criterion of truth and reason than the type and kind of opinions and customs current in the land where we live. There we always see the perfect religion, the perfect political system, the perfect and most accomplished way of doing everything.*

Montaigne most certainly wasn't the first to make note of our tendency to automatically assume the superiority of local beliefs and practices; Herodotus, the Greek historian of the fifth century BC, made very similar observations in his *Histories*, noting how all peoples are "accustomed to regard their own customs as by far the best." And in his famous Letter 93, which presents an early argument against religious toleration, the medieval Catholic theologian

Saint Augustine laments the way in which old customs produce a closed-minded resistance to alternative beliefs and practices that, he argues, is best broken by the threat of punishment. When the nineteenth-century sociologist William Graham Sumner later named this tendency "ethnocentrism," the term, and the allegation, became a mantra of twentieth-century cultural anthropology.

Ethnocentrism—our culture's tendency to twist our judgment in favor of homegrown beliefs and practices and against foreign alternatives—is not, I take it, a phenomenon in need of further empirical confirmation. It is quite obvious that we are all ethnocentric to at least some extent. I am a Canadian and grew up with free, government-provided health care—a system that seems both fair and feasible to most Canadians, including myself. As such, I have a hard time comprehending the ferocity with which so many have opposed health-care reform in the United States. But equally, someone raised in a conservative swath of Texas is just as likely to find my sense of what is "fair" highly dubious.

Philosophers have long been aware of the role of culture and upbringing in facilitating moral disagreements of this sort. And more recently, moral psychologists have begun to offer insightful accounts of the psychological forces that make such disagreements so impervious to resolution through reasoned debate. For instance, in his recent book, *The Righteous Mind: Why Good People Are Divided by Politics and Religion*, Jonathan Haidt argues that, far from being a way of holding our moral beliefs up to critical scrutiny, moral reasoning is generally something we use merely to convince others of long-held beliefs that we are unwilling to abandon. If we reflect on what it's actually like to argue with others who fundamentally disagree with us on moral or political matters, Haidt seems to get something right; often, no amount of persuasive reasoning, clear argument or exposed contradiction can shake us from what we already believe.

In light of the recent escalation of partisanship in the United States, not to mention other widening global ideological fissures, I think it's important that we reflect, however briefly, on what we should make of this fact, with regard to our own ethnocentrism. Is ethnocentrism something we're doomed to? Can we avoid it? If so, should we avoid it? Is it even a bad thing?

Philosophers have responded to the pervasive influence of culture on our moral beliefs in various ways. Many have embraced some form of skepticism. To take a contemporary example, John L. Mackie (1917–81) famously cited ethnocentrism as evidence that there are no objective moral facts, or at least none that we can access. If our moral beliefs are dictated by our culture or way of life, he argued, then it is senseless to think of ourselves as capable of discerning objective moral truths; what room is left for such facts to make an impact on our consciousness? Mackie thought of himself as an "error theorist"—because, in his view, anytime we make a moral judgment that purports to be objectively true we are inevitably wrong—but there are other skeptical ways of responding to the fact of ethnocentrism. Many have argued, for instance, that the influence of culture on our moral beliefs is evidence not of error theory but of moral relativism: the idea that the moral truth, for any given people, is determined by their culture—the set of shared practices and beliefs that they ascribe to. We know from various sources, including Plato's dialogues, that some ancient Greeks defended such a view. And contemporary philosophers like David Wong and Gilbert Harman are among its serious proponents.

Tempting as these skeptical reactions to ethnocentrism may seem at first glance, there are important reasons to be hesitant. For one, however obvious it may be that culture plays an important role in our moral education, it is nevertheless very hard to prove that our moral beliefs are entirely determined by our culture, or to rule out the possibility that cultures themselves take some direction from objective moral facts. Since it is these hard-to-prove claims that Mackie and other error theorists need to make their argument work, we should hesitate before jumping on board. Second, moral relativism, for its part, seems like an odd and unwarranted response to ethnocentrism. For it's not at all clear why the influence of culture on our moral beliefs should be taken as evidence that cultures influence the moral truth itself—so that, for instance, child sacrifice would be morally permissible in any community with enough members that believe it to be so. Not only does that conclusion seem unmotivated by the phenomenon under discussion, it would also paradoxically convert ethnocentrism into a kind of virtue (since assimilating the views of one's culture would be a way of tapping into the moral truth), which is at odds with the generally pejorative understanding of the term.

Most important of all is the fact that there are other, more straightforward and less overtly skeptical ways of responding to ethnocentrism. Chief among these, in my view, is the simple but humbling acknowledgment that ethnocentrism is a danger that confronts us all, but not one that should disillusion us from the pursuit of truth altogether. This is the sort of response to ethnocentrism one finds, for instance, in the work of the nineteenth-century English philosopher John Stuart Mill. Mill is quick to acknowledge the "magical influence of custom" on our thought, and the way in which local beliefs and practices inevitably appear to us to be "self-evident and self-justifying," but he does not see this as a reason to lapse into skepticism. Instead, and quite reasonably, he takes it to be evidence of both our intellectual laziness and our fallibility—the ever-present possibility that our beliefs might be wrong. The fact that our deepest-held beliefs would be different had we been born elsewhere on the planet (or even, sometimes, to different parents farther down the street) should disconcert us, make us more open to the likelihood of our own error, and spur us to rigorously evaluate our beliefs and practices against alternatives, but it need not disillusion.

In a more candid moment of "Des cannibales," of which there are many across Montaigne's writings, the author unabashedly admits to having forgotten a third observation that the native Brazilians shared with him in response to his question. His forgetfulness is a pity not just because it deprives us of a window onto a 500-year-old cultural confrontation that is fascinating in its own right, but also because it deprives us of a potential opportunity to do just what Mill recommends: reexamine our beliefs and practices, become alert to weaknesses and inconsistencies in our own thinking, discover something plausible in a culturally unfamiliar point of view and in so doing, become better than the ethnocentric creatures that we are.

What, to the Black American, Is Martin Luther King Jr. Day?

—Chris Lebron

I AM VERY HONORED TO BE ADDRESSING YOU HERE TODAY, THOUGH it is not without some trepidation.

You see, the distance between where I grew up, where I come from in the world, and where many of you sit is significant. That I am where I am in the world sometimes surprises me. So I consider it an especially pressing duty to be mindful of my journey; and, when possible, to remind others that such a journey is just that for some of us—a setting out without a clear sense that we will get where we intend to go.

Representing the point of view that I do—as a brown American from a lower-class background, with the good fortune today to walk the halls of one of America's most elite institutions as a teacher of philosophy—Martin Luther King Jr. Day is taken to represent a triumph. But here is an uncomfortable truth: It is a triumph of acceptable minimums rather than full respect for those who continue to wait for Dr. King's dream to become reality.

My purpose is to challenge the common belief that honoring of Martin Luther King Jr. means the same thing to all Americans. Recalling the sense of disconnect expressed by Frederick Douglass in his speech "What, to the Slave, Is the Fourth of July?"—between himself as a former slave and his white audience—I want to say there is also some distance between black and white Americans today, between "you" and "I," as it were, and that this day has increasingly become "yours," not mine.

That may seem narrow or bitter. You may argue that the holiday has taken greater hold in the nation over time. Who today questions the validity of this holiday? Many of us have been given a day off work to reflect on it. A blockbuster Hollywood movie about Dr. King's role in one of the civil rights movement's greatest victories is playing in theaters nationwide. Clothes, furniture, bedding and cars are on sale to honor the man. Martin Luther King Jr. Day, it seems, now belongs to more of the nation than ever before.

But I maintain that it does not fully belong in the most profound ways to many Americans, and to some of them, it does not belong at all.

I think it goes without question that not only has the idea of a post-racial America proven to be a myth, but that racial inequality remains a tragic mark on the character of this otherwise great nation—a nation founded on respect not only for what persons hope to accomplish in life but for what they are: humans owed rights, liberty and respect because of their humanity. The equal recognition of humanity has only intermittently taken hold with respect to black lives. The closeness of Emmett Till and Eric Garner attest to that.

This was Dr. King's great struggle in his life. While he indeed fought for the security of a full schedule of rights for black Americans, he was in fact fighting for something greater and more difficult to articulate—the hope that white Americans could extend a hand of brotherly and sisterly love to blacks. The mark of true love, for Dr. King, was to embrace strangers as familiars, and conversely, to deny that blacks' humanity was a new and strange thing. There is hope in the thought that Dr. King is fervently embraced by so many Americans today, and there is consolation that his struggle gave us the Civil Rights Act and Voting Rights Act.

My purpose today, however, is to reflect on the nature of this embrace. When you celebrate Dr. King, what are you cheering? Do you cheer the greatness of a man who fully knew his journey's destination was insecure? The greatness of a man who paid the ultimate price so that my son could vote and sit in class alongside your children? If so, I am happy to join you. Do you celebrate his struggle as a resounding success that ushered in a new age of race relations? Do you intend to show appreciation for the notion that he helped us move past a difficult moment in American history? If so, then I cannot join you. And I fear that I observe the tendency to celebrate not so much the man but the hope that claiming him for all Americans exculpates us from the sins of inhumanity that is racial marginalization.

To say today that racial inequality is wrong is easy. Anyone can say it, and, in fact, most people do. It is true, there was a time when to pronounce on the equality of all men and women, regardless of color, was not only disallowed but also treacherous territory, as Dr. King learned. But it is important to note that as truly great a person as Dr. King was, he was not the only person to face the danger that came with insisting on social justice. Nor were blacks as a group the only group to face that danger. As has been known, and as we are being reminded with the film "Selma," white Americans were key to the success of Dr. King's movement, and some paid an equally heavy price.

The actions of these Americans were deeply honorable, for they faced down the expectation that social power imposes upon us at all times—to stay the course rather than to agitate for change; to take comfort in small moral affirmations in the presence of our peers rather than to challenge the staid beliefs of the privileged. The actions of these Americans serve to remind us that there is hope in the ideas of humanity and compassion, but that without it, America threatens to be false to its past, to its present, leaving our future insecure.

These words might sound anachronistic, as if this were 1955, not 2015. In 1962, Dr. King remarked in his speech "The Case Against 'Tokenism'" that racial justice was an idea whose time had come. He wrote: "The issue is not *whether* segregation and discrimination will be *eliminated* but how they will pass from the scene."

Dr. King's conviction seems prescient as the Civil Rights Act remained two years away. But one wonders what to make of this conviction today as segregation not only remains alive and well in many parts of America's neighborhoods and schools, but is also in some cases worsening. One wonders what to make of the claim that discrimination will soon be a thing of the past when in the twenty-first century our best researchers have shown that a black individual with an "ethnic" sounding name faces poorer chances of being invited for a job interview than a white American even if the two résumés are identical. Yet anyone who thinks this is a shortcoming on Dr. King's part fails to employ the better parts of his or her critical judgment.

From Dr. King's perspective his faith—and that's what is was, faith—was in ways warranted: He watched a movement to claim for blacks equal status grow into one of American history's most momentous movements and stand down centuries of white supremacy. Though he faced headwinds, he also perceived that the promised land was at least in sight. No—the failing is not his. The fact that fifty-three years later neither segregation nor discrimination have been eliminated indicates the eagerness with which white Americans have adopted the idea that securing racial justice was a matter of the passing of a law and the martyrdom of a great man. But this clearly will not do.

DURING THE DAYS OF slavery one could identify a person analogous to the swine-drover in the meat market. This person—we might call him a man-drover—rather than ushering pigs to market to be sold as a transferable commodity, did so with blacks. It goes without question that this treatment was inhumane. It made blacks into something less than human, things to be traded as objects to fuel economic necessity.

You may think that these days are long past but consider the case of Ferguson, MO,—a city of 21,135 people, predominantly black, that served 32,975 arrest warrants for nonviolent offenses in 2013. This remarkable level of surveillance and interdiction incidentally generated for Ferguson more than $2.5 million in revenue from fines and court fees—the city's second largest source of revenue. I ask you, what is this except the return of the drover in the mask of state legitimacy? In a nation where blacks possess only on average a dime of wealth for every dollar of white wealth, how is this reclamation of scarce resources anything but the continuation of oppression by other means, the reduction of blacks to instruments of economic necessity and exploitation?

If this does not convince you, listen to the audio track of Eric Garner's last words. In a tragic sense, his plea—"I can't breathe"—is the soundtrack of black life under conditions of deep unfairness and disregard: When we use the breath we have to ask for the rights and respect that ought to be ours, we have little breath to accomplish much else. Everyday life becomes the double struggle of working not only for what we need but also for securing that to which we are entitled in any case. Dr. King may have seen the promised land, but we appear to be anchored off its coast.

What can get us on course? What can unmoor us from our current predicament toward the promise of genuine American freedom for all? Dr. King once said that the arc of the moral universe is long, but that it bends toward justice. I am concerned that his statement is sometimes taken to hold a view of historical necessity—that oppression has a shelf life, that marginalization has an expiration date.

Despite his religious convictions, Dr. King's life was marked by the relationship between moral sense and action. The arc of the moral universe is long but bends only where the actions of good and brave people put to shame and rest the beliefs of the morally lazy and untoward. That is why moral life is work, and that is why racial justice is hard to secure. The arc of the moral universe is no more predetermined than is our will to show gratitude for an act of kindness. A life of civic goodness is always near enough, but we must often stretch to fully grasp it—to merely see it and praise it from the comfort of self-congratulatory appreciation is empty and a disappointment to better moral sensibilities.

I would have greatly preferred to present thoughts more joyous than these, but joy in a time of injustice is a very great luxury, one indulged in by either the willfully blind or the callously indifferent. The rest of us must come to terms with what we face and where we are headed. It is as Dr. King says: The arc of the moral universe is long; and it does bend where dissatisfied courage triumphs over privileged contentment. Daily I pray for the courage to do my small part to bend the arc and bring us into right relationship with the good and the just. It is my duty. But it is not mine alone.

If this holiday is to someday belong to all of us, then you must also bear the burden. The great victory comes then: When the burden is shared, so then is the aspiration to show one another genuine love that Dr. King exhorted us to express. So then will his day become both yours and mine as he would have wished. And that is cause for celebration.

This essay is adapted from the transcript of a speech given by the author to the Greenwich, CT, YWCA on Jan. 15, 2015.

JANUARY 18, 2015

Is Real Inclusiveness Possible?

—Justin E. H. Smith

LIKE MANY INSTITUTIONS THAT HAVE BECOME MORE CONCERNED
with equality in the past few decades, academic philosophy today
aims to be more inclusive. In general, university departments are
now striving to consider the experiences and concerns of a broader
range of people than have traditionally played the social and professional role of the philosopher. This makes sense. In an increasingly
global intellectual landscape, the removal of barriers to entry for
previously excluded groups of people and schools of thought is productive and fair.

It may be, however, that the full implications of the project of
inclusiveness have not fully been grasped by the people promoting
it. A dwindling number believe that it would be enough to simply
change the make-up of philosophy departments without changing
the content. Increasingly, these two projects are seen as connected:
philosophy will not attract long-excluded groups of people if members of these groups do not see themselves—their traditions, standpoints, and idioms—represented in syllabi and in publications. But
what would it mean to reconceive philosophy in order to adequately
represent these?

Let us start by doing some math: not the number-crunching of
human resources or admissions offices, but the mathematics of infinite series.

There is a formula for calculating the value of π that runs as follows:

$$1 - \tfrac{1}{3} + \tfrac{1}{5} - \tfrac{1}{7} + \tfrac{1}{9} - \ldots = \pi/4.$$

This, to be precise, is an alternating series that converges toward a value of the ratio of the circle's circumference to its diameter. It is most commonly known as a "Leibniz series," since in its current formulation it owes much to work carried out by the German philosopher and mathematician G. W. Leibniz in the 1680s. This discovery had significant implications for Leibniz's philosophical reflections on the nature of the infinite and on the ontology of mathematical objects. But Leibniz could not have accomplished what he did in this domain without building on the work of the Scottish mathematician James Gregory, and so sometimes the discovery is hyphenated as the "Gregory-Leibniz series."

So can we simply add the single hyphenation to the name of the series and leave it at that? Alas, things are not so simple. Some centuries earlier, in the southern Indian region of Kerala, the mathematician Madhava of Sangamagrama (1350–1425), developed his own methods for calculating a variety of infinite series, including the expression for π. The discovery in question, therefore, should more accurately be called the "Madhava-Gregory-Leibniz series."

Can we stop here? One fears, in fact, that our naming practices could easily take on the infinite character of the very series the names are meant to pick out. We may indeed reasonably speculate that there were numerous intermediaries—Arabs, Persians, French and Italian Jesuits—whose names have been forever lost to the historical record, and who helped slowly to transmit Madhava's innovations from fourteenth-century India to seventeenth-century Europe.

A more serious impediment to full inclusiveness, to the aim of recognizing conceptual depth and profound insight wherever these occur, is that even in joining the names of Madhava and Leibniz (to leave the Scot out for now), we represent them as having had fundamentally the same idea, and moreover, because most of us working in

Europe or North America have a clearer understanding of Leibniz's broader intellectual project, we tend to allow the German thinker to define for us what precisely this idea was.

But what was Madhava's intellectual project? What did this Indian thinker's world look like? The Kerala school of mathematics, of which Madhava was a founder, was centrally concerned with astronomy, and understood mathematics in large part as a tool for the calculation of the motions of celestial bodies. In this sense, the Kerala school is not so different from its Greek or Arabic counterparts, which were generally as concerned with the mixed mathematics of music and astronomy as with the unworldly abstractions of "pure" mathematics.

But the difference between the Indian and the European chapters of the life of the infinite series becomes more clear when we consider the human affairs whose rhythm and sense it was the purpose of astronomical measurement to mark out. In particular, astronomy was of use to the calendrical calculation of feasts, holy days and new years.

Ultimately, too, it was this calculation that established and articulated the vast cosmic epochs held to extend back into deep mythical time. These epochs provided a framework for the understanding of everyday reality that was entirely unfamiliar to members of outside cultures. Thus as the Persian Muslim traveler and geographer al-Biruni observed in his tenth-century *Indica*: in their measurement of time "it is the intention of the Hindus that we should refer the years invented by them to certain periods of life, beginning with the coming into existence, and ending with destruction and death." But these questions are rooted in what we think of as "myth," and not at all in the direct observation of the empirical world.

The ultimate meaning of the infinite series for Madhava, then, and of the sum total of mathematical practices in which this meaning is embedded, would be grounded in the Sanskrit scripture of Vedas. A rigorously hyphenated name for the discovery would include some mention of these holy texts, too.

That the discoveries of mixed mathematics and their philosophical implications can be traced to religious calendry is no less certain in European history. Thus the contemporary American philosopher of science Michael Friedman, for example, drawing on J. L. Heilbron's excellent book *The Sun in the Church*, has compellingly argued that we can trace a straight line from the ancient preoccupation with the temporal rhythms of the church calendar, to the construction of medieval cathedrals as dual-purpose astronomical observatories, and on, in a few more interesting steps, to modern European philosophical reflections on the nature of space and time.

The experience of time and the conceptualization of the past have been very different in India than in Europe (for one thing, the past calculated by Indians was vastly deeper than the relatively recent creation reported in Genesis: In Indian philosophy a single cosmic cycle, or yuga, lasts between roughly 4 and 8 billion years), but in both cases the presumed sequence of development is the same: from the rhythmic rituals of a mostly agricultural form of life, through the practical solution of problems for the regimentation of that form of life, and on to the increasingly theoretical reflection on the nature of these problems, a reflection that is often called "philosophy."

In both historical cases as well, the cultural practices of which philosophy may be seen as a recent outcropping are neglected and even denigrated by the philosophers themselves. In the Indian case, Sanskrit, the language of commentary on the Vedas and of philosophy, was not only not spoken by the great majority of people, but was positively forbidden to members of lower castes involved in sustenance activities such as food production. In the Greek context, Aristotle would seek to justify the very existence of laborers, including agricultural laborers, by virtue of the fact that their work enabled the existence of a small number of men whose entire lives could be devoted to reflection. Socrates would be even more blunt in his characterization of philosophy as by definition an urban activity, and thus an activity more or less removed from the cycles of the seasons and of nature. As he puts it in the dialogue *Phaedrus*: "I am a lover of knowledge, and the men who dwell in the city are my teachers, and not the trees or the country."

So for better or worse the eighteenth-century historian and philosopher Giambattista Vico would seem to have had it just right when he wrote that "the order of ideas must follow the order of institutions." For Vico "the order of all progress from the first origins" is the one that moves from "the woods," to "cultivated fields and huts, next little houses and villages, thence cities, and finally academies and philosophers." This is the self-understanding of philosophy made explicit, one that continues to define the endeavor as a cultural practice. Philosophy remains rigidly anchored to the world's great metropolitan centers. It is sometimes attempted in villages, in forests and out on the tundra, but there it is always marked by the anxiety of aspiration to tap into something that is, properly speaking, happening somewhere else.

It is hard to calculate the loss that this exclusionary self-conception assures. At a minimum, it hides from the sight of philosophy all the forms of sense-making throughout the world that have not, for whatever reasons, yielded institutions or textual records (not only the Vedas, but also the Homeric epics, spent their first several centuries in purely oral form, just like the poetic traditions of so many cultures from Amazonia to Africa to Siberia). It excludes the vast cognitive and interpretive resources of peoples who live in closer contact with the forces and cycles of the natural world, whether as foragers or as pastoralists and farmers. And let us make no mistake: these resources are equal to those of the people in the academies praised by Vico. They are the product of exactly the same sort of brains, set into different circumstances, making sense of those circumstances using just the same mixture of practical and theoretical reflection to which the "men who dwell in the city" have access.

The exclusionary self-conception, finally, prevents the development of the project of comparative ontology, which would take seriously the widest possible range of ways of making sense of the world, and would take the broadest possible measure of these beliefs, without concern for the institutional affiliations, the literacy, or the geographical niche of their holders.

At present, the small gestures made toward greater inclusiveness can in fact lead only to somewhat more robust representation of people who are all already in most important respects members of the same society. It excludes at the outset the people whose way of life separates them from the institutions in which philosophy is practiced and transmitted.

No one is talking yet about inserting pastoralist metaphysics or forager epistemology into the curriculum. You might suppose, of course, that the prospect of such things amounts to a reductio ad absurdum—a reduction to absurdity—of the recently popular project of inclusiveness, that once the doors are opened to conceptual innovations and cosmologies that developed far outside the tradition of philosophy extending back to ancient Greece, then at this point philosophy as a discipline loses all cohesion. If it is everywhere, then by the same token it is nowhere.

But I do not mean this as a reductio. The adequate account of any conceptual innovation or discovery in philosophy would be the one that also gives an account of its place in the broader context of human culture and history, and that would reveal its inextricable connection to cultural practices and human concerns that at first glance appear rather far removed from the concerns of the philosopher. This is an impossible goal, of course, but we can at least tend toward it, as toward the limit of an infinite series, if we wish. If we do not learn to see this effort as intrinsic to the study of philosophy, the recent calls for greater inclusiveness of other standpoints within philosophy will remain mere half-measures.

JUNE 22, 2014

ON WOMEN

When Prostitution Is Nobody's Business

—Laurie Shrage

Moral and political philosophers distinguish among different forms of privacy: physical, informational and decisional. When it comes to sex, we tend to have a strong expectation that we'll be granted all three.

Physical privacy involves having access to a space, on a permanent or temporary basis, where we are permitted to do things, sexual or otherwise, without being viewed by others. Informational privacy grants a reasonable amount of control over who has access to our personal information, including information about our sexual lives, habits and partners. Decisional privacy is having freedom from undue interference from others in the decisions we make about our lives, and people commonly want to make decisions about their sexual activities and relationships without such interference from family members, friends, co-workers or governments.

By contrast, other social relations, such as market transactions, come with different expectations of privacy. Commerce typically takes place in public venues, and we expect there to be informational transparency about the goods and services we purchase. We often want market transactions to be scrutinized or regulated by third parties in order to insure that they are fair and equitable, especially when full transparency is not available, as in the cases of pharmaceuticals, health care and real estate. So for the greater good, all three types of privacy are limited during market transactions in ways that would be unreasonable in regard to private sexual activity.

But when sex and commerce meet, the rules regarding sexual and market privacy quickly get murky. For example, should exchanges of sexual services for monetary gain take place with guarantees of privacy or transparency? If the former, then we expect them to be free from the intrusion of others. If the latter, then we expect them to be subject to social regulation. But where, exactly, is the border between the private exchange of money or gifts and the impersonal profit-making of the market?

When sexual partners exchange money and gifts between themselves, we generally see this as a private exchange. However, what do we do if a person has several sexual partners, and regularly receives money and gifts from each of them? Traditionally, a woman who had more than one sex partner from whom she received various forms of material support was likely to have been regarded as a "public woman," that is, a prostitute, whore or sex worker. Although there has been significant social tolerance historically for men who have and support multiple mistresses, moral disapprobation for women who have multiple lovers has resulted in laws in which women who have several sex partners from whom they accept gifts can face arrest for prostitution.

Having multiple, casual or ongoing partners from whom one receives monetary support is not the same as running a brothel, or setting up a home business that advertises publicly and accepts customers based on their ability to pay. Yet the line between these kinds of activities may be hard, at times, to make out. For example, should a person who is, say, polyamorous, and has multiple lovers who economically support her, have a right to physical, informational and decisional privacy in regards to her sex life?

Consider the case of Brandy Britton, a former university professor and mother who was separated from her abusive husband. Britton sought dates and accepted gifts from men whom she entertained in her home, with a goal of staving off the foreclosure of her house. In 2006, she was subject to an undercover arrest and charged with four counts of prostitution. A week before she was to be tried in court, she committed suicide.

Or consider that some young women today choose to seek "sugar daddies," typically well-off men who can help them pay their college tuition and living expenses, by using online dating sites. In exchange, the women offer these men companionship and other forms of intimacy. Should the activities of these women, or Britton, be treated as a form of prostitution, which is a criminal offense in the United States?

Laws and customs in America have evolved to the point where fewer consenting adults are charged with a crime when they privately engage in nonmarital sex. Laws against adultery have mostly been repealed or are unenforced. *Eisenstadt v. Baird* (1972) recognized the right of unmarried people to have access to contraception, and therefore to engage in nonprocreative sex. *Lawrence v. Texas* invalidated state anti-sodomy statutes that targeted private, consensual, same-sex intimacy between adults.

Can we really draw a bright line between a person who has casual sex, in private, with various lovers, and a person who has sex in private, with various short-term and long-term lovers, from whom she accepts monetary support? Dating couples often exchange money and gifts. Such exchanges of money do not transform their relationships into business transactions.

Anita Allen has argued that when people belong to groups that have been socially stigmatized, they often find it more difficult to defend and demand respect for their privacy, particularly in courts of law. For example, women, African-Americans, lesbians and gay men, the disabled, the poor or working class, and especially people at the intersection of two or more of these categories often lose in court when their privacy rights have been violated. Promiscuous, unmarried women and girls are often publicly shamed as "sluts," and denied their rights to privacy when others morally disapprove of their lifestyle. Although men also perform sex work, they are rarely subject to arrest or detention, or in other words, invasions of their sexual privacy.

When we described the activities of someone like Britton or the dating "sugar babies" as "selling sex" or performing "sex work," we place their activities in the public sphere. While these women may have sexual relations with a number of short- and long-term boyfriends or girlfriends who give them gifts of money, they are not formally employed as sex workers in a commercial establishment, nor are they running a business. Services provided in the home or other private spaces are typically understood differently than labor performed in spaces designated for commerce or under contract with an employer. Why should this be different when sex is involved?

If the state were to stop prosecuting women who provide intimate companionship for their one or many lovers, who in turn pay their bills, it does not follow that the state would then have to grant licenses to businesses offering sexual companions on a commercial basis. Commercial and publicly visible exchanges of personal sexual services present different kinds of moral issues. Would such businesses be of value to society, and could the rights of all involved and uninvolved parties be protected? With informal arrangements in our home, where we have a legitimate expectation of sexual privacy, these questions are less relevant.

Moreover, if the state were to stop prosecuting people like Britton for socializing with a flow of lovers in private, this does not entail that we should tolerate people having sex in cars, on the streets or in other public places. People can relieve themselves in a variety of ways in private, which we do not allow in the street. Whether anyone would want to live next door to a person like Britton is a different matter than whether her lifestyle should be criminalized. Surely she could be subject to the same nuisance laws, community rules and norms of politeness as anyone else. This should be sufficient to keep relations among neighbors peaceful and respectful. Some people have swinger parties in their homes without provoking the ire of their neighbors. But if they do offend, complaints are usually handled in a civil, rather than criminal, context.

In a liberal, democratic society, our basic right to privacy and equal treatment under the law should protect people like Britton when they do not harm others and are not a public nuisance. Such a change in our response to private, sexual activities would align our policies with those in Britain and other countries that have adopted the British model, where providing sex for money and offering money for sex are not crimes, as long as these activities take place in private.

This is a different model than the Swedish one, which criminalizes offering money for sex, or the Dutch "harm reduction model," which permits and regulates commercial sex work establishments. These models have had mixed success in protecting the safety and dignity of sex workers, or in stopping trafficking and nonconsensual sex work.

This week, participants in an Amnesty International council meeting in Dublin are considering a proposal to endorse the decriminalization of consensual paid sex between adults. The proposal has elements of the both the British model, which rests on the idea that consensual sex between adults should be protected from state interference, and the Dutch model, which is based on the idea that criminalizing paid sex generates more harm than good. The policy draft I read emphasizes the organization's longstanding commitment to end trafficking, and to insure that, where paid sex exists, it is voluntary and safe.

Yet some prominent feminist groups have organized to oppose Amnesty International's proposed policy and to endorse the Swedish model of prohibition. Their opposition is based on the assumption that acts of paid sex are inevitably coercive and that the state should intervene in private sexual acts between adults to protect vulnerable people.

The first assumption has been strongly challenged by many sex worker civil and labor rights groups, and the second assumption is subject to the objection that it is overly paternalistic toward adult women. Moreover, opponents to Amnesty International's proposed policy overlook the fact that it remains neutral on the question of whether there should be public establishments for the purpose of buying and selling sex.

Amnesty International's proposed policy, like the British model, offers an intermediate step that recognizes that an act, such as sex exchanged for monetary support, can have different meanings depending on its context.

Either of these policies, if implemented, would change the way we respond to cases of people like Brandy Britton and the women seeking sugar daddies through online dating, whose activities deserve protection under contemporary moral and legal understandings of "privacy."

While we might believe that having sex for money is neither wise nor good, democratic and free societies now allow adults—married or unmarried—to make their own choices regarding why and with whom they have sex. It's time to stop policing the private, consensual sex lives of adult women who support themselves in morally unconventional ways.

AUGUST 10, 2015

On Abortion and Defining a "Person"

—Gary Gutting

THE RECENT REFERENDUM IN MISSISSIPPI SHOWED THAT MANY Americans—including many strong opponents of abortion—are reluctant to treat a fertilized egg as a human person. They are, in particular, unwilling to extend the full protection of our laws against murder to a fertilized egg. This might seem to be just a common sense reaction to an extreme position, but rejecting the personhood position has important consequences for the logic of the abortion debate. (In formulating these logical consequences, I am not taking a position on the morality of abortion. As always, logic can only force a choice between accepting a conclusion and denying the premises from which the conclusion follows.)

The standard critique of abortion asserts that it is murder: the intentional killing of an innocent person. The typical starting point for this critique is the obvious fact that killing a baby right after its birth is murder. What the argument then must show is that, as far as the morality of killing goes, there is no essential difference between the newborn baby and the child at earlier stages of development. Here one approach is to cite more advanced features of the newborn (like consciousness, the capacity to feel pain or the ability to survive outside the womb) that might be thought to give it moral standing. But this limits the case against abortion, since for any such feature, there are stages where the fetus (or, earlier, the embryo) does not have these features.

Accordingly, the case against the morality of *all* abortions, no matter how early, needs to appeal to features of the newborn that are present at *every* stage of development beyond the fertilization of the egg. Here the only plausible feature seems to be *having the DNA characteristic of the human species* (the structure that, in the natural course of things, will lead to the newborn baby).

The problem, however, is that a fertilized egg itself has this DNA. Therefore, if we grant that killing a fertilized egg is not murder, we must also agree that the mere fact that a fetus or embryo possesses human DNA does not show that killing it is murder. It also seems to follows that at least some early-term abortions are not murder, since it's hard to see any moral difference between a fertilized egg and, say, an embryo of two or three weeks.

A possible response is to claim that there is a person with full moral standing only once the fertilized egg has been implanted in the uterus (about five days after fertilization). But why think that implantation confers personhood? The only plausible reason seems to be that an implanted egg is on a natural path that will, if all goes well, lead to a full-term birth. But the same is true of a fertilized egg. So it's hard to see that the potential to develop into a newborn morally differentiates a fertilized egg before and a fertilized egg after implantation.

The basic problem is that, once we give up the claim that a fertilized egg is a human person (has full moral standing), there is no plausible basis for claiming that all further stages of development are human persons. The DNA criterion seems to be the only criterion of being human that applies at every stage from conception to birth. If we agree that it does not apply at the earliest stages of gestation, there is no basis for claiming that every abortion is the killing of an innocent human person.

Those convinced that abortion is murder can, of course, maintain that this entire line of argument merely shows that we must hold that the fertilized egg is a human person: abortion is always wrong and it wouldn't be if the fertilized egg weren't a person. But what the Mississippi referendum showed was that many of those strongly opposed to abortion do not believe this. They were not willing, for example, to forbid aborting pregnancies that result from rape or incest or that are necessary to save the mother's life. Many were also unwilling to charge fertility doctors who destroy frozen embryos with murder or to forbid after-fertilization birth control devices such as IUD's.

Couldn't proponents of a personhood amendment allow exceptions for such cases? Yes, but this would destroy the logic behind the amendment. It is, for example, obviously wrong to kill a newborn on the grounds that it was conceived through rape or incest. But then, given the rape/incest exception, it is not true that the fetus before birth has the same moral standing as the newborn. There are conditions under which it may be killed and the newborn may not. This contradicts the basic claim that there is a human person present from the time of fertilization through the birth of the baby.

I am not claiming that those who reject the personhood of a fertilized egg have no grounds for opposing abortion. But they cannot consistently claim that all abortions, even at very early stages or in special circumstances, are wrong. They can still regard some (later-term) abortions as the killing of an innocent human person, although, to establish this, they need to provide a criterion for personhood beyond that of having human DNA.

The above analysis does not settle the vexed question of abortion. That would require answering the question of what makes a person a person. But the analysis does show that those who do not agree that a fertilized egg is a person cannot argue that abortion is wrong because an embryo or fetus has human DNA. To maintain a strong anti-abortion position, they must find some other reason for thinking that abortion is murder.

NOVEMBER 30, 2011

Girlfriend, Mother, Professor?

—*Carol Hay*

I'M NOT THEIR MOTHER. AND I'M NOT THEIR GIRLFRIEND EITHER. I'm their university professor. At times I encounter students, both male and female, who don't quite grasp this, and I consequently find myself in a whole host of awkward situations, trying to subtly remind them that I'm neither going to make their bed nor go to bed with them.

The problem is that my students lack the cultural scripts to know how to deal with our teacher-student relationship. In 1925, Sigmund Freud coined the idea of the "Madonna-whore complex," according to which men are able to see women only as their saintly mothers or their sexual playthings. Whatever one thinks of Freud, we can all recognize some truth to this insight.

If I were to serve as their mother, I'd have only compassion and unconditional acceptance to offer, not intellectual lessons. And being their sexual plaything isn't an option either; playthings aren't generally accorded the kind of respect needed for effective teaching and learning, not to mention the respect I deserve after more than a decade of postsecondary education.

My male colleagues don't have these problems. There's no shortage of roles they can avail themselves of in trying to reach their students.

Male professors' strategies for reaching their male students harken back to Plato. In his *Symposium*, Plato describes the methods of paiderastia, the ancient Athenian practice of instilling wisdom and civic virtue in young men through romantic relationships with older men. Sure, some of those students might have genuinely lusted after their teachers, but Plato explains that the role of this lust was to set a student on the path to learning transcendental lessons—moving from a concrete appreciation of beautiful bodies to an ever more abstract appreciation of beautiful souls, beautiful laws and customs, then culminating in an appreciation of the form of beauty itself.

The sex has (for the most part) dropped out for us now, but a mentoring relationship between older and younger men remains one of the most accepted and effective ways of transmitting knowledge and power in a patriarchal society such as ours.

One of male professors' most effective strategies for reaching their female students is an old one, described by the feminist and existentialist philosopher Simone de Beauvoir in 1949. De Beauvoir argued that women crave men's authority to protect them from their own liberty. Existentialists are, in general, pretty pessimistic about people's tendency to live in bad faith. They think most people want to avoid the anxiety of taking existential responsibility for their lives, preferring instead to find a way to have someone else make their decisions for them.

De Beauvoir argues that a distinctively feminine manifestation of this existential inauthenticity is women's tendency to subsume their identity under the identity of the man they love. Consider women who take on a whole new set of hobbies and interests every time they start dating a new man. (Lest you think this is a thing of the past, my students assure me that they still see it all the time among their friends.) Why do so many women take on their husband's surname when they marry? An apt metaphor for all this, de Beauvoir says, is found in the fairy tale of the little mermaid, who gave up her fishtail and had her tongue cut out for the chance to be loved by a human man, only to find herself turned into sea foam after he spurned her.

Many a female student has been turned into sea foam. They lust after their professors and are, too often, greeted with open arms, but the ensuing erotic relationship, unlike the pederastic one, does little to help women realize any higher intellectual lesson. Instead, the beloved is frequently stuck—or more accurately, objectified—valued only on the basis of her physical appearance or sexual appeal. The contrast between this situation and the one articulated by Plato is stark: In the *Symposium*, Socrates makes it clear that while his students might fall in love with him, he views this love as merely a tool to help them grow up and ultimately wrest themselves from childish attractions.

Erotic relationships between female students and their male professors, however, are not usually an effective steppingstone to further intellectual pursuits for the student, who will be more likely to face accusations of "sleeping her way to the top" than to be taken seriously as an intellectual interlocutor. But such relationships serve to flatter the ego of many an aging male academic, even when they show enough restraint to keep things at the level of "harmless" flirtation.

Of course, not all male professors exploit the intimacy of the pedagogical relationship by permitting it to turn sexual. But there are plenty of advantages to reap even for those who stay on the right side of the line. In our culture, men are the keepers of the intellectual flame and can bestow it as they see fit. Male professors can take on a "father knows best" persona, or an avuncular one, and use their comfortable position of authority to inspire a student to delve deeper into an academic subject. Female professors have no such personae available to them. In our culture mothers dispense hugs, not pearls of wisdom, and when they do venture to have opinions we're likelier than not to roll our eyes at them for being nags or scolds. And we don't even have a word for the aunt-equivalent of "avuncular."

As female professors age, the typecasting changes: We move with depressing predictability from the role of girlfriend to the role of mother. Julinna Oxley, an associate professor at Coastal Carolina University, reports that when she first started teaching, her teaching evaluations would say things like "She's hot," or "She wears great skirts." Now, ten years later, she's lost her chili pepper on RateMyProfessors.com and her students look to her for advice in their personal lives and for extensions on assignments.

My students, thankfully, aren't just men. But there are even fewer cultural scripts on which to model the pedagogical relationship between female professors and their female students. Some of my female students are able to recognize the need for and benefits of finding a female mentor, but surprisingly few of them actually do. One explanation for this comes from feminist philosophers as old as John Stuart Mill and de Beauvoir, who argue that solidarity is particularly hard for women because they often have more in common with the men in their lives than with women across race, class or age boundaries.

Another explanation comes from contemporary feminist philosophers like Sandra Bartky, who describes the phenomenon of internalized oppression. Bartky argues that self-loathing is an inevitable result of living in a culture saturated with messages about the inferior status and value of people like you. Given this, it's no surprise that many of my female students find it no easier than their male counterparts to look up to someone who's not a man. Mermaids would rather cut out their tongues than spend a life stuck with other mermaids.

The problem is that we, as a culture, don't really know what a female professor is supposed to be. The archetypal professor is decidedly male—rumpled tweed jacket, argyle socks, bushy beard, pipe—and even if it were an option not much in this aesthetic is terribly appealing to a cisgender woman like me. In my more optimistic moments I try to see this cultural void as an opportunity—I'm lucky enough to have the chance to avoid falling into age-old stereotypes and to invent new, more appropriate roles. But most of the time it just feels like a desert. Feminists have been telling us for a very long time that women in positions of authority find themselves stuck between a rock and a hard place. Too assertive or confident and they'll call you a "bitch." Too passive or self-deprecating and they'll think you're a doormat and unfit to be taken seriously.

And Patricia Hill Collins, a philosopher of feminism and race, has argued that women of color face even more rigid limitations on their social roles, usually finding themselves stereotyped as "mammies, matriarchs, welfare recipients, [or] hot mommas." The problem is that there really isn't a middle ground for any of us here: We can't handle it when women aren't "nice," but being in a position of authority means that you're sometimes going to tell people things they don't want to hear. So, for example, taking male colleagues to task for abusing their power for sexual gain is one of the best ways to alienate a reader.

Sociologists such as Arlie Hochschild and philosophers such as Cheshire Calhoun have written about the "emotional work" for which women are responsible even in the workplace. Because women are thought to be naturally caring and empathetic they're expected not only to have their own emotional ducks in a row, they're also expected to take on the task of helping others manage their emotions—calming tempers, mending wounded egos, boosting confidence, mediating frictions, ensuring harmony. This work is essentially invisible and uncompensated. It's almost never a formal requirement listed on job descriptions or performance and tenure reviews, and it's so taken for granted that it tends to fall below the radar of even our informal moral accounting.

Alice MacLachlan, an associate professor at York University, tells a story about joking with a male colleague about how she always knew midterms were over because she had to bring out her backup box of tissues. He looked at her blankly, and it was only then that she realized none of her male colleagues had to replace their tissues at least once a semester after crying students had used them up. Women are expected to be kind and caring, so the bar is higher for what's expected of them, and they're penalized more harshly when they're perceived not to be.

Serena Parekh, an associate professor at Northeastern University, still cringes at the memory of receiving a bad teaching evaluation that criticized her for not being "nurturing" enough. The philosopher Claudia Card has argued that if we're going to upset these unfair cultural expectations women need to care less and men need to care more. This is wonderful advice about how we should try to revise our expectations when making moral assessments of a given professor's character, but it's risky practical advice for female professors to take, given that we know that women who fail to live up to expectations of caring will be vilified.

As a female professor, I've found that a bigger challenge than "leaning in" to my career has been figuring out how to avoid falling into roles that are far from my own choosing. We lack the cultural narratives to make sense of women in positions of social power or authority. The ones we do have haven't changed much since the days of Freud and de Beauvoir. This failure of cultural imagination affects women's political, economic and social prospects. It always has. The trick, as educators, is to start figuring out how to teach our students without losing them in the sea foam, so they can grow up to look for, or to be, something other than girlfriends and mothers.

JANUARY 25, 2016

The Disappearing Women

—*Rae Langton*

"How many philosophers does it take to change a light bulb?"

"It depends what you mean by 'change' . . ."

That joke pokes gentle fun at a popular caricature: the chin-stroking graybeard, with his fetish for word meanings, his practical irrelevance and his philosophy that "leaves everything as it is," as Wittgenstein said. The caricature is misleading, for philosophy also prides itself on its capacity to ask hard questions and challenge prejudice. Socrates was executed for stirring up trouble. Descartes began his *Meditations* with a rousing call to "demolish completely" a long-standing edifice of falsehoods—to uproot our "habit of holding on to old opinions" and look at the world with fresh, unbiased eyes.

That radical power has inspired many women in philosophy, and much political work. The English philosopher Mary Astell wrote irreverently, in 1700, that an opinion's age is no guide to its truth, that "a rational mind" is not made for servitude, and that a woman's obligation to a man "is only a Business by the Bye"—"just as it may be any Man's Business and Duty to keep Hogs." From Descartes's idea that we are *essentially thinking beings* she deduced a conclusion too daring for her peers: *colleges for women*. Husband-keeping is like hog-keeping: a contingent duty, not what a woman is made for.

Many women have, like Astell, found in philosophy a source of joyful challenge and liberation, fascinating in its own terms, with illuminating consequences for life and the social world. Given philosophy's ambitions, we might fondly expect a profession especially free from bias and welcoming to those targeted by prejudice. That hope is somewhat hard to square with its dearth of women.

There are many possible explanations. Bias is harder to notice than Descartes expected, being unconscious, near-universal and more readily revealed in the psychologist's lab than by the "natural light of reason."

There is the effort of juggling work and family life (but why philosophy, more than other disciplines?) There are startling reports of sexual harassment, at the website What Is It Like to Be a Woman in Philosophy (Worse than other fields? Who knows, but it should be *better!*). Some have looked to gender norms for an explanation, supposing that if "men are from Mars," they thrive better in our martial debating culture (but why philosophy, more than economics?). Some have, more plausibly, invoked a "perfect storm" of diverse factors (see Louise Antony's article "Different Voices or Perfect Storm: Why Are There So Few Women in Philosophy?").

That caricature of Philosophy must be partly to blame: the "man of reason" pictured as a serious, high-minded Dumbledore (for some nice correctives, see the site Looks Philosophical). When a field is group stereotyped, outsiders often feel less welcome. They often perform less well when something triggers group awareness. Stereotype threat can make anyone, from white athletes to black students, underperform, when appropriately primed. Philosophy itself may be a source of priming influence, with its mostly male lineup for reading lists, conferences and teachers (see Jennifer Saul's work on the psychological biases affecting philosophy).

Philosophy is often introduced through its history, beginning with Socrates, who banished the weeping women, as prelude to the real business of philosophizing. Other banishments followed, so it can be tempting to see an unbroken all-male succession, as course lists (including my own) still testify. That part, too, is misleading. Princess Elisabeth of Bohemia, in her notable correspondence with Descartes, offered the most enduring objection to Descartes's dualism: How can immaterial mind and material body interact? She is puzzlingly absent from standard editions that include his contemporary critics. Maria von Herbert provoked a deep question for Kant: Is moral perfection compatible with utter apathy? She is puzzlingly absent from the latest Kant biography, and her letters survive elsewhere for their gossip value (sex! suicide!). With omissions like these we let down philosophers of past, present and future. We feed the stereotype and the biases Descartes despised.

One more joke, then: "How many feminists does it take to change a light bulb?"

"It's not the light bulb that needs changing."

SEPTEMBER 4, 2013

A Feminist Kant

—Carol Hay

Iɴ ᴏɴᴇ ᴏғ ʜɪs ᴍᴏʀᴇ ᴍᴇᴍᴏʀᴀʙʟᴇ ᴇssᴀʏs, "Gᴇᴛᴛɪɴɢ Aᴡᴀʏ ғʀᴏᴍ Already Being Pretty Much Away from It All," David Foster Wallace describes a visit to the Illinois State Fair. The friend who accompanies him, whom he calls Native Companion because she's a local, gets on one of the fair's rides. While she's hanging upside down, the men operating the ride stop it so that her dress falls over her head and they can ogle her. After she gets off the ride, Wallace and Native Companion have a heated discussion about the incident. He thinks she's been sexually harassed and thinks something should be done about it.

Wallace asks, "Did you sense something kind of sexual-harassmentish going on through that whole little sick exercise? . . . this doesn't bother you? As a Midwesterner, you're unbothered?" to which Native Companion replies, "So if I noticed or I didn't, why does it have to be *my* deal? What, because there's [harassers] in the world I don't get to ride on The Zipper? I don't get to ever spin? . . . What's getting hot and bothered going to do about it except keep me from getting to have fun?" Then, Wallace: "This is potentially key. . . . The core value informing a kind of willed politico-sexual stoicism on your part is your prototypically Midwestern appreciation of fun . . . whereas on the East Coast, politico-sexual indignation *is* the fun. . . . I'm telling you. Personal and political fun merge somewhere just east of Cleveland, for women." Native Companion: "They might ought to try just climbing on and spinning and ignoring [them]. That's pretty much all you can do with [expletive]."

Situations like this are ubiquitous, and hardly the worst thing women have to put up with in a sexist society such as ours. But I've grown tired of discussing what's wrong with the carnies' behavior. (It's a textbook case of sexual harassment, and more than enough feminist ink has been spilled explaining why and how this sort of thing is morally unacceptable.) Instead, I want to ask a different set of questions: What is Native Companion obligated to do here? In general, are victims of oppression obligated to resist their oppression?

In short, yes. And the philosophical resources for this claim can be found in a somewhat surprising place: in the moral philosophy of the eighteenth-century German philosopher Immanuel Kant.

I wasn't always so optimistic about Kant's prospects. I first started thinking about these questions while I was in grad school, a feminist who was training to be an analytic philosopher. Analytic philosophers are generally friendly toward Kant (friendlier than many of them tend to be toward feminism, in any case). But most feminist philosophers make no secret of their dislike of him. They rightly decry the horrifically misogynistic things Kant actually said about women (there are some real doozies), and they argue that, among other things, he is committed to a conception of personhood that unfairly and inaccurately privileges our rationality and autonomy over the social, interdependent, embodied, and emotional aspects of our lives. This misrepresentation of human nature encourages us to think about people as fundamentally independent, and this, they argue, leads to the exploitation of those people (usually women) who are responsible for caring for those people who are not independent (children, the elderly, the disabled and infirm—all of us at some point in our lives, really).

Consulting yet another dead white male about the problems of oppression didn't initially strike me as the best idea. But I've now come to think that Kant's account of what our rational nature is, why it's valuable, how it can be compromised and deformed, and why it must be fostered and protected, should be of interest not only to feminists, but to anyone who cares about the victims of oppression, harassment, bullying, or abuse.

Kant argues throughout his moral philosophy that what's distinctive about us as human beings is our rational nature—our ability to set and pursue ends according to reason (or, more colloquially, our ability to figure out what we want, to figure out how to get it, and to ask ourselves whether we should want it). This rational nature, he argues, is what makes us morally valuable and what makes us deserve an important sort of respect.

This respect requires that we always be treated as an end and never merely as a means. As Kant puts it, "So act that you use humanity, whether in your own person or in the person of any other, always at the same time as an end, never merely as a means." We treat people as means whenever we ignore the ends they've set for themselves and instead use them for our own purposes. Kantian philosophers typically focus on how this morally impermissible use of another person involves deception and coercion. But Kant's moral framework can also be used to show what's wrong with other frustrations of rational nature, including those that pop up under oppression.

Feminists have been discussing the devastating psychological effects of sexist oppression for quite some time. Mary Wollstonecraft and J. S. Mill argued, in the eighteenth and nineteenth centuries respectively, that sexist social norms of genteel society and motherhood, combined with sexist legal institutions such as marriage and property, damaged women's rational capacities by depriving them of equal opportunities with men to develop their talents. Contemporary feminists have continued this discussion in a number of ways. Many focus on what happens when women internalize sexist oppression, when women come to believe in, are weakened by, and are motivated to fulfill the stereotypes that represent them as inferior. One way to think about these various harms is that they're instances where oppression has harmed women's rational nature in some way.

Of course, Kantianism is hardly the only philosophical framework with the resources to explain what's wrong with these harms.

What sets Kant apart from almost every other thinker in the Western philosophical canon is his ability to make sense of duties to the self, particularly the duty of self-respect. (Most non-Kantian philosophers think of duties as the sorts of things that you can only have to other people, not the sort of thing you can have to yourself.) Kant's duty of self-respect, first introduced in his 1785 *Groundwork of the Metaphysics of Morals*, is a duty each of us has to recognize the value of the rational nature within us and to respond accordingly. Just as we have a duty to respect others in virtue of their rational nature, we have a duty to respect ourselves.

Without this duty of self-respect, we could explain why someone like Native Companion has a duty to respond to the oppression of other women, simply by appealing a general duty to resist injustice. But we can't explain why she has a particular duty to resist her own oppression. Given that self-sacrifice is routinely expected of oppressed people in ways it's not expected of others (think, for example, of the ideal of the self-abnegating mother who unfailingly puts her family's interests before her own), establishing the duty of self-respect is especially important in these contexts.

What the marriage of Kantianism and feminism gets us, then, is this. Because we have an obligation to prevent harms to our rational nature, and because oppression can harm our capacity to act rationally, we have an obligation to resist our own oppression. Despite what Kant himself might've thought, we know that women's rational capacities are no different from men's. Thus, we can use Kantianism to explain why women are just as deserving of respect as men and why this respect is incompatible with sexist oppression.

So it looks like Native Companion is wrong. The duty of self-respect demands that she stand up for herself by resisting her oppression. Of course, this isn't the only duty that's operative here. The carnies have a duty to stop their immoral behavior; Wallace probably has a duty to stand up for his friend, and certainly has a more general duty to protest injustice; and Native Companion has a duty to other women to do what she can to undermine the manifestations of sexist oppression that all women face. But the duty of self-respect under oppression has received considerably less philosophical attention than these other duties.

The most obvious objection to this line of argument is that holding Native Companion responsible for resisting her oppression shifts the moral burden in this situation onto the party who hasn't done anything wrong—in effect, it blames the victim. But here, too, is a place where the resources of Kantianism are uniquely well-suited to help. In a later work, his 1797 *The Metaphysics of Morals*, Kant expands upon a distinction first introduced in his earlier *Groundwork*: a distinction between perfect and imperfect duties. Unlike perfect duties, imperfect duties aren't duties to perform specific actions. Instead, imperfect duties are duties to adopt certain general maxims, or principles of action, that can be satisfied by more than one action.

The obligation to resist oppression is this sort of duty: there are lots of things one can do to fulfill it. Native Companion could confront the carnies directly. She could lodge a formal complaint with the fair's management. We might even think that she actually is resisting her oppression internally by refusing to feel humiliated, refusing to let the carnies dictate when and how she can have fun, and refusing to believe that their sexually objectifying her demeans her moral status in any way. In some cases, there might be nothing an oppressed person can do to resist her oppression other than simply recognizing that there's something wrong with her situation. This is, in a profound sense, better than nothing. It means she hasn't acquiesced to the innumerable forces that are conspiring to convince her that she's the sort of person who has no right to expect better. It means she recognizes that her lot in life is neither justified nor inevitable.

DECEMBER 8, 2013

ON FAMILY

Think Before You Breed

—Christine Overall

As a young woman in my twenties I pondered whether or not to have children. Is there a way, I wondered, to decide thoughtfully rather than carelessly about this most momentous of human choices?

It's a tough decision because you can't know ahead of time what sort of child you will have or what it will be like to be a parent. You can't understand what is good or what is hard about the process of creating and rearing until after you have the child. And the choice to have a child is a decision to change your life forever. It's irreversible, and therefore, compared to reversible life choices about education, work, geographical location or romance, it has much greater ethical importance.

Choosing whether or not to procreate may not seem like the sort of decision that is deserving or even capable of analysis. The Canadian novelist Margaret Laurence wrote, "I don't really feel I have to analyze my own motives in wanting children. For my own reassurance? For fun? For ego-satisfaction? No matter. It's like (to me) asking why you want to write. Who cares? You have to, and that's that."

In fact, people are still expected to provide reasons *not* to have children, but no reasons are required to have them. It's assumed that if individuals do not have children it is because they are infertile, too selfish or have just not yet gotten around to it. In any case, they owe their interlocutor an explanation. On the other hand, no one says to the proud parents of a newborn, Why did you choose to have that child? What are your reasons? The choice to procreate is not regarded as needing any thought or justification.

Nonetheless, I think Laurence's "Who cares?" attitude is mistaken.

We are fortunate that procreation is more and more a matter of choice. Not always, of course—not everyone has access to effective contraception and accessible abortion, and some women are subjected to enforced pregnancy. But the growing availability of reproductive choice makes it clear that procreation cannot be merely an expression of personal taste.

The question whether to have children is of course prudential in part; it's concerned about what is or is not in one's own interests. But it is *also* an ethical question, for it is about whether to bring a person (in some cases more than one person) into existence—and that person cannot, by the very nature of the situation, give consent to being brought into existence. Such a question also profoundly affects the well-being of existing people (the potential parents, siblings if any, and grandparents). And it has effects beyond the family on the broader society, which is inevitably changed by the cumulative impact—on things like education, health care, employment, agriculture, community growth and design, and the availability and distribution of resources—of individual decisions about whether to procreate.

There are self-help books on the market that purport to assist would-be parents in making a practical choice about whether or not to have children. There are also informal discussions on websites, in newspapers and magazines, and in blogs. Yet the ethical nature of this choice is seldom recognized, even—or especially—by philosophers.

Perhaps people fail to see childbearing as an ethical choice because they think of it as the expression of an instinct or biological drive, like sexual attraction or "falling in love," that is not amenable to ethical evaluation. But whatever our biological inclinations may be, many human beings do take control over their fertility, thanks to contemporary means of contraception and abortion. The rapidly declining birthrate in most parts of the world is evidence of that fact. While choosing whether or not to have children may involve feelings, motives, impulses, memories and emotions, it can and should also be a subject for careful reflection.

If we fail to acknowledge that the decision of whether to parent or not is a real choice that has ethical import, then we are treating child-bearing as a mere expression of biological destiny. Instead of seeing having children as something that women *do*, we will continue to see it as something that simply *happens* to women, or as something that is merely "natural" and animal-like.

The decision to have children surely deserves at least as much thought as people devote to leasing a car or buying a house. Procreation decisions are about whether or not to assume complete responsibility, over a period of at least eighteen years, for a new life or new lives. Because deciding whether to procreate has ethical dimensions, the reasons people give for their procreative choices deserve examination. Some reasons may be better—or worse—than others.

My aim, I hasten to add, is not to argue for policing people's procreative motives. I am simply arguing for the need to think systematically and deeply about a fundamental aspect of human life.

The burden of proof—or at least the burden of justification—should therefore rest primarily on those who choose to have children, not on those who choose to be childless. The choice to have children calls for more careful justification and thought than the choice not to have children, because procreation creates a dependent, needy, and vulnerable human being whose future may be at risk. The individual who chooses childlessness takes the ethically less risky path. After all, nonexistent people can't suffer from not being created. They do not have an entitlement to come into existence, and we do not owe it to them to bring them into existence. But once children do exist, we incur serious responsibilities to them.

Because children are dependent, needy and vulnerable, prospective parents should consider how well they can love and care for the offspring they create, and the kind of relationship they can have with them. The genuinely unselfish life plan may at least sometimes be the choice not to have children, especially in the case of individuals who would otherwise procreate merely to adhere to tradition, to please others, to conform to gender conventions, or to benefit themselves out of the inappropriate expectation that children will fix their problems. Children are neither human pets nor little therapists.

Some people claim that the mere fact that our offspring will probably be happy gives us ample reason to procreate. The problem with this argument is, first, that there are no guarantees. The sheer unpredictability of children, the limits on our capacities as parents, and the instability of social conditions make it unwise to take for granted that our progeny will have good lives. But just as important, justifying having kids by claiming that our offspring will be happy provides no stopping point for procreative behavior. If two children are happy, perhaps four will be, or seven, or ten.

The unwillingness to stop is dramatized by the so-called Octomom, Nadya Suleman, who first had six children via in vitro fertilization, then ended up with eight more from just one pregnancy, aided by her reprehensible doctor, Michael Kamrava. Higher-order multiple pregnancies often create long-term health problems for the children born of them. It's also unlikely that Suleman can provide adequate care for and attention to her fourteen children under the age of twelve, especially in light of her recent bankruptcy, her very public attempts to raise money, and the impending loss of their home. Was Suleman's desire for a big family fair to her helpless offspring?

Consider also reality television "stars" Michelle and Jim Bob Duggar, the parents of nineteen children. The Duggars claim to have religious motives for creating their large family. But it's not at all clear that God places such a high value on the Duggar genetic heritage. Unlike Suleman, the Duggars don't struggle to support their brood, but mere financial solvency is not a sufficient reason to birth more than a dozen and a half offspring, even if the kids seem reasonably content.

People like the Duggars and Suleman might respond that they have a right to reproduce. Certainly they are entitled to be free from state interference in their procreative behavior; compulsory contraception and abortion, or penalties for having babies, are abhorrent.

But a right to non-interference does not, by itself, justify every decision to have a baby.

We should not regret the existence of the children in these very public families, now that they are here. My point is just that their parents' models of procreative decision making deserve skepticism. The parents appear to overlook what is ethically central: the possibility of forming a supportive, life-enhancing and close relationship with each of their offspring.

After struggling with our own decision about whether to procreate, in the end my spouse and I chose to have two children, whom we adore. The many rewards and challenges of raising kids have gradually revealed the far-reaching implications of procreative decision making. In choosing to become a parent, one seeks to create a relationship, and, uniquely, one also seeks to create the person with whom one has the relationship. Choosing whether or not to have children is therefore the most significant ethical debate of most people's lives.

JUNE 17, 2012

Is Forced Fatherhood Fair?

—Laurie Shrage

THIS WEEKEND MILLIONS OF AMERICANS WILL HAPPILY CELE-brate the role that fathers play in their families. For some families, though—specifically those in which dad's role was not freely assumed, but legally mandated—Father's Day can be an emotionally complicated occasion. And that somewhat messy reality raises a question that is worth examining today as the very definition of parents and families continues to undergo legal and social transformation.

Women's rights advocates have long struggled for motherhood to be a voluntary condition, and not one imposed by nature or culture. In places where women and girls have access to affordable and safe contraception and abortion services, and where there are programs to assist mothers in distress find foster or adoptive parents, voluntary motherhood is basically a reality. In many states, infant safe haven laws allow a birth mother to walk away from her newborn baby if she leaves it unharmed at a designated facility.

If a man accidentally conceives a child with a woman, and does not want to raise the child with her, what are his choices? Surprisingly, he has few options in the United States. He can urge her to seek an abortion, but ultimately that decision is hers to make. Should she decide to continue the pregnancy and raise the child, and should she or our government attempt to establish him as the legal father, he can be stuck with years of child support payments.

Do men now have less reproductive autonomy than women?

Should men have more control over when and how they become parents, as many women now do?

The political philosopher Elizabeth Brake has argued that our policies should give men who accidentally impregnate a woman more options, and that feminists should oppose policies that make fatherhood compulsory. In a 2005 article in the *Journal of Applied Philosophy* she wrote, "if women's partial responsibility for pregnancy does not obligate them to support a fetus, then men's partial responsibility for pregnancy does not obligate them to support a resulting child." At most, according to Brake, men should be responsible for helping with the medical expenses and other costs of a pregnancy for which they are partly responsible.

Few feminists, including Brake, would grant men the right to coerce a woman to have (or not to have) an abortion, because they recognize a woman's right to control her own body. However, if a woman decides to give birth to a child without securing the biological father's consent to raise a child with her, some scholars and policy makers question whether he should be assigned legal paternity.

Historically, it was important for women to have husbands who acknowledged paternity for their children, as children born to unmarried parents were deemed "illegitimate" and had fewer rights than children born to married parents. Today, the marital status of a child's parents affects that child's future much less. Nevertheless, having two legal parents is a significant advantage for a child, and establishing legal paternity for both married and unmarried fathers is a complicated but necessary part of our public policies.

As more children are born to unmarried parents, the social and legal preference for awarding paternity to the mother's husband becomes more outdated. When there is a dispute about fatherhood rights and obligations, the courts can use different criteria for assigning legal paternity. These include a man's marital or marriage-like relationship with the child's mother, his caregiving and support role in the child's life, and his biological relationship to the child.

The legal scholar Jane Murphy has argued that a new definition of fatherhood is emerging in our laws and court decisions which privileges a man's biological tie to a child over other criteria. In a 2005 article in the *Notre Dame Law Review*, Murphy wrote about paternity "disestablishment" cases in which men who have assumed the father role in a child's life seek genetic testing to avoid the obligations of legal fatherhood, typically when they break up with the child's mother. Her research shows that replacing the limited "mother's husband" conception of fatherhood with a narrow biologically based one still leaves many children legally fatherless.

Furthermore, Murphy explains how the new definition of "fatherhood" is driven by the government's goal of collecting child support from men whose biological offspring are in the welfare system, as well as lawsuits from men aiming to avoid financial responsibility for their dependents. Murphy, then, reasonably proposes that judges and legislators "recognize multiple bases for legal fatherhood" and be guided by "the traditional goals of family law—protecting children and preserving family stability." Murphy argues for revising paternity establishment policies so that fewer men become legal fathers involuntarily or without understanding the legal responsibilities they are assuming.

Murphy's proposed reforms would apply to men who have different kinds of ties to a child. They would protect a naïve man who, in a moment of exuberance with a girlfriend, allows his name to be put on a birth certificate, and a man whose only tie to a child is biological. Coercing legal paternity in such cases leads to painful "disestablishment" battles that are unlikely to be in the best interest of the child or promote stable family relationships. Murphy discusses cases in which legal fathers resort to violence or threats of violence against a mother and her children when child support orders are enforced against them.

I happen to be familiar with the social consequences of forced paternity because my mother worked in the district attorney's office in Santa Clara County, CA, in the 1970s and '80s. I remember the stories that she told about mothers on public assistance who lived in fear that a former abuser would return to harm them or their children because of the DA's enforcement of a child support settlement. Coerced paternity in such cases—where there has been little informed consent at the moment of assigning legal paternity—is typically costly to enforce and does not protect children or preserve family stability.

Feminists have long held that women should not be penalized for being sexually active by taking away their options when an accidental pregnancy occurs. Do our policies now aim to punish and shame men for their sexual promiscuity? Many of my male students (in Miami, where I teach), who come from low-income immigrant communities, believe that our punitive paternity policies are aimed at controlling their sexual behavior. Moreover, the asymmetrical options that men and women now have when dealing with an unplanned pregnancy set up power imbalances in their sexual relationships that my male students find hugely unfair to them. Rather than punish men (or women) for their apparent reproductive irresponsibility by coercing legal paternity (or maternity), the government has other options, such as mandatory sex education, family planning counseling, or community service.

Court-ordered child support does make sense, say, in the case of a divorce, when a man who is already raising a child separates from the child's mother, and when the child's mother retains custody of the child. In such cases, expectations of continued finiancial support recognize and stabilize a parent's continued caregiving role in a child's life. However, just as court-ordered child support does not make sense when a woman goes to a sperm bank and obtains sperm from a donor who has not agreed to father the resulting child, it does not make sense when a woman is impregnated (accidentally or possibly by her choice) from sex with a partner who has not agreed to father a child with her. In consenting to sex, neither a man nor a woman gives consent to become a parent, just as in consenting to any activity, one does not consent to yield to all the accidental outcomes that might flow from that activity.

Policies that punish men for accidental pregnancies also punish those children who must manage a lifelong relationship with an absent but legal father. These "fathers" are not "deadbeat dads" failing to live up to responsibilities they once took on—they are men who never voluntarily took on the responsibilities of fatherhood with respect to a particular child. We need to respect men's reproductive autonomy, as Brake suggests, by providing them more options in the case of an accidental pregnancy. And we need to protect children and stabilize family relationships, as Murphy suggests, by broadening our definition of "father" to include men who willingly perform fatherlike roles in a child's life and who, with informed consent, have accepted the responsibilities of fatherhood.

JUNE 12, 2013

"Mommy Wars" Redux: A False Conflict

—Amy Allen

THE "MOMMY WARS" HAVE FLARED UP ONCE AGAIN, SPARKED most recently by the publication of the English translation of Elisabeth Badinter's book, *The Conflict: How Modern Motherhood Undermines the Status of Women.* In it, Badinter argues that a certain contemporary style of mothering—a style that requires total devotion of mother to child, starting with natural childbirth and extending through exclusive and on-demand breastfeeding, baby wearing and cosleeping—undermines women's equality. Badinter claims that it does this in several ways: by squeezing fathers out of any meaningful role in parenting; by placing such high demands on mothers that it becomes nearly impossible to balance paid work with motherhood (especially once fathers have been sidelined); and by sending the message that day care, bottle feeding, sleep training and the other things that allow women to combine motherhood with paid work are harmful to children, and that the women who use them are selfish.

A post in the *Times'* Room for Debate forum earlier this month described the conflict staked out in Badinter's book as one of "motherhood vs. feminism." But what this discussion failed to capture is something that Badinter actually discusses in her book at some length—namely, that the debate over mothering is not just a conflict between feminists and women in general but rather a conflict *internal* to feminism itself.

Despite the fact that Badinter is frequently described in press coverage as "a leading French philosopher," the book could hardly be called a sophisticated philosophical analysis, especially not when compared with the kind of scholarship that is produced by feminist philosophers these days. The argument of the book is rather thin and much of the empirical evidence marshaled in support of that argument is unsystematic and anecdotal. Moreover, serious questions have been raised about Badinter's objectivity, particularly having to do with her arguments against breastfeeding, in light of her financial ties to corporations that produce infant formula, including Nestle and the makers of Similac and Enfamil.

Nevertheless, Badinter's book—and the discussion it has provoked—does manage to shed light on some profound challenges for feminist theory and practice.

Much work in second-wave feminist theory of the 1970s and 1980s converged around a diagnosis of the cultural value system that underpins patriarchal societies. Feminists argued that the fundamental value structure of such societies rests on a series of conceptual dichotomies: reason vs. emotion, culture vs. nature, mind vs. body and public vs. private. In patriarchal societies, they argued, these oppositions are not merely distinctions—they are implicit hierarchies, with reason valued over emotion, culture over nature, and so on. And in all cases, the valorized terms of these hierarchies are associated with masculinity and the devalued terms with femininity. Men are stereotypically thought to be more rational and logical, less emotional, more civilized and thus more fit for public life, while women are thought to be more emotional and irrational, closer to nature, more tied to their bodies, and thus less fit for public life.

Where second-wave feminists diverged was in their proposed solutions to this situation. Some feminists argued that the best solution was for women to claim the values traditionally associated with masculinity for themselves. From this point of view, the goal of feminism was more or less to allow or to encourage women to be more like men. In practical terms, this meant becoming more educated, more active in public life and less tied to the private sphere of the family, and more career focused.

Other feminists, by contrast, argued that this liberal assimilationist approach failed to challenge the deeply problematic value structure that associated femininity with inferiority. From this point of view, the practical goal of feminism was to revalue those qualities that have traditionally been associated with femininity and those activities that have traditionally been assigned to women, with childbirth, mothering and caregiving at the top of the list.

While both of these strategies have their merits, they also share a common flaw, which is that they leave the basic conceptual dichotomies intact. Hence, the liberal assimilationist approach runs the risk of seeming a bit too willing to agree with misogynists throughout history that femininity isn't worth very much, and the second cultural feminist approach, even as it challenges the prevailing devaluation of femininity, runs the risk of tacitly legitimating women's marginalization by underscoring how different they are from men.

This is why the predominant approach in so-called third-wave feminist theory (which is not necessarily the same thing as feminist philosophy) is deconstructive in the sense that it tries to call into question binary distinctions such as reason vs. emotion, mind vs. body, and male vs. female. Among other things, this means challenging the very assumptions by means of which people are split up into two and only two sexes and two and only two genders.

This short detour through the history of second-wave feminism suggests that the choice that has emerged in the debate over Badinter's book—that we either view attachment parenting as a backlash against feminism or embrace attachment parenting as feminism—is a false one. Neither vision of feminism challenges the fundamental conceptual oppositions that serve to rationalize and legitimate women's subordination.

Even if one accepts the diagnosis that I just sketched—and no doubt there are many feminist theorists who would find it controversial— one might think this is all well and good as far as theory goes, but what does it mean for practice, specifically for the practice of mothering? A dilemma that theorists delight in deconstructing must nevertheless still be negotiated in practice in the here and now, within

our existing social and cultural world. And women who have to negotiate that dilemma by choosing whether to become mothers and, if
they do become mothers, whether (if they are so economically secure
as to even have such a choice) and (for most women) how to combine
mothering and paid employment have a right to expect some practical insights on such questions from feminism.

This brings me to the question of the conflict to which Badinter
refers in her title. Many discussions of the book have focused on the
internal psychological conflict suffered by mothers who work outside
of the home—either by choice or by necessity—and feel guilty for not
living up to the unrealistic demands of the contemporary ideology of
motherhood. As a working mother of four children who has juggled
motherhood with an academic career for the last sixteen years, I am
all too familiar with this particular conflict, and I agree that it is
pernicious and harmful to women. But Badinter's book also points
to another kind of conflict, one that isn't primarily internal and psychological but is rather structural. This is the conflict between economic policies and social institutions that set up systematic obstacles
to women working outside of the home—in the United States, the lack
of affordable, high-quality day care, paid parental leave, flex time
and so on—and the ideologies that support those policies and institutions, on the one hand, and equality for women, on the other hand.

This is the conflict that we should be talking about. Unfortunately
this is also a conversation that is difficult for us to have in the United
States where discussions of feminism always seem to boil down to
questions of choice. The problem with framing the mommy wars in
terms of choice is not just that only highly educated, affluent, mostly
white women have a genuine choice about whether to become über
moms (though the ways in which educational, economic and racial
privilege structure women's choices is a serious problem that must
not be overlooked). The problem is also that under current social,
economic, and cultural conditions, no matter what one chooses,
there will be costs: for stay-at-home mothers, increased economic
vulnerability and dependence on their spouses, which can decrease
their exit options and thus their power in their marriages; for work-

ing mothers, the high costs of quality child care and difficulty keeping up at work with those who either have no children or have spouses at home taking care of them, which exacerbates the wage gap and keeps the glass ceiling in place. (Families with working mothers and fathers who are primary caregivers avoid some of these problems but have to pay the costs associated with transgressing traditional gender norms and expectations.)

If "the conflict" continues to be framed as one between women— between liberal and cultural feminists, or between stay-at-home mothers and working women, or between affluent professionals and working-class women, or between mothers and childless women— it will continue to distract us from what we should really be doing: working together (women *and* men together) to change the cultural, social and economic conditions within which these crucial choices are made.

MAY 27, 2012

The End of "Marriage"

—Laurie Shrage

THE INSTITUTION OF MARRIAGE HAS BECOME THE FOCUS OF PUB-
lic debate and reform, not just in the state-by-state political battles
familiar to us in the United States, but across the world. Some of the
long-standing practices currently being scrutinized both here and in
other countries include parental approval in the choice of a spouse,
permission for a husband to take more than one wife (polygyny),
temporary marriage, close relative (incestuous) marriage, strict or
permissive divorce terms, mandatory bride virginity, child marriage or betrothal and gender-structured marriage in which wives
and husbands have different duties and privileges and therefore
must be gender "opposites."

Marriage reform is typically part of a larger agenda for social
change. In earlier eras, challenges to bans on interfaith and interra-
cial marriage were tied to political movements promoting religious,
ethnic and racial equality and social integration. In the Middle East,
Africa, and Asia today, marriage reformers often aim to expand the
rights and liberty of girls and women, while in the Americas and
Europe, their primary aim is to advance social equality and respect
for lesbians and gay men.

While marriage reform is moving forward in many countries
(for example, to extend access to same-sex couples), many prominent legal and political theorists—such as Cass Sunstein, Richard Thaler, Martha Fineman, Tamara Metz, Lisa Duggan, Andrew

March and Brook Sadler (to name only some of those who have put their views in writing)—are proposing that the institution of marriage be privatized. More specifically, they propose that we eliminate the term *marriage* from our civil laws and policies, and replace it with a more neutral term, such as *civil union* or *domestic partnership*. The state would then recognize and regulate civil unions rather than civil marriage, and people would exchange marriage-like rights and duties by becoming "civilly united." Some private organizations, such as religious institutions, might still perform and solemnize marriages among their congregants, but these marriages would have no official state recognition.

The primary argument for this change of policy is that the state allegedly has no business regulating marriage, which is a complex cultural and religious practice. However, the state does have an interest in promoting private caregiving within families—the care of children, elderly parents and sick or disabled relatives. According to advocates for marriage privatization, the state can better pursue its interest in promoting nongovernmental forms of caregiving by establishing and regulating civil unions for all who qualify, and steering clear of defining, interfering with or regulating "marriage."

Of course, private lives are complicated. Many different kinds of families and households exist and are capable of providing care and nurturance to their members. This includes single-parent families, unmarried partners who care for each other and/or children, and nonspousal relatives—for example, siblings—who together care for parents and children. Those who advocate for replacing civil marriage with civil union maintain that the many tangible benefits of civil marriage (such as tax relief, benefit sharing and inheritance rights) should be available, not only to families headed by heterosexual couples, but to all families that relieve taxpayers of much of the cost of the care and nurturance of their members.

The aforementioned political theorists argue that the best way for the state to begin treating all families equally is for governments to avoid the highly contested terrain of licensing marriage and granting a package of rights only to citizens who achieve this status. Instead, they contend, governments should license civil unions for a wide range of caregiving units and extend the benefits that promote private caregiving to those units that gain this status. Caregiving units are defined in terms of the commitments of ongoing support that adults make to each other and their dependents, rather than in terms of the sexual/romantic attachments that happen to exist between a pair of adults.

This is an ingenious proposal that has many advantages. First, by eliminating "marriage" and revising state policies to focus on caregiving activities rather than sexual/romantic relationships, the state advances its legitimate interest in insuring that vulnerable citizens receive care and nurturing without illegitimately interfering in the private sphere of marriage. Our sexual, romantic or marital relationships are governed by values and beliefs that may not be shared by all citizens, and so noninterference in this sphere is generally a good policy. Keeping the government out of our bedrooms is especially important for democracies that value religious diversity and personal freedom.

Second, by licensing a wide range of caregiving units, the state treats families that are differently structured equally. Some families may be headed by a heterosexual married couple, but others may be organized around one or more nonromantically attached adults and there is no good reason for the state to prefer one caregiving arrangement over others. State support for diverse families is especially good for democracies that value social equality among citizens and equality of opportunity for all, no matter how one starts out in life.

So why not advocate for the end of civil "marriage"?

Unfortunately, this proposal has some serious problems. First, "privatizing" marriage will not cause it to disappear—it will just leave it to be regulated by private institutions, especially religious and ethnic ones. For many centuries, marriage has been the primary mechanism by which people who are not related "by blood" become relatives, and it is unclear that civil unions will acquire this social power. Many families will then be structured and governed primarily by private marriage customs and practices now freed of state regulation. Because of the deep and rich cultural significance of marriage, in many cases marriage arrangements will take precedence over the terms of civil unions. When these arrangements exist in tension with widely shared public values—like those that subordinate wives and daughters and limit their opportunities—privatizing and deregulating marriage will curtail the government's ability to promote gender equality within families structured by marriage. In other words, privatizing marriage will give private organizations, including inegalitarian ones, more influence over the institution of marriage without giving individuals negatively affected much protection by having access to civil union status.

Second, because civil unions are designed to include many kinds of households, their terms will need to be flexible and individually negotiated. Importantly, adults who are not in marriage-like relationships may not want to exchange the same set of rights as those who are, such as debt and income sharing. An inclusive institution of civil union, then, is likely to become equivalent to a system of privately negotiated domestic contracts that the state merely enforces and also protects from outside interference. The problem with this is that, when the terms of civil unions are individually rather than publicly negotiated, they will be less responsive to widely shared public values and beliefs. Moreover private negotiations will require hiring legal professionals to protect the interests of all parties, which will put civil unions outside the reach of many.

In short, the arguments against privatizing marriage are similar to those against privatizing formal schooling or all forms of public assistance. Private institutions may do socially valuable work, but because they are governed by their own rules, they may also engage in forms of discrimination that conflict with public values.

Those advocating for privatizing and deregulating marriage are operating with too narrow a vision of the state's (and society's) interest in recognizing families. I agree with marriage privatizers that the state should not promote marriage among adults as a way to establish parent responsibility or to avoid poverty. The state can pursue these aims less intrusively—by formalizing agreements of child support and custody between both unmarried and married parents (that is, independently of marriage). Indeed the terms of marriage are not comprehensive enough to cover this, though they traditionally assigned the bulk of childcare to wives. But not promoting marriage is different from deregulating or privatizing it. In countries or states where women have achieved formally equal rights, such as the United States, there is no need to support heterosexual marriage as a way to insure the well-being and security of women.

Sadly, for many women today, marriage rarely is a means to economic and social security and often puts these goals at risk. Wives who perform unpaid caregiving and place their economic security in the hands of husbands, who may or may not be good breadwinners, often find their options for financial support severely constrained the longer they remain financially dependent. Decades of research on the feminization of poverty show that women who have children, whether married or not, are systematically disadvantaged when competing for good jobs. Marriage is neither a recipe for economic security nor responsible parenting.

To help move the state away from promoting marriage as a way to advance its interest in protecting children, we need to design policies that support caregivers of all kinds and cooperative caregiving schemes among parents, whether they are married or unmarried, or civilly united or not. Flexible civil unions may work for some, marriage for others, but the state should offer a mechanism for formalizing coparenting agreements independently of the commitments that adults make to each other.

While many marriage privatizers are anxious to limit state control over sexual intimacy between adults, they seem to forget the importance of state regulation in protecting the fundamental rights of those whose intimate social relationships become abusive, coercive and exploitative. Public regulation of marriage is critical for protecting vulnerable citizens in such situations. Public reform of marriage is also critical for improving the general social condition of women and children in many countries today, as well as the social standing of lesbians and gay men. Having the state regulate only civil unions is much less certain to accomplish profound social change.

Imagine that the states had not repealed "head and master" laws (which gave a husband in a marriage ultimate control of the family's property) or made other changes that rendered spouses formally equal and profoundly changed the status of married women in American society. These changes include the right of married women to own property in their name and greater protections against domestic violence. They also include laws prohibiting credit and employment discrimination against married women. Suppose instead the states had simply privatized marriage and accomplished these reforms for people who become civilly united.

Under a system in which the state only recognizes and supports civil unions, shouldn't it still prohibit discrimination against women who are married and protect them against domestic violence, whether they are also civilly united or not? Shouldn't the state also restrict child marriage and nonconsensual marriage? And shouldn't the state also prohibit terms of marriage that require involuntary servitude from a spouse? Without these restrictions, the condition of married women and girls would be unlikely to improve much. But if the state has to regulate marriage to protect married women or minors in some ways, then it has not fully privatized marriage or eliminated "marriage" from our laws.

The state need not (and should not) use its power to coerce domestic and sexual intimacy (civil marriage or union) between coparents in order to advance its legitimate goal in protecting the welfare of children. Instead the state can pursue the latter goal less intrusively by formalizing schemes of cooperation among parents in different kinds of relationships. Moreover, the state should recognize the marriages of same-sex couples that desire to participate in this institution and make the commitments thought appropriate to it. Even if marriage becomes more inclusive in ways that protect equality and freedom for all, some caregivers will prefer more flexible civil union agreements, or only to formalize their child support and custody arrangement. Public regulation and recognition of all of these options is an important step toward achieving social justice for women, lesbians and gay men, ethnic and religious minorities and children.

My Parents' Mixed Messages on the Holocaust

—*Jason Stanley*

M Y CHILDHOOD WAS PRIVILEGED AND FORTUNATE. MY MOTHER was a court stenographer in criminal court, and my father was a professor of sociology at Syracuse University, who had written his doctoral thesis on British colonialism in Kenya. My parents divorced when I was young. But they each happily remarried, and in any case, when I was growing up in Syracuse in the 1970s and '80s, it was the kids of non-divorced parents who were weird. I was on the cross-country team, the math team. And my mother and my father survived the Holocaust.

As a child, this fact was not as salient to me as it is today.

I grew up hearing stories from my father of Central Park and the Ethical Culture Society. New York City in the 1940s and '50s seemed like a magical place. But between these stories were interspersed ones whose contrast couldn't have been stronger.

My father told me of watching Nazi marches from his grandparents' balcony, begging his grandparents to allow him to join. He told me what the signs on the streets said when he started learning to read. He told me of the fear of being in hiding, and of the lessons my grandmother gave him in how to dress quickly. More recently, reading family letters, I learned about the beatings he suffered on the streets of Berlin, his five-year-old hands outstretched to fend off the truncheon blows raining down on his head.

My mother's family is from eastern Poland. Her father served in the Polish cavalry and fled with his wife and first child when the German Army swept in. She was born in Siberia, where she spent the first five years of her life in a labor camp, surviving on potato peels.

When the war ended, she, her mother and sister were packed into the trans-Siberian railroad headed west. Her father had been taken to a separate camp before she was born. At each stop, they stepped off the train and onto the platform, praying that he had survived. One day, they stepped out of the train and there he was, bags packed. Every morning for weeks he had headed to the station, waiting to join his family, the daughter he had never met.

No one was waiting for them when they arrived in Warsaw. My grandparents had many siblings, each with large families of their own. As far as we know, no one survived. Warsaw was still a dangerous place to be Jewish. The children were put in an orphanage for their safety. One day in the late 1940s anti-Semites beat my grandfather almost to death. Soon after, United States visas arrived, and they set off for a new life in Brownsville, Brooklyn.

My parents explained to me that these pasts meant that they were not Holocaust survivors. My mother told me that in her labor camp, they were hungry, they were put to work, but no one was shooting or gassing them. When they went back to Poland, it was hard, and Jews were hated. But this, she explained, was the fate of Jews. Anti-Semitism was a permanent feature of the world, not special to the Holocaust.

My father's reaction to describing him as a Holocaust survivor was more severe. He angrily questioned my motivations. Was I seeking a special status as a victim? He urged me to reflect about how offensive this is to those who have to actually live under oppression. He argued powerfully against the stance of the victim. It was morally dangerous, he said, using the actions of Israelis and Palestinians toward one another as an example. He was scornful when he saw signs that I was taking the Holocaust to mean that Jews were special. "If the Germans had chosen someone else," he often said, "we would have been the very *best* Nazis."

Most frequently and passionately, he would reprimand me for

taking the Holocaust to be about *me*, or about *my family*. The Holocaust was about *humanity*. It was about what we are capable of doing to one another. It could happen again, it could happen here. The Holocaust was about *everyone*. Helping to prevent such events from occurring required agency and good moral sense, and good moral sense was not consistent with preferring one's own people.

My mother's most frequent advice was about knowing when to get out of a dangerous situation. The moment where one must accept that a situation is genuinely dangerous is usually well past the time when one can exit it. Her advice would come out especially during any patriotic moment. She was afraid I would develop an attachment to a country and would not flee early enough.

My mother and father both believed that normal people could do unimaginably terrible things. As a court stenographer in criminal court, my mother witnessed the racial injustice of the American legal system up close. I remember her sometime in the late 1980s saying to me with a rather flat affect, "They are targeting black people in this country." That didn't mean she was about to march out on the street in protest of injustice. That would be a completely incorrect interpretation of my mother. My mother believes that injustice is the normal, unchangeable state of things. My mother believes trust is foolishness. She thinks it is not only naïve to live as if justice were an attainable ideal; it is self-destructive. My mother believes they will kill you if they can.

My father was always critical of Israel's policies toward Palestinians, convinced that the establishment of the state of Israel was implicated in the horrors of colonialism. He was equally abhorrent of Palestinian violence toward Israeli citizens. I grew up hearing other American Jews speak of Palestinians in pre-genocidal ways; that Palestinians have always wanted to kill the Jews, and must therefore be kept locked away and controlled. Regular exposure to such talk has made me permanently afraid for the safety of the Palestinian people. Comparisons between Israeli treatment of Palestinians and Nazi treatment of Jews are absurd. But my background has made me sensitive to the grimmest of even remote future possibilities. I have exactly the same reactions when I hear such rhetoric directed against Israeli citizens.

I am a philosopher. My calling, at its very basic level, obligates me to question the beliefs with which I was raised. But on this topic—how to live—I was given two answers. Which view do evidence and reason command?

I accept the legacy of my father. But it is impossible for me to shut out my mother's concerns. Maybe the reality is that all groups are at war for power, and that to adopt an ethic of common humanity is a grave disadvantage. Maybe we should do what we can, but prioritize the safety of our families.

History speaks strongly on my mother's side. So does my anecdotal evidence. I am white Jewish-American; my sons and wife are black Americans. I cannot retreat from my commitment to these groups. Being interested in the equal dignity of other groups is an additional burden.

It takes work to feel the suffering of Palestinians when I hear of the anger they bear toward my fellow Jews, even though I recognize its clearly justifiable source. It takes much *more* work to feel the suffering of poor white Americans when I hear it coupled with a thoroughly unjustifiable racism directed against my children. Is it work that I should be doing? Or should I be doing the work of attending primarily to the flourishing of *my* children?

If equal human dignity for all groups is impossible, then my mother is right: Striving for it as an ideal is not only naïve, it is dangerous for our families. While we are striving, there will be violations, which we will then overlook at our peril. And yet, for all we know, equal human dignity *is* possible. And so taking my mother's view of life will most likely diminish this possibility.

A world in which this ideal is realized is no doubt far-off. The temptation to surrender it is strong. But history has provided us with too many events that show how important it is not to be complicit in making it unattainable.

AUGUST 20, 2016

ON EATING

The Meat Eaters

—*Jeff McMahan*

Viewed from a distance, the natural world often presents a vista of sublime, majestic placidity. Yet beneath the foliage and hidden from the distant eye, a vast, unceasing slaughter rages. Wherever there is animal life, predators are stalking, chasing, capturing, killing, and devouring their prey. Agonized suffering and violent death are ubiquitous and continuous. This hidden carnage provided one ground for the philosophical pessimism of Schopenhauer, who contended that "one simple test of the claim that the pleasure in the world outweighs the pain . . . is to compare the feelings of an animal that is devouring another with those of the animal being devoured."

The continuous, incalculable suffering of animals is also an important though largely neglected element in the traditional theological "problem of evil"—the problem of reconciling the existence of evil with the existence of a benevolent, omnipotent God. The suffering of animals is particularly challenging because it is not amenable to the familiar palliative explanations of human suffering. Animals are assumed not to have free will and thus to be unable either to choose evil or deserve to suffer it. Neither are they assumed to have immortal souls; hence, there can be no expectation that they will be compensated for their suffering in a celestial afterlife. Nor do they appear to be conspicuously elevated or ennobled by the final suffering they endure in a predator's jaws. Theologians have had enough trouble explaining to their human flocks why a loving God permits them to suffer; but their labors will not be over even if they are finally able to justify the ways of God to man. For God must answer to animals as well.

If I had been in a position to design and create a world, I would have tried to arrange for all conscious individuals to be able to survive without tormenting and killing other conscious individuals. I hope most other people would have done the same. Certainly this and related ideas have been entertained since human beings began to reflect on the fearful nature of their world—for example, when the prophet Isaiah, writing in the eighth century BCE, sketched a few of the elements of his utopian vision. He began with people's abandonment of war: "They shall beat their swords into plowshares, and their spears into pruning hooks: nation shall not lift up sword against nation." But human beings would not be the only ones to change; animals would join us in universal veganism: "The wolf also shall dwell with the lamb, and the leopard shall lie down with the kid; and the calf and the young lion and the fatling together; and a little child shall lead them. And the cow and the bear shall feed; their young ones shall lie down together: and the lion shall eat straw like the ox" (Isaiah 2:4 and 11:6–7).

Isaiah was, of course, looking to the future rather than indulging in whimsical fantasies of doing a better job of Creation, and we should do the same. We should start by withdrawing our own participation in the mass orgy of preying and feeding upon the weak.

Our own form of predation is of course more refined than those of other meat eaters, who must capture their prey and tear it apart as it struggles to escape. We instead employ professionals to breed our prey in captivity and prepare their bodies for us behind a veil of propriety, so that our sensibilities are spared the recognition that we, too, are predators, red in tooth if not in claw (though some of us, for reasons I have never understood, do go to the trouble to paint their vestigial claws a sanguinary hue). The reality behind the veil is, however, far worse than that in the natural world. Our factory farms, which supply most of the meat and eggs consumed in developed societies, inflict a lifetime of misery and torment on our prey, in contrast to the relatively brief agonies endured by the victims of predators in the wild. From the moral perspective, there is nothing that can plausibly be said in defense of this practice. To be entitled to regard ourselves as civilized, we must, like Isaiah's morally reformed lion, eat straw like the ox, or at least the moral equivalent of straw.

But ought we to go further? Suppose that we could arrange the gradual extinction of carnivorous species, replacing them with new herbivorous ones. Or suppose that we could intervene genetically, so that currently carnivorous species would gradually evolve into herbivorous ones, thereby fulfilling Isaiah's prophecy. If we could bring about the end of predation by one or the other of these means at little cost to ourselves, ought we to do it?

I concede, of course, that it would be unwise to attempt any such change given the current state of our scientific understanding. Our ignorance of the potential ramifications of our interventions in the natural world remains profound. Efforts to eliminate certain species and create new ones would have many unforeseeable and potentially catastrophic effects.

Perhaps one of the more benign scenarios is that action to reduce predation would create a Malthusian dystopia in the animal world, with higher birth rates among herbivores, overcrowding, and insufficient resources to sustain the larger populations. Instead of being killed quickly by predators, the members of species that once were prey would die slowly, painfully, and in greater numbers from starvation and disease.

Yet our relentless efforts to increase individual wealth and power are already causing massive, precipitate changes in the natural world. Many thousands of animal species either have been or are being driven to extinction as a side effect of our activities. Knowing this, we have thus far been largely unwilling even to moderate our rapacity to mitigate these effects. If, however, we were to become more amenable to exercising restraint, it is conceivable that we could do so in a selective manner, favoring the survival of some species over others. The question might then arise whether to modify our activities in ways that would favor the survival of herbivorous rather than carnivorous species.

At a minimum, we ought to be clear in advance about the values that should guide such choices if they ever arise, or if our scientific knowledge ever advances to a point at which we could seek to eliminate, alter, or replace certain species with a high degree of confidence in our predictions about the short- and long-term effects of our action. Rather than continuing to collide with the natural world with reckless indifference, we should prepare ourselves now to be able to act wisely and deliberately when the range of our choices eventually expands.

The suggestion that we consider whether and how we might exercise control over the prospects of different animal species, perhaps eventually selecting some for extinction and others for survival in accordance with our moral values, will undoubtedly strike most people as an instance of potentially tragic hubris, presumptuousness on a cosmic scale. The accusation most likely to be heard is that we would be "playing God," impiously usurping prerogatives that belong to the deity alone. This has been a familiar refrain in the many instances in which devotees of one religion or another have sought to obstruct attempts to mitigate human suffering by, for example, introducing new medicines or medical practices, permitting and even facilitating suicide, legalizing a constrained practice of euthanasia, and so on. So it would be surprising if this same claim were not brought into service in opposition to the reduction of suffering among animals as well. Yet there are at least two good replies to it.

One is that it singles out deliberate, morally motivated action for special condemnation, while implicitly sanctioning morally neutral action that foreseeably has the same effects as long as those effects are not intended. One plays God, for example, if one administers a lethal injection to a patient at her own request in order to end her agony, but not if one gives her a largely ineffective analgesic only to mitigate the agony, though knowing that it will kill her as a side effect. But it is hard to believe that any self-respecting deity would be impressed by the distinction. If the first act encroaches on divine prerogatives, the second does as well.

The second response to the accusation of playing God is simple and decisive. It is that there is no deity whose prerogatives we might usurp. To the extent that these matters are up to anyone, they are up to us alone. Since it is too late to prevent human action from affecting the prospects for survival of many animal species, we ought to guide and control the effects of our action to the greatest extent we can in order to bring about the morally best, or least bad, outcomes that remain possible.

Another equally unpersuasive objection to the suggestion that we ought to eliminate carnivorism if we could do so without major ecological disruption is that this would be "against Nature." This slogan also has a long history of deployment in crusades to ensure that human cultures remain primitive. And like the appeal to the sovereignty of a deity, it, too, presupposes an indefensible metaphysics. Nature is not a purposive agent, much less a wise one. There is no reason to suppose that a species has special sanctity simply because it arose in the natural process of evolution.

Many people believe that what happens among animals in the wild is not our responsibility, and indeed that what they do among themselves is none of our business. They have their own forms of life, quite different from our own, and we have no right to intrude upon them or to impose our anthropocentric values on them.

There is an element of truth in this view, which is that our moral reason to prevent harm for which we would not be responsible is weaker than our reason not to cause harm. Our primary duty with respect to animals is therefore to stop tormenting and killing them as a means of satisfying our desire to taste certain flavors or to decorate our bodies in certain ways. But if suffering is bad for animals when we cause it, it is also bad for them when other animals cause it. That suffering is bad for those who experience it is not a human prejudice; nor is an effort to prevent wild animals from suffering a moralistic attempt to police the behavior of other animals. Even if we are not morally *required* to prevent suffering among animals in the wild for which we are not responsible, we do have a moral *reason* to prevent it, just as we have a general moral reason to prevent suffering among human beings that is independent both of the cause of the suffering and of our relation to the victims. The main constraint on the permissibility of acting on our reason to prevent suffering is that our action should not cause bad effects that would be worse than those we could prevent.

That is the central issue raised by whether we ought to try to eliminate carnivorism. Because the elimination of carnivorism would require the extinction of carnivorous species, or at least their radical genetic alteration, which might be equivalent or tantamount to extinction, it might well be that the losses in value would outweigh any putative gains. Not only are most or all animal species of some instrumental value, but it is also arguable that all species have intrinsic value. As Ronald Dworkin has observed, "We tend to treat distinct animal species (though not individual animals) as sacred. We think it very important, and worth a considerable economic expense, to protect endangered species from destruction." When Dworkin says that animal species are sacred, he means that their existence is good in a way that need not be good *for* anyone; nor is it good in the sense that it would be better if there were more species, so that we would have reason to create new ones if we could. "Few people," he notes, "believe the world would be worse if there had always been fewer species of birds, and few would think it important to engineer new bird species if that were possible. What we believe important is not that there be any particular number of species but that a species that now exists not be extinguished by us."

The intrinsic value of individual species is thus quite distinct from the value of species diversity. It also seems to follow from Dworkin's claims that the loss involved in the extinction of an existing species cannot be compensated for, either fully or perhaps even partially, by the coming-into-existence of a new species.

The basic issue, then, seems to be a conflict between values: prevention of suffering and preservation of animal species. It is relatively uncontroversial that suffering is intrinsically *bad for* those who experience it, even if occasionally it is also instrumentally good for them, as when it has the purifying, redemptive effects that Dostoyevsky's characters so often crave. Nor is it controversial that the extinction of an animal species is normally instrumentally bad. It is bad for the individual members who die and bad for other individuals and species that depended on the existence of the species for their own well-being or survival. Yet the extinction of an animal species is not necessarily bad for its individual members. (To indulge in science fiction, suppose that a chemical might be introduced into their food supply that would induce sterility but also extend their longevity.) And the extinction of a carnivorous species could be instrumentally good for all those animals that would otherwise have been its prey. That simple fact is precisely what prompts the question whether it would be good if carnivorous species were to become extinct.

The conflict, therefore, must be between preventing suffering and respecting the alleged sacredness—or, as I would phrase it, the *impersonal* value—of carnivorous species. Again, the claim that suffering is bad for those who experience it and thus ought in general to be prevented when possible cannot be seriously doubted. Yet the idea that individual animal species have value in themselves is less obvious. What, after all, *are* species? According to Darwin, they "are merely artificial combinations made for convenience." They are collections of individuals distinguished by biologists that shade into one another over time and sometimes blur together even among contemporaneous individuals, as in the case of ring species. There are no universally agreed criteria for their individuation. In practice, the most commonly invoked criterion is the capacity for interbreeding, yet this is well known to be imperfect and to entail intransitivities of classification when applied to ring species. Nor has it ever been satisfactorily explained why a special sort of value should inhere in a collection of individuals simply by virtue of their ability to produce fertile offspring. If it is good, as I think it is, that animal life should continue, then it is instrumentally good that some animals can breed with one another. But I can see no reason to suppose that donkeys, as a group, have a special impersonal value that mules lack.

Even if animal species did have impersonal value, it would not follow that they were irreplaceable. Since animals first appeared on earth, an indefinite number of species have become extinct while an indefinite number of new species have arisen. If the appearance of new species cannot make up for the extinction of others, and if the earth could not simultaneously sustain all the species that have ever existed, it seems that it would have been better if the earliest species had never become extinct, with the consequence that the later ones would never have existed. But few of us, with our high regard for our own species, are likely to embrace that implication.

Here, then, is where matters stand thus far. It would be good to prevent the vast suffering and countless violent deaths caused by predation. There is therefore one reason to think that it would be instrumentally good if predatory animal species were to become extinct and be replaced by new herbivorous species, provided that this could occur without ecological upheaval involving more harm than would be prevented by the end of predation. The claim that existing animal species are sacred or irreplaceable is subverted by the moral irrelevance of the criteria for individuating animal species. I am therefore inclined to embrace the heretical conclusion that we have reason to desire the extinction of all carnivorous species, and I await the usual fate of heretics when this article is opened to comment.

SEPTEMBER 19, 2010

If Peas Can Talk, Should We Eat Them?

—Michael Marder

IMAGINE A BEING CAPABLE OF PROCESSING, REMEMBERING, AND sharing information—a being with potentialities proper to it and inhabiting a world of its own. Given this brief description, most of us will think of a human person, some will associate it with an animal, and virtually no one's imagination will conjure up a plant.

Since November 2, however, one possible answer to the riddle is *Pisum sativum*, a species colloquially known as the common pea. On that day, a team of scientists from the Blaustein Institutes for Desert Research at Ben-Gurion University in Israel published the results of its peer-reviewed research, revealing that a pea plant subjected to drought conditions communicated its stress to other such plants with which it shared its soil. In other words, through the roots, it relayed to its neighbors the biochemical message about the onset of drought, prompting them to react as though they, too, were in a similar predicament.

Curiously, having received the signal, plants not directly affected by this particular environmental stress factor were better able to withstand adverse conditions when they actually occurred. This means that the recipients of biochemical communication could draw on their "memories"—information stored at the cellular level—to activate appropriate defenses and adaptive responses when the need arose.

In 1973, the publication of *The Secret Life of Plants*, by Peter Tompkins and Christopher Bird, which portrayed vegetal life as exquisitely sensitive, responsive and in some respects comparable to human life, was generally regarded as pseudoscience. The authors were not scientists, and clearly the results reported in that book, many of them outlandish, could not be reproduced. But today, new, hard scientific data appears to be buttressing the book's fundamental idea that plants are more complex organisms than previously thought.

The research findings of the team at the Blaustein Institutes form yet another building block in the growing fields of plant intelligence studies and neurobotany that, at the very least, ought to prompt us to rethink our relation to plants. Is it morally permissible to submit to total instrumentalization living beings that, though they do not have a central nervous system, are capable of basic learning and communication? Should their swift response to stress leave us coldly indifferent, while animal suffering provokes intense feelings of pity and compassion?

Evidently, empathy might not be the most appropriate ground for an ethics of vegetal life. But the novel indications concerning the responsiveness of plants, their interactions with the environment and with one another, are sufficient to undermine all simple, axiomatic solutions to eating in good conscience. When it comes to a plant, it turns out to be not only a what but also a who—an agent in its milieu, with its own intrinsic value or version of the good. Inquiring into justifications for consuming vegetal beings thus reconceived, we reach one of the final frontiers of dietary ethics.

Recent findings in cellular and molecular botany mean that eating preferences, too, must practically differentiate between vegetal what-ness and who-ness, while striving to keep the latter intact. The work of such differentiation is incredibly difficult because the subjectivity of plants is not centered in a single organ or function but is dispersed throughout their bodies, from the roots to the leaves and shoots. Nevertheless, this dispersion of vitality holds out a promise of its own: the plasticity of plants and their wondrous capacity for regeneration, their growth by increments, quantitative additions or reiterations of already-existing parts do little to change the form of living beings that are neither parts nor wholes because they are not hierarchically structured organisms. The "renewable" aspects of perennial plants may be accepted by humans as a gift of vegetal being and integrated into their diets.

But it would be harder to justify the cultivation of peas and other annual plants, the entire being of which humans devote to externally imposed ends. In other words, ethically inspired decisions cannot postulate the abstract conceptual unity of all plants; they must, rather, take into account the singularity of each species.

The emphasis on the unique qualities of each species means that ethical worries will not go away after normative philosophers and bioethicists have delineated their sets of definitive guidelines for human conduct. More specifically, concerns regarding the treatment of plants will come up again and again, every time we deal with a distinct species or communities of plants.

In Hans Christian Andersen's fairy tale "The Princess and the Pea," the true identity of a princess is discovered after she spends a torturous night on top of twenty mattresses and twenty feather beds, with a single pea lodged underneath this pile. The desire to eat ethically is, perhaps, akin to this royal sensitivity, as some would argue that it is a luxury of those who do have enough food to select, in a conscious manner, their dietary patterns. But there is a more charitable way to interpret the analogy.

Ethical concerns are never problems to be resolved once and for all; they make us uncomfortable and sometimes, when the sting of conscience is too strong, prevent us from sleeping. Being disconcerted by a single pea to the point of unrest is analogous to the ethical obsession, untranslatable into the language of moral axioms and principles of righteousness. Such ethics do not dictate how to treat the specimen of *Pisum sativum*, or any other plant, but they do urge us to respond, each time anew, to the question of how, in thinking and eating, to say "yes" to plants.

APRIL 28, 2012

When Vegans Won't Compromise

—Bob Fischer and James McWilliams

I F A MAN COLLAPSES AT THE OPERA, SHOULD THE SHOW GO ON? This question came up after a friend observed a commotion in the mezzanine during an operatic version of *Romeo and Juliet*. At the moment Juliet launched into an aria called "Je veux vivre dans le reve" (I want to live in my dreams), a disturbance arose on the other side of the theater.

Our friend knew something was going on, but was not sure exactly what. From what he could gather, an audience member had passed out cold. What was the appropriate response?

Our friend did nothing. He suspected the man needed help, but absolved himself of the moral duty to get up and offer assistance. Plenty of other capable people were closer than he was. Perhaps, he thought, obligations don't stretch that far.

What about the patrons sitting next to the man? Calling 911 was obvious, and presumably someone did that. But what should have been done before the paramedics arrived? This question required weighing one man's life against the value of a performance—one that about 2,000 people were enjoying.

In the heat of the moment, those patrons chose not to interrupt the performance by calling out for a doctor. They let the show go on, allowing someone to drag the unconscious man out of his box to wait for the medics to arrive. These people probably understood how high the stakes were—or should have—but weighed the interests of the performers and theatergoers along with this one man's need for medical attention.

What should we make of their decision? Beauty matters, of course, and it would have been difficult for the performers to recreate it, and the audience to experience it, after such a disturbance. But a life ought to trump such aesthetic concerns, right?

That's certainly what you'd say if it were your father or son or brother who had passed out at the opera. We don't typically see this choice as a dilemma. Lives matter in a way that aesthetic experiences don't. But in the physical context of the theater, the opera lovers adhered—some would say too rigidly—to the traditional principle that the performance is sacred, that it ought not to be disturbed, or in more familiar terms, that "the show must go on."

STRICT ADHERENCE TO PRINCIPLE is often the mark of commitment; sometimes, it's the precursor to great change. But it has its costs. Consider, for example, an issue that's getting a lot of attention these days: animal rights. Activists argue that animals possess rights—that is, that their basic interests are inviolable in the same way that human interests are. And if you think this, it's hard not to see industrial agriculture, which kills billions of animals a year, as an especially heinous practice. Accordingly, these activists reject any compromises with welfare-oriented groups that aim to secure incremental improvements—such as larger cages—for animals raised and slaughtered in horrific circumstances.

Epitomizing this no-compromise position is the philosopher and law professor Gary Francione, who has written:

> By endorsing welfare reforms that supposedly make exploitation more "compassionate" or single-issue campaigns that falsely suggest that there is a coherent moral distinction between meat and dairy or between fur and wool or between steak and foie gras, we betray the principle of justice that says that all sentient beings are equal for purposes of not being used exclusively as human resources.

Francione urges those "who believe that animals are members of the moral community" to "make clear that veganism, defined as not eating, wearing, or using animals, is the nonnegotiable, unequivocal moral baseline . . ."

Francione isn't crazy: he's making the same inference that slavery abolitionists made in the nineteenth century. They claimed, as many animal activists do now, that it was pointless to call for the reform of an unjust institution. You don't fix unjust institutions; you dismantle them. Entirely. Now.

Moreover, Francione isn't alone. This form of abolitionism is becoming increasingly popular among ethicists who study animal rights, and although some of the major animal advocacy organizations take a more flexible stance, others certainly don't. They want to ban all use of animals, whether for food, research, or any other purpose. Some even want to get rid of companion animals, arguing that ownership is inherently exploitative.

We, too, think that animals have rights. We, too, are convinced that industrial agriculture is a grave evil. But we're also aware that there are moral costs in taking the high road. Absolute certainty and purity of principle can be detrimental to moral decision-making.

Most notably, purity of principle can lead us to ignore competing moral commitments that go beyond animals. Chief among them is the thought that we ought to do whatever we can for those least able to plead their own case—even if it's only providing larger cages for the soon-to-be-slaughtered.

This moral commitment must be allowed to shape—at least temporarily—our response to animal exploitation. But when someone insists, as Francione does, that these considerations are irrelevant or even harmful to the cause of animal rights, it begins to seem that the cause is no longer the welfare of the animals, but rather the moral position itself, in all its philosophical elegance. Activists, in this way, become so enamored with their most basic moral commitments that they sacrifice the victims to preserve the loveliness of a clean, hard line.

In that sense, the advocates of this form of absolutism resemble those who let the opera continue while a man in the audience lay unconscious. Their moral purity leads them to an odd place: They're willing to allow some preventable suffering for the sake of their ideology. But an ideology that leads you here has led you astray. A life trumps beauty, so the show shouldn't go on. Likewise, suffering trumps ideology, so we should enact the reforms we can, provided they alleviate that suffering.

After all, an abolitionist take on veganism, for instance, overlooks the reality of the world in which we live, the one we have inherited—one in which, for all intents and purposes, very few people choose to go vegan. This isn't because people have great ethical arguments against veganism; it's because most people don't take it seriously enough to argue against. The lack of social support for the movement makes the price even higher for those who do want to change. Estimates vary, but the odds are that less than three percent of Americans have gone vegan, and they lapse at an alarming rate. To respond to this reality with moral purity, to demand that the 97 percent step up and toe the line, would marginalize the cause of animals at the expense of a stubborn adherence to an ideal.

Instead, the moral answer—the pragmatic way to face the problem squarely—is to push for achievable goals based on reasons that vegans and non-vegans share. Ideas like Meatless Mondays, and other dietary programs that limit meat consumption, can be healthful, reduce demands on the earth's natural resources, and create (however indirectly) an improvement in the overall conditions for animals.

Strict veganism, of course, would be better on all counts. But any tactic that aims to lower demand for animal bodies has a moral benefit—not because it's the ideal, but precisely because it isn't. These compromises are responses to reality that lower demand for animal products far more than the vegan fringe, however ideologically pure, ever could.

We're not saying that the activists should become more moderate.

The point here isn't that the activist's principles are mistaken, but rather that those principles have to coexist with other moral commitments, and with the reality of the world as we find it, if he or she is to honor the beings for whom those principles were designed. Principles are lovely things, but when it comes to improving the lives of animals, sometimes the opera must be interrupted.

AUGUST 16, 2015

The Enigma of Animal Suffering

—Rhys Southan

O NE OF THE MOST PROVOCATIVE TACTICS USED BY OPPONENTS OF animal exploitation is to draw an analogy between human and animal suffering. Marjorie Spiegel's *The Dreaded Comparison: Human and Animal Slavery* finds parallels between white oppression of African slaves in America and human exploitation of nonhumans. Spiegel asserts that like human slaves, nonhuman animals are subjected to branding, restraints, beatings, auctions, the separation of offspring from their parents and forced voyages.

Charles Patterson's *Eternal Treblinka: Our Treatment of Animals and the Holocaust* mines another human tragedy for comparisons to animal husbandry. The "eternal" of the title hints at one difference between the Nazis' attempted eradication of Europe's Jews and the raising of animals for food—the latter is an ongoing cycle of breeding and killing and not a hate-fueled extermination campaign—but genocide and animal farming can both involve objectification and efficient mass killing.

Some animal rights activists also compare dairy production with sexual assault, because cows are often artificially inseminated to get them pregnant and continuously lactating.

Such analogies are shocking. But are they sound?

Our perception of the external, of disturbing images or scenes, is sometimes a projection of our own feelings as observers; it does not match what the subjects of such treatment actually experience.

Animal slaughter, for instance, looks gory and disturbing, but when the animals are knocked insensible first, the discomfort is our own—not theirs.

For human analogies to animal farming to have force, the *experience* of being a farmed animal should be equivalent to the human experience in superficially similar circumstances. Is it safe to assume that a cow raised for food suffers the same general humiliations, agonies and frustrated drive for freedom that a human slave or victim of sexual assault or genocide does? If not, arguments equating animal suffering to human suffering are logically flawed.

Animal activists tacitly admit that internal perception is essential when they talk about the importance of sentience. We dominate and slaughter plants, but few people care because it is assumed that our plant victims don't perceive any of it. We are not typically challenged to imagine ourselves as industrially raised stalks of corn, with our roots stuck underground, never able to sit or lie down, pecked at by crows and brutally harvested. With the physical attributes and cognitive abilities of a human, that would be torture, but we quite reasonably assume that it's not so bad for stiff, brainless stalks of corn.

It's not the exploitation in itself that's objectionable, then, but that the exploitation is experienced as harmful. This, however, raises the possibility that the domination and control of animals would be acceptable if we could do it without their minding it very much. Is there reason to believe this is so?

Yes, if we accept the following three premises:

1. *Even though animals feel physical and emotional pain, it is possible to raise them for food and kill them without causing them any more suffering than what we might expect a well-off human to experience.*

2. *Pigs, cows, chickens, lambs, goats and other farmed animals don't have the communication skills or access to information to figure out that the purpose of their lives, from the point of view of humans, is to use them as food.*

3. To have lived a happy but brief life is no worse than to have never lived at all.

The first premise might seem hard to accept, given the brutal realities of modern animal farming. Most farm animals are raised on intensive factory farms where they suffer for the majority of their short lives. Even small, high-welfare farms tend to subject their animals to at least some painful procedures like castration without anesthetic, dehorning or the separation of mothers and their new-born children.

Yet ultra-high-welfare animal products are a possibility, not a fantasy. Consider the highest level of the "5-Step" animal-welfare rating program at Whole Foods Market. For beef, this prohibits branding, castration, ear notching, separating mothers from calves for early weaning and long trips to the slaughterhouse. For pigs, this ensures they are never separated from their littermates, which is important because of how social pigs are. For chickens, it means they have plenty of space and don't have to endure physical alterations like debeaking.

Almost no farms meet these standards, but if more of us were willing to compromise on the price, taste, quantity and texture of the meat we eat, more farms like this could exist and thrive.

Advances in technology and breeding could also improve welfare. Selective breeding of cows who lactate for two or more years after giving birth, a practice called perennial dairying, could reduce the number of times a dairy cow needs to get pregnant to produce milk. Painless slaughter is already feasible when done carefully and would become easier if we were raising far fewer animals for food and didn't rush thousands through a single slaughterhouse in a day.

If we treat animals well throughout their lives and slaughter them in a non-stressful way, the second premise—that animals are unaware that we are raising them for food—seems to fall into place naturally. That it's possible to peacefully load animals onto trucks and lead them calmly to slaughter suggests that this is the case. In her book *Animals Make Us Human: Creating the Best Life for Animals,*

the animal scientist (and slaughterhouse designer) Temple Gran-
din writes:

> *Often I get asked, "Do cattle know they are going to die?" While
> I was still in graduate school I had to answer this question. To
> find the answer I watched cattle go through the veterinary chute
> at a feedlot and then on the same day I watched them walk up
> the chute at the Swift plant. To my amazement, they behaved the
> same way in both places. If they knew that they were going to die,
> they should have acted wilder with more rearing and kicking at
> the Swift plant. At the plant, the handling was better and they
> were often calmer there.*

If we can take animals to their deaths without their ever connect-
ing the dots, then with the best animal farming the existential angst
over their being exploited and doomed is almost certainly in our
heads, not in theirs.

Recently there have been high-concept proposals to take the
painless exploitation further. Some ideas include breeding genetically modified animals who are insensitive to pain, culturing nonsentient animal products in a lab, and giving chickens virtual reality
helmets so that they think they are living in a nice environment even
if they're not. These ideas may not be very practical yet, but they help
illuminate the principle that could allow animal farming but not
human slavery and genocide: Exploitation is harmful only when the
exploited are able to notice it and resent it.

Because the third premise—that to have lived a happy but brief life
is no worse than to have never lived at all—is a philosophical assertion and not a testable empirical question, it may not have a definitive answer. However, we could defend it by consulting the Greek
philosopher Epicurus and his Roman protégé Lucretius. Epicurus
argued that death was nothing to fear because when existence ends
for an individual, he ceases to experience anything and so cannot
suffer harm or deprivation from his death. Lucretius added to this his
"symmetry argument," that since there was nothing bad for us about

the time before we existed, we should see nothing bad for us about the time after we exist, and so we should no more regret dying earlier than we regret being born later. If prebirth nonexistence is identical to postmortem nonexistence, why accept the former and reject the latter? If we agree with Epicurus and Lucretius here, it doesn't seem cruel to breed animals into existence even while intending for their lives to be brief.

I realize that even a sudden mass acceptance of these three premises wouldn't satisfy all opponents of animal farming, because even if we remove physical and psychological suffering from the equation, there is still perhaps the intangible harm of symbolic injustice. Farm animals' existences, no matter how pleasant we can make them, are ultimately designed for our selfish benefit, and there might seem to be something sinister in that.

But just remember that it may seem sinister only to *us*. If farm animals lack the complex forms of communication and access to information that would allow them to realize that they exist to become food for us, and if they don't experience physical tortures along the way, then they avoid all the worst aspects of human exploitation.

This doesn't escape objections of unequal treatment of animals so much as raise the bar. Rejecting pro-human prejudice doesn't mean seeing animal husbandry as equivalent to human oppression, but if animals' ignorance of their own exploitation is our excuse to exploit them, we have a bullet to bite: We have to endorse exploitation for ourselves so long as we're blissfully unaware.

AUGUST 10, 2014

ON THE FUTURE

Is Humanity Getting Better?

—Leif Wenar

I.

Lᴏɴᴅᴏɴ, 1665. Tʜᴇ ᴄᴀᴘɪᴛᴀʟ sᴍᴇʟʟᴇᴅ ᴏꜰ ᴅᴇᴀᴛʜ ɪɴ ɪᴛs ʟᴀsᴛ ʟᴀʀɢᴇ outbreak of the Plague, the worst since the Black Death of the fourteenth century. The diarist Samuel Pepys mourned, "Every day sadder and sadder news of its increase. In the City died this week 7,496; and of all of them, 6,102 of the Plague. But it is feared that the true number of the dead this week is near 10,000—partly from the poor that cannot be taken notice of through the greatness of the number."

As the deaths mounted and the streets filled with waste, Londoners noticed that dogs and cats were everywhere in the city. And so the order went out from the Lord Mayor.

Kill the dogs and cats.

The Chamberlain of the City paid the huntsmen, who slaughtered more than 4,000 animals. But the dogs and cats were chasing the rats that were feeding on the waste—and the rats were carrying the fleas that transmitted the Plague. Now spared from their predators, the rats spread the affliction even more fiercely. The medical advice from London's College of Physicians—to press a hen hard on the swellings until the hen died—did not slow the disease. In the end, the Plague of 1665 is thought to have killed almost 20 percent of London's population (the equivalent of a million and a half people today). A great fire then consumed a third of the city.

Many humans and animals died in this crisis of ignorance. Now that we understand the Plague bacterium, we know what procedures and medicines will keep the disease from becoming epidemic. Ignorance, we might say, no longer plagues us.

Today, pestilence threatens us not because of our ignorance but because of the success of our systems. Our transportation networks are now so fast and far-flung that they transmit diseases worldwide before cures can catch up. The next epidemics will play on our strengths, not our weaknesses—fighting them will mean canceling flights, not killing fleas. This Horseman of the Apocalypse has dismounted and now travels coach.

The twentieth century marked an inflection point—the beginning of humanity's transition from its ancient crises of ignorance to its modern crises of invention. Our science is now so penetrating, our systems are so robust, that we are mostly endangered by our own creations. Our bomb-making is now informed by particle physics; our computers are becoming ever-better informed about our private lives.

In 1665, half a billion humans sweated to sustain the species near subsistence with their crude implements. Now our global economy is so productive that sixteen times that number—some 8 billion humans—will soon be alive, and most will never have known such poverty.

Indeed, our machines have multiplied so much that a new crisis looms because of the smoke coming off them as they combust. Future food crises, if they come, will be driven by anthropogenic climate change. Famine will descend not from the wrath of God but from the growth of gross domestic product. We ourselves are outfitting the Horsemen of the future, or perhaps it's better to say that we are creating them.

Our new crises of invention are so challenging because the bads are so tightly bound with the goods. Breaking the world's slave chains was a moral triumph; breaking the world's supply chains is not an option. Climate change is a crisis of invention. So many more people, living longer, eating better, traveling more to see the world and one another—is it not poignant that these human goods are engendering a mortal danger?

II.

Molecules are heavy and expensive; bits are fast and cheap. So if the past was about scarcity, the future should be about abundance—but the future may well be abundant with trouble. Whether humans can overcome their coming crises of invention will turn on the philosopher's old question of whether individuals are essentially good or evil, which is a hard question—but recent news will tempt many thumbs to turn downward.

A more positive answer emerges if we switch to a systems perspective, evaluating humanity as a whole as we would an ecosystem or a complex machine. What happens when humanity "adds" energy to itself—what happens when humanity produces and consumes more energy, as it's done massively in the transition from wood and muscle power to fossil fuels and alternatives?

The encouraging answer is that with more energy the species grows like crazy. And adding more energy has also activated some potentiality that has made humans generally more tolerant, more cooperative and more peaceful. Humans have, it's true, developed energy weapons powerful enough to destroy the entire system. Yet so far, they have not used those weapons to do so. So far, at least, more energy = more humanity.

Something is happening to our species, and especially over the last seventy years. The years since 1945 have seen many horrors: the partition of India, China's Great Leap Forward, the Vietnam War, the Biafran crisis, the Khmer Rouge and the Rwandan genocide, wars in Afghanistan, Iraq and Syria, mass slaughters, civilizational dictatorships, widespread famines and the grueling civil conflicts that have become watchwords for evil in our time. Today our screens overflow with chaos and hate, and today our screens follow us everywhere.

Yet this has also been the most prosperous time in human history by far. And by a long way the time with the greatest increase in democracy around the world. It has also been the most peaceful era in recorded human history. What Hegel called the slaughter-bench of history is becoming less bloody.

That thesis about "the most peaceful era in history" is naturally the hardest to believe, yet it's true. As Joshua Goldstein puts it in *Winning the War on War*, "We have avoided nuclear wars, left behind world war, nearly extinguished interstate war, and reduced civil wars to fewer countries with fewer casualties." Goldstein continues:

> *In the first half of the twentieth century, world wars killed tens of millions and left whole continents in ruins. In the second half of that century, during the Cold War, proxy wars killed millions, and the world feared a nuclear war that could have wiped out our species. Now, in the early twenty-first century, the worst wars, such as Iraq, kill hundreds of thousands. We fear terrorist attacks that could destroy a city, but not life on the planet. The fatalities still represent a large number and the impacts of wars are still catastrophic for those caught in them, but overall, war has diminished dramatically.*

The percentage of states perpetrating mass killings of civilians is also well down since 1945, and fatalities from armed assaults on civilians (and from genocide) are down since reliable records have been kept. And while the numbers on deaths from terrorism vary according to the definition of that word, all agree that the numbers of terrorism deaths are quite small compared with those caused by (increasingly rare) wars.

These statistics definitely do not prove that animus or madness has ended. No decent person would deny that violence is still much too high everywhere. And there is no guarantee that any of these positive trends will continue.

Still, the big picture of postwar history shows significant improvements in nearly all indicators of lived human experience. The average life span of humans is today longer than it has ever been. A smaller proportion of women die in childbirth than ever before. Child malnutrition is at its lowest level ever, while literacy rates worldwide have never been higher. Most impressive has been the recent reduction in severe poverty—the reduction in the percentage of humans living each day on what a tall Starbucks coffee costs in America. During a recent twenty-year stretch the mainstream estimate is that the percentage of the developing world living in such extreme poverty shrank by more than half, from 43 to 21 percent.

The real trick to understanding our world is to see it with both eyes at once. The world now is a thoroughly awful place—compared with what it should be. But not compared with what it was. Keeping both eyes open gives depth to our perception of our own time in history, and makes us better able to see where paths to more progress may be open.

III.

It would be ungenerous to be impatient with humanity, which—like each one of us—needs time to learn. It was quite a shock for humankind to wake one day with atomic weapons suddenly in its midst, especially as a world war was then ablaze. In 1945, humanity had little idea how to handle this novel existential threat. But it learned, through death and nightmares, and at least so far, it has done better than many first feared. With ever more crises of invention emerging, humanity will need to learn again, and it will need to learn quicker and better.

Humanity does learn, painfully and often only after thousands or even millions have died—like a giant starfish hurrying over a jagged reef, with only primitive vision, slicing off spines on its way, yet regenerating as it grows and slowly adapting its motion. The currents are pushing the starfish faster, the reefs ahead are sharper—humanity must become sharper, too. Mainly, humanity learns as identities alter to become less aggressive and more open, so that networks can connect individual capacities more effectively and join our resources together.

Many people are still beyond ruthless in pursuing their own interests, yet interests are now more pacific than they once were. Most people around you now do not want to kill you to get your phone, torture you until you profess their religion, or prey on your credulity until you join a racist gang. Some may—but not many. If these profound changes for the better remain unseen, it is likely because of what we now take for granted.

What we take for granted frames the size of our concerns. We've come to expect that mayors and police chiefs will not endorse, much less order, the lynching of minorities. Within that frame, racial profiling and deaths in police custody are top priorities. After decades, we've come to expect enduring peace among the great powers. Within that frame any military action by a major power, or a civil war in a resource-rich state, rightly becomes top news.

We can't relax; the upward trends in time's graphs may crest at any point. Yet batting away the positive facts is lazy, and requires only a lower form of intelligence. There are immense challenges: climate change, resource scarcity, overpopulation, and more. Still, these are the follow-on problems of species achievement, as the world gets more crowded and productivity grows. These are the burdens of our success. Something is happening—especially since World War II—as we add more energy to our species. What future generations might marvel at most will be if we, in the midst of it, do not see it.

FEBRUARY 15, 2016

Should This Be the Last Generation?

—Peter Singer

HAVE YOU EVER THOUGHT ABOUT WHETHER TO HAVE A CHILD? If so, what factors entered into your decision? Was it whether having children would be good for you, your partner and others close to the possible child, such as children you may already have, or perhaps your parents? For most people contemplating reproduction, those are the dominant questions. Some may also think about the desirability of adding to the strain that the nearly seven billion people already here are putting on our planet's environment. But very few ask whether coming into existence is a good thing for the child itself. Most of those who consider that question probably do so because they have some reason to fear that the child's life would be especially difficult—for example, if they have a family history of a devastating illness, physical or mental, that cannot yet be detected prenatally.

All this suggests that we think it is wrong to bring into the world a child whose prospects for a happy, healthy life are poor, but we don't usually think the fact that a child is likely to have a happy, healthy life is a reason for bringing the child into existence. This has come to be known among philosophers as "the asymmetry," and it is not easy to justify. But rather than go into the explanations usually proffered—and why they fail—I want to raise a related problem. How good does life have to be to make it reasonable to bring a child into the world? Is the standard of life experienced by most people in developed nations today good enough to make this decision unproblematic in the absence of specific knowledge that the child will have a severe genetic disease or other problem?

The nineteenth-century German philosopher Arthur Schopenhauer held that even the best life possible for humans is one in which we strive for ends that, once achieved, bring only fleeting satisfaction. New desires then lead us on to further futile struggle and the cycle repeats itself.

Schopenhauer's pessimism has had few defenders over the past two centuries, but one has recently emerged in the South African philosopher David Benatar, author of a fine book with an arresting title: *Better Never to Have Been: The Harm of Coming into Existence*. One of Benatar's arguments trades on something like the asymmetry noted earlier. To bring into existence someone who will suffer is, Benatar argues, to harm that person, but to bring into existence someone who will have a good life is not to benefit him or her. Few of us would think it right to inflict severe suffering on an innocent child, even if that were the only way in which we could bring many other children into the world. Yet everyone will suffer to some extent, and if our species continues to reproduce, we can be sure that some future children will suffer severely. Hence continued reproduction will harm some children severely, and benefit none.

Benatar also argues that human lives are, in general, much less good than we think they are. We spend most of our lives with unfulfilled desires, and the occasional satisfactions that are all most of us can achieve are insufficient to outweigh these prolonged negative states. If we think that this is a tolerable state of affairs it is because we are, in Benatar's view, victims of the illusion of Pollyannaism. This illusion may have evolved because it helped our ancestors survive, but it is an illusion nonetheless. If we could see our lives objectively, we would see that they are not something we should inflict on anyone.

Here is a thought experiment to test our attitudes to this view. Most thoughtful people are extremely concerned about climate change. Some stop eating meat or flying abroad on vacation in order to reduce their carbon footprint. But the people who will be most severely harmed by climate change have not yet been conceived. If there were to be no future generations, there would be much less for us to feel guilty about.

So why don't we make ourselves the last generation on earth? If we would all agree to have ourselves sterilized, then no sacrifices would be required—we could party our way into extinction!

Of course, it would be impossible to get agreement on universal sterilization, but just imagine that we could. Then is there anything wrong with this scenario? Even if we take a less pessimistic view of human existence than Benatar, we could still defend it, because it makes us better off—for one thing, we can get rid of all that guilt about what we are doing to future generations—and it doesn't make anyone worse off, because there won't be anyone else to be worse off.

Is a world with people in it better than one without? Put aside what we do to other species—that's a different issue. Let's assume that the choice is between a world like ours and one with no sentient beings in it at all. And assume, too—here we have to get fictitious, as philosophers often do—that if we choose to bring about the world with no sentient beings at all, everyone will agree to do that. No one's rights will be violated—at least, not the rights of any existing people. Can nonexistent people have a right to come into existence?

I do think it would be wrong to choose the nonsentient universe. In my judgment, for most people, life is worth living. Even if that is not yet the case, I am enough of an optimist to believe that, should humans survive for another century or two, we will learn from our past mistakes and bring about a world in which there is far less suffering than there is now. But justifying that choice forces us to reconsider the deep issues with which I began. Is life worth living? Are the interest of a future child a reason for bringing that child into existence? And is the continuance of our species justifiable in the face of our knowledge that it will certainly bring suffering to innocent future human beings?

JUNE 6, 2010

What Do We Owe the Future?

—Patrícia I. Vieira and Michael Marder

S AN SEBASTIÁN, SPAIN—CONTEMPORARY LIFE IS OVER-
loaded with visions of the future. Whereas Friedrich Nietzsche
bemoaned the surplus of historical sense, crushing old Europe under
the weight of its past, we are now suffering from an obsession with
what lies ahead. Personal and national debts are accruing as rapidly as our obligations to subsequent generations. We are awash in
reports that the global environmental crisis may soon reach a tragic
turning point. With the possibility of apocalypse peering at us from
every corner, how are we to face the time to come?

In the midst of this turmoil, a new futurology is afoot, arising
out of a growing confidence in our ability to divine what the future
wants and needs. Decisions on issues like environmental protection
or the control of human reproduction are made in the name of future
generations. As the Nietzschean latecomers on the scene of history,
whose pinnacle we deem ourselves to be, we are confident that our
absolute knowledge extends well beyond the temporal horizon of the
present. But how do we determine the interests of, and our obligations to, those not yet born? Are we really able to listen to what the
future tells or, more often, faintly whispers to us? And, more crucial still, why are the demands of the present neither pressing nor
absorbing enough in their own right?

It's true that the consequences of today's actions are going to have
a long-term impact. The effects of a disaster, like Fukushima, will

certainly outlast those responsible for the catastrophe. But does the enormous size of our temporal footprint mean that we can speak for human beings who are not yet alive? In other words, what are the epistemic and ethical grounds upon which our relation to the future can unfold?

To insist on any one notion of the future in political and philosophical debates risks turning it into an ideological instrument used to justify present policies. The discourse of anti-abortion advocates, for instance, emphasizes the rights of the unborn in order to regulate female sexuality. The reductio ad absurdum of this argument is the prohibition of any form of contraception by certain religious conservatives, who place abstract reproductive responsibilities above existing persons. Arguments like this turn future generations into mere pawns in the power games of the present.

And so, suffocating under the excessive burden of the future, we project our worries onto it, and usurp its proper space. In claiming to speak for the future, we represent it in a double sense: by electing ourselves as its delegates and at the same time turning it into an extension of the present.

Another dimension of the colonization of the future is its idealization as the be-all and end-all of our actions. The future is converted into a fetish that supplements the deficiencies and redeems the flaws inherent in the present. Since the coming generations have not yet attained empirical existence, the ones now living will never be able to measure up to their purported perfection.

This seemingly new phenomenon is actually a mutation of the old metaphysical tendency to debase the world here below at the expense of an otherworldly ideal: Plato's Ideas, Aristotle's unmoved mover, medieval philosophy's God, Hegel's Spirit and the rest. But the emerging metaphysical paradigm differs from its predecessors in that its fate is tied to historical becoming, rather than to the eternal principles of being. This temporal characteristic is illusory, since the future is postponed indefinitely. It always remains beyond the present, immune to contestation, much like the chimeras of old metaphysics.

Nothing is easier than appropriating the voices of those who cannot speak for themselves in the polemical struggle to define the present. In the context of colonization, as members of the Subaltern Studies group have pointed out, people deprived of the means for political expression risk being misrepresented by well-intentioned authority figures. Advocacy for the environment replays this pattern by ascribing particular interests to "voiceless" ecosystems and even individual species. Truly, the road to the future is paved with good intentions.

A healthy does of Epicureanism will go a long way toward curing the discursive inflation of the future. This is not to endorse a care-free attitude in public life, oblivious to ethical concerns. We suggest refocusing attention to the living beings, human and nonhuman, already in existence. At the least, the future should not be used as a diversion from what is.

The one defensible relation to this temporal modality would be to leave the greatest number of options available for generations to come, as Daniel Innerarity argues in *The Future and Its Enemies*. This minimalist approach would be sensitive to the future's open-endedness and acknowledge our inability to do justice to its sheer otherness. Only then will the future truly have a future.

OCTOBER 13, 2013

The Importance of the Afterlife. Seriously.

—Samuel Scheffler

I BELIEVE IN LIFE AFTER DEATH.

No, I don't think that I will live on as a conscious being after my earthly demise. I'm firmly convinced that death marks the unqualified and irreversible end of our lives.

My belief in life after death is more mundane. What I believe is that other people will continue to live after I myself have died. You probably make the same assumption in your own case. Although we know that humanity won't exist forever, most of us take it for granted that the human race will survive, at least for a while, after we ourselves are gone.

Because we take this belief for granted, we don't think much about its significance. Yet I think that this belief plays an extremely important role in our lives, quietly but critically shaping our values, commitments and sense of what is worth doing. Astonishing though it may seem, there are ways in which the continuing existence of other people after our deaths—even that of complete strangers—matters more to us than does our own survival and that of our loved ones.

Consider a hypothetical scenario. Suppose you knew that although you yourself would live a long life and die peacefully in your sleep, the earth and all its inhabitants would be destroyed thirty days after your death in a collision with a giant asteroid. How would this knowledge affect you?

If you are like me, and like most people with whom I have discussed the question, you would find this doomsday knowledge profoundly disturbing. And it might greatly affect your decisions about how to live. If you were a cancer researcher, you might be less motivated to continue your work. (It would be unlikely, after all, that a cure would be found in your lifetime, and even if it were, how much good would it do in the time remaining?) Likewise if you were an engineer working to improve the seismic safety of bridges, or an activist trying to reform our political or social institutions or a carpenter who cared about building things to last, what difference would these endeavors make if the destruction of the human race was imminent?

If you were a novelist or playwright or composer, you might see little point in continuing to write or compose, since these creative activities are often undertaken with an imagined future audience or legacy in mind. And faced with the knowledge that humanity would cease to exist soon after your death, would you still be motivated to have children? Maybe not.

Notice that people do not typically react with such a loss of purpose to the prospect of their own deaths. Of course, many people are terrified of dying. But even people who fear death (and even those who do not believe in a personal afterlife) remain confident of the value of their activities despite knowing that they will die someday. Thus there is a way in which the survival of other people after our deaths matters more to us than our own survival.

The explanation for this may seem simple: if the earth will be destroyed thirty days after we die, then everyone we care about who is alive at that time will meet a sudden, violent end. Spouses and partners, children and grandchildren, friends and lovers: all would be doomed. Perhaps it is our concern for our loved ones that explains our horror at the prospect of a postmortem catastrophe.

But I don't think this is the full story. Consider another hypothetical scenario, drawn from P. D. James's novel *The Children of Men*. In Ms. James's novel, humanity has become infertile, with no recorded birth having occurred in over twenty-five years. Imagine that you found yourself living in such circumstances. Nobody now alive is younger than twenty-five and the disappearance of the human race is imminent as an aging population inexorably fades away. How would you react?

As in the case of the asteroidal collision, many activities would begin to seem pointless under these conditions: cancer research, seismic safety efforts, social and political activism, and so on. Beyond that, as Ms. James's novel vividly suggests, the onset of irreversible global infertility would be likely to produce widespread depression, anxiety and despair.

Some people would seek consolation in religious faith, and some would find it. Others would take what pleasure they could in activities that seemed intrinsically rewarding: listening to music, exploring the natural world, spending time with family and friends and enjoying the pleasures of food and drink. But even these activities might seem less fulfilling and be tinged with sadness and pain when set against the background of a dying humanity.

Notice that in this scenario, unlike that of the asteroidal collision, nobody would die prematurely. So what is dismaying about the prospect of living in an infertile world cannot be that we are horrified by the demise of our loved ones. (They would die eventually, of course, but that is no different from our actual situation.) What is dismaying is simply that no new people would come into existence.

This should give us pause. The knowledge that we and everyone we know and love will someday die does not cause most of us to lose confidence in the value of our daily activities. But the knowledge that no new people would come into existence would make many of those things seem pointless.

I think this shows that some widespread assumptions about human egoism are oversimplified at best. However self-interested or narcissistic we may be, our capacity to find purpose and value in our lives depends on what we expect to happen to others after our deaths. Even the egotistic tycoon who is devoted to his own glory might discover that his ambitions seemed pointless if humanity's disappearance was imminent. Although some people can afford not to depend on the kindness of strangers, virtually everyone depends on the future existence of strangers.

Similarly, I think that familiar assumptions about human individualism are oversimplified. Even though we as individuals have diverse values and goals, and even though it is up to each of us to judge what we consider to be a good or worthy life, most of us pursue our goals and seek to realize our values within a framework of belief that assumes an ongoing humanity. Remove that framework of belief, and our confidence in our values and purposes begins to erode.

There is also a lesson here for those who think that unless there is a personal afterlife, their lives lack any meaning or purpose. What is necessary to underwrite the perceived significance of what we do, it seems, is not a belief in the afterlife but rather a belief that humanity will survive, at least for a good long time.

But will humanity survive for a good long time? Although we normally assume that others will live on after we ourselves have died, we also know that there are serious threats to humanity's survival. Not all of these threats are human-made, but some of the most pressing certainly are, like those posed by climate change and nuclear proliferation. People who worry about these problems often urge us to remember our obligations to future generations, whose fate depends so heavily on what we do today. We are obligated, they stress, not to make the earth uninhabitable or to degrade the environment in which our descendants will live.

I agree. But there is also another side to the story. Yes, our descendants depend on us to make possible their existence and well-being. But we also depend on them and their existence if we are to lead flourishing lives ourselves. And so our reasons to overcome the threats to humanity's survival do not derive solely from our obligations to our descendants. We have another reason to try to ensure a flourishing future for those who come after us: it is simply that, to an extent that we rarely recognize or acknowledge, they already matter so much to us.

Accepting the Past, Facing the Future

—Todd May

HOW DO WE RELATE TO OUR PAST, AND WHAT MIGHT THIS TELL us about how to relate to our future? One of the most provocative approaches to this question comes from Friedrich Nietzsche, whose doctrine of the eternal return asks this: "What if some day or night a demon were to steal after you into your loneliest loneliness and say to you: 'This life as you now live it and have lived it, you will have to live once more and innumerable times more' "? To ask myself the question of the eternal return is to wonder about the worth of what I have done, to inquire whether it would stand the test of being done innumerable times again.

There is, however, a more disturbing worry underneath this one. For me to be able to ask the question of the eternal return already supposes that I have come into existence; and the question may arise of whether I should affirm the conditions that brought me into existence, not innumerable times but even once. To see the bite of this worry, let me share a bit of my own past. Had Hitler not come to power in Germany, the Holocaust and World War II would not have happened. Had World War II not have happened, my father would not have signed up for officer's training school. Had he not signed up, he would not have gone to college, majored in economics, and then moved to New York for a job. And so he would not have met my mother. In short, without the Holocaust I would not be here.

We need not look very deeply to see how many people's existence requires the occurrence of the Holocaust. And as Peter Atterton has argued recently here, all of us can trace our existence back to some mass atrocity or another (if not the Holocaust, then perhaps to slavery or to the Crusades).

How, then, might we relate to the past, and specifically to the fact that we owe our existence to one or another historical atrocity (or, for that matter, to a host of other events: weather patterns, feelings of lust, etc.)? One suggestion, a pessimistic one, is offered by another philosopher, R. Jay Wallace, in his book *The View from Here*. Wallace argues that to affirm my existence, to say yes to it, requires that I affirm (among other unpalatable things) the past that led to it. To be sure, he does not claim that we must feel good about it. We might wish that our existence had come about another way. However, he argues that we cannot have what he calls "all-in regret" about it. It's unfortunate that our existence had to arise this way, but since that's the way it happened, affirming our existence requires affirming the past that led to it. It is no wonder that he calls his position one of "modest nihilism."

But must we affirm the past that led to our existence? Must we be modest nihilists? For one thing, it is open to us to say that it would have been better for us not to have been born and for the Holocaust not to have happened. From a more cosmic perspective (assuming that recent history would not have offered us a comparable horror), we might say that it would have been better had the Holocaust not occurred and that the planet be filled with people different from us. When Atterton concludes his column by saying that we have no right to exist, I take it this is precisely what he is claiming. And, as far as it goes, I agree with him.

But that is not where the question should make us most uncomfortable, and not where Wallace stakes his ground. To affirm our existence is not a matter of what we think would be cosmically or impersonally better. It is to say what we prefer, what we would choose. Would I prefer that the Holocaust or slavery or the Crusades not have happened and that I not exist? If I were somehow allowed to rewind the tape of history and then let it go forward again in a way that prevented one of these atrocities, and thus my existence, would I do it? That is a more troubling question for those of us who are attached to our lives.

I would like to think that, at least in my better moments, I would, however reluctantly, acquiesce to that deal. At those times where I have a more vivid encounter with the Holocaust, for instance, when at the Holocaust Memorial Museum in Washington I saw the shoes of many who had perished in the camps, I think I would, with difficulty, be willing to trade my existence for those of its victims. (It is another and even more vexing question of whether I would trade my childrens' lives to spare theirs, recognizing that my childrens' existence requires my own. But for reasons outside the scope of this essay, I believe that that is a question for my offspring to answer rather than me.) I don't know for sure what I would do, but I hope I would be able to rise to the occasion.

If this is right, then perhaps the proper attitude to take toward the monstrosities that gave rise to us might be called one of acceptance rather than affirmation. We are the products of histories we cannot change, histories that contain atrocities we cannot undo. We know that it would have been better if those horrors had not happened and, consequently, we had not been born, and in nobler moments we might even prefer that it had been that way. Our lives are rooted in tragedies that have no reparation, and in that they are inescapably tainted. We must accept this, but we need not affirm it. The difference lies in what we would have been willing to do, given the opportunity.

At this point, however, someone might ask why it matters what I, or any one of us, would do in an imaginary scenario that cannot possibly happen. The Holocaust happened; it cannot be prevented retroactively. So why should we take up any attitude toward our existence in relation to it? There are two reasons for doing so, one more philosophically reflective and the other more practical. The philosophically reflective reason is this: We condemn the Holocaust. I believe most of us would say that it should not have occurred. But had it not occurred, many of us would not be here. So what is our attitude toward the Holocaust, really? Do we really condemn it, or do we not? Asking the questions I am posing here will reveal to us aspects of who we are in ways that we may or may not find comfortable.

The second reason is practical. If we would be willing to sacrifice our existence for the sake of preventing past horrors, what would we be willing to sacrifice of ourselves to prevent horrors now and in the future? And why are so many of us (and I include myself here) not doing so? I should note here that the situation of the past is not exactly symmetrical to that of the future. There is a complication. If I had not existed, I would not technically have lost anything, because there would have been no "I" to lose it in the first place. (Of course, it's even more complicated than that. I have to exist to consider the possibility of my never having existed.) However, now that I do exist, in sacrificing myself I do stand to lose something—my future existence.

Nevertheless, with that caveat in mind, a willingness to sacrifice our existence in the past should be matched by a willingness to sacrifice at least something of value now or in the future to prevent or mitigate new atrocities. What would we be willing to sacrifice for the refugees from Syria or the potential victims of police violence, or the impoverished undocumented workers in our country—those whose troubles will help determine who our children and grandchildren are? What would we be willing to sacrifice to prevent the enormous consequences of climate change, which seem already to be multiplying their victims? And if we're not prepared to make some sacrifice, what does this in turn say about our relation to the horrors that gave rise to us? Our relation to the past and our relation to the future are not entirely distinct from each other. In asking about one, we offer answers—and perhaps not answers we would prefer to acknowledge—to the other.

As a new year is upon us, then, we might do better to renew rather than to forget our old acquaintance with the past, and allow that to be a guide to our future.

JANUARY 4, 2016

ACKNOWLEDGMENTS

Our gratitude for this book extends in four directions.

To the editors of the Opinion section of *The New York Times*, who have given The Stone the best possible home—a website read devotedly by millions—and who have patiently allowed it to exist and flourish.

To the readers of The Stone, who have proven to be legion, loyal and both appreciative and hard to please. Their devotion to and engagement with the work we publish—by way of their commenting, discussing and sharing—completes this virtuous circle.

To the contributors of The Stone, who kindly offer their hard-earned intellectual work to our project and our readers, for so little remuneration (but our great thanks), and who do service to all of us by remaining engaged with the world of ideas and the people who inhabit it.

To our editor, Philip Marino, and the entire team at Liveright Books, led by the tireless Bob Weil, and to Alex Ward, the *Times'* editorial director of book development, for their faith in our project and their support, skill and investment in making lasting documents (yes, attractive, well-edited books), and extending the life of the work these important thinkers have produced.

We are also grateful to Nemonie Craven and Rosie Welsh of the Jonathan Clowes agency for bringing us all together in this common purpose contractually.

—Peter Catapano and Simon Critchley,
New York,
2017

CONTRIBUTORS

AMY ALLEN is Liberal Arts Research Professor of Philosophy and Women's, Gender, and Sexuality Studies and head of the Philosophy Department at Penn State University.

LOUISE M. ANTONY is a professor of philosophy at the University of Massachusetts Amherst and former president of the Eastern Division of the American Philosophical Association. She has edited or coedited several books, including *Philosophers without Gods: Meditations on Atheism and the Secular Life*, *Chomsky and His Critics* and *A Mind of One's Own: Feminist Essays on Reason and Objectivity*. Antony has also published many articles on her research in the areas of philosophy of mind, feminism and philosophy of religion. She is cofounder and codirector of the Mentoring Program for Early-Career Women in Philosophy.

SEYLA BENHABIB has been Eugene Meyer Professor of Political Science and Philosophy at Yale University since 2001 and was an adjunct professor at the Yale Law School. She has previously taught at the New School for Social Research and Harvard University. Benhabib has written on German philosophy and the critical theory of the Frankfurt School, Hannah Arendt, democracy and cultural difference, and the rights of migrants and citizens. Her work has been translated into thirteen languages. Benhabib's book *Exile, Statelessness, and Migration: Jewish Themes in Political Thought* is forthcoming (Princeton University Press, 2018).

LAWRENCE BERGER has had a varied career as a professional economist and as a business school professor at the University of Iowa and the University of Pennsylvania's Wharton School. He recently completed a PhD in philosophy at the New School for Social Research and presently teaches philosophy at Marist College in Poughkeepsie, New York.

ANAT BILETZKI is Albert Schweitzer Professor of Philosophy at Quinnipiac University and a professor of philosophy at Tel Aviv University. She has written and edited several books, including *Talking Wolves: Thomas Hobbes on the Language of Politics and the Politics of Language* and *(Over)Interpreting Wittgenstein*. From 2001 to 2006 she was chairperson of B'Tselem—the Israeli Information Center for Human Rights in the Occupied Territories.

OMRI BOEHM is an assistant professor of philosophy at the New School for Social Research, working on Kant, early modern philosophy and the philosophy of religion. He is the author of *The Binding of Isaac: A Religious Model of Disobedience* and, most recently, *Kant's Critique of Spinoza*.

PAUL BOGHOSSIAN is Silver Professor of Philosophy at New York University. He works primarily in epistemology and the philosophy of mind but has also written about many other topics, including the aesthetics of music and the concept of genocide. He is the author of several books, including *Fear of Knowledge: Against Relativism and Constructivism* (Oxford University Press, 2006), *Content and Justification: Philosophical Papers* (Oxford University Press, 2008) and *Debating the A Priori* (with Timothy Williamson, forthcoming from Oxford University Press).

CARL CEDERSTRÖM is associate professor of organization studies at Stockholm Business School, Stockholm University. He is coauthor of *The Wellness Syndrome* (with André Spicer) and *Dead Man Working* (with Peter Fleming).

SIMON CRITCHLEY is Hans Jonas Professor of Philosophy at the New School for Social Research in New York and the author of many books. He is the moderator of The Stone and coeditor of this book.

NATHANIEL B. DAVIS is an officer in the United States Army and the director of Defense and Strategic Studies at the United States Military Academy at West Point. He deployed twice to Iraq and has been awarded the Bronze Star Medal. He holds a PhD in war studies from King's College London and a master of public administration from Harvard University.

FIRMIN DeBRABANDER is a professor of philosophy at the Maryland Institute College of Art in Baltimore and is the author of *Spinoza and the Stoics* and *Do Guns Make Us Free?*

FRANS DE WAAL is a biologist interested in primate behavior. He is C. H. Candler Professor in Psychology, director of the Living Links Center at the Yerkes National Primate Research Center at Emory University, in Atlanta, and a member of the National Academy of Sciences and the Royal Dutch Academy of Sciences. His latest book is *Are We Smart Enough to Know How Smart Animals Are?* (W. W. Norton, 2016).

ADAM ETINSON is a lecturer in the Department of Philosophy at the University of St Andrews. He has interests in ethics, political philosophy and social epistemology.

BOB FISCHER teaches at Texas State University. He's edited a number of books, including *The Moral Complexities of Eating Meat* (Oxford University Press, 2015), *College Ethics* (Oxford University Press, 2017), and *The Routledge Handbook of Animal Ethics* (Routledge, forthcoming), and he's the author of over twenty essays on animal ethics, moral psychology and modal epistemology.

SIMONE GUBLER is a doctoral candidate in philosophy at the University of Texas at Austin. She works in moral, political and legal philosophy, and is currently writing on the role of forgiveness in secular ethics and public life.

GARY GUTTING is a professor of philosophy at the University of Notre Dame and an editor of *Notre Dame Philosophical Reviews*. He is the author, most recently, of *Talking God: Philosophers on Belief* (W. W. Norton, 2016) and writes regularly for The Stone.

CAROL HAY is an associate professor of philosophy and the director of Gender Studies at the University of Massachusetts Lowell and the author of *Kantianism, Liberalism, and Feminism: Resisting Oppression*. She is currently writing a book entitled *The Stories We Tell About Women*.

WILLIAM IRWIN is Herve A. LeBlanc Distinguished Service Professor and chair of Philosophy at King's College (Pennsylvania). He is the author of *The Free Market Existentialist: Capitalism without Consumerism* (2015) and the libertarian novel *Free Dakota* (2016). He is also the general editor of the Blackwell Philosophy and Pop Culture series.

JOHN KAAG is a professor of philosophy at the University of Massachusetts Lowell and the author of *American Philosophy: A Love Story* (Farrar, Straus and Giroux, 2016).

SEAN D. KELLY is Teresa G. and Ferdinand F. Martignetti Professor of Philosophy and former chair of the Department of Philosophy at Harvard University. He is the author of numerous scholarly articles and the coauthor, with Hubert Dreyfus, of *All Things Shining: Reading the Western Classics to Find Meaning in a Secular Age*.

SARAH KREPS is an associate professor of government at Cornell University.

JENNIFER LACKEY is Wayne and Elizabeth Jones Professor of Philosophy at Northwestern University. Her research focuses primarily on issues in social epistemology, such as questions about how moral and political issues bear on our status as knowers. Lackey also teaches classes at Stateville Correctional Center, which is a maximum-security men's prison outside of Chicago.

RAE LANGTON is Knightbridge Professor of Philosophy at the University of Cambridge, and a Fellow of Newnham College. She taught at the Massachusetts Institute of Technology from 2004 to 2012. Her most recent book, *Sexual Solipsism: Philosophical Essays on Pornography and Objectification*, was published by Oxford University Press in 2009.

CHRIS LEBRON is the author of *The Color of Our Shame: Race and Justice in Our Time* and *The Making of Black Lives Matter: A Brief History of an Idea*. He is a professor of African-American studies and philosophy at Yale University.

JUDITH LICHTENBERG is a professor of philosophy at Georgetown University with a focus in ethics and political philosophy. She is the author of *Distant Strangers: Ethics, Psychology, and Global Poverty* (2014).

MICHAEL P. LYNCH is director of the Humanities Institute and a professor of philosophy at the University of Connecticut. He is the author of *The Internet of Us*, *In Praise of Reason* and *Truth as One and Many*.

ANDREW F. MARCH is a Berggruen Fellow at the Edmond J. Safra Center at Harvard Law School and a Law and Social Change Fellow at Harvard Law School's Islamic Legal Studies Program. He works on contemporary political philosophy and Islamic ethics and political thought. He is the author of *Islam and Liberal Citizenship: The Search for an Overlapping Consensus* and numerous articles on political philosophy and Islamic political thought.

MICHAEL MARDER is Ikerbasque Research Professor at the University of the Basque Country (UPV/EHU), Vitoria-Gasteiz, Spain, and a professor-at-large at the Humanities Institute of Diego Portales

University, Santiago, Chile. His most recent book is *Energy Dreams: Of Actuality.*

GORDON MARINO is director of the Hong Kierkegaard Library and a professor of philosophy at St. Olaf College. A boxing trainer, he covers boxing for the *Wall Street Journal* and is the editor of *Ethics: The Essential Writings* (Modern Library Classics, 2010).

JOEL MARKS is a professor emeritus of philosophy at the University of New Haven and a scholar at the Interdisciplinary Center for Bioethics at Yale University. He has written four books about living without morality: *Ethics without Morals: In Defense of Amorality, It's Just a Feeling: The Philosophy of Desirism, Bad Faith: A Philosophical Memoir* and *Hard Atheism and the Ethics of Desire: An Alternative to Morality.*

TODD MAY is Class of 1941 Memorial Professor of the Humanities at Clemson University and the author of, most recently, *A Fragile Life: Accepting Our Vulnerability, A Significant Life: Human Meaning in a Silent Universe* and *Nonviolent Resistance: A Philosophical Introduction.*

JUSTIN P. McBRAYER is a professor of philosophy at Fort Lewis College, the liberal arts college for the state of Colorado. He thinks that the greatest challenges for the modern world aren't scientific or technological but philosophical.

JEFF McMAHAN is White's Professor of Moral Philosophy and a Fellow of Corpus Christi College at the University of Oxford. Previously a Rhodes Scholar, he is the author of many works on ethics and political philosophy, including *The Ethics of Killing: Problems at the Margins of Life* (2002) and *Killing in War* (2009).

JAMES McWILLIAMS is an historian and writer based in Austin, Texas. His books include *The Modern Savage: Our Unthinking Decision to Eat Animals* (Thomas Dunne Books), *Just Food: Where Locavores Get It Wrong* *and How We Can Truly Eat Responsibly* (Little, Brown) and *A Revolution in Eating: How the Quest for Food Shaped America* (Columbia University Press), among others. His writing has appeared in *the Paris Review Daily, Harper's, the Washington Post, Slate, The American Scholar, Texas Monthly, The Atlantic, Virginia Quarterly Review* and at newyorker.com. He has a column at *Pacific Standard,* where he is a contributing writer. His literary nonfiction has appeared in *The Millions, Quarterly Conversation, The New York Times Book Review* and *Hedgehog Review.*

STEVEN NADLER is William H. Hay II Professor of Philosophy and Evjue-Bascom Professor in Humanities at the University of Wisconsin–Madison. His most recent books are *A Book Forged in Hell: Spinoza's Scandalous Treatise and the Birth of the Secular Age*; *The Philosopher, the Priest, and the Painter: A Portrait of Descartes* and (with Ben Nadler) the graphic book *Heretics! The Wondrous (and Dangerous) Beginnings of Modern Philosophy* (all from Princeton University Press).

PEG O'CONNOR is a professor of philosophy and gender, women, and sexuality studies at Gustavus Adolphus College in St. Peter, Minnesota. Her interests include Wittgenstein's approach to ethics and the philosophy of addiction. Her book *Life on the Rocks: Finding Meaning in Addiction in Recovery* was published by Central Recovery Press in 2016.

CHRISTINE OVERALL is a professor emerita of philosophy and holds a university research chair at Queen's University, Kingston, Ontario. Her publications are in bioethics and feminist philosophy. She is the editor or coeditor of five books, including *Pets and People: The Ethics of Our Relationships with Companion Animals* (Oxford University Press, 2017), and the author of six, including *Why Have Children? The Ethical Debate* (MIT Press, 2012).

STEVEN PAULIKAS is an Episcopal priest and rector of All Saints Church in Brooklyn, New York. His doctoral research at the University of

Oxford examines the role of evil in the works of Paul Ricoeur. He was previously a journalist based in Vilnius, Lithuania.

PETER RAILTON is Distinguished University Professor and Perrin Professor of Philosophy at the University of Michigan, Ann Arbor. His writing ranges from philosophy of science to ethics and meta-ethics to aesthetics and the philosophy of action. He is the author of *Facts, Values, and Norms* (Cambridge University Press, 2003) and coauthor of *Homo Prospectus* (Oxford University Press, 2016).

ALEX ROSENBERG is R. Taylor Cole Professor and Philosophy Department chair at Duke University. He is the author of twelve books in the philosophy of biology and economics. W. W. Norton published his book *The Atheist's Guide to Reality* in 2011, and Lake Union published his novel *The Girl from Krakow* in 2015, and his second novel, *Autumn in Oxford*, in 2016.

CAROL ROVANE is a professor of philosophy at Columbia University and the author of *Metaphysics and Ethics of Relativism* and *The Bounds of Agency: An Essay in Revisionary Metaphysics*.

MICHAEL RUSE is Lucyle T. Werkmeister Professor of Philosophy at Florida State University. He has written extensively on the history and philosophy of evolutionary biology, most recently in *Darwinism as Religion: What Literature Tells Us about Evolution* (Oxford University Press, 2017) and in *On Purpose* (Princeton University Press, 2017). He was a witness for the ACLU in 1981 in Arkansas, in a case successfully keeping the teaching of creationism in biology classes out of state-funded schools. He was the founding editor of the journal *Biology and Philosophy*.

AGATA SAGAN is an independent researcher.

SAMUEL SCHEFFLER is University Professor of Philosophy at New York University. He has written five books, including, most recently, *Death and the Afterlife* (2013).

ROY SCRANTON is the author of *Learning to Die in the Anthropocene: Reflections on the End of a Civilization* (City Lights, 2015) and the novel *War Porn* (Soho Press, 2016).

NANCY SHERMAN is University Professor of Philosophy at Georgetown University, a Guggenheim Fellow (2013–2014) and has served as the inaugural Distinguished Chair in Ethics at the United States Naval Academy. She is the author, most recently, of *Afterwar: Healing the Moral Wounds of Our Soldiers*. Her other books on related themes are *The Untold War: Inside the Hearts, Minds, and Souls of Our Soldiers* and *Stoic Warriors: The Ancient Philosophy Behind the Military Mind*. She is a Fellow at NYU Center for Ballet and the Arts (spring 2017).

LAURIE SHRAGE is a professor of philosophy at Florida International University.

PETER SINGER is currently Ira W. DeCamp Professor of Bioethics at Princeton University and a laureate professor at the University of Melbourne. He is well known for his text *Animal Liberation* (1975) and, most recently, is the author of *Ethics in the Real World*.

JUSTIN E. H. SMITH is University Professor of Philosophy at the Université Paris Diderot—Paris 7. He is the author, most recently, of *Nature, Human Nature, and Human Difference: Race in Early Modern Philosophy*.

RHYS SOUTHAN has written for *Essays in Philosophy*, *Aeon* and *Philosophy Now*. He is currently a master's student in philosophy at the University of Oxford and is planning to write his thesis on the ethics of killing animals.

AMIA SRINIVASAN teaches philosophy at University College London and is a Fellow of All Souls College, Oxford. She works mainly on epistemology, metaphilosophy and social and political philosophy. Her writing has appeared in the *London Review of Books*, the *Times Literary Supplement*, *Nation* and *Tank* magazine.

JASON STANLEY is Jacob Urowsky Professor of Philosophy at Yale University. He is the author of three books for Oxford University Press, *Knowledge and Practical Interests*, *Language in Context* and *Know How*, and one book for Princeton University Press, *How Propaganda Works*.

PATRÍCIA I. VIEIRA is an associate professor of Spanish and Portuguese, comparative literature, and film and media studies at Georgetown University, and an associate research professor at the Center for Social Studies (CES) of the University of Coimbra. Her most recent book is *States of Grace: Utopia in Brazilian Culture*. For more information, visit www.patriciavieira.net.

CHRISTY WAMPOLE is an assistant professor of French at Princeton University. Her research focuses primarily on twentieth- and twenty-first-century French and Italian literature and thought. She is the author of *The Other Serious: Essays for the New American Generation* and *Rootedness: The Ramifications of a Metaphor*.

RIVKA WEINBERG is a professor of philosophy at Scripps College, Claremont, California. She received her BA in English and philosophy from Brooklyn College, CUNY, in 1993, and her PhD in philosophy from the University of Michigan, Ann Arbor in 2001. As a philosopher and bioethicist, Weinberg specializes in ethical and metaphysical issues regarding birth, death and meaning.

LEIF WENAR's degrees in philosophy are from Harvard and Stanford Universities, and he is currently chair of Law and Philosophy at King's College London. He is the author of *Blood Oil: Tyrants, Violence, and the Rules That Run the World* (Oxford University Press).

AARON JAMES WENDLAND is an assistant professor of philosophy at the National Research University Higher School of Economics. He is the coeditor of *Heidegger on Technology* (Routledge, forthcoming) and *Wittgenstein and Heidegger* (Routledge, 2013), and his research interests include phenomenology, existentialism, ethics and the philosophy of art.

EDWARD O. WILSON is Honorary Curator in Entomology and University Research Professor Emeritus, Harvard University. He has received more than one hundred awards for his research and writing, including the U.S. National Medal of Science, the Crafoord Prize and two Pulitzer Prizes. His most recent book is *Half-Earth: Our Planet's Fight for Life* (Liveright, 2017).

GEORGE YANCY is a professor of philosophy at Emory University. He has written, edited and coedited numerous books, including *Black Bodies, White Gazes*; *Look, a White!* and *Our Black Sons Matter*, coedited with Maria del Guadalupe Davidson and Susan Hadley.